New Discourses in Medieval Canon Law Research

Medieval Law and Its Practice

VOLUME 28

The titles published in this series are listed at *brill.com/mlip*

New Discourses in Medieval Canon Law Research

Challenging the Master Narrative

Edited by

Christof Rolker

BRILL

LEIDEN | BOSTON

Cover illustration: *Gratiani decretum cum glosa.* München, Bayerische Staatsbibliothek München, Clm 23552, fol. 259v (detail). Licence: CC BY-NC-SA. With kind permission of the Bayerische Staatsbibliothek München.

Library of Congress Cataloging-in-Publication Data

Names: Rolker, Christof, 1979–, editor.
Title: New discourses in medieval canon law research : challenging the master narrative / Edited by Christof Rolker.
Description: Leiden : Brill, 2019. | Series: Medieval law and its practice ; 28 | Includes bibliographical references and index.
Identifiers: LCCN 2019001641 (print) | LCCN 2019001804 (ebook) | ISBN 9789004394384 (ebook) | ISBN 9789004389939 (hardback : alk. paper)
Subjects: LCSH: Canon law—History. | Law, Medieval. | Canon law—Study and teaching—Europe—History.
Classification: LCC KBR160 (ebook) | LCC KBR160 .N49 2019 (print) | DDC 262.9—dc23
LC record available at https://lccn.loc.gov/2019001641

Typeface for the Latin, Greek, and Cyrillic scripts: "Brill". See and download: brill.com/brill-typeface.

ISSN 1873-8176
ISBN 978-90-04-38993-9 (hardback)
ISBN 978-90-04-39438-4 (e-book)

This book is printed on acid-free paper and produced in a sustainable manner.

Contents

List of Illustrations VII
Abbreviations VIII
Notes on Contributors XI

Introduction 1
Christof Rolker and Andreas Thier

1 Fournier's Model and Its Merits 4
Christof Rolker

2 Law and Reform: The Transmission of Burchard of Worms' *Liber decretorum* 33
Kathleen G. Cushing

3 New Narratives for the Gregorian Reform 44
Greta Austin

4 Clerical Networks and Canon Law: The Beauvais Election Controversy of 1100–04 58
John S. Ott

5 The Role of Hagiography in the Development of Canon Law in the Reform Era 83
Tatsushi Genka

6 Of Scholasticism and Canon Law: Narratives Old and New 105
John C. Wei

7 The *Decretum* of Gratian: A Janus-Faced Collection 127
Stephan Dusil

8 Using the 'Old Law' in Twelfth-Century Decretal Collections 145
Danica Summerlin

Canon Law before Gratian: A Bibliographical Appendix 171
Christof Rolker
General Index 204
Index of Canonical Collections and Decretal Collections 210
Index of Manuscripts 213

Illustrations

Tables

6.1 Parallels in the inscriptions of the *Sententiae Sidonis* and its formal sources 121
6.2 Texts 1–4 in the *Sententiae Sidonis*, Gratian, and the *Sic et non* 122
6.3 Variants in Text 2 in the *Sententiae Sidonis*, Gratian, and the *Sic et non* 123
6.4 Variants in Text 3 in the *Sententiae Sidonis*, Gratian, and the *Sic et non* 123
6.5 Variants in Text 1 in the *Sententiae Sidonis*, Gratian, and the *Sic et non* 124
6.6 Variants in Text 4 in the *Sententiae Sidonis*, Gratian, and the *Sic et non* 125
7.1 Formal sources of D. 31 and D. 32 of Gratian's *Decretum* 138

Figure

8.1 Paris, Bibliothèque nationale, nouvelles acquisitions françaises 1761, fol. 29v: manuscript of the first recension of the Decretum Gratiani 140

Abbreviations

1 Canon Law Collections, Sentence Collections, and Decretal Collections

2L/8P	The so-called *Collection in Two Books / Eight Parts*, partly ed. Jean Bernhard, “La collection en deux livres (Cod. Vat. lat. 3832),” *Revue de Droit canonique* 12 (1962), 9–601
3L	*Collectio canonum trium librorum*, ed. Giuseppe Motta, 2 vols, MIC Corpus collectionum 8 (Vatican City, 2005–08)
4L	The *Collection in Four Books*, a derivative of *74T* (unedited)
5L	The Beneventan *Collection in Five Books* (unedited)
12P	The *Collection in Twelve Parts*, closely related to Burchard’s *Decretum* (unedited)
74T	*Diuersorum patrum sententie siue Collectio in LXXIV titulos digesta*, ed. John T. Gilchrist, 2 vols, MIC Corpus collectionum 1 (Vatican City, 1973); tr. as *The Collection in Seventy-Four Titles: A Canon Law Manual of the Gregorian Reform*, tr. John T. Gilchrist, Mediaeval Sources in Translation 22 (Toronto, 1980)
183T	*Liber canonum diuersorum sanctorum patrum siue Collectio in CLXXXIII titulos digesta*, ed. Giuseppe Motta, MIC Corpus collectionum 7 (Vatican City, 1988)
Abbo of Fleury	Abbo of Fleury, *Collectio canonum*, ed. in PL 139:473–508
Anselm of Lucca	Version ‘A’ of Anselm’s *Collectio canonum*, partly edited in *Anselmi episcopi Lucensis collectio canonum una cum collectione minore*, ed. Friedrich Thaner, 2 vols (Innsbruck, 1906–15)
Anselmo dedicata	The *Collectio Anselmo dedicata*, imperfectly ed. Jean Claude Besse, *Histoire des textes du droit de l’Église au Moyen-Age de Denys à Gratien: Collectio Anselmo dedicata: étude et texte* (Paris, 1960); also partly ed. Giuseppe Russo, *Tradizione manoscritta di Leges romanae nei codici dei secoli IX e X della Biblioteca capitolare di Modena* (Modena, 1980)
Bonizo of Sutri	*Bonizo von Sutri, Liber de vita christiana*, ed. Ernst Perels, Texte zur Geschichte des römischen und kanonischen Rechts im Mittelalter 1 (Berlin, 1930)

Breviarium extravagantium	The *Breviarium extravagantium* (or *Compilatio prima*) compiled by Bernard of Pavia, ed. in *Quinque compilationes antiquae, nec non Collectio canonum Lipsiensis*, ed. Emil Friedberg (Leipzig, 1882; repr. Graz 1956), pp. 1–66
Burchard of Worms	Burchard's *Decretum* or *Liber decretorum* (= *LD*): *Burchardi Wormatiensis ecclesiae episcopi decretorum libri XX* [...]. *Ergänzter Neudruck der* Editio princeps *Köln 1548*, ed. Gérard Fransen and Theo Kölzer (Aalen, 1992)
Compilatio prima	See *Breviarium extravagantium*
Deusdedit	*Die Kanonessammlung des Kardinals Deusdedit*, 1: *Die Kanonessammlung selbst*, ed. Victor Wolf von Glanvell (Paderborn, 1905) [all published]
Farfa Collection	*Collectio canonum regesto Farfensi inserta*, ed. Theo Kölzer, MIC Corpus collectionum 5 (Vatican City, 1982)
Gratian, *Decretum*	*Decretum magistri Gratiani*, ed. Emil Friedberg, Corpus iuris canonici 1 (Leipzig, 1879; repr. Graz, 1956)
D. 1, c. 2	Distinctio 1, capitulum 2
C. 2, q. 3, c. 4	Causa 2, questio 3, capitulum 4
d.a.c./d.p.c. 5	Dictum ante/post capitulum 5
Ivo of Chartres, *Decretum*	Ivo of Chartres, *Decretum*, ed. Martin Brett et al. at https://ivo-of-chartres.github.io/
LD	See Burchard of Worms
Liber extra	Ed. in *Decretalium collectiones / Decretales Gregorii*, ed. Emil Friedberg, Corpus iuris canonici 2 (Leipzig, 1881; repr. Graz, 1956)
Panormia	*Panormia*, ed. Martin Brett et al. at https://ivo-of-chartres.github.io/
Polycarpus	Gregory of San Grisogono, *Polycarpus*. A provisional edition by Uwe Horst is available at http://www.mgh.de/datenbanken/leges/kanonessammlung-polycarp/
Pseudo-Isidore	*Decretales Pseudo-Isidorianae et Capitula Angilramni*, ed. Paul Hinschius (Leipzig 1863)
Regino of Prüm	*Reginonis abbatis Prumiensis libri duo de synodalibus causis et disciplinis ecclesiasticis*, ed. Friedrich G.A. Wasserschleben (Leipzig, 1840; repr. Graz, 1964); also partly ed. and tr. as *Das Sendhandbuch des Regino von Prüm*, ed. and tr. Wilfried Hartmann, Ausgewählte Quellen zur deutschen Geschichte des Mittelalters 42 (Darmstadt, 2004)

Sententie Magistri A.	Partly ed. in Pauline Henriëtte Joanna Theresia Maas, *The Liber sententiarum Magistri A.: Its Place amidst the Sentences Collections of the First Half of the 12th Century*, Middeleeuwse studies 11 (Nijmegen, 1995), pp. 224–93
SN	Peter Abelard, *Sic et non: A Critical Edition*, ed. Blanche B. Boyer and Richard McKeon (Chicago, 1976)
Tripartita	The *Collectio Tripartita* attributed to Ivo of Chartres, ed. Martin Brett et al. at https://ivo-of-chartres.github.io/

2 Other Abbreviations

AA SS	*Acta sanctorum* [...], Antwerp 1643–1770, Brussels 1780–86, Tongerlo 1794, Brussels 1845–
BHL	Bibliotheca hagiographica latina
CC	Corpus Christianorum
CCCM	Corpus Christianorum: Continuatio mediaevalis, Turnhout 1971–
CC Hagiographies	Corpus Christianorum Hagiographies: histoire internationale de la littérature hagiographique latine et vernaculaire en Occident des origines à 1550, Turnhout 1994–
CCSL	Corpus Christianorum: Series latina, Turnhout 1953–
JL, JK, JE	*Regesta pontificum romanorum ab condita ecclesia ad annum post Christum natum MCXCVIII*, ed. Philipp Jaffé, rev. ed. by Samuel Löwenfeld, Friedrich Kaltenbrunner and Paul Ewald, 2 vols (Leipzig, 1885–88).
MGH	Monumenta Germaniae Historica
Const.	Constitutiones et acta publica imperatorum et regum
Epp. sel.	Epistolae selectae
Fontes iuris	Fontes iuris Germanici antiqui in usum scholarum separatim editi
LL	Leges
SS	Scriptores
SS rer. Lang.	Scriptores rerum Langobardorum
MIC	Monumenta Iuris Canonici
PL	*Patrologiae latinae cursus completus*, ed. Jean-Paul Migne, 221 vols (Paris, 1844–64).
WH	The Walther-Holtzmann-Kartei, available at http://www.kuttner-institute.jura.uni-muenchen.de/holtzmann_formular.htm.

Notes on Contributors

Greta Austin
Professor of the History of Christianity in the Department of Religious Studies, and Director of the Gender & Queer Studies Program, University of Puget Sound.

Kathleen G. Cushing
Reader in Medieval History, Keele University.

Stephan Dusil
Associate professor of Legal History, University of Leuven.

Tatsushi Genka
Associate professor of the History of Medieval Canon Law, University of Tokyo.

John S. Ott
Associate professor, Portland State University.

Christof Rolker
Professor for Historische Grundwissenschaften, University of Bamberg.

Danica Summerlin
Lecturer in medieval history at the University of Sheffield.

Andreas Thier
Professor of Legal History, Ecclesiastical Law, Legal Theory and Private Law, University of Zurich.

John C. Wei
Law clerk for the U.S. Court of Appeals for the Fifth Circuit.

Introduction

Christof Rolker and Andreas Thier

This volume comprises the contributions to a conference held at Zurich University in July 2014 on canon law history in the period between 1050 and 1150 and the fundamental changes in legal culture in this time. Well-known effects of this transformation are the rise of centralized papal government, the emergence of the university, the development of a new legal hermeneutics and, with the *Decretum Gratiani* around 1140, the compilation of a law-book that was to remain in use for centuries. What has been called the 'Renaissance of the twelfth century' (Haskins),[1] the 'theory of papal monarchy',[2] the 'papal revolution in law' (Berman),[3] 'scholastic humanism' (Southern)[4] or the emergence of a 'persecuting society' (Moore)[5] is all based, at least in part, on these dramatic shifts in legal culture. Unsurprisingly, the studies quoted above rely on the handbook literature produced by canon law historians. What is perhaps surprising, however, is that there is no up-to-date manual of canon law history. Faut de mieux, both specialists and non-specialists still depend on the famous *Histoire des collections canoniques en Occident dépuis les Fausses Décrétales jusqu'au Décret de Gratien* by Paul Fournier and Gabriel Le Bras published in 1931–32.[6] A core element of their narrative was the assertion

1 Charles Homer Haskins, *The Renaissance of the Twelfth Century* (Cambridge, Mass., 1927).

2 John A. Watt, "The Theory of Papal Monarchy in the Thirteenth Century: The Contribution of the Canonists," *Traditio* 20 (1964), 179–317; Walter Ullmann, *The Growth of Papal Government in the Middle Ages*, 3rd ed. (London, 1970), esp. ch. 9; Kenneth Pennington, *Pope and Bishops: The Papal Monarchy in the Twelfth and Thirteenth Centuries*, (Philadelphia, Penn., 1984); Colin Morris, *The Papal Monarchy: The Western Church from 1050 to 1250*, Oxford History of the Christian Church (Oxford, 1989).

3 Harold Joseph Berman, *Law and Revolution: The Formation of the Western Legal Tradition* (Cambridge, Mass. and London, 1983); a broad range of contributions addressing Berman's narrative is found in *Rechtsgeschichte—Legal History* 21 (2013), which are introduced with an editorial by Thomas Duve, "Law and Revolution—Revisited," ibid., pp. 156–59, available at http://dx.doi.org/10.12946/rg21/156–159.

4 Richard W. Southern, *Scholastic Humanism and the Unification of Europe*, 1: *The Foundations* (Oxford, 1995), 2 (with notes and additions by Lesley Smith and Benedicta Ward): *The Heroic Age* (Oxford, 2001).

5 Robert Ian Moore, *The Formation of a Persecuting Society: Power and Deviance in Western Europe, 950–1250* (Oxford, 1987).

6 Paul Fournier, with the collaboration of Gabriel Le Bras, *Histoire des collections canoniques en Occident dépuis les Fausses Décrétales jusqu'au Décret de Gratien*, 2 vols (Paris, 1931–32). A reprint has been published by Scientia (Aalen) in 1972.

 | DOI:10.1163/9789004394384_002

that the popes from Leo IX to Paschal II, with Gregory VII as a central figure, followed a long-term strategy of centralized, papal reform, and that canon law played a central role for this strategy. According to Fournier and Le Bras, both the compilation of new collections and the new legal hermeneutics were inspired by the papacy, and specifically meant to foster (papal) reform.

This model is repeated, for example, by more recent textbooks of legal history.[7] Or, to take a well-known example from a different field of scholarship, Harold Berman's concept of a 'papal revolution in law' very directly adopts Fournier's model, and helped to establish it well beyond the specialized field of canon law history.[8]

Various specialized studies (including those by the contributors to the proposed volume) have corrected various elements of the *Histoire*, and a growing consensus has been reached concerning its core narrative being based on assumptions no longer shared by modern scholarship. The participants of the conference took this as a starting point, and, going beyond criticism of the *Histoire*, have developed both individually and collectively alternative models to describe the dramatic changes in legal culture.

To provide the modern reader with a starting point of the model so widely discussed and criticized more than a century after it was developed, the first contribution in this volume is devoted to the genesis and the achievements of Fournier's model as found in the *Histoire* (Rolker). Several contributions (Austin, Wei) discuss traditional perspectives on rule making and legal knowledge during the period in question, and put them in a broader historiographical context like, e. g., the predominance of modernization narratives in 20th century historiography. Other essays (Cushing, Summerlin) focus on processes of rule-making and the transmission of legal norms. Here, it will be demonstrated that the pre-Gratian tradition remained very influential also after the creation of Gratian's *Decretum*, while the traditional narrative of the rise of *ius novum*, created by 12th century papacy, has to be revised. On the one hand, the early twelfth century indeed saw important changes in legal method, as Dusil makes clear. Another contribution, however, puts the position of the papacy within the church 1050–1150 in a new perspective: Ott's studies show how local conflicts influenced the ecclesiastical practice more than the much-debated struggle between emperor and pope. Such a focus on

7 E.g. Péter Erdö, *Geschichte der Wissenschaft vom kanonischen Recht. Eine Einführung*, ed. Ludger Müller, Kirchenrechtliche Bibliothek 4 (Münster, 2006), pp. 40–41.

8 See Berman, *Law and Revolution* (see above, n. 3), p. 202: "The systematization of the law of the church in the late eleventh and the twelfth century was closely related to the Papal Revolution in all its aspects."

the plurality within the church hierarchy provides an important alternative to the dated model of a centralized 'Gregorian' church. At the same time, this argument corresponds to the importance of plurality in late 11th ecclesiastical legal culture, which is of paramount importance in the doctrine of Bernold of Konstanz on the hierarchy of legal sources (Genka).

In conclusion, the following points might be highlighted: (1) The concept elaborated by Fournier and Le Bras follows a narrative of progress. (2) Their model is inconsistent with modern scholarship in church history and general medieval history. Rather than assuming top-down, centralized papal 'reform', scholarship agrees that regional ecclesiastical politics followed autonomous logics and was more or less independent from papal influences. The evolution of legal knowledge in the church—as represented in methodological concepts and collections of normative texts—reveals a conceptual width, which cannot be explained sufficiently by papal control. Instead, there were several ecclesiological approaches and different layers of textual traditions of ecclesiastical rules, which remained important in the whole period under discussion. A concept of differentiation might be helpful as analytical approach for further investigation of these phenomena. (3) The findings in the contributions give weight to the idea to focus on the diversity of legal texts and legal knowledge. Taken together, they will help to establish concepts of legal pluralism as the basis for future research.

CHAPTER 1

Fournier's Model and Its Merits

Christof Rolker

At our conference at Zurich, 'the master narrative' in high medieval canon law history was at issue. In this context, 'the' master narrative is a model for legal development in the high Middle Ages found in many, indeed in most handbooks of canon law history.[1] It goes back to the French legal historian Paul Fournier and is best known from the version enshrined in the two-volume *Histoire* he wrote in collaboration with his pupil Gabriel Le Bras.[2] Well before the *Histoire* appeared in 1931–32, Fournier had sketched his model in several major articles.[3] By the time the *Histoire* was published, Fournier had studied

1 Alfons Maria Stickler, *Historia iuris canonici latini*, 1: *Historia fontium* (Turin, 1950; repr. Zurich, 1970); Willibald M. Plöchl, *Geschichte des Kirchenrechts*, 3 in 5 vols (Vienna and Munich, 1960–70), 2:405–13; Antonio García y García, *Historia del derecho canónico: el primer milenio* (Salamanca, 1967); Constant van de Wiel, *History of Canon Law* (Leuven, 1991); Jean Gaudemet, *Église et cité: histoire du droit canonique* (Paris, 1994); James A. Brundage, *Medieval Canon Law* (London and New York, 1995), chapters 1–2; Peter Erdö, *Die Quellen des Kirchenrechts. Eine geschichtliche Einführung*, Adnotationes in ius canonicum 23 (Frankfurt, 2002); Gian Luigi Falchi and Brian Edwin Ferme, *Introduzione allo studio delle fonti dell'utrumque ius*, Studia et documenta. Sectio iuris romani et historiae iuris 3 (Vatican City, 2006); Brian Edwin Ferme, *Introduction to the History of the Sources of Canon Law: The Ancient Law up to the Decretum of Gratian*, Gratianus (Montréal, 2007). The multi-volume *Histoire du droit et des institutions de l'Église en Occident* edited by Gabriel Le Bras also adopts Fournier's model, if more indirectly. While it covers canon law from the earliest time to the twentieth century, none of its twelve volumes is devoted to pre-Gratian collections, thus supplementing rather than replacing the work Le Bras had co-authored with Fournier (see next note). In addition, the general introduction clearly shows that Le Bras still was faithful to Fournier's model; see Gabriel Le Bras, *Prolégomènes*, Histoire du droit et des institutions de l'Église en Occident 1 (Paris, 1955), esp. at p. 160. At the Second International Congress of Medieval Canon Law, Le Bras expressed the need for a revised new edition of the *Histoire*, but also pointed out the difficulties of such an enterprise; see the discussion on John Joseph Ryan, "Observations on the pre-Gratian Canonical Collections: Some Recent Work and Present Problems," in *Congrès de droit canonique médiéval: Louvain et Bruxelles 22–26 Juillet 1958*, ed. Stephan Kuttner, Henri Wagnon, and Gérard Fransen, Bibliothèque de la revue d'histoire ecclésiastique 33 (Löwen, 1959), pp. 88–103.

2 Paul Fournier, with the collaboration of Gabriel Le Bras, *Histoire des collections canoniques en Occident dépuis les Fausses Décrétales jusqu'au Décret de Gratien*, 2 vols (Paris, 1931–32).

3 Paul Fournier, "Le premier manuel canonique de la réforme du XIe siècle," *Mélanges d'archéologie et d'histoire de l'École française de Rome* 14 (1894), 147–223 and 285–90; idem, "Les collections attribuées à Yves de Chartres," *Bibliothèque de l'École des Chartes*, 57 (1896),

 | DOI:10.1163/9789004394384_003

more pre-Gratian collections than probably any other scholar of his time. The *Histoire* often repeats verbatim passages from Fournier's articles, and neither the preface nor the footnotes leave any doubt that the *Histoire* was mainly his work.[4] It is therefore just to label the narrative found here and adopted by so many handbooks as 'Fournier's model'.

Given that Fournier's model in its key elements dates back to the nineteenth century, it is in itself remarkable how influential it is still today, and even scholars who reject many of Fournier's assumptions and doubt his conclusions still find it a model worth discussing. Indeed, while there are numerous studies that have explicitly challenged Fournier's interpretation of specific collections, and rejected his overall conclusions, so far no clear alternative model has been proposed that would have found wider acceptance. In this situation, Andreas Thier and I brought together a number of scholars with expertise in different fields of early and high medieval canon law history. In this sense the conference was also a way of paying respect to Paul Fournier and his model. It is therefore only apt to begin our collection with an article devoted to the details of his model, its genesis, and its merits. In order to do so, I will first sketch Fournier's academic career and provide some background for his studies on pre-Gratian canon law, before moving on to the *Histoire* itself and the 'model' it contains.

1 Paul Fournier and the Study of Medieval Canon Law in France (*c.*1880 to *c.*1930)

Paul Fournier (1853–1935) is best known for his contribution to the history of medieval canon law.[5] Indeed, there can be little doubt that he already in

---

645–98, *Bibliothèque de l'École des Chartes* 58 (1897), 26–77, 293–326, 410–44, and 624–76; idem, "Un tournant de l'histoire du droit 1060–1140," *Nouvelle revue historique de droit français et étranger* 40 (1917), 129–80; idem, "Les collections canoniques romaines de l'époque de Grégoire VII," *Mémoires de l'Institut National de France, Académie des Inscriptions et Belles-Lettres* 41 (1918), 271–397. These (and other) important articles by Fournier were reprinted in his *Mélanges de droit canonique*, ed. Theo Kölzer, 2 vols (Aalen, 1983), 2:551–633 ("Premier manuel"), 1:451–678 ("Collections attribuées à Yves"), 2:373–424 ("Un tournant"), and 1:393–447 ("Collections canoniques romaines"), respectively.

4 See *Histoire* (see above, n. 2), pp. IX–X on Le Bras' contribution.

5 On Fournier, see above all Gabriel Le Bras, "Paul Fournier et l'histoire de l'Église de France," *Revue d'histoire de l'Église de France* 21 (1935), 532–49. See also the chapter on him the forthcoming volume *Great Christian Jurists in French History*, ed. Olivier Descamps and Rafael Domingo (Cambridge, 2019), written by Brigitte Basdevant-Gaudemet and Rafael Domingo which the latter kindly made available to me before publication. A shorter account is Jean Gaudemet, "Avant-propos," in Fournier, *Mélanges*, ed. Kölzer (see above, n. 3), 1:5–11.

his lifetime established himself as the leading authority in this field: he held the chair for canon law history at Paris, his *Histoire* co-written with his pupil Gabriel Le Bras became a set text for anyone interested in medieval canon law, he had an influential role in the *Société d'histoire du droit* (which he co-founded), the *Société d'histoire de l'Église de France* and the important *Revue historique du droit français et étranger*. He received a number of honorary degrees and was elected member of prestigious institutions both in France and abroad, including the *Legion of Honour*, the *Académie des inscriptions et belles-lettres*, and the *Institut de France*. In other words, Fournier's academic career very visibly was crowned by success.

Yet to understand his work, and in particular the *Historie*, it is equally important to remember that when Fournier began his scholarly career, it was far from clear that his studies would, one day, become classic texts in the field of the medieval history of canon law. In fact, there was no such academic sub-discipline by the time Fournier became interested in canon law history. Since the French Revolution of 1789, canon law had been banned from French universities, and medieval canon law history had a marginal role at best here. Legal history, as taught at French universities, was above all the history of Roman law, and general history was focussed on political history. In late-nineteenth century France, praise for the French Revolution and republican values went often hand in hand with anti-clerical sentiment, and this also extended to historiography: the role of the church in history was often depicted as negative, not least in widely-read accounts like Michelet's *Histoire de France*.[6]

It was this general background in which Fournier began his studies and soon turned to medieval canon law. He studied law from 1871 at Paris, and in 1875 also enrolled at the newly-founded *École des chartes*. In 1878, he submitted his doctoral thesis on Roman law, and the year he qualified as *archiviste-paléographe*. His thesis in law was devoted to Roman law, while his *École des chartes* thesis, published in 1880, was a very substantial study on the ecclesiastical courts in medieval France.[7] *Agrégé* in 1880, Fournier almost immediately was appointed professor for Roman law at Grenoble. Here, he taught Roman law and French legal history for more than three decades, but continue to publish on canon law history, above all analyses of pre-Gratian collections. Apart from his doctoral thesis, he does not seem to have published on Roman law.

6 Jules Michelet, *Histoire de France* (Paris, 1855), pp. 166–72.

7 Paul Fournier, *Des collèges industriels dans l'Empire romain* (Paris, 1878) and idem, *Les officialités au moyen-âge: étude sur l'organisation, la compétence et la procedure des tribunaux ecclésiastiques ordinaires en France, de 1180 à 1328* (Paris, 1880).

Instead, he continued to study above all medieval canon law. As already mentioned, Fournier's first major study was dedicated to medieval officialities. When he published it in 1880, he felt that this topic went against the *Zeitgeist*,[8] and compared to the vast majority of theses submitted at the *École de chartes*, its topic was indeed unusual.[9] Yet in the 1880s and 1890s, when Fournier published a series of seminal studies of various pre-Gratian collections (most notably his analysis of the *Collection in 74 Titles* and the Ivonian collections, respectively[10]), the general attitude towards medieval church history was slowly changing. Already in the early 1880s, a number of young catholic scholars had turned to medieval canon law topics, including (apart from Fournier) Jules-René Menu, Gustave Dupont, and Adhémar Esmein. Menu had done his thesis on the canonical collections attributed to Ivo of Chartres, and Dupont edited the register of the officiality of Cerisy; both published their books in 1880, the same year as Fournier's book on episcopal courts appeared in print.[11] Esmein, Fournier's senior by five years, was the first of the four to make an academic career. In 1881 he was appointed professor for law in Paris and joined the editorial board of the influential *Revue historique du droit français et étranger*; after the reform of the French universities in 1886 he started to teach canon law history at the *École superieure*,[12] where he later was appointed professor, too. His interests ranged widely, but canon law history was one of his areas of specialization, making him probably the first French scholar since 1789 to have made an academic career by studying canon law history.

The topics these young scholars turned to—the canon law of marriage, ecclesiastical courts and procedures, the question of investiture—corresponded to a more general interest in these issues in late-nineteenth-century Europe.

---

8 Fournier, *Officialités*, p. 1 (indeed the very first sentence): "Les temps où nous vivons semble peu favorable aux études d'histoire et de droit écclesiastique."

9 See N. N., "Chronique et mélanges," *Bibliothèque de l'École des Chartes* 40 (1879), 132–35, at p. 132 for a list.

10 Fournier, "Le premier manuel" and idem, "Collections attribuées à Yves de Chartres" (see above, n. 3, for both articles).

11 Jules-René Menu, "Le droit canon au onzième siecle: recherches et nouvelle étude critique sur les recueils de droit canon attribués à Yves de Chartres" (diss. theol., Paris, 1880); *Le registre de l'officialité de Cerisy*, ed. Gustave Dupont (Caen, 1880).

12 See N.N., "Rapport sur l'École pratique des hautes études, 1885–1886," *Annuaires de l'École pratique des hautes études* (1885), 3–225, here at pp. 223–24. His full name is Jean Paul Hippolyte Emmanuel Adhémar Esmein; in the reports, he is often referred to as 'Jean', but in his publications he preferred 'Adhémar'. He is best known for his *Le mariage en droit canonique* (Paris, 1891), 2nd ed., 2 vols (Paris 1929–35), but his early publications also include "La question des investitures dans les lettres d'Yves de Chartres," *Bibliothèque de l'École des Hautes-Études: sciences religieuses* 1 (1889), 139–78.

In France as in Germany and Italy, interest in medieval ecclesiastical history grew in the context of contemporary conflicts between the catholic church and secular governments, and also of conflicts within the catholic church both before and after the First Vatican Council of 1869–71. Civil marriage, the appointment of bishops, the relation between civil and ecclesiastical courts, and papal supremacy were among the topics which were both at the centre of heated political debate and a growing number of historical studies. Emil Friedberg is perhaps the best-known example of a canon law scholar who combined interest in medieval marriage legislation, the textual history of Gratian's *Decretum* and politics of the *Kulturkampf*.[13]

Fournier was very well aware of the German-language scholarship and the *Kulturkampf*, and like his (mainly protestant) counterparts saw historical scholarship as contributing to the debates of nineteenth-century politics. While still holding a chair for Roman law, and also having an academic side-interest in local history, Fournier established himself as a leading expert for the early medieval collections in France. From the mid-1880s on, he published analyses of almost every major collection compiled up to the twelfth century (with the notable exception of Gratian's *Decretum*). He carefully established the manuscript tradition of these collections, often distinguishing between various versions of the same collections; he then described the content and structure of the relevant collection, including comments on the sources the materials were taken from and way the material was arranged and, in some cases, manipulated. Given the state of the research at the time, the almost total absence of printed editions, and the limited time Fournier could spent with the manuscripts, his analyses are remarkably precise. Fournier's studies on the Ivonian collections, for example, surpassed all existing analyses of these collections, and the model of their relation he proposed was only challenged almost exactly a century later.[14] While many of these studies are 'technical' in nature—above all in establishing textual links to other collections and complicated questions of dating these interrelated works—many of these articles already contain the historical narrative which was spelled out in greatest clarity in the *Histoire*.

---

13 See Stefan Ruppert, *Kirchenrecht und Kulturkampf. Historische Legitimation, politische Mitwirkung und wissenschaftliche Begleitung durch die Schule Emil Ludwig Richters*, Ius Ecclesiasticum 70 (Tübingen 2002), especially chapter four (on Friedberg himself).

14 Fournier, "Collections attribuées à Yves de Chartres" (see above, n. 3). The model was first questioned by Martin Brett, "Urban II and the Collections Attributed to Ivo of Chartres," in *Proceedings of the Eighth International Congress of Medieval Canon Law: San Diego, University of California at La Jolla, 21–27 August 1988*, ed. Stanley Chodorow, MIC Subsidia 9 (Vatican City, 1992), pp. 27–46.

As will be analysed in detail below, Fournier mainly understood canon law collections as sources for the relation between secular and religious authorities, or 'church and state', as the common short-hand in contemporary politics and historiography was.[15] Indeed, it probably was Fournier's expertise on canon law and the question of 'church and state' in the Middle Ages which Fournier's growing reputation and success was based on. The concept of *laicité* continued to spark controversies in France, and the 1905 laws on the separation of church and state in particular were opposed by many catholics who perceived them as de facto being direct against their religion. Yet unlike the time Fournier published his first studies on medieval canon law, around 1900 there was considerable scholarly interest in what was often seen as the pre-history of these conflicts in medieval times. In any case, Fournier in 1914 was appointed professor at Paris (succeeding Esmein), and in 1920 a chair for canon law history was created for him. This was a very significant move given that since the French Revolution canon law had been banned from French universities. It may well be that this was facilitated by Fournier's role as advisor to the French government after World War I. When Alsace-Moselle became French again in 1919 it acquired (and retains until today) a local law code which in some respects is strikingly different from the rest of France. Namely, the 1905 laws on the separation of church and state did not apply here; instead, many pre-1918 and indeed pre-1871 laws were retained. As a result, the Alsace-Moselle region is the only part of France where religious education is mandatory, theology is taught at universities, ministers (priests, pastors and rabbis) are paid by the state and bishops are appointed by the government. Here, Fournier's expertise on the history of 'church and state' was very welcome.

Starting with what most contemporaries, certainly including some of his academic teachers, regarded as an obscure field of studies, Fournier made a remarkable career. Yet it should not be forgotten that this success mostly came late in his life. He was in his late sixties when he gave the inaugural lecture for his chair in 1921. By this time, he had completed his analyses of pre-Gratian collections. Indeed, Fournier published markedly less after 1921, apart of course

15 See, for example, his choice of title for the short version of his École thesis: Paul Fournier, "Les conflits de juridiction entre l'église et le pouvoir séculier de 1180 à 1328," *Revue des questions historiques* 27 (1880), 432–64. Likewise, Esmein and later Monod stressed conflicts between 'church and state' in their studies on episcopal elections in the late elventh century: Esmein, "La question des investitures" (see above, n. 12) and Bernard Monod, "L'Église et l'État au XIIe siècle: l'élection épiscopale de Beauvais de 1100 à 1104: Étienne de Garlande et Galon," *Mémoires de la société academique du département de l'Oise* 19 (1904–06), 53–74. On the Beauvais election (and Monod's study), see John Ott's article in this volume.

from writing the *Histoire* which appeared only in 1931–32, shortly after he had retired at the age of 76. The *Histoire* was one of Fournier's last publications, a magisterial synthesis of four decades of research.

2 General Outline of the *Histoire*

2.1 *Pre-Gratian Collections as Sources in their Own Right*

So the *Histoire* can rightly be seen as the sum of Fournier's studies in canon law history. It is based on an analysis of the canonical collections compiled in Western Europe up to the mid-twelfth century; apart from shorter notes on the earlier period, it mainly covers collections from the Pseudo-Isidorian Forgeries up to the *Decretum Gratiani*—excluding the *Decretum* itself but including a number of collections contemporary to or even slightly younger than it. The conventional short hand for all these works is 'pre-Gratian collections'.[16] As for the content, the *Histoire* covers 'canonical' collections in a very wide sense—'law books' containing only conciliar and papal legislation, penitential books, collections of more theological *sententiae*, and works containing any combination of these materials. Taken together, Fournier and Le Bras present the analysis of some one-hundred collections—most of them anonymous, and many only known to specialists both then and now. When the *Histoire* appeared, it was the most complete account of the pre-Gratian collections since the Ballerini brothers and Gallandi had published their works,[17] and until recently it has not been replaced.[18]

Compared to other overviews on canon law history of the nineteenth and early twentieth centuries, both the emphasis on collections (rather than dogma or institutions) and the chronological scope are significant. As the term 'pre-Gratian' suggests, these collections before had predominantly been studied with regard to the genesis of the *Decretum Gratiani*. Fournier and Le Bras, in contrast, studied them as sources in their own right, and by focussing on the

16 The concept was there with Berardi for the latest: Carlo Sebastiano Berardi, *De variis sacrorum canonum collectionibus ante Gratianum* (Turin, 1752). Until today, it is widely used, normally including (as here) some collections compiled after the *Decretum Gratiani* was made. The *Histoire*, interestingly, does not use the term.

17 Pietro and Girolamo Ballerini, "De antiquis tum editis tum ineditis collectionibus et collectoribus canonum ad Gratianum usque," in *Sancti Leonis Magni Romani pontificis opera*, ed. iidem (Venice, 1757), pp. i–cccxx; Andrea Gallandi, *De vetustis canonum collectionibus dissertationum sylloge: quibus virorum doctissimorum cura et studio elucubratis, de iuris ecclesiastici origine atque progressi luculenter differitur* (Venice, 1778).

18 See the on-going *History of Medieval Canon Law* edited by Wilfried Hartmann and Kenneth Pennington.

collections up to but excluding Gratian gave prominence to works otherwise often ignored. For in the second half of the nineteenth century, both the Pseudo-Isidorian Forgeries and Gratian had been subject to a number of path-breaking studies, and Hinschius and Friedberg produced editions that are still used today.[19] A few canon law collections were also studied for their part in the 'rediscovery of the Digest',[20] or as textual witnesses to lost papal registers.[21] Other collections compiled from the ninth to the twelfth century were given some attention as far as they played an immediate role in the compilation of Gratian.[22] In any case, these studies were highly specialized; handbooks of legal history would typically mention pre-Gratian collections only in passing,[23] often depicting them as quite primitive.[24] Medieval canon law in particular had a bad reputation for some legal scholars.[25] Independent of this, most legal

---

19 *Decretales pseudo-Isidorianae et Capitula Angilramni*, ed. Paul Hinschius (Leipzig, 1863); *Decretum magistri Gratiani*, ed. Emil Friedberg (Leipzig, 1879).

20 Most importantly, by Friedrich Carl von Savigny, *Geschichte des römischen Rechts im Mittelalter*, 2nd ed., 6 vols (Heidelberg, 1815–31) and later Max Conrat (Cohn), *Geschichte der Quellen und Literatur des römischen Rechts im frühen Mittelalter* (Leipzig, 1891).

21 In the context of the compilation of Jaffé's *Regesta* and the preparation of the MGH editions, many collections were scrutinized, but perhaps none more than the *Collectio Britannica*. See Paul Ewald, "Die Papstbriefe der Brittischen Sammlung," *Neues Archiv der Gesellschaft für ältere deutsche Geschichtskunde* 5 (1880), 275–414 and 505–96, Theodor Mommsen, "Bemerkungen zu den Papstbriefen der Britischen Sammlung," *Neues Archiv der Gesellschaft für ältere deutsche Geschichtskunde* 15 (1890), 187–88 and Harry Bresslau, "Bemerkungen zu den Papstbriefen der Britischen Sammlung," *Neues Archiv der Gesellschaft für ältere deutsche Geschichtskunde* 15 (1890), 189–93.

22 E.g. Augustin Theiner, *Über Ivo's vermeintliches Decret. Ein Beitrag zur Geschichte des Kirchenrechts, und ins Besondere zur Critik der Quellen des Gratian* (Mainz, 1832); Emil Ludwig Richter, *Beiträge zur Kenntnis der Quellen des kanonischen Rechts* (Leipzig, 1834); Friedrich Wilhelm Hermann Wasserschleben, *Beiträge zur Geschichte der vorgratianischen Kirchenrechtsquellen* (Leipzig, 1839); Joseph Julius A. Hermann Hüffer, *Beiträge zur Geschichte der Quellen des Kirchenrechts und des römischen Rechts im Mittelalter* (Münster, 1862).

23 For example, Johann Friedrich Schulte, *Das katholische Kirchenrecht*, 2 vols (Giessen, 1856–60). Maassen's account would potentially have constituted an important exception, had more than the first volume appeared: Friedrich Maassen, *Geschichte der Quellen und der Literatur des canonischen Rechts im Abendlande bis zum Ausgange des Mittelalters*, 1: *Die Rechtssammlungen bis zur Mitte des 9. Jahrhunderts* (Graz, 1870).

24 Conrad Franz Roßhirt, *Geschichte des Rechts im Mittelalter. Erster Theil: Canonisches Recht* (Mainz, 1846), pp. 72–73: "Alle Schriftsteller vor Gratian hatten die vorhandenen Quellen willkürlich aneinander gestellt, wie z. B. Regino, Burchard, Ivo und der Verfasser der tripartita."

25 See Frederick Pollock and Frederic William Maitland, *The History of English Law before the Time of Edward I*, 2 vols (Cambridge, 1898), 1:24 on the *Decretum Gratiani* and the *Liber extra*: "The canonist emulated the civilian and for a long while maintained in the

historians agreed that great changes in the history of law were brought about by the forging (as in the case of Pseudo-Isidore), rediscovery (as in the case of the Digest) or the compilation (as in the case of the *Decretum Gratiani*) of major works, not in the mass of often anonymous collections that emerged in diverse places. Thus, as far as such collections from the early and high Middle Ages were studied, they were mainly of interest for papal letters, conciliar legislation, Roman law or other materials they contained—not as historical sources that were interesting in themselves.

Fournier and Le Bras, in contrast, studied the pre-Gratian collections in their own right. They made clear that these collections were the result of serious engagement with canonical tradition, and claimed them to have had a significant impact on canon law, and indeed on ecclesiastical history in general. For this approach, it was crucial that Fournier assumed that collections could reveal the compiler's intentions. Already in his earliest studies on pre-Gratian collections Fournier had asked for the 'originality' of these works,[26] and crucially, both in these articles and in the *Histoire*, this extended to minor, anonymous collections which before Fournier were hardly ever studied this way, if at all. Indeed, from early on Fournier studied even individual copies of canonical collections as separate works made for specific purposes and expressing original ideas.[27]

Thus, a large group of collections otherwise given less attention was treated prominently by the *Histoire*. The effect of this was even stronger due to the unusual decision not to cover Gratian.[28] This prepared the ground for a model of legal change that did not focus on the towering figure of Gratian. Indeed, Fournier famously argued that the 'turning point' of medieval legal history was the second half of the eleventh century—and not in the mid-twelfth century.[29] Gratian's *Decretum* in this view was only a 'synthesis' (Fournier) of earlier achievements, indeed one put together by a 'mediocre compiler'

field of jurisprudence what seemed to be an equal combat. Unequal it was in truth. The Decretum is sad stuff when set beside the Digest and the study of Roman law never dies."

26 E.g. Fournier, "Premier manuel" (see above, n. 3), p. 202 ("originalité de la collection"). In the *Histoire*, all major collections are studied for their 'originality' and 'fundamental ideas'.

27 An early example is Paul Fournier, "Une forme particulière des *Fausses Décrétales*, d'après un manuscrit de la Grande-Chartreuse," *Bibliothèque de l'École des Chartes* 49 (1888), 325–49.

28 Fournier in *Histoire* (see above, n. 2), 1:VIII announced that Le Bras would publish a monograph on Gratian which famously never appeared.

29 See Fournier, "Tournant d'histoire," p. 159. Already idem, "Premier manuel," p. 290 hinted at the importance of the Gregorian collections (namely *74T*) for Gratian. See above, n. 3 for both articles.

(Le Bras).[30] According to Fournier's model, Gratian owed much to the compilers of pre-Gratian collections like Bernold of Konstanz, Ivo of Chartres and Alger of Liège.[31] Between the 1090s and the time of Gratian, Fournier and Le Bras claimed, there was very little innovation in canon law.[32] Instead, the decisive change was brought about by the collections compiled between the ninth and the early twelfth centuries—the very period many legal scholars still regarded as 'Dark Ages' of legal history.[33]

2.2 *"Non pas l'histoire sèche des manuscrits, mais celle des idées": From Textual Analysis to the History of Ideas*

So the *Histoire* gave prominence to the pre-Gratian collections, much more so than many contemporary legal scholars were ready to do. This was only possible because Fournier developed a new approach to analyse these collections. It was based on solid source criticism. The *Histoire*, and even more so the specialized studies it built upon, show that Fournier took great care to establish for any collection he studied the date and place of origin, the number of extant manuscripts, the formal and the material sources, the selection criteria and arrangement of the canons, the treatment of individual texts (including their inscriptions and rubrics), and other formal aspects. In many cases, his analysis was the first since at least the eighteenth century. Even if lacking most scholarly resources available today for such an enterprise, Fournier came to conclusions that have stood the test of time remarkably well. Even more importantly, however, Fournier went beyond the analysis of the manuscript tradition, intertextual relations, and source criticism of the pre-Gratian collections. The key assumption that made his model stand out among the legal scholarship of his time, and also made the *Histoire* attractive to many non-specialist historians, was the approach to study them as transmitting not

30 Fournier, "Tournant d'histoire" (see above, n. 3), p. 159 ("synthèse"); Gabriel Le Bras, "Le *Liber de misericordia et justitia* d'Alger de Liège," *Nouvelle revue historique de droit français et étranger* 45 (1921), 80–118, here p. 117 ("compilateur d'esprit médiocre"). See also idem, "Alger de Liège et Gratien," *Revue des sciences philosophiques et théologiques* 20 (1931), 5–26.

31 Fournier, "Tournant d'histoire" (see above, n. 3), p. 159 (Gratian "redevable aux idées exposées par Yves, Bernold et Abélard de la méthode qu'il adopta et qui assura le succès de son œuvre"); *Histoire* (see above, n. 2), 2:359 (works of Ivo, Bernold and Alger as "ébauches de l'œuvre qui devait, quelques années plus tard, être réalisée dans des proportions très vastes par le maître bolonais Gratien").

32 *Histoire* (see above, n. 2), 2:351: "Entre Yves de Chartres et Gratien, les auteurs de collections canoniques n'élargissent guère ni leur curiosité ni leur information, ni leurs procédés."

33 See Pollock and Maitland, *History of English Law* (see above, n. 25), ch. 1 (with the heading "The Dark Age in legal history").

just texts but 'ideas' and expressing individual 'tendencies'.[34] Indeed, Fournier went on to call certain collections 'handbooks' and 'instruments' of reform,[35] containing both the 'spirit' of reform and the specific normative texts that were useful to implement reform.

So how did Fournier and Le Bras establish 'tendency', 'spirit' and 'main idea' of a given collection? In practice, they combined internal and external evidence, with sometimes very different weight given to single aspects. In the case of collections with named compilers, the life and works of the compiler were given considerable attention. In many cases, these compilers had also written prefaces to introduce their collection, and relatively frequently had left other writings as well. Very frequently, the *Histoire* would stress how a given collection expressed the same guiding principles that also appeared to motivate the compilers' political action, in particular stressing what was known about the relation of the compiler either to secular rulers or the papacy. This approach was anything but unusual and based largely on the same sources that had been exploited by literary histories from medieval times to the *Histoire littéraire*.

A second approach to establish the 'tendency' of a compiler was to study forgeries and textual manipulation. In the case of forgeries, and in particular with the Pseudo-Isidorian Forgeries, such an approach was fairly conventional well before Fournier engaged with the subject in some of his earliest publications on canon law history.[36] The Forgeries had attracted many, often contradictory interpretations, not least concerning the ecclesiology they contained—was the stress on papal primacy in the False Decretals taken as evidence for the 'papal' tendency (even a Roman origin) of the forgeries, or was the exaltation of the papacy itself a means towards a different end, namely episcopal

34 *Histoire* (see above, n. 2), 1:8: "Non pas l'histoire sèche des manuscrits, mais celle des idées qu'ils transportent."

35 Ibid.: "instruments entre les mains des réformateurs"; see also Fournier, "Premier manuel" (see above, n. 3).

36 Paul Fournier, "La question des fausses décrétales," *Nouvelle revue historique de droit français et étranger* 11 (1887), 70–104 and 12 (1888), 103–09; idem, "De l'origine des Fausses Décrétales," in *Congrès scientifique international des catholiques, tenu à Paris, avril 1888*, 2 vols (Paris, 1888), 2:403–19; idem, "Forme particulière" (see above, n. 27). For him, like many others, the starting point must have been Hinschius' summary of the controversy: Paul Hinschius, "De collectione decretalium et canonum Isidori Mercatoris," in *Decretales pseudo-Isidorianae et Capitula Angilramni*, ed. idem (Leipzig, 1863), pp. XI–CCXXXVIII, here at pp. CCXIII–CCXXIX. Hinschius was very clear that the sheer scope of the collection, its complexity and the internal contradictions strongly warned against looking for 'the' intention of the forgeries (ibid., p. CCXV).

liberties?[37] In the context of the present article, the most interesting point about Fournier's early articles on these issues is less the conclusion he reached (that the forgeries were 'Roman' in nature but originated in northern France). Rather, it seems an attractive hypothesis that this debate on the 'tendency' of the Pseudo-Isidorian Forgeries provided Fournier with a model he applied to all pre-Gratian collections. Most of them did, of course, not introduce masses of newly forged materials, as Pseudo-Isidore had done, but the way Fournier studied even minute textual manipulation in other collections could well have been inspired by these debates. For example, he paid great attention to the changed inscriptions in a relatively small number of canons in Burchard's *Decretum* which had in common that they concealed the secular law origin of the canons in question and passed them as conciliar legislation. Partly, Fournier took this as evidence that Burchard was quite unscrupulous when it came to the integrity of his proof texts;[38] mainly, however, he took these seemingly small manipulations (which did not affect the main text of the canons in question) as evidence that Burchard, however loyal he personally may have been to the emperor, also insisted on the superiority of divine legislation—and for this reason passed canons from secular law as ecclesiastical sources so that his *Decretum* conveyed the impression that indeed all relevant canonical material stemmed from ecclesiastical authorities only.[39] While in the case of Burchard's manipulations there exceptionally was a certain scholarly tradition Fournier could build on,[40] he was the first to extend this approach to all collections.

Yet most pre-Gratian collections were not only anonymous but also relatively free from textual manipulations, so neither of these approaches would help to establish their 'tendency'. Indeed, the *Histoire* could not have been written the way it was, had Fournier not developed methods to establish the 'tendency' of anonymous collections that presented largely unaltered proof texts. One of

37 Emil Seckel, "Pseudoisidor," in *Real-Encyklopädie für protestantische Theologie und Kirche*, 24 vols (Berlin, 1896–1913), 16:1265–307. The *Histoire* (see above, n. 2), 1:232–33, in contrast, treats the pro-episcopal elements in Pseudo-Isidore as being less important.

38 *Histoire* (see above, n. 2), 1:381.

39 Fournier (ibid.) also quoted evidence to the contrary e.g. the canons which Burchard selected or, in very few cases, manipulated so they affirmed the joint action of secular rulers and ecclesiastical authorities, e.g. in the assembly of synods.

40 Karl Wilhelm Nitzsch, *Ministerialität und Bürgerthum im 11. und 12. Jahrhundert* (Leipzig, 1859), esp. p. 123; Julius Harttung, "Beiträge zur Geschichte Heinrichs II.: Die Synode von Seligenstadt und Burchards Decretum," *Forschungen zur deutschen Geschichte* 16 (1876), 587–93; Albert Hauck, "Ueber den liber decretorum Burchard's von Worms," *Berichte über die Verhandlungen der Königlich Sächsischen Gesellschaft der Wissenschaften zu Leipzig. Philologisch-historische Classe* 46 (1894), 65–86; idem, *Kirchengeschichte Deutschlands*, 5 vols (Berlin, 1887–1920), here at 3:435–40.

the guiding principles to achieve this was looking for selection criteria that seemed to govern any given collection. In this context, Fournier and Le Bras assumed that the inclusion of certain materials was a sign of endorsement and, even more interestingly, that the absence of certain materials often was to be explained by the opposition either to the texts themselves, or to the source they came from, or indeed to other collections that disseminated these canons.

This assumption had far-reaching consequences, and it was genuinely novel. Even as far some legal scholars and church historians may have studied some collections in a similar way, they were quite reluctant to make use of these methods.[41] In any case it was only Fournier who in the late 1880s and early 1890s turned this into a systematic approach to understand all pre-Gratian collections. The basis, to be sure, was relatively conventional: any such an analysis required first to carefully establish both the material and the formal sources, the selection criteria could vary greatly. Trained as a *chartist*,[42] and well familiar with the highly developed techniques of studying complex textual transmission, Fournier from the beginning of his career was well-placed to do the necessary manuscript studies. Yet the decise step was, as the *Histoire* put it, to go beyond the 'dry history of texts'[43]—namely, by using the minute analysis of textual interdependencies to look for the selection criteria applied by the respective compiler.

In many cases, Fournier and Le Bras assumed, the *topic* of the canons in question was decisive. Very frequently, they would quote single texts found in a collection as evidence of the compiler's intention[44]; likewise, the absence of certain proof texts (especially if it was almost certain the compiler knew them) is frequently taken as a sign that the compiler was either not particularly interested in the subject matter or indeed opposed the relevant legislation for one reason or the other.[45] By the same token, the sheer number of canons dealing with a given offence in the *Histoire* serves as an indicator of the compiler's preoccupations; if a collection contained an unusually high share of

41 While many German-speaking scholars of the time (e.g. Conrat, Hauck, Mirbt, Sackur, Sdralek, Seckel, and Thaner) were of course very familiar with both canon law and other sources of the so-called Investiture Contest, the studies on Burchard mentioned above are the only ones published before the 1890s that come close to Fournier's approach. Mirbt, for one, certainly was very well placed to study the canonical collections for their tendencies explicitely declined to so: Carl Mirbt, *Die Publizistik im Zeitalter Gregors VII.* (Leipzig, 1894), pp. 620–21: "Ausdrücklich sei hervorgehoben, dass eine Würdigung der Streitschriftsteller als Kanonisten nicht beabsichtigt ist."

42 For his academic career see above, pp. 6–10.

43 *Histoire*, 1:8 (as quoted above, n. 34).

44 See, for example, *Histoire* (see above, n. 2), 1:8 (on Burchard of Worms).

45 Ibid. (on Ivo of Chartres).

canons on a certain topic, the compiler is commonly said to promote 'reform' in this area. So if, for example, a collection included a certain number of canons dealing with clerical celibacy, this would often be taken as sign that the compiler supported the 'reform of the clergy'. The repetitiveness of pre-Gratian collections, sometimes quoted as a sign of a lack of legal culture, thus was taken as a hint of personal preferences.[46] As in the case of single texts, Fournier and Le Bras did also interpret (relative) silence on an issue as expressions of a lack of interest or indeed a form of opposition. For example, Fournier stressed that Burchard of Worms retained relatively little of the numerous canons dealing with papal primacy found in one of the earlier collections he took his material from (namely the tenth-century *Anselmo dedicata*). From this, Fournier concluded that while Burchard may have acknowledged papal primacy as such, his *Decretum* also was shaped by the intention to curb papal influence.[47] Such arguments are not limited to comparisons with known sources; for example, although none of Burchard's sources (or indeed any previous or contemporary collection) contained any canon law material dealing with investiture, Fournier repeatedly pointed at this 'gap' to establish which positions Burchard allegedly held in ecclesiastical politics.[48] He also assumed that contemporaries read collections in this way, and indeed that compilers anticipated that a large number of canons on an issue would be read as 'zealous' insistence on the canon law in question.[49]

A different kind of selection criterion Fournier and Le Bras paid attention to was the treatment of canonical texts depending on the sources they ultimately came from (the so-called *fontes materiales* or 'material sources'), or appeared to come from. Again, the assumption was that if a collection

46 Similar arguments were raised in the context of the Pseudo-Isidorian forgeries. See e.g. Seckel, "Pseudoisidor" (see above, n. 37), p. 279: "Die unendlichen Wiederholungen seiner Lieblingsgedanken, in denen Ps. seine Tendenzen offen zur Schau trägt, sind zutreffend auf das Prinzip der „Massenwirkung" (Wasserschleben) zurückgeführt worden."

47 See *Histoire* (see above, n. 2), 1:389–90. Contrasting the sheer number of canons on papal primacy in the *Anselmo dedicata* to the handful of texts found in Burchard's *Decretum*, they conclude: "C'est la pauvreté opposée à la richesse; évidemment cette pauvreté fut voulue par l'auteur du Décret."

48 Paul Fournier, "Le Décret de Burchard de Worms: ses caractères, son influence," *Revue d'histoire ecclésiastique* 12 (1911), 451–73 and 670–701, here at p. 690; the article is reprinted Fournier, *Mélanges de droit canonique*, ed. Kölzer (see above, n. 3), 1:393–447. See also idem, "Tournant d'histoire" (see above, n. 3), p. 134 and *Histoire* (see above, n. 2), 1:420: "Burchard ne mentionne ni les exemptions monastiques pour en prendre la défense, ni l'investiture par la crosse et l'anneau pour la réprouver."

49 Fournier, "Décret de Burchard" (see last note), p. 470 and *Histoire* (see above, n. 2), 1.390: "Si l'évêque de Worms a posé nettement le principe de la primatie romaine, il se garde d'y insister, comme s'il voulait éviter toute apparence de zèle sur un point délicat."

(compared to what was available to the compiler) contained an unusually high or low share of canons from certain sources, that this was the result of the compiler's choice, and often reflected which sources he regarded as reliable and which not. Fournier seems to have developed this conviction very early on, as it can already be found in one of his earliest canon law articles.[50] Again, the *Histoire* frequently draws on negative evidence in this context; e.g. the absence of transalpine materials in the collection of Anselm of Lucca or that of recent papal and synodal legislation in the *Farfa Collection* are explained by 'reservation' and 'hostility' towards the material sources of these texts.[51] Fournier and Le Bras very frequently argue how a compiler treated materials coming from specific material sources to establish the 'tendency' of a collection; no argument is used with greater frequency in the *Histoire*.

A third and final selection criterion used to establish the 'tendency' of a collection is the preference for certain 'formal sources' or *fontes formales*, that is, the very collections the compiler was actually taking his material from—whatever its ultimate source (or *fons materialis*) may have been. Already by asking which collection a compiler preferred over others as his formal source, Fournier and Le Bras assumed that the 'tendency' they established for pre-Gratian was also transparent for contemporary users of these works. Otherwise, medieval compilers could hardly have favoured or disfavoured earlier collections depending on whether they shared the tendency expressed therein. The most famous instance of this aspect of Fournier's model could be that the Gregorian compilers greatly preferred other Gregorian collections (namely the *Collection in 74 Titles*) over Burchard's *Decretum* in particular because they disagreed with Burchard's ecclesiology and other 'idées fondamentales' expressed in that collection.[52] Along the same lines, Fournier had asserted

---

50 Namely Fournier, "Forme particulière" (see above, n. 27), stressing that the abbreviated version of the Pseudo-Isidorian forgeries retained all material that seemed to come from papal letters or general councils.

51 *Histoire* (see above, n. 2), 2:32 (Anselm of Lucca "n'emploie qu'avec extrême réserve les matériaux d'origine insulaire ou transalpine") and 121 (Gregory of Catino "systématiquement passé sous silence la législation réformatrice qui s'était développée à Rome dans la dernière moitié du XIe siècle"), respectively.

52 Fournier, "Décret de Burchard" (see above, n. 48), pp. 691–92; idem, "Collections canoniques romaines" (see above, n. 3), p. 276; *Histoire* (see above, n. 2), 2:6. For criticism, see Detley Jasper, "Burchards Dekret in der Sicht der Gregorianer," in *Bischof Burchard von Worms, 1000–1025*, ed. Wilfried Hartmann, Quellen und Abhandlungen zur mittelrheinischen Kirchengeschichte 100 (Mainz, 2000), pp. 167–98. One could even doubt that Fournier's translation is accurate, see Christof Rolker, *Canon Law and the Letters of Ivo of Chartres*, Cambridge Studies in Medieval Life and Thought, Fourth Series 76 (Cambridge 2010), p. 64. It is worth noting that Fournier, while claiming frequently that the Gregorians

that pro-imperial but not Gregorian polemicists would use Burchard for their proof texts.[53] Indeed the same kind of argument, if sometimes articulated less dramatically, is found throughout the *Histoire*. It is most visible in cases where neither the compiler's biography nor the topics a collection covered are quoted to establish its 'tendency', but the very fact that it relies on certain formal sources. This is the case with many of the lesser collections (which are often only studied this way) but also more prominent collections like the *Caesaraugustana* which is described as a Gregorian reform collection mainly on account of the use of other Gregorian collections, not by establishing that it was paying special attention on the topics of the reform.[54]

2.3 *'Ardent Partisans' and Other Groups*

Fournier's model asserted that all collections, at least all 'major' ones, expressed specific ideas and tendencies, which could be explained by the circumstances of their compilation and above all the political intentions of the respective compiler. This in theory was an approach that stressed diversity rather than unity of the collections, as potentially every single collection was shaped by highly individual ideas. In practice, however, the *Histoire* stressed the unity of many collections much more than their diversity. Different as the compilers may have been, they were not working on their own; they were part of communities, networks and groups, and both the compilers and the collectors were shaped by predispositions shared with others.

Sometimes, compilers would express not so much individual sentiments but rather acted as representatives of the order they belonged to by their office's virtue. So if Abbo of Fleury in his collections devoted much more attention to monastic liberty and gathered many authorities protecting monks from

would in general not quote from Burchard, in fact had compiled a long list of collections (including 'Gregorian' ones) that did exactly that: Paul Fournier, "Études critiques sur le Décret de Burchard de Worms," *Nouvelle revue historique de droit français et étranger* 34 (1910), 41–112, 213–21, 289–331, and 564–84.

53 Fournier, "Décret de Burchard" (see above, n. 48), p. 390, n. 391; for a correction of this view, see Jasper, "Burchards Dekret."

54 In fact, the only 'tendency' that is established on the basis of selecting materials on account of their content (not their source) is unrelated at best to Gregorian reform as understood by Fournier and Le Bras: Paul Fournier, "La collection canonique dite *Caesaraugustana*," *Nouvelle revue historique de droit français et étranger* 45 (1921), 53–79, here at p. 75, apparently on basis of the selection criteria behind the ninth book of the *Caesaraugustana* tentatively asserts that it supported the regular clergy rather than monks in what he described as "les conflits très vifs qui [...] mettaient aux prises les moines et les clergé séculier." All other characteristics of the collection, in contrast, are based explicitly on the formal sources the *Caesaraugustana* was compiled from.

interference from the local bishop, while Burchard of Worms devoted only a small part of his *Decretum* to monastic affairs and, as far as he did, mainly gathered authorities on the visitation and control of monastic property by the local bishop, they both acted according to the different roles they had as abbot and bishop.[55]

More frequently, though, the *Histoire* pointed to individual relations and friendship to explain the peculiarities of specific collections. For example, if Burchard's *Decretum* contained at least some elements expressing distance from secular power, Fournier argued that Burchard had accepted this from his collaborator Olbert, who in turn was influenced by his friend Wazo of Liège who was known for his criticism of Henry III.[56] For Fournier, it was apparently less important that the conflict he quotes took place more than two decades after the *Decretum* was finished (namely in 1044), or that Wazo is not known to have clashed with Henry before his election as bishop in 1041. Fournier was likewise convinced that pupils could be expected to produce collections very similar to those of their teachers, only that they were more likely to make mistakes. For example, the collections attributed to Ivo of Chartres in many respects were very similar but one of them (the *Panormia*) contained a remarkable number of misattributions; for Fournier, this could best be explained by the work of less experienced pupils nonetheless sharing the same convictions as their master.[57] Or to take another example, the similarities in the teaching of Bernold, Ivo and Alger according to Fournier could be explained by the fact that they all had been in contact with Urban II.[58] In other cases, collections expressing similar ideas were explained as the result of a collaborative enterprise. Based on a detailed textual analysis, Fournier concluded that Anselm of Lucca, Bonizo of Sutri and Deusdedit exchanged intermediate collections to help each other, and in an unusually speculative move also claimed that Ivo of Chartres had access to these materials.[59]

---

55 *Histoire* (see above, n. 2), 1:326 and 391, respectively.

56 Ibid., 1:391 (repeated almost verbatim from Fournier, "Décret de Burchard," p. 461; see above, n. 48): "Nous ne saurions nous empêcher de penser que si le *Décret* décèle, sur certains points, une tendance plutôt réservée à l'égard du pouvoir civil, c'est dans l'influence d'Olbert, inspirée par Wazon, et plus ou moins acceptée par Burchard, qu'il faut en chercher la cause."

57 *Histoire* (see above, n. 2), 2:92–93 and 102–03.

58 Fournier, "Tournant d'histoire" (see above, n. 3), p. 157 (Bernold and Ivo "développèrent les idées émises par le pontife suprême"); the claim is repeated in *Histoire* (see above, n. 2), 2:358–59 but notably absent from the more detailed discussion of legal theory by Le Bras in the chapter on Alger, Bernold and Ivo (ibid., pp. 335–44).

59 *Histoire* (see above, n. 2), 1:10 (Anselm, Deusdedit, Bonizo), 77 (Ivo) and 105 (Ivo), respectively.

The latter group of compilers are indeed described as an almost uniform group, namely as 'partisans ardents' (a very frequent epithet in the *Histoire*) of the Gregorian reform. The *Histoire* also highlighted how both Gregorian and imperial polemicists drew on canon law collections for proof texts, and indeed Fournier assumed that both sides relied on 'their' collections.[60] Stressing the personal and textual links between canon law and polemic, Fournier's model thereby predicted that there were not only 'Gregorian' but also 'imperial' (or 'anti-Gregorian') collections. Indeed, already in one of his earliest articles on eleventh-century canon law Fournier had dealt with this question. In the same year he published his famous analysis of the *Collection in 74 Titles* as the 'first manual of reform',[61] he also published an article on the *Farfa Collection* as the product of the pro-imperial (indeed 'anti-reform') party.[62]

While these aspects—the office a compiler held, his personal contacts, and political allegiance—all may explain why collections often express the values and interests of specific groups rather than individuals, it is also important to stress that the *Histoire* does not make this a very strong argument. Except in the case of Burchard (representing 'episcopal reform' and the group of imperial bishops in particular), the *Histoire* rarely makes a case that specific collections were shaped by the interests of groups defined by their place in the ecclesiastical hierarchy. Friendship and personal contacts are also only relatively rarely quoted, mainly in cases where there was no textual evidence for the 'tendency' explained this way.[63] Above all, the frequent use of the term 'partisan' does not mean that the *Histoire* thought that most collections were compiled as 'partisan collections' driven by the interest of specific social groups. In the case of the *Farfa Collection*, the *Histoire* indeed asserts that it

---

60 Fournier, "Décret de Burchard" (see above, n. 48), p. 690; *Histoire* (see above, n. 2), 1:5. As mentioned above, many German-speaking scholars of the time had ignored the relation between canon law and polemics of the late eleventh century, e.g. Mirbt, *Publizistik*, pp. 620–21 (as quoted above, note 41).

61 Fournier, "Premier manuel" (see above, n. 3). On the collection itself, see below.

62 Idem, "La collezione canonica del regesto di Farfa," *Archivio della Società Romana di Storia Patria* 17 (1894), 285–301, p. 300 ("monumento di legislazione canonica destinato all'uso di uno dei più importanti monasteri del partito imperiale"); *Histoire* (see above, n. 2), 2:121 ("parti des adversaires de la Réforme," "milieu rebelle à l'Église," "parti qui opposait à la Papauté une résistance obstinée").

63 In particular, the idea that the Ivonian collections were inspired by the Gregorian reform was very difficult to establish from internal evidence, as the Ivonian collections shared much more material with non-Gregorian collections than with Gregorian ones, and the selection criteria according to Fournier's standards often suggest opposition to rather than affirmation of what Fournier described as key issues of the Gregorian reform (lay investiture, papal primacy, papal legates): *Histoire* (see above, n. 2), 2:109–14.

was produced by, and for, a specific group; but the *Histoire* is unequivocal that the 'partisans de la Réforme' were a different case. Indeed for two reasons, according to Fournier and Le Bras, these 'partisans' were not compiling partisan collections. First, any real church reform (that is, 'Reform') was not driven by partisan interest, but the greater good of the whole church; and secondly, the similarities between these collections were explained not by interaction within the reform party but by shared values that motivated the compilers. The difference between 'reform' and 'Reform' was one of ideas, not between social groups.

2.4 *From 'reform' to 'Reform': The Historical Narrative of the* Histoire

This is not the place to discuss Fournier's own political and religious convictions, which evidently shaped his academic work. Yet to understand the difference between 'reform' and 'Reform' in 'Fournier's model', one certainly has to take in account his general perception of ecclesiastical history. As stated in the *Histoire*, Fournier saw the history of the church as a perennial struggle between decadence and progress, marked by tensions between fragmentation and unity, punctuated by alternating periods of anarchy and order.[64] 'Reform', in this context, was the general term for all tendencies (and even modest attempts) towards unity, stability, and order.

Already the subtitles of the single volumes of the *Histoire* ('From Carolingian Reform to the Gregorian Reform') and chapter heading like 'Anarchy and Reform' leave little doubt that this view deeply shaped the historical narrative of his masterpiece. The *Histoire* is a story of reforms and Reforms, with the pre-Gratian collections being both the product and the media of these reforms.

The plural is important here. While Fournier's use of the term 'reform collection' was very generous,[65] he carefully differentiated *which* reform a given collection belonged to. The *Histoire* distinguished between major and minor collections, and for all of the former (and some of the latter) established which reform movement it belonged to. The first volume of the *Histoire* dealt with collections produced or inspired by the Carolingian reform, the Pseudo-Isidorian reformers, and a reform movement associated with Emperor Henry II; the second volume exclusively dealt with the Gregorian Reform era. It is the attachment of all (major) pre-Gratian collections to these reform movements

---

64 *Histoire* (see above, n. 2), 2:109–14 and 360; see Fournier, "Question" (see above, n. 36), p. 100.

65 See in particular *Histoire* (see above, n. 2), 1:IX and 352–61. Fournier's early articles on Pseudo-Isidore (idem, "Question"; idem, "Origine"; see above, n. 36 for both articles) and even his *thèse* are also instructive in this context: Fournier, *Officialités* (see above, n. 7).

that integrates legal history and church history, and therefore contains the crucial elements of the historical narrative of Fournier's model.

2.5 *'Carolingian Reform' and 'Pseudo-Isidorian Reform'*

Given Fournier's view of alternating phases of anarchy and order, it is not surprising that the *Histoire* in its preliminary chapters provides a very grim picture of early medieval church history, that is, the time before the Carolingian reform. The Merovingian age according to the *Histoire* period was marked by 'disorder' and 'anarchy' both at a textual and at the societal level. The canonical collections compiled were useless at best,[66] and many of the penitential books that gained influence were positively dangerous; their spread is described in terms of conquest and infection.[67] Even the Carolingian reform only temporarily changed the state of the Frankish church for the better,[68] mainly because it put the local churches in contact with the papacy again.[69] Like other scholars before them, Fournier and Le Bras saw the rediscovery, dissemination and recombination of canonical collections (namely the *Hadriana-Dionysiana*, the *Hispana* and the *Dacheriana*) as part of this reform; some of the new ('Roman') penitentials and a number of minor canon law collections are also described as 'inspired' by the same reform. Somewhat less conventionally, Regino's *Libri duo* are also counted as a belated expression of the Carolingian reform, partly on account of his material sources, partly because of his 'tendency' to accept royal intervention in church affairs.[70] In the end, Carolingian reform failed, or rather was perverted, as it effectively meant legalizing the seizure of church property and interference of royal and noble houses with church affairs.[71] While the collections rediscovered or newly compiled in the context of the reform were no doubt reform collections, they all showed defects; above all, they failed to centralize church law, which Fournier and Le Bras saw as a decisive criterion of any real reform.[72]

---

66 *Histoire* (see above, n. 2), 1:85 on the *Collectio Hibernensis*.

67 Ibid., 1:85 ('invasion'), 86 ('conquêtes'), 87 ('contagion').

68 Ibid., 1:85.

69 Ibid., 1:85 and 251.

70 Ibid., 1:251 on Regino being "dominé par les idées maîtresses de la Réforme carolingienne, comme le prouve la place prépondérante qu'il donne aux capitulaires, aux conciles et aux écrits pénitentiels du IXe siècle." For Regino's position on royal legislation as another important 'tendency', see *Histoire*, 1:267.

71 Ibid., 1:121–22.

72 Ibid., 1:122: "malgré leur rigoureuse orthodoxie, il est permis de les [the *Hadriana, Hispana* and *Dacheriana* collections, CR] placer en marge de la tradition unitaire." At best, they 'provisionally' and 'imperfectly' achieved some reform goal according to Fournier (ibid., p. 120).

Rather, it was only with the Pseudo-Isidorian forgers (or 'réformateurs isidoriens', as the *Histoire* prefers to call them) that church reform began in earnest. The failure of the Carolingian reform, as far as it was led by secular rulers, according to the *Histoire* made a new reform necessary, and this time by an ecclesiastical party that did not rely on secular rulers but rather on 'Roman' authority. Unlike the Carolingian reforms, this was church 'Reform' with a capital 'R'.[73] The main goal of the reformers, the *Histoire* asserted, was freedom of the church from secular interference and the restitution of church property.[74] For this, the forgers relied on papal authority.[75] They did not, Fournier insisted, strengthen (let alone invent) papal primacy.[76] Rather, papal primacy according to Fournier was well established and only quoted by the forgers to strengthen their own case.[77] In general, while the forgers may have produced new texts, by doing so they restored ancient law.[78] The orientation towards the papacy and ancient church law, not the place of origin or active papal support made this movement 'Roman' in nature.[79] To implement reform, it was crucial to spread these materials, and to replace existing texts—namely 'suspect' penitential canons and conciliar canons of the Frankish church.[80]

However, especially if measured by these standards, the reform largely failed. Neither did penitential canons disappear from the canonical collections, nor did the Pseudo-Isidorian forgeries (despite all the copies the *Histoire* duly mentioned) have a decisive impact on newly-compiled collections.[81]

73 See ibid., 1:120–22 on Carolingian reforms with the help of secular rulers "hostile à la Réforme." Indeed, only reforms inspired by Pseudo-Isidore and/or Gregorian ideas are consistently spelled with a capital 'R' in the *Histoire*; all other reforms (Carolingian, episcopal, imperial, local) are not.

74 Ibid., 1:120–22; see Paul Fournier, "Études sur les fausses décrétales," *Revue d'histoire ecclésiastique* 7 (1906), 33–51, 301–16, 543–64, 761–84, and *Revue d'histoire ecclésiastique* 8 (1907), 19–56, here at p. 301.

75 *Histoire* (see above, n. 2), 1:132; according to Fournier, even bishops themselves were well aware that episcopal reforms were doomed to fail (ibid., p. 120). In his earlier study on Pseudo-Isidore, Fournier had stressed that all 'successful reformers' had had turned to Rome for guidance and inspiration; bishops together with secular rulers are described as potential opponents of reform: Fournier, "Question" (see above, n. 36), p. 103.

76 *Histoire* (see above, n. 2), 1:133 and 231–33; see already Fournier, "Question" (see above, n. 36), p. 100 and idem, "Études" (see above, n. 74), pp. 26–27.

77 See esp. Fournier, "Question" (see above, n. 36), p. 100.

78 *Histoire* (see above, n. 2), 1:232.

79 Ibid.

80 Ibid.

81 Ibid. Fuhrmann famously summarized his own analysis of the evidence as "many manuscripts but little impact" of the Forgeries: Horst Fuhrmann, *Einfluß und Verbreitung der pseudoisidorischen Fälschungen. Von ihrem Auftauchen bis in die neuere Zeit*, 3 vols, Schriften der Monumenta Germaniae historica 24 (Stuttgart, 1972–74), 1:232; idem, "The

The only exception was the *Anselmo dedicata*, which the *Histoire* on account of its high share of Pseudo-Isidorian material, the large number of canons asserting papal primacy and the absence of 'dubious' (i.e. non-Roman) proof texts call a collection expressing 'purely ecclesiastical' reform inspired by Pseudo-Isidore.[82] All other collections compiled between Pseudo-Isidore and the early eleventh century are explicitly called 'minor' collections.[83] With the exception of the collection of Abbo of Fleury,[84] none of them is described as expressing any specific 'idea'; at best, these collection helped to disseminate (already existing) reform ideas.[85] Repeatedly, indeed almost invariably, the *Histoire* stressed that these collections had no discernible influence on later collections, were mostly short, and lacked internal structure.[86] Fournier and Le

Pseudo-Isidorian forgeries," in Detlev Jasper and Horst Fuhrmann (eds.), *Papal Letters in the Early Middle Ages*, History of Medieval Canon Law (Washington, D.C., 2001), pp. 135–95, at p. 184.

82 *Histoire* (see above, n. 2), 1:235 and 234, respectively.

83 *Histoire* (see above, n. 2), 1:234 ('collections majeures' vs. 'collections mineures') and pp. 268–362 (description of 'minor' collections).

84 *Histoire* (see above, n. 2), 1:234.

85 E.g. the collection in Milan, Biblioteca Ambrosiana, A 46 is described as 'farrago' (ibid.), but given the high share of Pseudo-Isidorian materials, it is also said to be "en général inspiré de l'esprit qui animait les réformateurs pseudo-isidoriens" (ibid., p. 331). Likewise, the collection in Vatican City, Biblioteca Apostolica Vaticana, Vat. lat. 3830 is described as "produit de l'esprit de réforme propagé à cette époque dans les monastères italiens, et encouragé par Henri II" (ibid., p. 454) apparently on account of the formal and material sources. In both cases, there is little other evidence to support these claims.

86 It is therefore striking that the *Collection in Twelve Parts* (= *12P*) is counted among the 'minor' collections; it is a very substantial, fairly well-structured collection extant in several manuscripts, as Fournier knew very well. Yet, the *Histoire* (see above, n. 2), 2:442 stressed that its influence was limited (at least compared to the exceptionally successful *Decretum* of Burchard of Worms) and soon 'outdated': "L'influence de la collection en douze livres, à la différence de celle du Décret, ne fut guère sensible [...]. D'ailleurs, avant qu'elle eût le temps de se faire accepter, le mouvement grégorien, auquel notre collection est étrangère, devait s'affirmer, la cause de la réforme entrait ainsi dans une phase nouvelle, et pour ses partisans, la *Collectio XII partium* se trouvait arriérée et démodée." If Fournier's analysis of the *12P* is unusually vague, this may partly have to do with the structure of *12P* but also that scholarship on the collection only relatively recently had moved beyond what the Ballerini brothers had written about this collection (Ballerini and Ballerini, "De antiquis collectionibus," here at PL 56:322; see above, n. 17). Fournier himself had long seen *12P* as one of many Burchard-derivatives; see Paul Fournier, "De quelques collections canoniques issues du *Décret* de Burchard," in *Mélanges Paul Fabre: études d'histoire du moyen âge* (Paris, 1902), pp. 189–214, p. 214; by 1911, he knew the Troyes manuscript of *12P*–Troyes, Médiathèque du Grand Troyes (olim Bibliothèque municipale), Fonds ancien 246–but did not recognize it as a *12P* copy. Rather, he treated it as another Burchard-derivative (idem, "Décret de Burchard," p. 689; see above, n. 46). Ten years later, he had developed the model that was repeated in the *Histoire*; see idem, "La collection

Bras concluded that the reform that produced the Pseudo-Isidorian Forgeries was short-lived.[87]

2.6 *'Imperial Reform'*

The result of this was 'anarchy'—both at a textual level (collections which were often abridged, without clear structure and contained sometimes contradictory canons from very diverse sources[88]) and in secular and ecclesiastical affairs at large.[89] This, according the *Histoire*, gave rise to a new reform movement which was promoted by episcopal and monastic reformers, but mainly by Emperor Henry II.[90] The collections Fournier and Le Bras identified as expressing the ideals of this reform are Burchard of Worms and the South-Italian *Collection in Five Books* (= *5L*), an interesting coupling given that the two emerged far apparat from each other in quite different environments and share little materials; in the case of *5L*, the main link to Henry II are five (of well above 1,000!) canons taken from an imperial council held in early 1014.[91] In the case of Burchard, his biography made it very easy to link him to Henry, but Fournier also argued that some elements of his *Decretum* showed his reservation towards the emperor.[92] The argument that both collections represented 'imperial reform' was partly based on the treatment of the Pseudo-Isidorian material by Burchard and its absence from *5L*, and on the positive attitude of both collections towards imperial legislation. This, however, according to the *Histoire* also explained one of the main weaknesses of this reform, as it relied on secular rulers and failed to sufficiently insist on papal supremacy.[93] This was also the main reason why

canonique dite 'Collectio XII partium': étude sur un recueil canonique allemand du XIe siècle," *Revue d'histoire de l'Église de France* 17 (1921), 31–62 and 229–59.

87 *Histoire* (see above, n. 2), 1:235.

88 Ibid., 1:235; see also ibid., 1:61 on disorder in the penitentials causing 'anarchie' in society.

89 Ibid., 1:61 ('anarchie renaissait dans l'Église'). See also the comments on "la tendance centrifuge, qui produit l'anarchie" (ibid., 1:360).

90 Ibid., 1:360 ('réforme imperiale').

91 Myron Wojtowytsch, "Die Kanones *Henrici regis*. Bemerkungen zur römischen Synode vom Februar 1014," in *Papsttum, Kirche und Recht im Mittelalter. Festschrift für Horst Fuhrmann zum 65. Geburtstag*, ed. Hubert Mordek (Tübingen, 1991), pp. 155–68 argued that it could have taken place in Rome rather than in Ravenna, as was traditionally thought.

92 Fournier, "Études critiques" (see above, n. 52), pp. 572–74.

93 *Histoire* (see above, n. 2), 2:355 on Burchard and *5L*: "[…] ni l'une ni l'autre n'établissaient solidement dans l'Église la suprématie d'un centre législatif et judiciaire, seul capable d'en refaire et d'en conserver l'unité. Les recueils qu'elles engendrèrent souffraient des mêmes vices et de la même impuissance."

they, still according to the *Histoire*, lost influence almost immediately after the papal reform began with the pontificate of Leo IX.[94]

2.7 *The 'Gregorian Reforms' and the 'Turning Point' in Canon Law History*

The most important reform in Fournier's model no doubt is the Gregorian Reform—always spelled with a capital 'R' in the *Histoire* and always referring to the 'reform programme' thought to be common to the popes from Leo IX to Paschal II and their supporters. Yet it was Gregory VII whose name was (and often still is) attached to it; for Fournier like for many scholars, Gregory's pontificate began with Leo IX, as Fliche put it.[95] The *Histoire* certainly reinforced the already widely-held believe that the Gregorian reform movement was an almost all-encompassing, centralized enterprise under the firm direction of the pope.[96] What the *Histoire*, for the first time, argued was that the collections compiled in the century before Gratian were an integral part of the Gregorian reform. On the one hand, they were almost all (either directly or indirectly) 'inspired' by the reform; on the other hand, they were themselves media of the reform, disseminating and implementing both general ideas and specific goals of the reform. The main goal of the reform and the reform collections, according to the *Histoire*, was the freedom of the church from secular interference, the reform of the clergy and—both as an instrument and as an end in its own right—the establishment of a strong papacy. All this was laid out in ancient church law, which the compilers under papal direction rediscovered, and increasingly also in the legislation of the reform popes themselves, which the compilers in Fournier's view were eager to disseminate. At the same time, the

94 The idea has been criticized severely, as both collections continued to be copied and used intensely; see, for example, Horst Fuhrmann, "Über den Reformgeist der 74-Titel-Sammlung (Diversorum patrum sententiae)," in *Festschrift für Hermann Heimpel*, 3 vols, Veröffentlichungen des Max-Planck-Instituts für Geschichte 36 (Göttingen 1972), 2:1101–20.

95 See the opening sentences in Augustine Fliche, *Études sur la polémique religieuse à l'époque de Grégoire VII* (Paris, 1916), p. 1: "Pour la plupart des historiens qui ont traité de la réforme religieuse du XIe siècle, le pontificat de Grégoire VII commence dès 1048 [*sic*], avec l'avènement de Léon IX. C'est au moine Hildebrand que reviendrait l'honneur de toutes les idées et de toutes les initiatives qui orientèrent l'Èglise vers la réforme à laquelle il attache son nom." A now classic criticism of the idea of a supposed 'Gregorian reform programme' is John T. Gilchrist, "Was There a Gregorian Reform Movement in the Eleventh Century?," *Study Sessions of the Canadian Catholic Historical Association* 37 (1970), 1–10; repr. in idem *Canon Law in the Age of Reform, 11th–12th Century*, Variorum Collected Studies Series 406 (Aldershot, 1993), no. VII.

96 Fliche in particular was impressed by the *Histoire*; see his enthusiastic review: *Revue d'histoire de l'Église de France* 19 (1933), 219–26.

reformers strove to purge canonical tradition from legislation that was not (at least implicitly) approved of by the papacy.[97] This, in Fournier's model, also explained why the reformers sought to replace the influential *Decretum* of Burchard of Worms.[98] Alongside the 'new' texts (including rediscovered ancient traditions), and almost as a side effect, this also led to the development of new legal hermeneutics, again directly inspired by the reform papacy according to Fournier and Le Bras. This, in a nutshell, is the key argument of the second volume of the *Histoire* and probably the argument for which Fournier and Le Bras are best known until today. Special attention is therefore needed to understand this argument which was absolutely novel by the time Fournier first articulated it,[99] and won wide acceptance for a long time.[100]

Let us look at the *Histoire* and the collections in detail. Again, the division of materials deserves close attention. The first volume of the *Histoire* had mainly distinguished between 'major' and 'minor' collections, and studied the 'tendency' of the former to establish how the collections conceived, disseminated and adopted concepts of reform. Volume two of the *Histoire* is similar but not identical. While in the first volume the 'major' collections are clearly those which are extant in more copies than any 'minor' collection, in volume two different criteria apply. Importantly, there are at least three different groups of collections. The first chapter of the second volume treats a group of four Italian collections which according to Fournier and Le Bras have in common that they were inspired by the 'pure' spirit of the Gregorian reform movement, namely the *Collection in 74 Titles* (= *74T*) and the collections of Atto of San Marco, Anselm of Lucca and Deusdedit. They are 'major' collections in the sense that the *Histoire* treats them as important, but as far as their dissemination is concerned, and also concerning their quality and structure, they are very different from each other; only one is extant in a two-digit number of manuscripts. The second group of collections are those attributed to Ivo of Chartres which were 'inspired' (as Fournier insisted) by the Gregorian reform but showed a marked reserve towards many Gregorian positions.[101] All

97 *Histoire* (see above, n. 2), esp. 2:4–14.

98 Fournier, "Tournant d'histoire" (see above, n. 3), pp. 131–39; *Histoire* (see above, n. 2), esp. 2:4–14 and 355.

99 The most important early article is Fournier, "Premier manuel"; the earliest fully-fledged version is found in idem, "Tournant d'histoire," and idem, "Collections canoniques romaines." See above, n. 3 for all three articles.

100 A well-known revival of the key argument is Harold Joseph Berman, *Law and Revolution: The Formation of the Western Legal Tradition* (Cambridge, Mass. and London, 1983). See also the works mentioned in n. 1 above.

101 *Histoire* (see above, n. 2), 2:109–14.

three were used in the compilation of relatively many other collections, and the *Panormia* was exceptionally influential; in addition, both the *Tripartita* and the *Panormia* supplied Gratian with his material. The next two chapters are devoted to a large number of 'local' collections; Fournier and Le Bras divide them into Italian and non-Italian collections, and further sub-divide both chapters by whether or not they were influenced by the Italian collections or the Ivonian ones, respectively. A fifth chapter, finally, treats the relation between canon law and theology, and in this context analyses collections like that of Alger of Liège which otherwise is often treated as a canonical collection.

This fifth chapter mainly is important for the claim that the reform papacy inspired the development of new methods ultimately applied by Gratian (but also Abelard and Peter Lombard).[102] The main argument concerning the compilation of collections as part of the Gregorian reform is contained in the previous chapters, and most importantly in the relation between the collections dealt in these chapters. Every chapter is contributed to a distinct part of Fournier's main thesis.

The claim that Gregory VII himself played a role in the compilation of any canon law collection was mainly argued for the Italian collections in the first chapters; three of the four compilers were well-known supporters of Gregory, namely Atto of San Marco, Anselm of Lucca and Deusdedit, and for the anonymous *74T* Fournier had argued vehemently that it was compiled at the curia of Leo IX.[103] For all four collections, Fournier could quote internal evidence supporting the idea that these collections were 'Gregorian', too.[104] However, for the claim that the Gregorian reform had a decisive impact on

102 Fournier, "Tournant d'histoire" (see above, n. 3); Le Bras, "Alger de Liège et Gratien" (see above, n. 30); *Histoire* (see above, n. 2), 2:334–50. The classic reply is Stephan Kuttner, "Urban II and the Doctrine of Interpretation: A Turning Point?," *Studia Gratiana* 15 (1972), 55–85: repr. in idem, *The History of Ideas and Doctrines of Canon Law in the Middle Ages*, 2nd ed., Variorum Collected Studies Series 113 (London, 1992), no. IV. See also Rolker, *Canon Law* (see above, n. 52), pp. 295–303.

103 Paul Fournier, "Une collection canonique italienne du commencement du 12e siècle," *Annales de l'enseignement supérieur de Grenoble* 6 (1894), 343–438; *Histoire* (see above, n. 2), 2:16. This has largely been disproven by Linda Fowler-Magerl, "The Use of the Letters of Pope Gregory I in Northeastern France and Lorraine before 1100," in *"Ins Wasser geworfen und Ozeane durchquert". Festschrift für Knut Wolfgang Nörr*, ed. Mario Ascheri et al. (Cologne, 2003), pp. 237–60; see also Fuhrmann, "Reformgeist" (see above, n. 92).

104 But see Fuhrmann, "Reformgeist" (see above, n. 92); Kathleen G. Cushing, *Papacy and Law in the Gregorian Revolution: The Canonistic Work of Anselm of Lucca*, Oxford Historical Monographs (Oxford, 1998); eadem, "Polemic or Handbook? Recension Bb of Anselm of Lucca's Collectio canonum," in *Bishops, Texts and the Use of Canon Law around 1100: Essays in the Honour of Martin Brett*, ed. Bruce Clark Brasington and Kathleen G. Cushing, Church, Faith and Culture in the Middle Ages (Aldershot, 2008), pp. 69–77.

canon law, Fournier could hardly rely on these three collections, as their influence was limited. Notably the collection of Atto of San Marco which Fournier at many occasions quoted as the exemplar of a Gregorian collection stood out as having extremely limited influence.[105]

Here, the Ivonian collections came into play; while the collections, as Fournier himself conceded, were markedly less 'Gregorian' than the Italian collections discussed before,[106] and contained little material coming either from these collections or the reform papacy, they were very influential indeed, both directly and via numerous collections including, above all, the *Decretum Gratiani*. What they lacked in 'purity' they made up in influence; given the lack of textual links to the reform, it was all the more important first that Ivo was a Gregorian and secondly that the collections (namely the *Panormia*) attributed to him were indeed his own work.[107]

Just as the Ivonian collections were one step removed from the 'pure' idea of reform, the 'local' collections were even further apart, and also lacking in quality, originality, and influence. In the *Histoire*, they are mainly studied as disseminating the texts and ideas they in turn took from 'major' collections.[108] For example, in a sub-chapter on 'cisalpine collections influenced by Ivo', six collections are said to have been influenced, if indirectly, by the Gregorian reform because they draw (though not exclusively, and in different degrees) on the Ivonian collections.[109] Yet the eight 'cisalpine collections independent of Ivo' treated together in another sub-chapter also turn out to be reform collections 'inspired' ultimately by the Gregorian reform.[110] So more or less

105 It is extant in only one manuscript; the rather radical claims in the preface, which Fournier frequently cites, have no parallel in any other collection. On the preface, see Fournier, "Décret de Burchard" (see above, n. 46), p. 692, idem, "Tournant d'histoire" (see above, n. 3), p. 137, and *Histoire* (see above, n. 2), 2:6 and 21–24.

106 *Histoire* (see above, n. 2), 2:109–14.

107 I have challenged both claims elsewhere: Rolker, *Canon Law* (see above, n. 52).

108 Interestingly, this includes several collections which elsewhere are seen as rather 'major' collections, above all the *Liber* of Bonizo of Sutri.

109 See *Histoire* (see above, n. 2), 2:265–313.

110 Ibid. According to Fournier, the collection of Lanfranc "contenait la substance de l'œuvre réformatrice d'Isidore" (ibid., p. 228); it is quoted as proof that the development of canon law in England in the eleventh and twelfth centuries was fundamentally in line with that of continental Europe (ibid., p. 229). The *Collection in Seventeen Books* is described as an abridged version of Burchard brought in line with (Gregorian) reform: "En réalité, notre recueil est un Burchard abrégé et complété dans l'esprit de la Réforme" (ibid., p. 233). The *Collection in Four Books*, reworking *74T* with Pseudo-Isidorian material and letters of Gregory I, for this reason is said to be "fidèle aux inspiration de l'esprit romain, qui était celui de la Réforme, par conséquent de la collection en 74 titres" (ibid., p. 237). The *Collection of Tarragona* compiler, using *74T* and *Liber pontificalis*, is called a "partisan

all 'minor' collections show that the 'major' works were read and used in many places. Unspectacular as every single one may be, their diversity, their geographical dispersal and their sheer number gave credibility to Fournier's claim that the reform had had, in whatever form, a profound impact and indeed changed the law of the church.

Clearly this was a top-down-model, beginning with the 'purest' form of the reform (that is, the *idea* of reform), inspiring a small number of collections containing a 'pure' version of it which in turn is taken up in collections that for one reason or the other only preserved some of this purity, but contributed to its wide dissemination. The gradual diluting of the reform is explained as a 'necessity of life'—not all compilers were able to accept the radical claims, and many (namely Ivo of Chartres) are said to deliberately have made 'compromises' which allowed the reform to win wider acceptance, although at the cost of losing some of its purity.

All methods outlined above to establish 'tendencies' are applied, but in very different combinations. For the Italian Gregorian collections, both textual parallels to programmatic Gregorian texts and the compilers' biographies were crucial to argue that they were the spearhead of the Gregorian reform in law. In the case of the Ivonian collections, the main argument hinges on Ivo's personality and the question of authorship in particular for the *Panormia*. The 'local' collections, finally, are studied by different methods, but most frequently the textual relations to either the Ivonian collections or *74T* is quoted to establish their place in the hierarchy of reform collections.

3 Summary

Fournier's articles and later the *Histoire* presented the reader with a novel way to interpret pre-Gratian collections otherwise often seen as rather inpenetrable by many historians. It also connected the history of canon law with the history of ideas and a (rather ultramontane) narrative of church reform. Different

dévoué du Saint-Siège et de la Réforme" (ibid., p. 247). The Bordeaux collection, combining Burchard with *74T*, exceptionally, is not described as having a specific tendency; only its appendix is highlighted as "décidément favorables à la primauté du Pontife romain" (ibid., p. 250). The *Collection in Thirteen Books* is called a Gregorian collection, "l'œuvre d'un partisan détermine de la réforme ecclesiastique et de l'autorité pontificale" (ibid., p. 258). For the Arras collection, no reform tendency is stated but Fournier highlights that the most recent material are letters of Gregory VII (ibid., p. 260). The Saint-Victorine *Collection in Nine Books* too according to Fournier is a reform collection "dévoué à la cause de la Réforme et la mémoire de Grégoire VII" (ibid., p. 265).

aspects of Fournier's model were, and still are, attractive to different audiences. For his contemporaries, the questions of church reform, 'church and state', 'Investiture Contest' and the personality of Gregory VII may have been most important in their judgement of the *Histoire*. In the controversies over Gregory VII which continued well into the twentieth century, the close link between the reform papacy, ancient church law and high medieval canonical collections the *Histoire* proposed were particularly attractive for those who read it as an apology of Gregorian reform as both necessary and just.[111] Yet in the long run it was probably more important that the *Histoire* had much to offer for historians working with very different methods and on topics well beyond the Gregorian reform. For many scholars working mainly on the textual tradition of canonical texts, Fournier's model was attractive as it gave new significance to their minute analyses; but it was likewise attractive for the history of ideas, as a whole new genre of sources could now be studied for the transmission of ideas. And although Fournier and Le Bras themselves did not exploit this aspect, it also contained clues how canonical collections could be linked to a study of social groups which used collections to define themselves, to maintain cohesion and to act collectively.

These merits are independent from the doubts that have been raised concerning many of Fournier's claims pertaining to specific collections, and for this reason any references to such doubts have been consigned to the footnotes in this article. Likewise, while Fournier almost always used his then novel method to fit almost all pre-Gratian collections in his historical narrative of perennial reform, the merits of his model do not depend on the grand narrative enshrined in the *Histoire*. We need not adopt either Fournier's view on church history, nor his assumption about 'Reform', and certainly not his specific view of the Gregorian reform to adopt his methods. One does not even need to share his optimism that most collections had one and only one 'tendency'; in fact, while Fournier was sometimes very bold in his interpretations and quick to label collections as 'inspired by Gregorian reform', he also in many cases was ready not to pronounce any judgement, came to conclusions that ran against his own assumptions, and in several cases provided evidence for quite contrary interpretations. If scholars in the past two decades in particular have argued against Fournier's historical narrative of 'reform', they often relied on Fournier's methods, and this way have confirmed the merits of Fournier's model.

111 See Augustine Fliche, *La Réforme grégorienne*, 3 vols (Leuven and Paris, 1924–37) in particular.

CHAPTER 2

Law and Reform: The Transmission of Burchard of Worms' *Liber decretorum*

Kathleen G. Cushing

The *Liber decretorum* of Bishop Burchard of Worms (hereafter *LD*) was one of the most important canon law collections of the eleventh and early twelfth centuries until the compilations associated with Ivo of Chartres came into widespread use.[1] Yet even given the popularity and transmission of the *Panormia*, it is clear that *LD* continued actively to be read and consulted after this, especially in Italy. For example, whilst Gratian made scant use of *LD*, a considerable proportion of the *paleae*—the additions or 'chaff' added to the *Decretum Gratiani* by masters at Bologna—was in fact derived from Italian manuscripts of Burchard.[2] Moreover, manuscript evidence shows that *LD* continued to be copied (either in full or in abbreviations) throughout the twelfth and early thirteenth centuries and there are more than 35 references to *LD* manuscripts (for the most part no longer extant) in old library catalogues dating from the twelfth to the eighteenth centuries.[3] No doubt, there were considerably more that have not survived. At the same time, scholars such as Weigand, Landau and Summerlin among others have drawn attention to the continuing use of pre-Gratian collections—or the 'old law'—by the decretists in glosses and in decretal collections, thereby underlining the extent to which the *ius novum* did not mean the end of appeals to the older collections, including Burchard.[4] Indeed there is likely a connection between Gratian's neglect of

1 I am grateful to Professor Peter Landau for his comments on an earlier version.

2 Peter Landau, "Burchard de Worms et Gratien: A propos des sources immédiates de Gratien," *Revue de droit canonique* 48 (1998), 233–45, where he argues that Burchard accounts for some ten canons and revised his earlier contention of no use as in his "Vorgratianische Kanonessammlungen bei Dekretisten und in frühen Dekretalensammlungen," in *Proceedings of the Eighth International Congress of Medieval Canon Law: San Diego, University of California at La Jolla, 21–27 August 1988*, ed. Stanley Chodorow, MIC Subsidia 9 (Vatican City, 1992), pp. 93–116.

3 Lotte Kéry, *Canonical Collections of the Early Middle Ages (ca. 400–1140): A Bibliographical Guide to the Manuscripts and Literature*, History of Medieval Canon Law (Washington, D.C., 1999), pp. 145–47.

4 Landau, "Vorgratianische Kanonessammlungen bei Dekretisten" (see above, n. 1), pp. 93–116; Rudolf Weigand, *Die Glossen zum 'Dekret' Gratians. Studien zu den frühen Glossen und*

 | DOI:10.1163/9789004394384_004

Burchard and the attention it found after 1150, mostly among the decretists. For example, the noted canonist and decretalist, Bernard of Pavia (a man educated at Bologna under Bazianus, Gandulphus and perhaps even Huguccio himself), availed himself of Burchard's *LD* when compiling his *Breviarium extravagantium* or *Compilatio prima* in the 1190s. Whilst the prevailing master narrative might imply that Bernard's use of 'Brocarda' or Burchard could be deemed personal, idiosyncratic or indeed even 'antiquarian', Bernard of Pavia's decretal collection, as Summerlin argues below, was the first to be widely used in the schools and the stability of the text (which existed in more than a handful of manuscripts) suggests that its users had no qualms about continuing to appeal to the old law.[5] Whilst other examples are offered by Summerlin, it is a clear indication of the extent to which Burchard and other 'old law' continued to be read alongside, used to supplement and inform the *ius novum* and indeed the *ius commune*. Indeed, the ongoing copying of the *Decretum Gratiani* in the later twelfth and thirteenth centuries provides compelling evidence of this phenomenon, especially if we accept Gratian as the culmination of the old law and not necessarily the start of the new law, spurred on by the recovery of Justinian's *Digest*.[6] The problem remains, however, that the historical master narrative of the development of medieval canon law especially in the eleventh and twelfth centuries indelibly influenced by Paul Fournier has not been sufficiently adjusted to reflect the textual and historical realities.

Paul Fournier devoted considerable scholarly attention to Burchard's *LD* in extended critical articles on its sources, character and influence, all reprinted in his *Mélanges de droit canonique* and also summarized in the exceptionally influential (possibly too much so) *Histoire des collections canoniques en Occident dépuis les Fausses Décrétales jusqu'au Décret de Gratien*, co-authored with Gabriel Le Bras.[7] Fournier recognized the pivotal role played by Burchard in compiling a practical, indeed user-friendly compendium for pastoral care, but found the collection theoretically unsophisticated and on the whole dismissed

Glossenkompositonen, 2 vols, Studia Gratiana 26–27 (Rome, 1991). See Danica Summerlin, "Using the 'Old Law'" in the present volume.

5 Danica Summerlin, "Using the 'Old Law'" in the present volume.

6 For a different perspective, see Kenneth Pennington, "The 'Big Bang': Roman Law in the Early Twelfth Century," *Rivista internazionale del diritto commune* 18 (2007), 43–70. See also Bruce Clark Brasington, *Order in the Court: Medieval Procedural Treatises in Translation*, Medieval Law and its Practice 21 (Leiden, 2016), pp. 52–58.

7 Paul Fournier, *Mélanges de droit canonique*, 2 vols, ed. Theo Kölzer (Aalen, 1983); Paul Fournier, with the collaboration of Gabriel Le Bras, *Histoire des collections canoniques en Occident dépuis les Fausses Décrétales jusqu'au Décret de Gratien*, 2 vols (Paris, 1931–32). Le Bras' principal contribution was up to the eleventh century.

the collection as lacking 'le droit théorique'.[8] As Christof Rolker discusses in chapter 1 in more detail, Fournier's relentlessly teleological narrative of the development of the western legal tradition where all roads led from the Pseudo-Isidorian *Decretals* 'jusqu'au Gratien' (most notably seen in *Histoire des collections canoniques*) continues to cast a long shadow and his master narrative has remained seductively influential.[9] He contended that critical legal acumen in canon law was first revealed in the polemical and ideological orientation of the 'Gregorian' canon law collections, which, in turn, fed into the proto-scholasticism of the Ivonian *Decretum* which Fournier believed was a preparatory work for the *Panormia*. This proto-scholastic approach was then 'realized' as a fundamentally scholastic and indeed even proto-jurisprudential approach to canon law as a legal science in its own right in what he believed to be the Ivonian *Panormia*. This theoretically-sophisticated approach together with the decisive advent of Roman law within the canonical tradition then triumphed, according to Fournier, in Gratian.[10] This of course is a simplistic and somewhat unjust characterization of Fournier's historical trajectory, but one made for a purpose. For Fournier, Burchard had to be relegated into an unsophisticated pre-reform context and indeed he argued that *LD* was eclipsed by the far less widely-transmitted Gregorian collections, quite in the face of the manuscript transmission. As Detlev Jasper has shown, if it actually had been the Gregorian reformers' intention to supplant *LD*, they failed abysmally, especially in Italy.[11]

---

8 Paul Fournier, "Le Décret de Burchard de Worms: ses caractères, son influence," *Revue d'histoire ecclésiastique* 12 (1911), 451–73 and 670–701, here at p. 453.

9 Christof Rolker, "Fournier's Model and its Merits," in the present volume.

10 There is much debate on the nature and timing of the recovery of Roman law and the idea of a 'big bang' (as Pennington, "Big Bang," above note 6). As Abigail Firey, among others, has noted, "there is danger in seeming to reduce 'law' and 'jurisprudence' to learned law and the written opinions of professional jurists, a danger in envisaging this law as universal and prescriptive" (Abigail Firey, "Getting Rid of the Lawyers with High Explosives: The Strange History of Medieval Canon Law," paper presented at the Medieval Academy of America's annual meeting, Chicago, 26–28 March 2009). I am grateful to Abigail Firey for permission to cite this unpublished paper here. For a lucid summary of the debates, see Brasington, *Order in the Court* (see above, n. 6), pp. 56–57 and the literature he cites in notes 20–21.

11 Detlev Jasper, "Burchards Dekret in der Sicht der Gregorianer," in *Bischof Burchard von Worms, 1000–1025*, ed. Wilfried Hartmann, Quellen und Abhandlungen zur mittelrheinischen Kirchengeschichte 100, pp. 167–98. See also Kathleen G. Cushing, "Law, Penance, and the 'Gregorian' Reform: The Case of Padua, Biblioteca del Seminario Vescovile MS 529," in *Canon Law, Religion and Politics: Liber Amicorum Robert Somerville*, ed. Uta-Renate Blumenthal, Anders Winroth and Peter Landau (Washington, D.C., 2012), pp. 28–40.

This chapter seeks to argue that the transmission of Burchard provides a very useful mechanism with which to challenge the Fournier model and to think about a new discourse in medieval canon law research, as part of an argument in which continuity rather than change is more important. At the same time, its looks to suggest that Gratian (in various stages) was a significant development but one that extended the nature, purpose and audience of canon law without necessarily eradicating the nature, purpose and audience of the 'old law' that continued to be read throughout the twelfth century and beyond. In this way, one might say that Gratian 'matters' more in hindsight in terms of scale, the scholastic tradition and in modern historiography. This is in no way to underestimate the great significance of Gratian, the *Decretum Gratiani* and its stimulation of legal learning, especially after 1150. Yet Gratian has become a towering divide and the historical narrative of early medieval canon law leads inexorably to him only then to explode in a progressive, historical big bang in which law becomes jurisprudence that then marches through the decretists to the decretalists and to *Liber extra*. Our thinking about the development of the western legal tradition, moreover, has been further clouded by the problematic transmission of Gratian, which, when we scrutinize it, is extraordinary in terms of the sheer number of manuscripts, abbreviations, and commentaries, etc. but also perhaps restricted to a quite selective audience, chiefly but of course not solely the schools, although here as well thinking about production and provenance might prove useful.[12] For historians of canon law, change, evolution and linear development are perhaps inescapably the general default position and this may be the problem. To stress just continuity, however, would be simplistic and inadequate. Yet, it is clear that the 'old law' did not disappear with the 'new' and we must find ways creatively to tell this story. The process by which what we might term the applied or practical theology of the earlier middle ages, where compilers and users of canon law 'looked beyond their texts into a world the [later] lawyers were rarely to enter'—as Martin Brett memorably put it—became the jurisprudential system of legal norms of the schools, the curia and professional lawyers requires more from us than plotting

12 There needs to be further work on the production and use of canon law collections by monks. For example, the extant first recension manuscripts of the *Decretum Gratiani* have monastic provenances, although the manuscripts themselves are late. See Anders Winroth, *The Making of Gratian's Decretum*, Cambridge Studies in Medieval Life and Thought, Fourth Series 49 (Cambridge, 2000), pp. 18–32. See Kathleen G. Cushing, "Monastic 'Centres' of Law? Some Evidence from Eleventh-Century Italy," in *From Learning to Love: Schools, Law and Pastoral Care in the Middle Ages*, ed. Tristan Sharp, Abigail Firey and Isabelle Cochelin (Toronto, 2017), pp. 315–26 and Christof Rolker's forthcoming volume of the *History of Medieval Canon Law*.

causality in a chronological narrative.[13] It demands reflection more than has been done not simply on the ostensible purpose of a text (its sources, methods, etc., something at which Fournier did excel) but especially on its readers, their use, indeed consumption, of that text, all of which changed over time. Indeed, as Brett has reminded us, behind every copy, version, excerpt, abbreviation and manuscript, there is a reader. The influence and tranmission of a collection such as *LD* offers a useful test case study, but one that could clearly be applied to other collections.

1 Burchard and the Transmission of the *Liber decretorum*

Burchard was born in Hesse sometime in the mid-tenth century (*c.*965) to a noble and well-connected family. He became a canon at the cathedral in Koblenz and may also have studied there at the monastic school of either Sankt Kastor or Sankt Florian. He seems to have been something of a peripatetic scholar and at some point studied at the cathedral school in Mainz where he came under the patronage of Archbishop Willigis (975–1011) who appointed him to several positions including treasurer and provost of Sankt Viktor at Mainz. Elevated to the see of Worms by Otto III in February 1000, Burchard in many ways resembles the typical imperial bishop of the Ottonian-Salian *Reich*: close to and dependent upon imperial patronage but also a reformer in his own right with keen concerns for ecclesiastical discipline along with his bishopric's rights and its peoples as shown notably in his *Lex familiae Wormatiensis* of 1024–25, a short code of the customary laws governing the *familia* of Worms. Burchard died in 1025.

To have a sense of the significance of *LD*, it is useful first of all to think quantitatively: compiled between 1012 and 1023 (with Hartmut Hoffmann and Rudolf Pokorny suggesting between 1015 to 1020 on palaeographical grounds), its popularity is borne out not just by its subsequent use as a formal source but also by its widespread transmission.[14] The collection remains extant in more than 80 copies with some 20 fragments some of which consist of single leaves

13 Martin Brett, "Finding the Law: The Sources of Canonical Authority before Gratian," in *Law before Gratian: Law in Western Europe c. 500–1100*, ed. Per Andersen, Mia Münster-Swendsen and Helle Vogt, Proceedings of the Carlsberg Academy Conference on Medieval Legal History 3 (Copenhagen, 2007), pp. 51–72.

14 Hartmut Hoffmann and Rudolf Pokorny, *Das Dekret des Bischofs Burchard von Worms. Textstufen—Frühe Verbreitung—Vorlagen*, MGH Hilfsmittel 12 (Munich, 1991). For further literature and manuscripts see Kéry, *Canonical Collections* (see above, n. 3), pp. 134–48. See Greta Austin, *Shaping Church Law around the Year 1000: The* Decretum *of Burchard*

and, as noted above, there is evidence that many additional copies existed. For the purposes of comparison, the *Panormia* exists in some 150 copies whilst the total number of extant Gratian manuscripts (in multiple forms) stands at more than 600, of which Weigand postulated that more than 150 date from the twelfth and first half of the thirteenth centuries.[15] Although Burchard was explicit in his *Preface* that the collection should not pass beyond the boundary of his bishopric and that it was intended for use/study by his prelates, *LD* was quickly transmitted and in the form of the Frankfurt manuscript moved rapidly beyond Worms to southern Germany to Burgundy and to Italy. Burchard himself may have had a role in its early dissemination.[16]

Burchard's collection was especially valued in Italy and nearly half the extant manuscripts are of Italian origin.[17] It is known, for instance, that Abbot Rudolf I of Nonantola (1002–35) had acquired a copy and that another was at the Cathedral of Parma by the mid-eleventh century. The early use of Burchard in Italy can also be seen in minor canonical collections such as the *Collectio capitula Veronensis* (second quarter of the eleventh century), in the *Collectio canonum* of Biblioteca Apostolica Vaticana, Vat. lat. 3830 (mid-eleventh century), in the *Collectio canonum Barberiniana* (begun between 1050 and 1073 and augmented in two later stages), in the *Collection in 183 Titles* (after 1063; hereafter *183T*),[18] and Joseph Ryan long ago argued for its wider

---

of Worms, Church, Faith and Culture in the Medieval West (Aldershot, 2009) with a comprehensive bibliography.

15 Weigand, *Die Glossen zum Dekret Gratians* (see above, n. 4). See also Winroth, *Making of Gratian's Decretum* (see above, n. 11), pp. 9–15.

16 Austin, *Shaping Church Law* (see above, n. 14), pp. 26–28.

17 The classic work on the transmission of Burchard is Otto Meyer, "Überlieferung and Verbreitung des Dekrets des Burchard von Worms," *Zeitschrift der Savigny-Stiftung für Rechtsgeschichte, kanonistische Abteilung* 24 (1935), 141–83, which was extended by Hubert Mordek, " Handschriftenforschungen in Italien I. Zur Überlieferung des Dekrets des Bischofs von Worms," *Quellen und Forschungen aus italienischen Archiven und Bibliotheken* 51 (1971), 626–51; Gérard Fransen, "Le *Décret* de Burchard de Worms: Valeur du texte de l'édition. Essai de classement des manuscrits," *Zeitschrift der Savigny-Stiftung für Rechtsgeschichte, kanonistische Abteilung* 63 (1977), 1–19; idem, "Le *Décret* de Burchard," in *Burchardi Wormatiensis ecclesiae episcopi decretorum libri XX ex consiliis et orthodoxorum patrum decretis* [...], ed. Gérard Fransen und Theo Kölzer, Aalen 1992, pp. 25–42; See also Hoffmann and Pokorny, *Dekret des Bischofs Burchard* (see above, n. 14).

18 On these collections, see Linda Fowler-Magerl, *Clavis Canonum: Selected Canon Law Collections before 1140: Access with Data Processing*, MGH Hilfsmittel 21 (Munich, 2005), pp. 94, 95–97, 98, 101; *Liber canonum diversorum sanctorum patrum sive Collectio in CLXXXIII titulos digesta*, ed. Joseph Motta, MIC Corpus collectionum 7 (Vatican City, 1988); Mario Fornasari, "*Collectio canonum Barberiniana*," *Apollinaris* 36 (1963), 127–41 (analysis) and 214–97 (edition), and Kathleen G. Cushing, "'Intermediate' and Minor Collections: The Case of the *Collectio Canonum Barberiniana*," in *Readers, Texts and*

circulation in Italy before 1050 given the use of the collection made by Peter Damian in his letters.[19] As well as being copied as a unique collection, *LD* was also combined especially in central and southern Italy with the *Collection in Five Books* and its derivatives, later with the *Collection in 74 Titles*, and with other penitential and liturgical collections, a number of which date from the mid-eleventh century onwards.[20]

It is also clear that a number of different versions (if ultimately dependent on the Frankfurt version) were circulating quite early in Italy that we now refer to as the so-called Italian Order of Worms, Type B. This version, although with variants and additions, includes Burchard's preface, the text of *LD* interrupted by the distinctive *Ordo synodalis 5* with the canons from the Council of Seligenstadt (1023) at the conclusion of an often (if not always) abbreviated book 20.[21] There are further sub-groups such as one that circulated in Tuscany which informed Vat. lat. 3830, the *Colllection in Two Books/Eight Parts* and Anselm of Lucca which can be identified by consistent variations in the inscriptions, e.g. the attribution of a Gelasian decretal to Hormisdas. Gerard Fransen also noted copies of the collection marked by four *lacunae*, that he termed 'deteriores', which seem to have originated in northern Italy before *c.*1090 although its archetype may be even earlier.[22]

The transmission of Burchard elsewhere in Europe, however, was less immediate and less extensive. Only some 13 of the extant manuscripts are French and none of these date before 1050. Here we also see a geographical divide in that southern French copies were ultimately dependent on Italian models whereas in northern France the so-called German version of Order of Worms, Type B prevailed. Burchard's influence and reception in northern France, however, was not negligible as can be seen in the revised *Collectio Atrebatensis* of Paris, Bibliothèque nationale, lat. 18221 and the *Atrebatensis* (*c.*1093), but its principal influence was indirect and derived from its reception

---

Compilers in the Earlier Middle Ages: Studies in Medieval Canon Law in Honour of Linda Fowler-Magerl, ed. Martin Brett and Kathleen G. Cushing, Church, Faith and Culture in the Medieval West (Aldershot, 2009), pp. 73–86.

19 John Joseph Ryan, *Saint Peter Damiani and his Canonical Sources: A Preliminary Study in the Antecedents of the Gregorian Reform* Pontifical Institute of Medieval Studies. Studies and Texts 2 (Toronto, 1956), pp. 13 and 160.

20 See Roger E. Reynolds, "Penitentials in South and Central Italian Canon Law Manuscripts of the Tenth and Eleventh Centuries," *Early Medieval Europe* 14.1 (2006), 65–85, esp. pp. 76–84 and literature cited there.

21 For the 'Order of Worms, type B', see Rudolph Pokorny in Kéry, *Canonical Collections* (see above, n. 2), pp. 137–42; on *Ordo 5*, see Herbert Schneider, *Die Konzilsordines des Früh- und Hochmittelalters*, MGH Ordines de celebrando concilio (Hanover, 1996), esp. p. 235.

22 Fransen, "*Décret* de Burchard" (see above, n. 17), pp. 8–12.

into the Ivonian collections, especially the *Decretum* and those dependent on it. England, as in so many ways, was again 'exceptional' and was essentially a directly Burchard-less world until the circulation there of the *Panormia* which was of course a vehicle of Burchardian material albeit in very different form taken from the Ivonian *Decretum*.

2 Burchard and His 'Readers'

In terms of its audience, it is clear that *LD* was especially valued in episcopal circles: it was a practical, user-friendly collection, ideally suited to episcopal administration, and useful in conducting councils as Eberhard I of Konstanz (d. 1046) noted in his copy of the collection. The penitential clearly also extended its pedagogical if not necessarily its practical influence. Compilers such as that of the *183T*, Anselm of Lucca and later Ivo of Chartres would be considerably influenced by *LD* and it is certainly the case that most but not all extant copies are from episcopal rather than monastic libraries. But there were other readers of Burchard in the eleventh and twelfth centuries. Monasteries both in Italy and elsewhere did possess copies of *LD*; monks and abbots, after all, needed canon law quite as much as bishops and other clergy for a variety of practical reasons: to defend their privileges, liberties and exemptions in disputes with bishops and others, and even—it can be contended—for pedagogical purposes. And, as already stressed above, *LD* found many readers among the decretists and decretalists, for example in the late twelfth century at the Cistercian monastery of Alcobaça in Portugal, itself a centre of canon law study where decretal collections were compiled and at Saint-Remi in Reims around 1180.[23]

It is important to remember, however, that *LD* was not simply copied without perhaps an implicit critique. Italy of course offers the best example for comparisons because of its widespread transmission, and its variations such as the *deteriores* noted above. But one of the striking things about the reception of Burchard in Italy are what can be called the Burchard derivatives. By this I refer to those collections that amalgamated or else copied together parts of Burchard (and very often simply Book 19, the so-called *Corrector sive medicus*) with other collections such as the *Collection in Five Books* and from

23 See Kéry, *Canonical Collections* (see above, n. 3), pp. 138 and 136, respectively. See also Peter Landau, "Die Dekretsumme 'Tractaturus Magister' und die Kanonistik in Reims in der zweiten Hälfte des 12. Jahrhunderts," *Zeitschrift der Savigny-Stiftung für Rechtsgeschichte, kanonistische Abteilung* 100 (2014), 132–52.

the later eleventh century, ones that combined Burchard with the *Collection in 74 Titles*, e.g. Rome, Biblioteca Vallicelliana, F2 and F8; Montecassino, Archivio dell'Abbazzia, 216 and Rome, Biblioteca Casanatense, 2010.[24] All of these derivative compilations give us evidence of readers for whom—for reasons about which we can only speculate—*LD* perhaps did not entirely meet their needs. Others seem to have rejected the collection outright, for example Atto of San Marco, at whose church a copy of *LD* was likely available. In his preface to the *Breviarium* compiled at Rome *c.*1075, Atto can be seen as criticising Burchard for the use of canons of dubious authority from transalpine councils and other apocryphal texts.[25]

Other eleventh- and twelfth-century 'readers' suggest a reflective or even selective attitude, one that would be useful to extend to understanding *LD*'s decretist and decretalist readers.[26] The *Collectio canonum* of Vat. lat. 3830 and the *Collectio canonum Barberiniana* use Burchard in interesting ways. The *183T* compiled perhaps at Lucca in the decade after 1063 makes considerable use of Burchard in blocks, but supplements these with Ps.-Isidorian decretals, texts from the *Code*, the *Institutes* and the *Epitome Iuliani* along with extensive materials from Gregory I's *Register* and excerpts from St Augustine. The collection of Anselm of Lucca, moreover, clearly valued Burchard as an important and authoritative formal source—but not the only one. As has been shown elsewhere, the relationship of Burchard and Anselm Book 11, the penitential, is especially instructive. Although Burchard acts as a comprehensive source in many ways in this book, the blocks of texts do not always follow the original sequence.[27] Anselm's use, moreover, of other material, in particular the late eighth/early ninth-century tripartite penitential

---

24 See Reynolds, "Penitentials," (see above, n. 20) pp. 76–85.

25 *Breviarium*, ed. Angelo Mai, *Scriptorum veterum nova collectio e Vaticanis codicibus edita* 6.2 (Rome, 1832), 60–61. Mai believed that the condemnation referred to the Roman penitential, whereas Fournier believed that it referred to Burchard: Fournier, "Le Décret" (see above, n. 8), p. 692. Given that Atto named both the Roman Penitential and Burchard before his famous line: 'Multa tamen ibi, licet vera, falso nomine auctoris titulantur, alia re ipsa falsa leguntur, alia vero turpissima scribuntur, quae sanctis viris solet esse pudor dicere et pudor audire', I would suggest (as many scholars agree) that it could be an explicit criticism of Burchard.

26 As is currently being undertaken by Danica Summerlin. See her "Using the 'Old Law'" in the present volume. For Founier's hermeneutic, see Christof Rolker, "Fournier's Model and its Merits" in the present volume.

27 Kathleen G. Cushing, "Anselm of Lucca and Burchard of Worms: Re-Thinking the Sources of Anselm 11, *De Penitentia*," in *Ritual, Text and Law: Studies in Medieval Canon Law and Liturgy Presented to Roger E. Reynolds*, ed Kathleen G. Cushing and Richard F. Gyug, Church, Faith, and Culture in the Medieval West (Aldershot, 2004), pp. 225–39.

known as the *Capitula iudiciorum*, suggests not blind or automatic copying but deliberate selections—on grounds about which we can only speculate—that reflected a need for supplementary sources. Ivo of Chartres' reconfiguration of Burchard in the *Decretum* and the use of Burchard by Gregory of San Grisogono for the *Polycarpus* offer further evidence of careful and critical reading, though both are beyond the scope of the present chapter.

It is of course difficult to understand how compilers 'read' Burchard. Many of the collections noted above lack prefaces and ostensible discussion of authorial intent. It is perhaps unwise to be too doctrinaire in insisting that editorial decisions about formal sources and the presentation of canons reflects systematic legal reasoning or deliberate canonistic erudition, but at the same time they must do so in some if not many cases. Those who chose not to use or to neglect the collection are even more unfathomable. For example, we can only speculate about why—given the extensive Italian transmission of *LD*—Gratian made such minimal use of it. That said, as Landau has demonstrated, Gratian's formal sources were quite restricted: Anselm, *Tripartita, Panormia, Polycarpus* and the *Collection in Three Books*, with other sources used for specific parts of the *Decretum*, e.g. Alger of Liège and the *Sententiae Magistri A.*[28] (This is essentially the case for both the first and the second recensions.) Whether *LD* was simply not available or was 'rejected' is probably unknowable, although the ways in which the *Decretum* was constructed may have been a factor. As Titus Lenherr has shown, Gratian seems not to have used all his sources at the same time (some in the beginning and some later); a contention corroborated by Winroth for the first recension.[29]

3 Conclusions

If the 'old law' was characterized by compilers and readers who looked beyond the texts into the real world and who read/used those texts in that context, as the author of the first recension of Gratian's *Decretum* could also be argued to do,[30] where did they go in the world of the *ius novum*? Even more important,

28 Landau, "Vorgratianische Kanonessammlungen bei Dekretisten" (see above, n. 2), pp. 93–116.

29 Titus Lenherr, *Die Exkommunikations- und Depositionsgewalt der Häretiker bei Gratian und den Dekretisten bis zur 'Glossa Ordinaria' des Johannes Teutonicus*, Münchener theologische Studien. Kanonistische Abteilung 42 (Munich, 1987), here at pp. 12–17. See Winroth, *Making of Gratian's Decretum* (see above, n. 11), pp. 17–18.

30 See Anders Winroth, "Marital Consent in Gratian's *Decretum*," in *Readers, Texts and Compilers in the Earlier Middle Ages: Studies in Medieval Canon Law in Honour of Linda*

where should they be situated in a new narrative of the development of medieval canon law? Were these compilers theologians, lawyers or something else sitting uneasily in between these supposedly separate spheres as older narratives have suggested?

If the boundaries between law and theology were still not clear cut after the 1140s (and certainly less so before), we need to think about how compilers came to their collections trained in theology as much as law and whose preoccupations with preparing the priesthood for *cura animarum* (as Burchard made clear in his Preface to *LD*) spoke both to the classroom as much as to the practical or applied theologians and continued to do so. It is not enough to say that when canon law as 'applied theology' became jurisprudence the concerns of the supposedly theoretically unsophisticated old law became the province of theologians and *summae confessorum* whilst the practical ramifications of the chasm between law and reality played itself out in local ecclesiastical courts, the papal courts or were handled by judge delegates *in partibus*. The counterpart to such a narrative would state that, in the *ius novum*, law became the theoretical and professional jurisprudence of the schools where law was first and foremost an academic discipline whose proponents engaged probably little with the world, apart perhaps from those lawyers who ended their teaching careers as bishops. Whilst I simplify for effect, this remains an enduring if too uncomplicated narrative. In the end, Western Christendom remained in the twelfth century and beyond a place where compilers, commentators, readers, students and users of canon law had to look beyond learned texts and scholastic disputes so as to bridge the gap between normative rules and the often messy realities of lived human experience, as Burchard did, along with probably many of his subsequent readers.[31] As historians, we need to find a way to accommodate their stories in a narrative of the western legal tradition that takes into account a multiplicity of understandings of what constituted learned law in the eleventh and twelfth centuries.

Fowler-Magerl, ed. Martin Brett and Kathleen G. Cushing, Church, Faith and Culture in the Medieval West (Aldershot, 2009), pp. 111–21.

31 An intriguing example are Burchard's *interrogationes* involving superstition, magic and remnants of paganism in Book 19.5 of *LD* which have no legal or penitential precedents and which may well reflect practices prevalent in the Rhineland in the late tenth and early eleventh centuries. See Bernadette Filotas, *Pagan Survival, Superstitions and Popular Cultures in Early Medieval Pastoral Literature* (Toronto, 2005), pp. 56–57. The extensive correspondence of Bishop Ivo of Chartres offers many examples of looking into the 'real world', see Christof Rolker, *Canon Law and the Letters of Ivo of Chartres*, Cambridge Studies in Medieval Life and Thought, Fourth Series 76 (Cambridge, 2010). See also Winroth, "Marital Consent in Gratian's *Decretum*," especially pp. 119–21.

CHAPTER 3

New Narratives for the Gregorian Reform

Greta Austin

The master narrative about the Gregorian Reform generally represents the Gregorian Reform as pivotal in the history of Western law. Paul Fournier formulated a highly influential version of the master narrative in his "Un tournant" article of 1917.[1] He recapitulated this in his *Histoire* with Gabriel Le Bras. Fournier elegantly explained changes in Western law and traced these changes to the Gregorian Reformers and to the rediscovery of Roman law. According to Fournier's model, canonists' notions of law, and their methods of legal interpretation, remained simplistic and arbitrary until the Gregorian Reform. The popes and their supporters unearthed new legal texts, including Roman law, in order to underpin their new claims to authority. The Gregorians' rediscovery of Roman law inspired a second generation of canonists under Urban II, particularly Ivo of Chartres, to develop new systematic methods of jurisprudence. For Fournier, Ivo not only wrote the first systematic treatise on jurisprudence, one which anticipated early scholasticism. Ivo also created a canon law collection, the *Panormia*, which put those principles into action. For Fournier, the *Panormia* laid the groundwork for Gratian's *Decretum* and a new period of 'classical' canon law, one which culminated ultimately in the codification of church law.

Fournier's narrative has been widely influential. Here I will talk only about one use of Fournier, that of Harold Berman, an American law professor with wide-ranging interests. In his book on the history of Western law, Berman took Thomas Kuhn's model of scientific revolutions, and applied Kuhn's model to the history of law.[2] For Berman, the Gregorian Reform was a 'revolution' in law. The Gregorian Reform, Berman claimed, caused the Western legal system to come into being.[3] Berman's book won a prize from the American

1 Paul Fournier, "Un tournant de l'histoire du droit 1060–1140," *Nouvelle revue historique de droit français et étranger* 41 (1917), 129–80; repr. in idem, *Mélanges de droit canonique*, ed. Theo Kölzer, 2 vols (Aalen, 1983), 2:373–424.

2 Thomas S. Kuhn, *The Structure of Scientific Revolutions* (Chicago, 1962). This essay will not discuss the critiques of Kuhn's theory. For one such critique, see https://www.thenewatlantis.com/publications/the-structure-of-scientific-revolutions-at-fifty.

3 Harold Joseph Berman, *Law and Revolution: The Formation of the Western Legal Tradition* (Cambridge, Mass. and London, 1983), p. 123.

 | DOI:10.1163/9789004394384_005

Bar Association. His *New York Times* obituary described him as altering "beliefs about origins of Western law."[4] Berman's book covers many subjects, but this paper focuses on his discussion of the Gregorian Reform as a kind of 'big bang' that gave birth to the Western legal tradition.

Fournier and Berman are useful representatives of the master narrative, at least in part because one came out of the civil law tradition and the other out of the Anglo-American common law tradition. Berman is instructive also because he defined 'Western law' precisely as a 'legal system' which possesses particular characteristics. For Berman, the crucial features of a legal system are methods of handling texts, and 'legal institutions', especially a professionalized body of specialists who have been trained in a professional system.[5] He showed himself to be a product of the common law tradition, which focuses on institutions and methods. Conversely, Fournier focused on the entrance of Roman law and on systematization, which paved the ground for codification.[6]

Many aspects of the narrative are under siege today.[7] This paper begins by discussing some flaws with the master narrative first formulated by Fournier. To develop these new narratives, we should start by learning from the master narrative—what are its flaws? How can we avoid these? In critiquing the master narrative, there are two ways to approach it:

1) Does contemporary research support Fournier's claims about the history of Western law? Here we set aside whether their assumptions and methods are correct.
2) Conversely, let us set aside whether the evidence works or not, and ask a different question. When they told their stories about how the Gregorian Reform changed (Fournier) or gave birth to (Berman) Western law, what were their assumptions about 'law'? What did they think law

---

4 *New York Times*, November 18, 2007, http://www.nytimes.com/2007/11/18/us/18berman.html?_r=0.

5 Berman, *Law and Revolution* (see above, n. 3), pp. 4–5. Berman looks for a legal system, which has "legal institutions and procedures, legal values, legal concepts, legal rules." These result in governance, they allocate rights and duties, and they resolve conflicts. Berman goes on to identify characteristics of all legal 'systems': a distinction between the legal institution and other types of institutions; the existence of specialists or legal professionals; a professional system for training jurists; the transformation of those institutions by legal learning (pp. 7–9).

6 Paul Fournier, with the collaboration of Gabriel Le Bras, *Histoire des collections canoniques en Occident dépuis les Fausses Décrétales jusqu'au Décret de Gratien*, 2 vols (Paris, 1931–32), here at 2:357; see also ibid., p. 361.

7 William North and Maureen Miller have organized a series of 'Rethinking Reform' panels at the Kalamazoo International Congress on Medieval Studies, and these panels have provided important jumping off points for rethinking the master narratives.

was? What did they look for in 'law'? And then, by extension, how should new narratives about law and reform define law? How should they look for 'reform'? In the conclusion, this paper proposes a few new directions for narratives which could replace the old Fournier story, which over-emphasizes and anticipates the later vertical structure of the papacy. The new ways of describing the eleventh-century movements might avoid triumphalist views of Western progress, as well as teleological approaches which often over-anticipate later developments, such as the eventual monarchical papacy. Instead, new narratives might focus more on the local and regional demands for the rule of law—as much to the 'horizontal' structures as well as the vertical structures of the medieval Church and its law.

1 New Research and the Old Master Narrative

Let us ignore, for the moment, Berman and/or Fournier's starting definitions of law, and thus what they look for in the history of law. Instead, let us ask: What does new research say about their narrative? In what directions does that new research point us for constructing new narratives? This paper singles out only a few examples of problems highlighted by recent research.[8]

Problem #1: Canon Law Occupied a Vital Place in the Church before the Gregorian Reform

Fournier saw the Gregorian Reform as a period of 'profound transformation' in the growth and systematization of church law.[9] Fournier singled out collections like the *Collection in 74 Titles* and those compiled by Anselm of Lucca and Deusdedit as 'establishing uniformity' and as modeling 'the Gregorian spirit' of reform.[10] Yet the *Collection in 74 Titles* is a monastic, not a papal reforming,

8 Peter Clarke provides an excellent overview in his entry on 'Canon Law' for the *Routledge History of Medieval Christianity, 1050–1500*, ed. Robert N. Swanson (Abingdon and New York, 2015), pp. 77–89, here at pp. 78–80.

9 *Histoire* (see above, n. 6), 2:355.

10 *Histoire* (see above, n. 6), 2:355.

collection,[11] and Deusdedit survives in only one medieval manuscript.[12] Only Anselm of Lucca seems to have exercised both considerable influence in terms of manuscript dissemination and effect on later collections.[13] Fournier underplayed the extent to which Burchard's *Decretum*—a collection which for him represented the uninspired 'before' against which the glorious 'after' of the reforming collections shone more brightly—continued to be copied even after the 'reforming collections' of the later eleventh century,[14] and the extent to which Burchard's collection supplied texts to those 'reforming' collections.[15] Burchard's collection exercised an enormous influence, and its influence is only now beginning to be fully appreciated.

Generally, as with the work on Burchard, recent research suggests that canon law was thriving before the papal reform movements. Papal reformers participated in that growth and contributed to it, such as in Anselm's work, but did not initiate it. As an early and influential sceptic of the master narrative, Martin Brett pointed out a "vast undergrowth of canonical interest" during the later eleventh and early twelfth centuries.[16] Brett's work points to a 'middle- and bottom-up' more than a 'top down' model of legal growth.

The model of legal growth itself might need to be re-thought as well, since such an "undergrowth of canonical interest" might have existed far longer than previously thought. Historians of medieval canon law (the author included),

---

11 Linda Fowler-Magerl, "The Use of the Letters of Pope Gregory I in Northeastern France and Lorraine before 1100," in *"Ins Wasser geworfen und Ozeane durchquert". Festschrift für Knut Wolfgang Nörr*, ed. Mario Ascheri et al. (Cologne, 2003), pp. 237–60; Christof Rolker, "The *Collection in Seventy-Four Titles*: A Monastic Canon Law Collection from Eleventh-Century France," in *Readers, Texts and Compilers in the Earlier Middle Ages: Studies in Medieval Canon Law in Honour of Linda Fowler-Magerl*, ed. Martin Brett and Kathleen G. Cushing, Church, Faith and Culture in the Medieval West (Aldershot, 2009), pp. 59–72.

12 Lotte Kéry, *Canonical Collections of the Early Middle Ages (ca. 400–1140): A Bibliographical Guide to the Manuscripts and Literature*, History of Medieval Canon Law (Washington, D.C., 1999), pp. 229–30.

13 Kathleen G. Cushing, *Papacy and Law in the Gregorian Revolution: The Canonistic Work of Anselm of Lucca*, Oxford Historical Monographs (Oxford, 1998).

14 See Kathleen G. Cushing's paper "Law and Reform: The Transmission of Burchard of Worms' *Liber decretorum*" in this volume.

15 Christof Rolker, *Canon Law and the Letters of Ivo of Chartres*, Cambridge Studies in Medieval Life and Thought, Fourth Series 76 (Cambridge 2010), p. 66.

16 Martin Brett, "Canon Law and Litigation: The Century before Gratian," in *Medieval Ecclesiastical Studies in Honour of Dorothy M. Owen*, ed. Michael J. Franklin and Christopher Harper-Bill, Studies in the History of Medieval Religion 7 (Woodbridge, 1995), pp. 21–40, at p. 34.

often relying on models which look for change, tend to compare a 'before' to an 'after.'[17] These models may inherently underestimate the contributions of earlier periods. Indeed, the contemporary research on canon law during the Carolingian, Ottonian and early Salian periods increasingly suggests continuity in canonical activity, rather than sudden growth during the Reform period. Scholars have historically neglected these periods because of the long shadow cast by, as Abigail Firey writes,

> a larger narrative shaped to accentuate the creativity and expansion of the universe of medieval legal studies after the publication of Gratian's *Decretum*, which so effectively integrated canonistic and Roman legal perspectives.[18]

This larger narrative also caused Carolingian (as well as many pre-Gratian collections) to be assessed anachronistically according to later standards. As Firey points out,

> The plethora of Carolingian collections, and the scholarly presumption that proper law should be systematised and codified, diminished appreciation of Carolingian canon law. To those for whom notable legal achievement displays uniformity, central authority, and fixity, the canon law of the Carolingian epoch seemed chaotic, indeterminate in scope and sources, and variable in its textual representation.[19]

Considerably more work remains to be done to understand better Carolingian and Ottonian and Salian canon law on their own terms. Even so, the accomplishments of these periods are already becoming clear. For instance, the on-going research of Wilfried Hartmann has demonstrated the depth and breadth of canonical work during the later ninth and tenth centuries.[20]

17 Greta Austin, *Shaping Church Law around the Year 1000: The* Decretum *of Burchard of Worms*, Church, Faith and Culture in the Medieval West (Aldershot, 2009).

18 Abigail Firey, "Canon Law in the Carolingian Era," in *The Cambridge Companion to Medieval Canon Law*, ed. Anders Winroth and John C. Wei, p. 1 (draft numbering). Thanks to Prof. Firey for allowing me to consult this article before publication.

19 Firey, "Canon Law," p. 2 (draft numbering).

20 Hartmut Hoffmann has documented the extensive activity of Ottonian scriptoria: *Buchkunst und Königtum im ottonischen und frühsalischen Reich*, 2 vols, Schriften der Monumenta Germaniae historica 30 (Stuttgart, 1986) and *Schreibschulen und Buchmalerei. Handschriften und Texte des 9.–11. Jahrhunderts*, Schriften der Monumenta Germaniae historica 65 (Hanover, 2012). The study focusing on canonical activity during this period is, above all, Wilfried Hartmann, *Kirche und Kirchenrecht um 900. Die Bedeutung der*

This period not only produced the landmark collections of Regino of Prüm and the *Anselmo dedicata*, but also witnessed a wide range of legal production linked to the Church, be it through synodal decrees and decisions, episcopal capitularies, penitentials, and a variety of legal collections and dossiers.[21] In short, canon law occupied a vital place in the Church before the papal reform movement.

Problem #2: Before the Gregorian Reform, Church Law was Being Systematized, and Jurisprudential Methods were Being Developed

For both Berman and Fournier, the papal reformers laid the groundwork for the birth of legal science, in which professionals began to lay out legal principles and to develop methods for interpreting texts.[22] Such methods did not exist previously, according to most versions of the master narrative.

Before the Gregorian Reform, however, there is evidence that thinkers engaged with interpretative questions in canon law and theology. Abbo of Fleury had already pointed out the problem of conflicting texts, and suggested some methods for addressing these. Like Gratian, but in a much more limited sense, Abbo had included commentary on canonical texts.[23] Similarly,

---

spätkarolingischen Zeit für Tradition und Innovation im kirchlichen Recht, Schriften der Monumenta Germaniae historica 58 (Hanover, 2008).

21 Hartmann, *Kirche*; Greta Austin, "The Bishop and the Law of the Church, 900–1050," in *The Bishop Reformed: Studies in Episcopal Culture and Power in the Central Middle Ages (900–1215)*, ed. John Ott and Anna Trumbore Jones (Aldershot, 2007), pp. 39–56; eadem, "Canon Law in the Long Tenth Century, 900–1050," in *The Cambridge Companion to Medieval Canon Law*, ed. Anders Winroth and John C. Wei (Cambridge, forthcoming).

22 See Fournier, "Un tournant" (see above, n. 1), especially at p. 165, as well as his comments in *Histoire*, 2:358 (see above, n. 6), "A dire vrai, c'est la restauration de l'herméneutique juridique qui sera la conséquence des principes posés par Urbain II." Similarly, he commented, "Si tel fut un des résultats des recherches provoquées par Grégoire VII, ce fut là sûrement un résultat fort imprévu, et qui, par les consequences si importantes qu'il entraîna, ne répondit nullement aux aspirations des chefs du movement réformateur du XIe siècle" (ibid., p. 14). Berman, *Law and Revolution* (see above, n. 3), p. 120, on the universities, wrote: "The emergence of modern Western legal systems in the late eleventh and the twelfth centuries was closely related to the emergence of the first European universities. There, for the first time in western Europe, law was taught as a distinct and systematized body of knowledge, a science, in which individual legal decisions, rules, and enactments were studied objectively and were explained in terms of general principles and truths basic to the system as a whole."

23 Abbo's *Collectio canonum*, canon 8, points out that canons conflict, and then suggests a method for addressing this: "unde considerandus est terrarium situs, qualitas temporum, infirmitas hominum, et aliae necessitates rerum, quae solent mutare regulas diversarum provinciarum. Potestate etiam multa mutate sunt pro communi utiliate ecclesiarum, quae nemo reprehendit fidelium," that is, "… one has to consider the site of countries,

Burchard of Worms worked to eliminate conflicts and to address questions of the authority of texts.[24] Regino of Prüm took a different approach: he included a variety of texts and left "to the judgment of the reader what he prefers to select and approve as most important."[25] In other words, a user (like the archbishop of Mainz) would be able, on his own, to identify legal answers from a range of texts. These texts might conflict, but the user would know how to find a legal answer. Many huge pre-Gregorian legal compendia, like the *Collection in Twelve Parts*, might have simply given readers an enormous selection of texts. Readers could then identify their own legal answers. These compendia thus may assume considerable legal discretion, as well as methods for addressing issues. In short, before the papal reforming movements, church law was not in such a sorry state of disrepair as Berman and Fournier represented it to be.

Problem #3: There is not a Clear, Causal Link between the Gregorian Reform and the Rise of Jurisprudential Reasoning

First, contemporary research on Ivo and the canon law collections attributed to him problematizes Fournier's model. For Fournier, Ivo provided a crucial bridge between the Reformers and early scholastic thought.[26] But Christof Rolker has challenged this picture: "Ivo was not a reformer in Fournier's sense;

---

the quality of the times, the weakness of man, and other necessities of matter, which habitually change the rules of the various provinces. By lawful power much has also been changed on behalf of the general expediency of the churches, which no believer would censure" (trans. from Marco Mostert, *The Political Theology of Abbo of Fleury: A Study of the Ideas about Society and Law of the Tenth-Century Monastic Reform Movement*, Middeleeuwse studies en bronnen 2 (Hilversum, 1989), p. 117). On Abbo see, inter alia, *Abbon, un abbé de l'an mil*, ed. Anne Dufour and Gilette Labory, *Bibliothèque d'histoire culturelle du Moyen Âge* 6 (Turnhout, 2008), esp. Franck Roumy, "Remarques sur l'œuvre canonique de Abbon de Fleury," at pp. 311–41; Elizabeth Dachowski, *First among Abbots: The Career of Abbo of Fleury* (Washington, D.C., 2008), and Mostert, *Political Theology*.

24 Austin, *Shaping Church Law* (see above, n. 17).

25 See Regino's preface in *Reginonis abbatis Prumiensis libri duo de synodalibus causis et disciplinis ecclesiasticis*, ed. Friedrich G.A. Wasserschleben (Leipzig, 1840; repr. Graz, 1964), p. 2: "lectoris iudicio dereliquens, quid potissimum eligere ac approbare malit [...]"; trans. Robert Somerville and Bruce Clark Brasington, *Prefaces to Canon Law Books in Latin Christianity: Selected Translations, 500–1245* (New Haven and London, 1998), p. 94.

26 Fournier, "Un tournant" (see above, n. 1), pp. 159–66. Kuttner followed Fournier in asserting that the *Panormia* was "more instrumental than other treatises of the same period in disseminating these methods and principles," that is, of "general doctrines of interpretation": Stephan Kuttner, "The Revival of Jurisprudence," in *Renaissance and Renewal in the Twelfth Century*, ed. Robert Louis Benson and Giles Constable (Oxford, 1982), pp. 299–323, here at p. 311; repr. in idem, *Studies in the History of Medieval Canon Law*, Variorum Collected Studies Series 325 (Aldershot, 1990), no. III.

he did not compile the *Panormia*; and his genuine works display few, if any, 'pre-scholastic' traits."[27] Rolker calls for less of a focus on 'great men' like Ivo, and for a "story starting with the interests of scribes and readers—and the very plurality of these interests."[28]

Second, the rediscovery of Roman law does not seem to have led directly to a rebirth of jurisprudence. For Fournier, the rediscovery of Roman law, specifically the *Digest*, significantly changed the 'evolution of canon law'. Roman law provided the "methods and new categories" for a new scientific study of church law.[29] But the re-entry of Roman law seems to have been more limited than Fournier acknowledged. Even in Gratian 1, Roman law played a relatively minor role.[30] In the Ivonian collections, Roman law also played a fairly limited role as well.[31] Fournier's narrative is also problematic in that it works implicitly from early modern understandings of Antiquity as the measure of intellectual achievement.

Thus, on many fronts, scholars have challenged the evidence supporting Fournier's master narrative. These challenges should provide important starting points for new narratives.

---

27 Rolker, *Canon Law* (see above, n. 15), p. 296.

28 Rolker, *Canon Law* (see above, n. 15), p. 298.

29 According to Fournier, the Gregorians' enterprising research in the service of the Reform led to the reappearance of the *Digest*. The *Digest* entered canonical collections and acquired "une place assez importante. Cependant la découverte des *Pandectes* fut le signal de la renaissance de l'étude du droit romain et du renouveau de son enseignement, fait capital, qui, non seulement devait transformer la législation de la plupart des nations de l'Occident, mais eut sa répercussion dans l'évolution du droit canonique, auquel il donna des methods et des categories nouvelles et qu'il dota ainsi d'un enseignement véritablement scientifique," *Histoire*, 2:13–14 (see above, n. 6). See also Fournier, "Un tournant" (see above, n. 1), p. 151.

30 Anders Winroth, "Roman Law in Gratian and the *Panormia*," in *Bishops, Texts and the Use of Canon Law around 1100: Essays in the Honour of Martin Brett*, ed. Bruce Clark Brasington and Kathleen G. Cushing, Church, Faith and Culture in the Middle Ages (Aldershot, 2008), pp. 183–90.

31 In the books on homicide and just war in Ivo's *Decretum* and the *Panormia* formerly attributed to Ivo, Roman law added relatively few new ideas. These collections borrowed the basic framework of categorizing offenses and crimes in terms of homicide from the early eleventh-century collection of Burchard of Worms, who in turn relied extensively upon Regino of Prüm's *Libri duo*. Ivo's *Decretum* and the *Panormia* had less elaborate schemata than Burchard in terms of the practical rules about homicide. Their main contribution was to provide canons on just war that were new to the canonical tradition. Those discussions of just war, however, came extensively from patristic texts. Augustine is quoted far more than Roman law in the sections on just war in the *Decretum* and the *Panormia*.

1) Legal interest was growing before the Gregorian Reform.
2) Similarly, thinkers were dealing with hermeneutical questions before the Gregorian Reform.
3) More attention should be paid to the 'horizontal' picture of various textual communities,[32] rather than to Great Men, as John Wei points out in his paper.[33] The third part of this paper will take up these points.

2 Berman and Fournier's Starting Assumptions about Law

Berman and Fournier shared an interest in law which was not separated clearly from religion. Each emphasized different aspects of the Reform, based on their background in either the civil law or common law traditions. Berman in particular rejected the Enlightenment "concept of law as something wholly instrumental."[34] Berman, a Jewish convert to Christianity, saw law as deriving some of its authority not from its instrumentality, but from its grounding in religion: "in all societies, though in widely varying ways, law draws on the sense of the holy partly in order to commit people emotionally to the sense of the just".[35] Berman recognized that American society is pluralistically religious and no longer predominantly white and protestant, and he made clear that he was not calling for a return to a 'golden age'.[36] For Berman, law had power because of its transcendent meanings and values, as grounded in religion:

> The radical separation of legal and religious institutions does not require the radical separation of legal and religious values. It does not require the total secularization of law and the total spiritualization of religion.[37]

Berman saw law and religion as distinct but still drawing upon each other. He defined "religion and law in the broadest possible terms—religion as man's

32 See Martin Brett, "Editions, Manuscripts and Readers in Some Pre-Gratian Collections," in *Ritual, Text and Law: Studies in Medieval Canon Law and Liturgy Presented to Roger E. Reynolds*, ed Kathleen G. Cushing and Richard F. Gyug (Aldershot, 2004), pp. 205–24, here at p. 219.

33 John Wei, "Of Scholasticism and Canon Law: Narratives Old and New,".

34 Harold J. Berman, "Law and Religion in American Constitutional History," in *Faith and Order: The Reconciliation of Law and Religion*, Emory University Studies in Law and Religion 3 (Atlanta, 1993), p. 215.

35 Ibid., p. 19.

36 Ibid., p. 224.

37 Ibid., p. 216.

sense of the holy, law as man's sense of the just."[38] People obey laws because of their transcendent values: "in all societies, though in widely varying ways, law draws on the sense of the holy partly in order to commit people emotionally to the sense of the just."[39] Thus, for Berman, revivifying the religious elements of law could potentially solve social ills, including the problem of repeat offenders being incarcerated rather than reintegrated into their communities—a prescient critique of the current American punitive justice system that has enjoyed increasingly loud support in recent years.[40] Berman's work in *Law and Revolution* thus arose out of his broader concern to demonstrate the religious foundations of contemporary law, which he traced all the way to the Gregorian Reform.

To the scholarly critiques of the Fournier narrative about the Gregorian Reform, described in this essay earlier, Berman might respond as follows: "Yes, 'law' did exist before the Gregorian Reform, but it was not *really* law in the Western sense of a legal *system*." Berman asserted that no "legal system—a distinct, integrated body of law, consciously systematized"—existed before the Gregorian Reform.[41] Until the Gregorian Reform, Berman claimed, "there was no independent, integrated, developing body of legal principles and procedures clearly differentiated from other processes of social organization and consciously articulated by a corps of persons specially trained for the task."[42] If we set aside the evidence laid out above, Berman's argument 'works'. Berman defined the Western legal system in modern terms. Berman's definition of law also focuses on institutions and professionalization, as well as on legal methods. Berman's definition of Western law, then, seems very much shaped by his background in the Anglo-American common law.

Conversely, Fournier, writing in the civil law tradition, argued for an 'evolution' of law, in which the Gregorian Reform marks a dramatic 'turning point'. The Gregorian Reform, for Fournier, marked the rediscovery of Roman

38 Ibid., p. 19.

39 Ibid.

40 Ibid., p. 15: "a recognition of the dialectical interdependence of law and religion leads us in the opposite direction—in the direction of fundamental social, economic, and political change and of new legal solutions for the acute problems confronting us," such as "unemployment, racial conflict, crime, pollution […]."

41 Berman, *Law and Revolution* (see above, n. 3), p. 49. Before the Gregorian Reform, Berman wrote (ibid., p. 50), "legal rules and procedures […] were largely undifferentiated from social custom and from political and religious institutions. No one had attempted to organize the prevailing laws and legal institutions into a distinct structure. Very little of the law was in writing. There was no professional judiciary, no professional class of lawyers, no professional legal literature. Law was not yet consciously systematized."

42 Berman, *Law and Revolution* (see above, n. 3), p. 50.

law. Its achievements eventually led to codification of the canon law. Fournier described the *Code of Canon Law* of 1917 as achieving the Roman work of the unification of canon law—a project in which the Gregorian Reform played a crucial role.[43]

For Fournier and Berman, the Gregorian Reform was very important, but they focused upon different aspects of it. Berman stressed the professionalization and specialization of the teaching of canon law—hallmarks of the common law tradition. Fournier emphasized jurisprudential methods and Roman law—hallmarks of the civil law tradition. Both Fournier and Berman began with modern (and different definitions) of 'law', and then worked to identify these characteristics of modern law, in embryonic form, during the Gregorian Reform.

Thus, Fournier and Berman bring us to the question of definitions, which underpin implicitly or explicitly all new narratives. How should new narratives define 'law'? Church law? Similarly, what was the Gregorian Reform? What is reform? This paper focuses primarily on the first question, that of 'what is law'. Yet the Gregorian Reform itself is a term much under siege, as other papers in this volume point out. Reform, too, is a much contested term; it often implicitly measures medieval thought against the standards of modernity or Antiquity. For the purposes of this paper, I leave aside now the question of 'reform'.

In formulating new narratives, we need to pay particular attention to that question of defining law. All new narratives must begin with the question—what are we looking for in the Middle Ages when we tell new stories about church law? Are we looking for the history of us and 'our' law, so to speak? Or, on the other hand, are we trying to understand what medieval people understood by church law, and to understand the range of meanings involved in those terms, for different audiences?

To put it another way, there are essentially two ways of thinking about how new narratives might define church law. One, like Berman and Fournier, we could work backwards from modern Western conceptions of law (and there are many such definitions, which differ, of course). Two, we could adapt an understanding of law as, very generally, a system of rules, in which law is what people say it is. So this definition of church law would be harder to create, because it would involve surveying the pluralities of ideas about church law in various places and times, as Brett and Rolker suggest: understanding localized and varied understandings of church law, on their own terms.

The second approach may be more fruitful for developing new narratives—that of defining church law as medieval people saw it, rather than reading the

43 *Histoire* (see above, n. 6), 2:360.

present back into the past. The Berman and Fournier approach, of defining law in contemporary terms, has a number of problems. First, such a model of evolution (Fournier) or transformation (Berman) tends towards a sunny teleological history, one in which church law only improves. Implicit here is the assumption that our contemporary legal model is the ideal, best one, and that law has been 'evolving' towards that improved point. It is a somewhat narcissistic view of the past, to praise whatever seems to be 'modern' and 'like us'. Second, such a view of history tends to find what one wants to find. If you anticipate an end result, it is easier to find people who 'anticipate' or 'lay the groundwork' for that particular result. Third, Fournier and Berman actually stress *different* aspects of legal accomplishment. They see what they want to see in the Gregorian Reform. In this way, the Gregorian Reform (or any other period) becomes a blank slate onto which moderns project themselves. And fourth, modernity (or antiquity) becomes the measuring-stick of progress and 'reform'. Only what 'worked'—what was 'rational', modern, etc.—becomes important, without paying attention to the plurality and messiness on the ground. Because of these concerns, then, I suggest that a better starting point for new narratives might be to define law as 'what people thought it was', and to study a plurality of understandings of church law.

3 Starting Points for New Narratives about Church Law

A second discussion question would be the following: What was the so-called Gregorian Reform? For the purposes of this paper, I define it as a series of overlapping movements, centreed around Rome, of varying intensities during the second half of the eleventh century. The reformers worked for 'a reorientation of loyalties', which not only fought against various issues like "simony, clerical unchastity, ecclesiastical property, and freedom from lay control", but also worked to create "boundaries, both for and between different parts of society", to borrow Kathleen Cushing's definition.[44]

And yet another discussion question would be the following: What about narratives in general? Is there one 'metanarrative' that can describe church law? Or are we in a postmodern world in which the master narrative has fragmented, and in which no one narrative can describe the local and the specific? "We tell ourselves stories in order to live", wrote the essayist Joan

44 Kathleen G. Cushing, *Reform and the Papacy in the Eleventh Century: Spirituality and Social Change* (Manchester and New York, 2005), pp. 35–36.

Didion.[45] Historians, too, live by stories. In his review of *Law and Revolution*, Edward Peters points out the benefits of large-scale narratives: "It must first be said of Berman's study that he has indeed made the effort and taken the risk of setting forth a broad historical account—and that he will be criticized for the way in which he has done it."[46] So new stories do seem in to be in order—and the plural is deliberate, rather than one *new* 'master narrative'.

The research suggests some directions for new narratives. A pattern emerges across the history of church law during the Middle Ages: that church law would eventually shift from 'horizontal' and legally pluralistic, to 'vertical' and unified under a papal monarch. Before the Reform, church law—like the Church itself—was 'horizontal', with many local users. In the tenth and early eleventh centuries, church law was legally pluralistic and localized: practiced, collected, and/or ignored in many small worlds with overlapping boundaries. The bishop of Rome was the ultimate authority, but primarily in theory and not as a matter of practice. His letters were generally not diffused and copied widely; they usually reached only a fairly small number of recipients. The papal reformers' contribution was to re-energize a vision of a hierarchically structured state centralized under the bishop of Rome. The reformers might have capitalized on a general demand for law, which the Church, as one of the dominant institutions in the social field of the period, could carry out. But I do not think the papal reformers (nor Roman law) invented that legal interest, nor jurisprudential methods in the West. That interest and those methods pre-dated the Reforming period of the eleventh century. This narrative of horizontal to vertical differs from Berman or Fournier, because the Gregorian Reform plays a relatively minor role. The story is that of continuity, rather than of sharp disjunctures (Fournier) or beginnings (Berman).

The collections described collectively as the *Panormia* itself might provide a model for describing the pluralistic and 'horizontal' narrative of law during the long eleventh century. There is no one stable text of the *Panormia*. Rather, there are *Panormias*, plural, which differ sometimes considerably from each other.[47] Studying the *Panormia* requires us to abandon one metanarrative and to look at many different narratives—many different users, in various places,

45 Joan Didion, "The White Album," in *The White Album* (New York, 1979), p. 11.

46 Edward Peters, review of *Law and Revolution*, in *Harvard Law Review* 98 (1985), 686–96, here at p. 687. Peters calls for historians to improve on Berman at p. 696.

47 See Martin Brett and Bruce Brasington's provisional edition of the *Panormia*, available at https://ivo-of-chartres.github.io/ with date/revision stamp 2014–06–03 / b8a41.

with a wide range of interests and needs.[48] Similarly, perhaps there was no one singular 'canon law', but rather a plurality of church laws, a dynamic set of texts, traditions, and customs upon which local users drew variously and differently.

In addition, the *Panormia* might well be a model for thinking about the changes in church law during this period. It includes many texts not found in Regino or Burchard. And in the later eleventh century, we *do* see a change: that many new texts entered the canonical tradition.[49] The Church Fathers comprised many of the new texts,[50] but Roman law was also present in the *Panormias*.[51] So the *Panormia*—one of the most widely-copied collections of the twelfth century—does represent change, but a change that attests not to a more 'vertical' structure, but instead to greater messiness, greater diversity, and a wider set of topics—for instance, the introduction of just war into the subject of homicide which Burchard and Regino had already treated. In comparison to the layout of Burchard's *Decretum*, the *Panormia* disappoints. It is much less 'user-friendly' than the *Decretum*—the rubrics are wildly inconsistent and varying, many copies lack rubrics entirely or after book three, there are often not running headers or tables of contents, and so forth. So the *Panormia* points to more 'messiness'—less of a clean singular narrative, and a localized, horizontally-structured plurality of church law. The *Panormia* has, in a sense, come full-circle. Fournier saw it as exemplifying the 'spirit of Reform',[52] but instead the *Panormias*, plural, might well exemplify the diversity and complexity of the 'horizontal' nature of church law's users and communities during the long eleventh century.

48 Martin Brett's work has been seminal; see, e.g. "Editions, Manuscripts and Readers" (see above, n. 32), and "Creeping up on the *Panormia*," in *Grundlagen des Rechts. Festschrift für Peter Landau*, ed. Richard H. Helmholz et al., Rechts- und Staatswissenschaftliche Veröffentlichungen der Görres-Gesellschaft N. F. 91 (Paderborn, Munich, Vienna, and Zurich, 2000), pp. 205–70.

49 Peter Landau, "Wandel und Kontinuität im kanonischen Recht bei Gratian," in *Sozialer Wandel im Mittelalter: Wahrnehmungsformen, Erklärungsmuster, Regelungsmechanismen*, ed. Jürgen Miethke and Klaus Schreiner (Sigmaringen, 1994), 215–33; *Histoire* (see above, n. 6), 2:12.

50 Peter Landau, "The Development of Law," in *The New Cambridge Medieval History, c. 1024–1098*, 4/1, ed. David Luscombe and Jonathan Riley-Smith (Cambridge, 2015), pp. 113–47, here at p. 121.

51 Winroth, "Roman Law" (see above, n. 30).

52 *Histoire* (see above, n. 6), 2:Préambule.

CHAPTER 4

Clerical Networks and Canon Law: The Beauvais Election Controversy of 1100–04

John S. Ott

Many scholars, both within and outside the field of canon law, are currently in the midst of a sustained period of questioning about the value and validity of one of the quintessential historical paradigms of the Middle Ages—namely, the nearly continuous presence and role of reform in religious life, above all of the so-called 'Gregorian' reform of the late eleventh century. We have begun reflecting on what insights we gain, and what we overlook, by continuing to embrace 'reform' as an explanatory or causal factor in the institutional and legal evolution of the medieval church.[1] Intellectual unease over the reform label is nothing new. Since at least the 1960s, historians and legal scholars have been squeamish about using it without serious qualification, whether applying it to mentalities, individuals, institutions, legal collections, or political agendas.[2] In his 1988 synthesis *Die westliche Kirche vom 10. bis zum frühen 12. Jahrhundert*, Gerd Tellenbach asked: What is the church reform movement? Did it have a clear and consistent program? Were there one or many reform parties? Following a rapid survey of the vast reform vocabulary, he offered

1 I shall henceforward dispense with the use of inverted commas to qualify the term. In addition to probing this question with respect to canon law at the workshop that produced this volume, Julia Barrow, Kate Cushing, Maureen C. Miller, William North, and Steven Vanderputten—to name only a few—have been active in organizing panels, conferences, seminars, and research groups on the subject. See the recent assessments of Maureen C. Miller, "The Crisis in the Investiture Crisis Narrative," *History Compass* 7:6 (2009), 1570–80; and Leidulf Melve, "Ecclesiastical Reform in Historiographical Context," *History Compass* 13:5 (2015), 213–21.

2 Works that question traditional assumptions about reform or raise questions about those assumptions include Christopher M. Bellitto and Louis I. Hamilton, eds., *Reforming the Church before Modernity: Patterns, Problems and Approaches*, Church, Faith and Culture in the Medieval West (Aldershot, 2005), pp. xiv–xvi, here at p. xxiii; Cinzio Violante, "La réforme ecclésiastique du XIe siècle: une synthèse progressive d'idées et de structures opposées," *Le Moyen Âge* 91 (1991), 355–65; Ovidio Capitani, "Esiste un' 'età gregoriana'? Considerazioni sulle tendenze di una storiografia medievistica," *Rivista di storia e letteratura religiosa* 1 (1965), 454–81.

 | DOI:10.1163/9789004394384_006

the apt conclusion that the term is "confusing and obscure, because what is actually meant by the referent remains unproven, vague, and indeterminate."[3]

In the field of canon law, similar hesitations are also being voiced over the applicability of once widely accepted ascriptions such as 'reform collection' to denote legal compendia.[4] Scholarly assessments of the *Diversorum patrum sententiae*, or *Collection in Seventy-Four Titles* (= *74T*) afford a convenient case in point.[5] Dubbed by Paul Fournier in the late nineteenth century a 'canonical manual' or 'first manual' of reform owing to its many canons on simony (canons 111–37, 221–23), qualifications for clerical office (cc. 138–59), clerical fornication (cc. 170–73), and papal primacy (cc. 1–23, 174–85)—and for its known use among the clerics in Gregory VII's friendship circle—*74T* until recently carried this label, with implications for scholars' understanding of its purpose (papally-led reform) and place of origin (Italy).[6] Renewed examination of *74T* by Linda Fowler-Magerl and Christof Rolker upended these certainties; Rolker has now

3 *Die westliche Kirche vom 10. bis zum frühen 12. Jahrhundert*, Die Kirche in ihrer Geschichte 2, F1 (Göttingen, 1988), pp. 133–36, at p. 134 ("Dieses riesige Vokabular ist oft verwirrend und verschleiernd, weil unbelegt, vage und unbestimmt bleibt, was man unter dem Bezugswort eigentlich versteht."); English trans. by Timothy Reuter, *The Church in Western Europe from the Tenth to the Early Twelfth Century* (Cambridge, 1993), pp. 157–64. See also Tellenbach's earlier overview, "'Gregorianische Reform': Kritische Besinnungen," in *Reich und Kirche vor dem Inverstiturstreit. Vorträge beim wissenschaftlichen Kolloquium aus Anlaß des achtzigsten Geburtstags von Gerd Tellenbach*, ed. Karl Schmid (Sigmaringen, 1985), pp. 99–113. With reference to legal collections, see Kathleen G. Cushing, *Papacy and Law in the Gregorian Revolution: The Canonistic Work of Anselm of Lucca*, Oxford Historical Monographs (Oxford, 1998), pp. 11–17; John T. Gilchrist, "Was There a Gregorian Reform Movement in the Eleventh Century?," *Study Sessions of the Canadian Catholic Historical Association* 37 (1970), 1–10, esp. pp. 5–6. Steven Vanderputten has raised a trenchant critique of scholars' often unsupportable approach to institutional reform as a unified process in his *Monastic Reform as Process: Realities and Representations in Medieval Flanders, 900–1100* (Ithaca, N.Y., 2013), pp. 3–11, 186–89. For a rejoinder, see John Howe, *Before the Gregorian Reform: The Latin Church at the Turn of the First Millennium* (Ithaca, N.Y., 2016), pp. 8–10.

4 Readers should refer to the contribution of Christof Rolker, "Fournier's Model" in this volume for a splendid historiographical survey of this interpretive paradigm.

5 John Gilchrist, trans., *The Collection in Seventy-Four Titles: A Canon Law Manual of the Gregorian Reform*, Mediaeval Sources in Translation (Toronto, 1980), pp. 3–13. One might also point to recent reassessments of Burchard of Worms' *Decretum*, for which see Greta Austin, *Shaping Church Law around the Year 1000: The* Decretum *of Burchard of Worms*, Church, Faith and Culture in the Medieval West (Aldershot, 2009), pp. 235–36. For a recent state-of-the-art in canon law studies, aimed at scholars unfamiliar with the field, see Kriston R. Rennie and Jason Taliadoros, "Why Study Medieval Canon Law?," *History Compass* 12:2 (2014), 133–49.

6 Paul Fournier, "Le premier manuel canonique de la réforme du XIe siècle," *Mélanges d'archéologie et d'histoire de l'École française de Rome* 14 (1894), 147–223 and 285–90 (also separately published); see also in this volume Rolker, "Fournier's Model".

made a strong case for the collection's monastic origins and use.[7] Both scholars believe the collection originated well north of the Alps.

Re-examining our assumptions about the characteristics and intentions of reform, whether legal or institutional, marks an important first step in freeing our analysis from presumed certainties about the purpose and motivations of individuals, institutions, and texts. But we are quickly confronted by another obstacle, particularly with respect to the promulgation of canon law: knowing how, when, and in what way the law was applied in the reform and administration of local churches and religious communities, or to resolve inter-institutional disputes. The mere existence of a legal collection or acknowledged legal expertise of an individual furnishes few guarantees as to how these assets were used, or even *if* they were used, in specific circumstances or conflicts. Moreover, recourse to the law represented but one possible avenue open to litigants for resolving their disputes, and then perhaps not the most effective or desirable one. Even when appeal to legal judgment represented a viable option in dispute resolution, disputing parties might bypass it altogether in favour of strategies like mediation, negotiation, confrontation, or threat.[8]

This essay re-visits and re-examines one of the better-known episcopal election controversies in Francia at the turn of the twelfth century, namely, the long-running dispute that divided the church of Beauvais between 1100 and 1104.[9] The Beauvais election crisis offers an appealing case study. In addition to being well documented and a flashpoint in the reform debate, the leading canonist of the late eleventh century, Ivo of Chartres, was smack in the middle of it. Other bishops with a demonstrable expertise in canon law also became involved. My goal is to highlight the value in giving close readings of legal sources and their use (or non-use) in deeply embedded social contexts, and to ask when canon law was employed in dispute resolution, and when not—and if not, why not. Raising these questions not only calls into relief the limited

7 Linda Fowler-Magerl, "The Use of Letters of Pope Gregory I in Northeastern France and Lorraine before 1100," in *"Ins Wasser geworfen und Ozeane durchquert". Festschrift für Knut Wolfgang Nörr*, ed. Mario Ascheri et al. (Cologne, 2003), pp. 237–60; Christof Rolker, "The *Collection in Seventy-Four Titles*: A Monastic Canon Law Collection from Eleventh-Century France," in *Readers, Texts and Compilers in the Earlier Middle Ages: Studies in Medieval Canon Law in Honour of Linda Fowler-Magerl*, ed. Martin Brett and Kathleen G. Cushing, Church, Faith and Culture in the Medieval West (Aldershot, 2009), pp. 59–72.

8 See the editors' introduction (pp. 1–35), bibliography (pp. 287–319), and essays collected in *Conflict in Medieval Europe: Changing Perspectives on Society and Culture*, ed. Warren C. Brown and Piotr Górecki (Aldershot and Burlington, 2003).

9 I originally treated this episode, in less detail and with a different focus, in John S. Ott, *Bishops, Authority and Community in Northwestern Europe, c. 1050–1150*, Cambridge Studies in Medieval Life and Thought, Fourth Series 102 (Cambridge, 2015), pp. 134–42.

applicability of the reform label to individuals and movements long saddled with it; more importantly, it cautions us against assuming that canon law was necessarily applied, or even deemed a useful tool, in resolving institutional disputes that hinged on legal issues. Bernard Monod pointed this out over a century ago when he observed of the Beauvais controversy that "everyone [involved] violated the old canon law before, during, and after the election."[10] This essay presents in lieu of traditional interpretations a close analysis of the interpersonal dynamics of the episcopal circle at the heart of the debate, and opens up an opportunity to move assessment of the conflict beyond determining 'victor and vanquished'.[11]

1 The Disputed Election at Beauvais, 1100–04

The figures at the centre of the broken election at Beauvais were Stephen of Garlande, an archdeacon of Paris and brother to the royal seneschal, and Galo, abbot of Saint-Quentin of Beauvais, a house of regular canons headed from *c.*1078 until 1094 by Ivo of Chartres.[12] Scholars once routinely saw these men as proxies and adversaries in an institutional struggle between the Frankish *regnum* and its monarchs, Philip I and his son (the future king) Louis VI, and

10 Bernard Monod, "L'Église et l'État au XIIe siècle: l'élection épiscopale de Beauvais de 1100 à 1104: Étienne de Garlande et Galon," *Mémoires de la Société académique d'archéologie, sciences et arts du département de l'Oise* 19 (1904), 53–74, at p. 74.

11 Warren C. Brown and Piotr Gorecki, "What Conflict Means: The Making of Medieval Conflict Studies in the United States, 1970–2000," in *Conflict in Medieval Europe*, ed. iidem (Aldershot and Burlington), pp. 1–35, at p. 6. Evaluation of who 'won' or 'lost' the Beauvais conflict once seemed essential (e.g., to Monod, "L'Église et l'État," pp. 64–74). Rolf Sprandel, *Ivo von Chartres und seine Stellung in der Kirchengeschichte*, Pariser Historische Studien 1 (Stuttgart, 1962), p. 163, referred to Ivo as the "am Ende erfolgreiche Gegner" of the king and Stephen; Olivier Guyotjeannin, *Episcopus et comes: affirmation et déclin de la seigneurie épiscopale au nord du royaume de France (Beauvais-Noyon, X[e]—début XIIIe siècle)* (Geneva, 1987), p. 78, concluded there was neither "vainqueur ni vaincu."

12 On the Garlande family, see Éric Bournazel, *Le gouvernement capétien au XIIe siècle: structures sociales et mutations institutionnelles* (Paris, 1975), pp. 35–40, 112–15. For the date of Ivo's abbacy, see Sprandel, *Ivo von Chartres*, 7–8; Paris, Bibliothèque nationale de France, nouvelles acquisitions françaises 1921, fol. 115r (notice of 26 June 1078). Ivo remained the titular abbot of Saint-Quentin for four years after his election as bishop of Chartres, only remitting his abbacy to the bishop of Beauvais in 1094; see Yves de Chartres, *Correspondance, 1: 1090–1098* [all published], ed. and trans. Jean Leclercq, Les classiques de l'histoire de France au Moyen Âge 22 (Paris, 1949), pp. 126–29 (no. 31). While this practice was not unusual—Audebert, the archbishop of Bourges (1093–1097), was also abbot of Déols for example—it was not strictly speaking canonical.

Pope Paschal II (1099–1118).[13] Stephen and Galo will not directly concern us, however. Instead, this essay focuses on the relationships of four bishops orbiting the conflict, all of whom have been called reformers, and were active in the production and transmission of canon law.[14] Those prelates were Lambert of Arras (1094–1115), John of Thérouanne (1099–1130), Archbishop Manasses II of Reims (1096–1106), and the aforementioned Ivo of Chartres (1090–1115). Each became involved in the Beauvais election controversy for different reasons: Manasses, as metropolitan, both because of his lawful role in consecrating the bishop-elect and his critical standing as a political pivot between the pope and king; Lambert and John, because the contending parties appealed to them for help; and Ivo, because of his activism on behalf of his former church, and because he detested Stephen of Garlande and was the friend and patron of Galo of Saint-Quentin.[15]

The figure who dominated the scene and did more than any other prelate to establish a collegial, regional episcopal network in the province of Reims at this time was Lambert of Guines, the bishop of Arras.[16] Lambert laid the

13 In addition to Monod, "L'Église et l'État" (see above, n. 10), earlier studies include Pierre Imbart de la Tour, *Les élections épiscopales dans l'église de France du IXe au XIIe siècle: étude sur la décadence du principe électif (814–1150)* (Paris, 1890; repr. Geneva, 1974), which makes only passing reference to Beauvais; Achille Luchaire, *Louis VI le Gros: annales de sa vie et de son règne (1081–1137)* (Paris, 1890), pp. clxi–clxvi; Bernard Monod, *Essai sur les rapports de Pascal II avec Philippe Ier (1099–1108)* (Paris, 1907), pp. 27–34, 74–9, 89–92; Willi Schwarz, "Der Investiturstreit in Frankreich," *Zeitschrift für Kirchengeschichte* 43 (1924), 92–150 and 255–328; Alfons Becker, *Studien zum Investiturproblem in Frankreich. Papsttum, Königtum und Episkopat im Zeitalter der gregorianischen Kirchenreform (1049–1119)*, Schriften der Universität des Saarlandes (Saarbrücken, 1955), pp. 114–21. More recent assessments, taking into account local politics, include Guyotjeannin, *Episcopus et comes* (see above, n. 11), pp. 75–78; and Jay Rubenstein, *Guibert of Nogent: Portrait of a Medieval Mind* (New York and London, 2002), pp. 90–92.

14 The vast body of research on Ivo's contributions to canon law, including important recent revisions concerning his putative authorship of collections long ascribed to him, is to a considerable extent surveyed in the recent publications and editions of Christof Rolker, *Canon Law and the Letters of Ivo of Chartres*, Cambridge Studies in Medieval Life and Thought, Fourth Series 76 (Cambridge 2010); Bruce Clark Brasington, *Ways of Mercy: The Prologue of Ivo of Chartres: Edition and Analysis*, Vita regularis. Editionen 2 (Münster, 2004); and Martin Brett, "Creeping up on the *Panormia*," in *Grundlagen des Rechts. Festschrift für Peter Landau*, ed. Richard H. Helmholz et al., Rechts- und Staatswissenschaftliche Veröffentlichungen der Görres-Gesellschaft N. F. 91 (Paderborn, Munich, Vienna, and Zurich, 2000), pp. 205–70, among others.

15 Ivo refers to the church of Beauvais as "mater mea [...] quae in Christo me genuit, quae lacte suo me aluit"; see PL 162:112 (no. 102).

16 A fuller treatment of Lambert and his circle may be found in Ott, *Bishops, Authority and Community*, pp. 111–19, 130–32. See also the remarks of Claire Giordanengo in *Le registre de*

foundations for a powerful company of prelates to take office in the waning years of the eleventh century. He had a direct or indirect role in the elevation to office of half the prelates of the province around 1100, including the archbishop Manasses II, and in that tight-knit circle he acted as a father-figure.[17] The closeness of Lambert's bond with Manasses II is indicated in a letter of the archbishop to Lambert on the eve of his consecration, in which he beseeched him to "come and throw yourself into our loving embraces. For I burn and clamour to be promoted to the diaconate and priesthood by the imposition of your hands."[18] Repeated appeals in letters to Lambert to his *fraternitas*, *auctoritas*, and *sanctitas* tell us that fellow bishops and laymen alike admired his charismatic power as well as his political sagacity and command of the law.

We are well-informed, if somewhat one-sidedly, about the events at Beauvais thanks to Ivo of Chartres, whose voluminous correspondence and intervention in the affair have deeply coloured our understanding of events. Because its details have been refracted through Ivo's letters, scholars have consequently seen the controversy from his point of view, including his articulation of the motives of those involved. This led Bernard Monod, for example, to identify Manasses of Reims, whom Ivo upbraided for his conduct, as King Philip's creature and an agent of royal interests.[19] We will examine this insinuation more carefully below.

The essential events were these. Following a vacancy of perhaps half a year, the canons of Beauvais elected as their bishop Stephen of Garlande, a royal chaplain and archdeacon of Paris. The canons made their choice despite the trenchant objections of Ivo of Chartres, whose intervention in the ecclesiastical business of his former diocese had continued long after he left the abbey of Saint-Quentin of Beauvais in 1090.[20] Stephen's partisans in the chapter, who

---

Lambert, évêque d'Arras (1093–1115), ed. and trans. Claire Giordanengo, Sources d'histoire médiévale 34 (Paris, 2007), pp. 39–41.

17 Rolker, *Canon Law* (see above, n. 14), pp. 241–42, notes Lambert's predominant role in the absolution of Philip I for his unlawful marriage to Bertrada of Montfort; Laurent Morelle, "La pratique épistolaire de Lambert, évêque d'Arras (1093–1115)," in *Regards sur la correspondance (de Cicéron à Armand Barbès)*, ed. Daniel-Odon Hurel (Rouen, 1996), pp. 37–57, at p. 48. From 1103 until his death, Lambert was the senior bishop (in terms of tenure in office) in the province of Reims.

18 *Registre*, ed. Giordanengo (see above, n. 16), pp. 342–43 (no. 10). Manasses required a special dispensation from Urban II because he was *infra ordines*.

19 Monod, *Essai* (see above, n. 13), p. 31, asserts for example that "Manasses, deaf to the orders from Rome as to the prayers of his fellow bishop, remained resolutely on the king's side, against the pope, against the reformists, against canon law."

20 For further context on Ivo's involvement, see Sprandel, *Ivo von Chartres* (see above, n. 11), pp. 161–69.

included the capitular officers, insisted that the election had been executed canonically and had the full support of the people and clergy.[21] They presented their candidate before a provincial council convened by Manasses at Soissons sometime before August 1100.[22] The bishops in council seem to have agreed with the choice, but the canons of Beauvais quickly ran into other unspecified problems (*multa et innumera incommoda*). They wrote to Lambert of Arras, hoping he would influence the papal legates John and Benedict, who were on their way to convene a council at Poitiers, and through them win the pope to their side.[23] The source of their *innumera incommoda* was no doubt Ivo, for the bishop of Chartres pursued a similar course of action after the election, writing to the same legates and to Pope Paschal to convince them of its illegitimacy and Stephen's lack of fitness.[24] As becomes clear from his letters (nos. 87 and 89) to John, Benedict, and Paschal, Ivo had a fairly slender basis on which to dispute the canonicity of the electoral process itself. He raised no procedural objections; moreover, no legal prerogative permitted him to intervene unilaterally in the electoral affairs of another diocese. Nevertheless,

21 The dignitaries named were the archdeacons Lisiard and Roger, the cantor Drogo, and the dean Hugh. We know regrettably little about this group. Lisiard was the uncle of Guibert of Nogent, whose family belonged to the minor nobility around Clermont-en-Beauvaisis. The dean Hugh was the brother of the vidame of Gerberoy, Garnier, and also related to the lords of Vignory. (On the *vidames* of Gerberoy, which lies about 20 km northwest of Beauvais, see Guyotjeannin, *Episcopus et comes*, pp. 109–12; see above, n. 11.) It is highly probable that Ivo knew these men, nearly all of whom had held office for many years prior to 1100, from his time at Saint-Quentin. Hugh had been dean and Roger archdeacon since at least 1072; Drogo was cantor from *c.*1078 until 1108/09, when he became a canon at Saint-Quentin. Lisiard was archdeacon from no later than 1095, and possibly since the 1080s. See William Mendel Newman, *Les seigneurs de Nesle en Picardie (XIIe–XIIIe siècle): leurs chartes et leur histoire*, 2 vols (Philadelphia, 1971), 1:239, 248, 252, 258.

22 The date of the provincial council may be inferred from two of Ivo's letters (nos. 84 and 87; PL 162:105–08). In the former, written before 29 July 1100, he alludes to the fact that he has business to discuss with the legates; in the latter, he affirms that the business concerns the Beauvais election.

23 It is not entirely clear whether Lambert attended the provincial council at Soissons, because the canons mention the council's business in a way that suggests he was unfamiliar with what had happened there. On the council at Poitiers, see Theodor Schieffer, *Die päpstlichen Legaten in Frankreich vom Vertrage von Meersen (870) bis zum Schisma von 1130*, Historische Studien 263 (Berlin, 1935), pp. 163–68. Monod, "L'Église et l'État" (see above, n. 10), misidentifies the legates as John bishop of Gubbio and Benedict cardinal-priest of Santa Eudoxia; they were in fact John, cardinal-priest of Santa Anastasia and Benedict, cardinal-priest of Santa Pudenziana. See Rudolf Hüls, *Kardinäle, Klerus und Kirchen Roms, 1049–1130*, Bibliothek des Deutschen Historischen Instituts in Rom 48 (Tübingen, 1977), pp. 146–47, 200–01.

24 PL 162:107–08 (no. 87), 109–11 (no. 89), 112–13 (no. 92).

to Paschal Ivo aired two legal and moral complaints, namely that Stephen was only in minor orders—"not yet even a subdeacon"—and that he was of disreputable character, having once been excommunicated by the papal legate Hugh of Lyon for his 'public adultery' ("publice olim de adulterio publico infamatum, et […] ecclesiae communione privatum").[25] With the legates and pope alerted to Ivo's concerns, the election ground to a halt. Stephen remained unconsecrated, and the bishop of Chartres and the canons of Beauvais began to lobby the provincial bishops, particularly Lambert, John, and Manasses, for help. In order to understand how the dispute proceeded, we must examine in turn how Ivo, the canons of Beauvais, and the provincial bishops utilized the law, suasion, and their personal connections to move the controversy in their favour.

2 Making the Case against Stephen of Garlande: Ivo's Approach

Intervening in episcopal electoral politics was nothing new for Ivo. He had been doing it for years, both within his province of Sens and in the province of Reims.[26] Not only had Ivo involved himself, he had frequently done so on behalf of candidates who faced various canonical impediments. Most recently, the bishop of Chartres had endorsed—over the reluctance of Pope Urban II—the promotion of the previous candidate to the see of Beauvais, Ansellus (1096–99), who, it seems, had been married and/or had children. In a letter from 1096 addressed to Hugh of Lyon, Ivo argued that Ansellus' advantageousness (his *utilitas*) to the church of Beauvais and the peace of the realm should outweigh qualms about his canonical eligibility.[27] A central feature of Ivo's conception of church law was the necessity that its pastors differentiate whether a 'rigorous'

25 PL 162:110 (no. 89): "procul a sacris ordinibus inventum, utpote nondum subdiaconum." See also PL 162:108 (no. 87) and 117 (no. 97). Hugh of Lyon had most recently exercised legatine powers in France from late 1093 or early 1094 off and on through 1097; see Schieffer, *Die päpstlichen Legaten*, pp. 153–62; Kriston R. Rennie, *Law and Practice in the Age of Reform: The Legatine Work of Hugh of Die (1073–1106)*, Medieval Church Studies 17 (Turnhout, 2010), pp. 42–51. Stephen's infamy was thus relatively old news in 1100, though no doubt raised by Ivo for the benefit of the new pope. This letter was perhaps Ivo's second or third to Paschal, who had been consecrated within the previous year, on 13 August 1099.

26 Rolker, *Canon Law* (see above, n. 14), pp. 238–39.

27 PL 162:66–67 (no. 55); *Correspondance*, ed. Leclercq (see above, n. 12), pp. 222–27: "electum suum [scil. Ansellus, JSO] quem utilem sibi in recolligendis bonis suis," and "cum ecclesia ad praesens aeque utilem sibi non inveniat quem cum pace regni et consensu ecclesiae in episcopum eligat." On Ansellus' election in 1096, see also Guyotjeannin, *Episcopus*

or a 'dispensatory' application of the law was appropriate in a given context, with the goal of avoiding schism within the church.[28] This meant that a judge, whether bishop or pope, should exercise his discretion when deciding whether to overlook potentially disqualifying conditions of a particular candidate for the episcopate in favour of securing the person most 'useful' for the local or universal church's well-being.[29] Quoting from Augustine, Ivo wrote:

> The princes of churches often pass judgment more severely according to the tenor of the canons; and they tolerate many things from the necessity of the times. They often give dispensation for the utility of persons or to avoid harm to the people.[30]

Judges might offer dispensation; however, this did not in Ivo's mind mean that they should act without counsel from others. Indeed, Ivo's understanding of dispensation invited, even demanded, that wise councillors interject their voices, and the bishop of Chartres was ever ready to offer his. In Ansellus' case, Ivo's argument eventually carried the day. Ansellus was consecrated bishop of Beauvais in June 1099, only to die a few months later.

Ivo proceeded to lay out his case against Stephen of Garlande through a multi-pronged strategy, sending letters first to the papal legates John and Benedict, then to Paschal, and eventually to Manasses of Reims. Ivo's initial letters to the legates and pope (nos. 87 and 89), composed before the council held at Poitiers in late November 1100, are similar. In both, he notes that he

---

et comes (see above, n. 11), p. 75 and n. 39. Ivo in this letter seems to have made use of material from the *Collectio Britannica* (Rolker, *Canon Law*, p. 152; see above, n. 14).

28 Brasington, ed., *Ways of Mercy* (see above, n. 14), pp. 26–89, esp. pp. 41–44. See also Rolker, *Canon Law* (see above, n. 14), pp. 167–71.

29 Brasington, ed., *Ways of Mercy* (see above, n. 14), pp. 77–78. On the concept of 'utilitas', which had a long ecclesiological history, see in the first instance Yves Congar, "Quelques expressions traditionnelles du service chrétien," in *L'épiscopat et l'Église universelle*, ed. idem and Bernard-Dominique Dupuy, Unam Sanctam 39 (Paris, 1962), pp. 101–32, at pp. 113–23; Ovidio Capitani, "'Ecclesia romana' e riforma: 'utilitas' in Gregorio VII," in *Chiesa, diritto e ordinamento della 'Societas Christiana' nei secoli XI e XII: atti della nona settimana internazionale di studio Mendola, 28 agosto–2 settembre 1983* (Milan, 1986), pp. 26–66.

30 *Correspondance*, ed. Leclercq (see above, n. 12), p. 224 (no. 55), and Ivo's *Prologue*, in Brasington, *Ways of mercy* (see above, n. 14), pp. 61–62 and (for the text) 125: "Multa quoque principes ecclesiarum pro tenore canonum districtius iudicant multa pro temporum necessitate tolerant multa pro personarum utilitate uel strage populorum uitanda dispensant."

cannot keep silent concerning the state of the church of Beauvais. He must speak out, as a faithful son of the church and because the canons of Beauvais had acted in contempt of a formal interdiction against illicit elections issued by both the legates and Paschal himself.[31] Ivo was clearly priming his audience for the face-to-face meetings to come, and he urgently noted to John and Benedict that Stephen was preparing to send emissaries to Rome to 'deceive' the pope and sway curial officials 'with gifts or promises'.[32]

At this point, Ivo limited his arguments against Stephen's candidacy to detailing the archdeacon's unsuitability for office (his layman's behaviour, including gambling and womanizing, lack of major orders, and the fact that he was unlettered) and to making broad appeals for the need to maintain canonical rigor in episcopal elections.[33] There was no need to cite canon law specifically, because to Ivo the archdeacon's disqualifications were patently obvious, and he sent Paschal copies of earlier letters of Hugh of Lyon pronouncing Stephen's adultery. Ivo reinforced his arguments with scriptural admonitions, particularly from Ezekiel, whose call for pastors to rise up like a wall before the Lord's house he employs in his letter to John and Benedict.[34] These he presumably reiterated to the legates in person at Poitiers.

31 PL 162:108 (no. 87) and 110 (no. 89): "quod adversus litteras domni papae et vestras de electione vel assumptione episcopi illicita prohibentes." I locate these letters chronologically very close in time: after the provincial synod in Soissons, after Ivo's initial letter to the legate John (no. 84, composed before 29 July 1100), and before 23 November, the opening of the legatine council. When the papal interdict had been pronounced is unclear. Paschal's October 1100 council at Melfi is a possibility, but no legislation from it remains. See Uta-Renate Blumenthal, *The Early Councils of Pope Paschal II, 1100–1110*, Pontifical Institute of Medieval Studies. Studies and Texts 43 (Toronto, 1978), pp. 7–11.

32 PL 162:108 (no. 87): "Praedictus enim intrusus festinate ut cito Romam vadat, aut mittat, et palatinos quibus poterit muneribus vel promissionibus flectat in suam partem, et domnum papal quacunque poterit machinatione decipiat."

33 PL 162:108 (no. 87): "Cui [Stephen, JSO] si ad episcopalem ministrationem aliquando apostolic auctoritate patuerit aditus, manifestum est temporibus nostris exitiale silentium impositum esse canonicis legibus." Compare PL 162:110 (no. 89, to Paschal): "haec [Stephen's conduct, JSO] quae vera et manifesta sunt ad repulsionem ejus sufficient, si apostolica et canonica instituta vigorem suum non amittunt." Monod, "L'Église et l'État" (see above, n. 10), p. 58, believes Ivo's letter no. 89 to Paschal was composed after Poitiers; here I disagree.

34 Ibid. (Ezekiel 13:5). He further refers to 'incircumcisi clerici' who must be repulsed by papal authority; see Ezekiel 32:19–32 for repeated uses of this adjective.

3 Making the Case for Stephen of Garlande: The Beauvais Canons' Approach

At least initially, the chapter of Beauvais appears to have been united in its choice of the archdeacon of Paris as its next bishop, and presented their candidate to the prelates assembled in the provincial council at Soissons. There, the bishops assented and presumably set a date for Stephen's consecration at Reims.[35] Already, however, the canons had been aware that Ivo had raised objections to Stephen in his letters to the legates and pope, and they in turn asked for a letter of recommendation from the bishops in council.[36] The canons then composed a supplicatory letter to Lambert of Arras, who had apparently not been present at Soissons.[37] Aware that Lambert was headed to Poitiers, they asked him to intercede on their behalf before the papal legate John, his 'close friend'.[38] Writing on behalf of "the entire congregation of the church of Beauvais, the bishop's vassals, and all the people of the same city", the canons presented several arguments in defence of the canonicity of

35 The council's assent is implied in the canons' letter to Lambert of Arras (*Registre*, ed. Giordanengo, no. 62, pp. 412–15; see above, n. 16), wherein they note that the bishops in council had agreed to send a letter to Paschal confirming their support of the election. The canons must have anticipated some objections, perhaps on the basis of their earlier rejection of Stephen as a candidate for the position. The background to this latter event is murky. However, it is possible that Stephen had been forwarded for the canons' consideration by the king or prince during the difficult election of 1096 that ultimately saw Ivo back Ansellus. We learn from a later letter of the bishop of Chartres (no. 95, see below) that the archdeacon Lisiard had, during Hugh of Lyon's legation of 1093/94–97, vigorously opposed Stephen. This may have been because at that time Lisiard was promoting his nephew Guibert, the future abbot of Nogent, for the post. See Rubenstein, *Guibert of Nogent* (see above, n. 13), pp. 88–90, who locates Guibert's involvement in Beauvais electoral politics to the period around 1100. Circumstantial evidence appears to favour an earlier date, however, perhaps 1096.

36 *Registre*, ed. Giordanengo (see above, n. 16), no. 62, pp. 414–15. Their letter refers obliquely to their concern that 'certain people' ('aliquorum intrusione') might question their choice, which I read as a reference to Ivo's resistance.

37 The canons' letter describes to Lambert what had happened at the provincial council.

38 *Registre*, ed. Giordanengo (see above, n. 16), no. 62, pp. 414–15: 'familiari amico vestro'. Indeed, John had already written to Lambert, expressing his friendship and ordering him to come to Poitiers; *Registre*, ed. Giordanengo (see above, n. 16), no. 60, pp. 410–11. Lambert's connection to John is unclear, but the legate seems to have come from Burgundy, and he, Lambert, and John of Thérouanne were all present in Rome for Urban II's synod of 24 March 1099. See Hüls, *Kardinäle, Klerus und Kirchen Roms* (see above, n. 23), p. 146; Lotte Kéry, *Die Errichtung des Bistums Arras, 1093/1094*, Francia Beihefte 33 (Sigmaringen, 1994), pp. 188–89; Alfons Becker, *Papst Urban II. (1088–1099)*, 3 vols, Schriften der Monumenta Germaniae historica 19 (Stuttgart, 1964–2012), 2:200–01.

Stephen's election.[39] First, they reassured Lambert that the archdeacon had been chosen by the common will and counsel of the clergy and people, free of the taint of simony, and that he had been reluctant to assume the honour.[40] Then the authors took a page from Ivo's own legal philosophy, arguing that Stephen was a candidate both "suitable and upright" ("utilem et honestum virum"). 'Utilis' had been the very word the bishop of Chartres had earlier employed in advocating for the promotion of Ansellus to the see of Beauvais. It is even possible that the canons of Beauvais had a copy of Ivo's letter promoting Ansellus to Hugh of Lyon, or other of his legal writings, in front of them.[41]

The letter concluded by noting that Beauvais must return to peace through the intervention of its mother, Reims, and its other sisters, the churches of the archdiocese.[42] Ivo had repeatedly used similar rhetoric to different ends, excusing his electoral interference on the grounds that the church of Beauvais had 'given birth' to him in Christ and was his 'mother and nursemaid'.[43] In referring to the archdiocesan church as 'its mother' and to the other diocesan churches in familial terms as 'sisters' (much as bishops were accustomed to addressing one another fraternally in their correspondence), the canons made use of a time-tried expression of ecclesiastical hierarchy.[44] In an age where appeals to Rome as the 'mother of all churches' were exceedingly common, however, the emphasis placed on Beauvais' metropolitan church of Reims as

39 *Registre*, ed. Giordanengo (see above, n. 16), no. 62, pp. 412–13: "omnisque congregatio Belvacensis ecclesiae, casati etiam cum universo populo ejusdem civitatis." The term 'casatus' embraced a wide range of figures in the episcopal entourage, to which the term 'vassals' does not really do justice; see Guyotjeannin, *Episcopus et comes* (see above, n. 11), pp. 96–99.

40 As Giordanengo, *Registre* (see above, n. 16), pp. 35–36 points out, Lambert's letters frequently key in on the details of episcopal elections, the canonicity of which, at least with respect to the letter of law, he, like Ivo, was keenly interested in. On the use of this terminology to mark a canonical election, see Imbart de la Tour, *Les élections épiscopales* (see above, n. 13), pp. 10–12. Reluctance to take office was another traditional sign of fitness to rule.

41 Compare Ivo's *Correspondance*, ed. Leclercq (see above, n. 12), p. 224, and Lambert's *Registre*, ed. Giordanengo (see above, n. 16), pp. 412–13.

42 *Registre*, ed. Giordanengo (see above, n. 16), pp. 414–15: "Necesse est ut Belvacensis ecclesia per sanctam Remensem ecclesiam, utique matrem suam, et caeteras sorores suas curae pastoralis sollicitudine perveniat ad quietem."

43 PL 162:112 (no. 92, to Paschal); 121 (no. 102, to Manasses).

44 On maternal language and imagery as expressive of church hierarchies, see Megan McLaughlin, *Sex, Gender, and Episcopal Authority in an Age of Reform, 1000–1122* (Cambridge, 2010), pp. 124–28, 139–52.

its mother may signal the canons' desire to have their election controversy settled locally.[45]

That the canons had both anticipated and were responding to Ivo's legal arguments is evident in the next letter he sent to Paschal (no. 92), sometime after the council at Poitiers.[46] Ivo had been present at Poitiers, as had Lambert of Arras, and it seems certain that the canons of Beauvais sent representatives, including their archdeacon Lisiard, to argue their case before the legates.[47] Stephen himself may have attended.[48] One would like to know what was said in that audience hall! Happily, Ivo's follow-up letter to the pope (no. 92) gives us an idea. The bishop of Chartres had been handed a resounding defeat.[49] Citing Ivo's own principles, the canons apparently argued that although Stephen was not in orders, his usefulness (*utilitatem*) to Beauvais should supersede this impediment. Moreover, even if the archdeacon were guilty of criminous behaviour, he had neither confessed to nor been convicted of anything. Furthermore, Ivo had no jurisdiction in the province of Reims and should not be interceding before the pope or filling his ears 'with inordinate pleas'. Finally, the canons professed themselves ready to respond to any objections, should those accusations be canonically made. Ivo's, they implied, had not, and technically speaking they were correct.[50] Ivo ends his letter by making a significant concession: the bishop-elect should present himself before the pope, "either to receive mercy or submit to judgement." Should Paschal extend

45 Ibid., pp. 148–52.

46 PL 162:112–13 (no. 92). The letter was probably sent in late 1100 or very early 1101. Note that my reading of both this letter and Ivo's subsequent missive to Paschal differs slightly from the reading of Luchaire, *Louis VI*, clxii, and Monod, "L'Église et l'État" (see above, n. 10), pp. 57–58, who follows Luchaire in some respects.

47 On the prelates attending the council, see Odette Pontal, *Les conciles de la France capétienne jusqu'en 1215* (Paris, 1997), p. 244. Lisiard's presence is strongly implied by Ivo's letter (no. 92), in which he singles out the fact that the archdeacon, although at one time opposed to Stephen, had now become his advocate; see PL 162:113 (no. 92).

48 See below, n. 52 (on Stephen's probable presence at Poitiers).

49 This is further affirmed when Ivo wrote to Paschal (PL 162:127–28, no. 9) following the council, complaining that the legates "non tantum non possunt curanda curare, sed nec curanda prospicere," and asking that Paschal appoint Hugh of Lyon as his representative in their place. Of course, Hugh had earlier opposed Stephen of Garlande's attempt to secure the see of Beauvais, and was on very friendly terms with Ivo, which accounts for Ivo's preference.

50 PL 162:112–13 (no. 92): "Postulat autem eadem Ecclesiae in persona electi sui unam tantum imperfectionem remitti, videlicet quod in sacris ordinibus non est inventus cum in caeteris ejus integritatem praedicet, utilitatem commendet. Si autem in eo aliquid criminosum, vel quod sacris canonibus obviet, repertum fuerit, pro hujusmodi non est nostrum apud sedem justitiae intercedere, nec vestrum inordinatis precibus aurem praebere."

mercy to Stephen, Ivo noted sarcastically that the pope would be "mercifully rush[ing] headlong toward the wretched ruination of the Church"—a not-so-subtle assertion that even if Stephen's candidacy were legally valid, his consecration would be a huge mistake.[51] He later affirmed that this was precisely his intent in writing: not to consent to the canons' electoral choice, but to urge Paschal to look past the legal argument and reject Stephen on other, perhaps moral or political, grounds.[52]

Ivo got what he wanted. Overturning both the decision reached at the provincial council of Soissons and the sentiment in favour of the canons' case at Poitiers, Paschal wrote to the bishop of Chartres and church of Beauvais annulling the election, letters that Ivo eagerly publicized "to nearly all the churches of our kingdom."[53] It is important at this point to note that the papal prerogative for intervention in local councils and episcopal elections was well established by 1100.[54] Legal compendia favoured by Gregory VII and his successors asserted that provincial councils could be annulled by papal fiat and that they had no constitutional powers.[55] Yet nothing suggests that Manasses had acted against canon law, broken with apostolic authority or deviated from his jurisdiction as metropolitan, which necessarily included

51 PL 162:113 (no. 92): "quatenus sic judicium ex misericordia temperetis, ut quantum salvo honore vestro potestis, miserabilibus Ecclesiae ruinis misericorditer occurratis." Then follows a thinly veiled threat of resistance: "Sic enim volumus amicis prodesse, ut auctoritati et honestati sedis apostolicae in nullo velimus obesse."

52 See PL 162:115 (no. 95). Referring to his previous letter (no. 92), in which he urged Paschal not to permit the ruin of the Church, Ivo wrote that "[i]mportunitate enim sua [Stephen's, JSO] extorsit a me litteras," a statement that makes sense if (a) Stephen had been present at Poitiers, and (b) if Ivo had been compelled there to admit the weakness of his case and agree that Stephen should be judged in Rome. Ivo then says that the letters "ei nullo modo profuturas, imo multum credidi obfuturas, si intelligentem haberem lectorem, et commodem expositorem." He reiterates in another letter (no. 97, to Lambert of Arras and John of Thérouanne) that his point in writing had not been to promote Stephen so much as to subtly denounce him before the pope. Paschal had missed that point completely (compare letter no. 95, col. 115, in which Ivo notes that he had endured "in me propter eum [Stephen] paterna invectione" from the pope for now supporting Stephen), but nevertheless had done what Ivo hoped he would do: suspend the election.

53 PL 162:115 (no. 95): "me publicante [Paschal's letters, JSO] fere omnibus nostri regni Ecclesiis ad laudem divini nominis." It's hard not to detect a certain smugness in Ivo's tone here.

54 Imbart de la Tour, *Les élections épiscopales* (see above, n. 13), pp. 476–89.

55 Raymonde Foreville, "The Synod of the Province of Rouen in the Eleventh and Twelfth Centuries," in *Church and Government in the Middle Ages: Essays Presented to C.R. Cheney on his 70th Birthday*, ed. Christopher N.L. Brooke et al. (Cambridge, 1976), pp. 19–39, at pp. 19–20, citing Deusdedit's *Collectio canonum* (c.1083–87) and Gratian.

the power to consecrate the bishops-elect of his province.[56] At this point, sometime relatively early in 1101, the Beauvais election controversy entered new territory. Ivo threw his weight behind Paschal, arguing on behalf of the pope's ultimate authority to overturn conciliar elections and abrogate the law, even when it had been followed validly. He did so in full contravention of at least some of his own established legal principles, and indeed, Paschal had rejected Stephen for apparently moral reasons, not legal ones.[57] Archbishop Manasses now found himself on the defensive, his council's decision and freedom to consecrate having been overturned, but not for legal cause. Standing on his *own* legal principles, and no doubt perturbed that Ivo's meddling had led to his humiliation, he began to delay. Much of what happened next hinged on his decisions and his relationship with the bishop of Chartres. Caught in the middle were the provincial bishops, Lambert of Arras and John of Thérouanne, whom Ivo saw as the key to unlocking the entire puzzle.

4 Ivo of Chartres and the Episcopal Cohort of Reims

The election of Stephen of Garlande having been voided by papal fiat, a party of the Beauvais canons moved to hold a new election. Other stakeholders, including Stephen himself, the cantor Drogo, King Philip, and Prince Louis, mounted a vigorous resistance. Anticipating that Manasses would join this resistance, Ivo wrote to his old friends, the bishops of Arras and Thérouanne, who were connected by close personal and professional bonds to the archbishop.[58] He urged Lambert and John in language at once flattering and vaguely incriminatory to pressure Manasses to permit the new election. "It was always [your] custom", Ivo said to them, implying that they had betrayed

56 See Jean Gaudemet, *Le gouvernement de l'Église à l'époque classique*, 2: *Le gouvernement local*, Histoire du droit et des institutions de l'Église en occident 8/2 (Paris, 1979), p. 27, citing Gratian's sources at n. 105.

57 Ivo repeatedly held that it was up to the ultimate judge to decide on the suitability of a candidate, but in this case there was no *a priori* legal reason why Stephen should have been rejected, since the objections that had been raised could be easily countered. Instead, the pope acted on his moral authority (it appears), which in part explains why Ivo for the most part avoided making legal arguments thereafter.

58 Lambert and Ivo were two of the only bishops to speak out against Philip's adulterous marriage to Bertrada of Montfort in 1092 (for which see Myriam Soria Audebert, *La crosse brisée: des évêques agressés dans une Église en conflits* (*royaume de France, fin X*[e]*–début XIII*[e] *siècle*), Culture et société médiévales 6 (Turnhout, 2005), pp. 74–78, 168–71, 177–82), and they exchanged heartfelt letters on other occasions; *Registre*, ed. Giordanengo (see above, n. 16), pp. 334–37 (no. 5); 490–93 (no. 119).

their principles, "to reject with perfect hatred any wolves sneaking into the Lord's sheepfold, and like faithful hounds in God's house fight them wherever apparent."[59] The bishop of Chartres urged John and Lambert to compel Manasses to pressure the canons of Beauvais into a second election, and if necessary admonish him to fulfil his office "so that what ought to be done by him should not fall to the hands of others."[60] Manasses evidently ignored any requests put to him, and so it was without archiepiscopal support that a second election was held at Beauvais and a rival candidate put forward: Galo, abbot of Saint-Quentin and Ivo's protégé.

King Philip objected to this new election, of course, at least partly on the grounds that Galo was of modest birth, and swore he would never see Galo invested at Beauvais.[61] Manasses did not move to consecrate Galo, eliciting a second lengthy and admonitory letter from the bishop of Chartres.[62] Ivo laid out two arguments, one pastoral and supported by biblical authorities, the other legal and, for the first time in his exchanges with the archbishop, supported by canonical sources. In his moral and pastoral exhortations, Ivo, citing Ezekiel, reminded Manasses of his duty to recall the lost sheep of his flock and to cull the sick.[63] Ivo then reminded Manasses that if he did not do what he should—that is, consecrate Galo—he would cede this honour to another person. Assuming Manasses were not anathematized, this could only

59 PL 162:117 (no. 97): "Quoniam igitur vestra semper fuit lupos in ovilia Dei subintrantes perfecto odio reprobare, et eos sicut fideles in domo Dei canes ubi licuit impugnare."

60 Ibid.: "Quod si praeblandiente desidia facere distulerit, aut dissimulaverit, monendus est a vobis quatenus sic honorificet ministerium suum, ut quod per eum faciendum est, per manus non impleatur aliorum." At approximately the same time—which could hardly have been a coincidence—Paschal renewed the privileges of the church of Arras and confirmed its independence from Cambrai (PL 163:69–70, no. 48; JL 5867, 708). This letter was probably hand-delivered by John of Thérouanne, who happened to be at Rome dealing with business of his own.

61 Philip also continued to make use of the episcopal goods of Beauvais; PL 162:123 (no. 104) and 124 (no. 105): "quod Galo in vita ejus nunquam futurus esset Belvacensis episcopus." See here Monod, *Essai* (see above, n. 13), pp. 30–31. On Galo's situation I will have little further to add, but the narrative may be followed in Monod, "L'Église et l'État" (see above, n. 10), pp. 61–64. Reference to Galo's modest background is made in Ivo's letter no. 102 (PL 162:121). That this should be the major sticking point in Manasses' reluctance to recognize the election is hard to believe, but it offered a convenient excuse to disqualify Galo. Meanwhile, Stephen of Garlande was distributing exotic furs to his supporters in the chapter (PL 162:123, no. 104).

62 PL 162:120–22 (no. 102, probably composed mid-1101).

63 PL 162:121: "Vestrum est enim dissipatas oves in die nubis et caliginis per avia quaerere, et ad ovile, quantum ad vos pertinent reducere [...]. Vestrum est oves morbidas quae contagione sua plurimas perdunt, ab ovili interim removere." Compare Ezekiel 34:12.

have meant consecration by the pope.[64] As for his legal sources, Ivo restricted himself to two, both concerning the involvement of laymen (kings, specifically) in episcopal elections. The first, from the Fourth Council of Constantinople (869–70), prohibited the nomination or consecration of bishops owing to the "power and intrigues of civil authorities", and declared any such elections void.[65] The same canon appears in the *Tripartita A* attributed to Ivo and in his *Decretum*, both of which were probably composed before the letter.[66] The remaining, imprecise, reference is to unidentified capitularies of Charlemagne and Louis the Pious conceding the election of bishops to churches and the sanctioning of elections in provincial councils. Within the Ivonian corpus, it appears uniquely here.[67] Their inclusion by Ivo in his letter to Manasses indicates that Philip's vow to prevent Galo from assuming office had presented him with the legal opening he needed, a fact confirmed by Ivo in another letter to Paschal.[68]

From Manasses' perspective, it would have been hard to miss the irony in Ivo's imprecations. First, in urging him to oversee a new election and by implying that his prerogative as metropolitan would be superseded if he did not, Ivo casually overlooked the fact that Manasses' privilege of confirming elections had already been trampled, largely thanks to Ivo himself. Second, even while Ivo was busy injecting himself into the affairs of a province where he had no legal jurisdiction or position, he presumed to lecture Manasses on canon law and had also recently rebuked him for becoming involved in the diocesan affairs of his own suffragans. Two years earlier at the council of Saint-Omer in 1099, Manasses had butted heads with his fellow bishops when he unilaterally granted the count of Flanders and his vassals the right to seize the consorts and wives of any clerics who refused to dissolve their conjugal relationships. Manasses' demand was apparently based on a canon from Urban II's 1089

64 PL 162:121: "consecrationem electi praedictae ecclesiae acceleraretis, ne differendo, vel non faciendo quod vestrum est, honorem vestrum alteri detis." This was, incidentally, the very route by which Ivo was finally able to assume his own office. On Ivo's consecration by Urban II, see Sprandel, *Ivo von Chartres* (see above, n. 11), p. 86.

65 Fourth Council of Constantinople (869–70), c. 12: "potentia et praeceptione principum factas penitus interdicentibus." For an edition and translation, see *Decrees of the Ecumenical Councils*, 1, *Nicaea I to Lateran V*, ed. and trans. Norman P. Tanner (London and Washington, D.C., 1990), p. 175.

66 Rolker, *Canon Law* (see above, n. 14), p. 316; see also pp. 107, 135–37, 144–45. The canon is also found in the *Panormia*.

67 PL 162:121 (no. 102): "Francorum etiam reges Carolus et Lodovicus electiones episcoporum Ecclesiis concesserunt, quod et in suis capitularibus scriptum reliquerunt, et in conciliis episcoporum provincialibus sanciri permiserunt."

68 PL 162:123 (no. 104).

council at Melfi (c. 12), but from the perspective of at least some of the bishops in the archdiocese (and perhaps Lambert and John, whose dioceses were located within the county of Flanders) it gave undue licence for both lay and archiepiscopal interference in internal diocesan affairs, and they complained that Manasses had established this prerogative without their consent or counsel.[69] When the bishops' protests fell on deaf ears, they sent a letter to Ivo seeking his legal advice and complaining about Manasses' threatening treatment of the bishop of Soissons, who may have objected most loudly to the archbishop's initiative. Ivo advised the bishops to stand firm together, then forwarded a chastening letter to the archbishop. Manasses eventually backed down.[70] Finally—and probably encapsulating for the archbishop of Reims the absurdity of Ivo's position in the entire Beauvais affair—Ivo had supported Manasses' *own* election in 1096, despite the fact that, like Stephen of Garlande, Manasses had not been in major orders and was, at least according to one witness, 'marginally lettered'.[71]

---

69 These events are known to us thanks to a letter of Manasses to Robert (*Registre*, ed. Giordanengo, no. 59, pp. 408–11; see above, n. 16), and two letters from Ivo of Chartres, to the provincial bishops of Reims and to Manasses (PL 162:104–07, nos. 83 and 85). They are all undated, but likely were composed in mid- to late 1100. The letter of Manasses to Robert was written once Robert had returned from the holy land (no later than 20 June 1100, perhaps as early as 8 February 1100). *Registre*, ed. Giordanengo, p. 408 (no. 59): "absque consensu consilioque eorumdem coepiscoporum nostrorum." The canon in question says nothing about excommunication, only loss of clerical orders and seizure of wives. The provincial bishops seem primarily to have been concerned about their compromised jurisdictional autonomy vis-à-vis lay authorities. See Robert Somerville in collaboration with Stephan Kuttner, *Pope Urban II, the* Collectio Britannica, *and the Council of Melfi (1089)* (Oxford, 1996), pp. 256, 261–62, 287–89; Anne Llewellyn Barstow, *Married Priests and the Reforming Papacy: The Eleventh-Century Debates*, Texts and Studies in Religion 12 (New York and Toronto, 1982), p. 100.

70 PL 162:104 (no. 83). That Ivo's sympathies lay with the provincial bishops is apparent in his salutation "reverendis in Christo fratribus diocesis Remensis episcopis," especially when compared to the ironic greeting he extended to Manasses, "reverendo Remorum archiepiscopo [...] charitatis visceribus abundare" (compare Luke 1:78). Ivo urged solidarity: "vestrum est tam pro vobis quam pro confratre vestro Suessionensi episcopo pondus earum [the archbishop's threats, JSO] animadvertere, et in periculo ejus periculum vestrum studiose praecavere."

71 For Ivo's letter on Manasses' behalf, see *Correspondance*, ed. Leclercq (see above, n. 12), pp. 194–97 (no. 48). On the condition of Manasses' learning, similar to Ivo's description of Stephen of Garlande's, see the *Chronicon s. Andreae Castri Cameracesi*, ed. Ludwig C. Bethmann, MGH SS 7:544: "parum quidem litteratus, sed elemosinis et curae pauperum studiose deditus." Lambert of Arras had just as enthusiastically supported Manasses' fast-track consecration despite these impediments; see *Registre*, ed. Giordanengo (see above, n. 16), pp. 346–49 (no. 13).

Unmoved by Ivo's pleas and arguments, and just as Galo and his supporters were preparing to travel to Rome to obtain a papal consecration, Manasses summoned the two parties to mediation (*dicitur pacem volens componere*). Although Ivo generally supported ecclesiastical due process, especially when it suited his interests,[72] to him this smacked of intentional delaying tactics done in the king's favour, and he told Paschal as much in a new letter.[73] While Ivo's letter hints broadly that the archbishop was standing on procedure, what seems to make him even more anxious is that Paschal might recognize the council's decision, for here he injected an admonitory passage from scripture for the pope's benefit:

> It therefore remains, most beloved Father, that for the sake of your power and authority you come to the aid of the Church as you had started to, and as the clergy have reasonably requested, and that you should make your counsel crystal clear, so that your detractors and those plotting against you should not start to whisper about you, "Here is a man who starts to build but cannot bring the work to completion". LUKE 14:30[74]

What was clear to Ivo at this point was that the election controversy at Beauvais and the reconciliation of Philip to the Church had become linked in the pope's mind. His next letter to Paschal consisted primarily of a series of canonical authorities which argued for the legitimacy of absolving individuals from their oaths, which Paschal might use to release Philip from the oath he had sworn that Galo would never become bishop of Beauvais.[75] This twist suggests that the king, perhaps in Manasses' council, had raised the difficulty that should he break his vow, he would commit a sin. To this, the bishop of Chartres could only throw up his hands in exasperation. "If a canonical election can be annulled by a sacrament of this sort", he lamented to Paschal, "there will be no elections in

72 Rolker, *Canon Law* (see above, n. 14), pp. 196–99. For Ivo's understanding of judicial procedure, see now Bruce Clark Brasington, *Order in the Court: Medieval Procedural Treatises in Translation*, Medieval Law and its Practice 21 (Leiden, 2016), pp. 42–50.

73 PL 162:123 (no. 104): "Unde electores ejus [Galo's, JSO] ad paternitatem vestram jam confugissent, nisi quia metropolitanus eorum eos detinet condicto die inter contradictores et electores, sicut dicitur pacem volens componere, vel forsitan propter voluntatem regis rem callide impedire."

74 Ibidem: "Superest ergo, dilectissime Pater, ut pro potestate et auctoritate vestra, sicut coepistis, Ecclesiae, prout clerici rationabiliter postulaverint, succurratis, et consilium vestrum inconfusibile faciatis, ne insidiatores et detractors vestri, subsannando de vobis dicere incipient: 'Hic homo caepit aedificare, et non potuit consummare.'"

75 PL 162:124 (no. 105).

the future in the kingdom of the Franks except those done by simony or violent imposition."[76]

In spite of Ivo's complaints, there was no reason that Galo's election should *not* be debated in the provincial synod, and a peaceful resolution attempted, before the case passed to Rome. Nor is there an obvious reason why Manasses should not have attempted to broker an agreement on his own initiative.[77] The outcome is in any case clear: Manasses never consecrated Galo, and the pope appeared willing to compromise. Ivo became desperate, and the tone of his subsequent letter to Paschal is bleak. Despite his best efforts, "those men"—perhaps a reference to Stephen and his supporters—"wishing to rot in their own excrement, brought to us beseeching letters from the holy see, I do not know by what machinations, seeking to palliate his wickedness and defend his disobedience."[78] Worn down by the opposition and despairing of his efforts, Ivo set out with Galo for Rome. They got as far as the Alps. There the bishop of Chartres heard rumors that his enemies had prepared ambushes for him, so he sent Galo, "who was more adept at hiding himself in suspect places", perhaps because he was less well known than Ivo, to deliver his message to the pope in person. Ivo returned to Chartres.[79]

When Galo arrived in Rome, the pope declared him bishop of Beauvais and sent him to Poland as a legate, effectively tabling the matter and clearing a path toward reconciliation with Philip I over his unlawful marriage.[80] More than two years later, and having never occupied the see, Galo was transferred to the vacant diocese of Paris. Beauvais' multi-year hiatus without a bishop

76 Ibid.: "si tali sacramento annullari potest canonica electio, nulla ulterius in regno Francorum futura est, nisi aut simoniaca aut violenta intrusio."

77 Monod, "L'Église et l'État" (see above, n. 10), p. 61 and n. 6, following Ivo on this point, calls this move "une ruse habile." He sees Manasses' negotiation and refusal to consecrate Galo as resulting from his desire to maintain his position with respect to the king and the pope, rather than as a defence of his own ecclesiastical prerogative.

78 PL 162:128–29, at 128 (no. 110): "Ipsi in stercoribus suis computrescere cupientes, litteras a sede apostolica, nescio quibus subreptionibus impetratas nobis deferunt ad palliandum malitiam suam, vel defendendam inobedientiam." I take this as a reference to Stephen, though it could refer to the king or one of Stephen's partisans.

79 PL 162:129 (no. 110): "Domnum itaque Gualonem confratrem et coepiscopum nostrum, qui in suspectis locis ad occultandum se aptior est." The precise meaning in nevertheless unclear.

80 Probably in late 1102 or early 1103. See Pierre David, "Un disciple d'Yves de Chartres en Pologne—Galon de Paris et le droit canonique," in *La Pologne au VIIe Congrès international des sciences historiques, Varsovie 1933*, 2 vols (Warsaw, 1933), 1:99–113.

in residence finally came to an end in 1105 with the election of Geoffrey 'of Pisseleu', a clerk with connections to the royal household.[81]

5 Law and Compromise

The electoral controversy at Beauvais in 1100–04 traditionally has been assessed primarily in terms of whether the pope, or the king, more effectively imposed his will in the clash between *regnum* and *sacerdotium*. Bernard Monod, who carried out the most detailed study more than a century ago, concluded that both Philip and Paschal only really succeeded in negating the other's decisions, rather than carrying the day by the force of their legal arguments or authority. A 'simple compromise' resulted.[82] Monod considered Manasses' role in the affair 'strange', and concluded that he stayed deaf to Paschal's orders, resolutely positioning himself "against the reformists, against the majority of the clergy, against his fellow bishops, against canon law."[83] In fact, Manasses appears to have stood his ground in defence of his legal privilege and acted with a fair degree of autonomy—hence Ivo's vexed appeal to him to move the second election forward. Moreover, his fellow bishops Lambert and John, whose reputations in Rome were virtually spotless, seem to have supported Manasses on these grounds and even interceded directly before Paschal on his behalf, assuring the pope, in a letter hand-carried to Rome by John in 1101, that Manasses "venerated the decrees of the apostolic see, loved truth, feared God, honoured men religious and of good testimony, and showed himself to be especially devoted to the care of the poor", this last part a totally irrelevant character reference.[84] Manasses' actions did not open a schism within

81 That is, it came to an end for everyone except Ivo, who quickly found himself writing to the new bishop to protest the latter's installation of one Odo as Galo's successor at Saint-Quentin "against my request and your promise" ("contra petitionem etenim meam et promissionem vestram")—suggesting a *quid pro quo* may have been arranged; PL 162:156 (no. 151). On Geoffrey's origins, see Guyotjeannin, *Episcopus et comes* (see above, n. 11), p. 78, who suggests he may have been a royal chaplain or chancellor; he may also have been a canon from Orléans. What is certain is that he was not one of the capitular dignitaries of Beauvais.

82 Monod, *Essai* (see above, n. 13), p. 92.

83 Monod, "L'Église et l'État" (see above, n. 10), p. 62; idem, *Essai* (see above, n. 13), pp. 75–76.

84 PL 163:454 (no. 6), and *Registre*, ed. Giordanengo (see above, n. 16), pp. 420–21 (no. 67). Monod, *Essai* (see above, n. 13), p. 78 suggests that Manasses ceded his right to transfer Galo from Beauvais to Paris to the pope, but since there is no evidence that the archbishop recognized Galo as lawful bishop of Beauvais, his exact sentiments on the transfer must be left to speculation.

the episcopal ranks of the province or bring about direct retributive action from Paschal,[85] and the archbishop remained on excellent terms with both Lambert and John.[86] It is a testament to the solidarity of this group, or at least to the esteem in which Paschal held the opinion of the bishops of Arras and Thérouanne, that the pope seems not to have pressured Manasses any further. He sent him no more letters in the affair, and delegated Lambert of Arras the responsibility of reconciling Philip to the Church.[87]

What lessons, then, does the Beauvais election dispute of 1100–04 hold for us concerning church reform and the law? One observation that emerges from the documents is that Ivo and the canons of Beauvais knew that to make their cases they had to co-opt the collegial solidarity that bound the bishops of Arras and Thérouanne to Manasses. Perhaps one of the more unanticipated outcomes of the whole affair is the degree to which Manasses and his suffragans largely maintained a middle ground in defence of their episcopal and metropolitan privilege, despite immense political pressure from Ivo, Paschal, and Philip. If historians have concluded that the election controversy ended in a 'stalemate', it is because they have seen it primarily through the eyes of these three figures. Ultimately, however, Lambert and John, despite their reputation as reformers and their friendship with Ivo, rallied to their archbishop and refused to put other agendas before the proceedings of the provincial council.

Ostensibly, the entire controversy at Beauvais hinged on the canonical fitness of Stephen of Garlande. But as Monod pointed out long ago, the contending parties applied legal arguments selectively, or ignored the law altogether as a means of resolving the dispute. Christof Rolker has more recently shown that Ivo, for example, believed in synodal authority and respecting the ecclesiastical hierarchy—until it did not suit his needs. His

85 Moreover, Manasses appears to have continued to insist on his procedural powers as metropolitan vis-à-vis the church of Beauvais and its elections until at least 1104; see Ivo's final letter to him at PL 162:151 (no. 145): "Unde consulendo suggerimus, et suggerendo consulimus, ut rigorem justitiae quem nunc tandem [...] erga Belvacensem ecclesiam nescio quo impellente intendistis, consultiori moderatione remittatis."

86 As evidenced in the letters Manasses and Lambert exchanged from 1101 onward; see *Registre*, ed. Giordanengo (see above, n. 16), pp. 422–29 (nos. 68–70), 430–32 (no. 74), and the charters they witnessed together. See for these the editions in Patrick Demouy, "Actes des archevêques de Reims d'Arnoul à Renaud II, 997–1139," 2 vols (unpublished thèse de doctorat, Université de Nancy II, 1982), vol. 2/2, no. 135 (1103), p. 368; no. 136 (1103), p. 371.

87 PL 163:128 (no. 116), letter of 5 October 1104 (JL 5979, 717). Paschal also commissioned John of Thérouanne and Lambert to judge other local disputes; see for example PL 163:127 (no. 113), letter of 25 April 1104 (JL 5976, 717). It is also possible to read Paschal's delegations of John and Lambert as reflecting a lack of confidence in Manasses, but I suspect it has more to do with their good reputations than the archbishop's standing.

views on archiepiscopal prerogative were likewise mixed, and Ivo was willing to sacrifice legal consistency in favour of contingency and the discretion of episcopal and papal authority.[88] In his letters to Lambert, Manasses, and John, he generally avoided using legal arguments. In the course of the controversy he cites legal precedent to Manasses and Paschal on only two occasions, and only when faced with clear setbacks to his position.[89] In light of the voluminous correspondence Ivo produced during the four years of his involvement with the episcopal election at Beauvais, he sought virtually no remedy in the law. He offers his most developed legal argument, in which he cites Ambrose's *De officiis*, Augustine's sermon on the beheading of John the Baptist, Jerome's *Commentary on Jeremiah*, and an extract from Anastasius Bibliothecarius' commentary on the acts of the Second Council of Nicaea (787), against Philip's claim to be bound by his oath not to allow Galo to assume office.[90] To Manasses he cites a single canon, and alludes broadly to another. All of his citations are connected to or concern the king.

Thus, much as the Beauvais election was *about* the law, its transaction did not involve legal arguments. Or, more precisely, virtually all the legal points in the case could be countered with other sources or arguments. The disputants therefore explored other avenues for resolving the conflict, and that meant personal pressure tactics and appeals, using personal and intimate language, with the focus on the provincial bishops. And whereas historians once saw these events as avatars for the conflict between 'Church and State' or 'Church Reform', ideology and principled positions had little to do with its negotiation or eventual resolution.[91]

As historians think about how to replace inadequate models of reform in canon law and other fields, I suggest that a renewed focus on regional episcopal networks would be profitable. Writing about reform has for a long time resembled institutional history in a 'statist' mode, with the law as its handmaiden. We must replace the prevailing narrative of reform in both legal and ecclesiastical history with one that stresses regional complexity and uniqueness and considers the history of law embedded within a broader social history of the clergy, much as modern historians have begun to examine 'a

88 Rolker, *Canon Law* (see above, n. 14), pp. 193–204, 208.

89 In letters 102 (to Manasses) and 105 (to Paschal), and covering the period from 1100–04.

90 PL 162:124. These canons appear elsewhere in Ivo's work, notably the *Decretum*. See Rolker, *Canon Law* (see above, n. 14), pp. 316–17.

91 If one were to identify the individual who most consistently maintained his position, apart from the king, it would be the Archbishop Manasses.

Europe of regions' rather than a Europe of states.[92] Linda Fowler-Magerl has recently proposed one type of model. Noting the proliferation and copying of legal texts along the Via Francigena, which linked Rome to Canterbury and passed through the dioceses of Thérouanne, Arras, and Reims, Fowler-Magerl has suggested that scholars pay attention to road networks and the physical connections between places.[93] Her examples from the province of Reims of work transmitted along the Via Francigena include widely diffused collections like *Sinemuriensis* (also known as *Collectio Remensis*), compiled at Reims; the more local *Collection in Nine Books* and the *Collection in Ten Parts*, both perhaps produced at Thérouanne; and the *Collectio Atrebatensis*, of Arras.[94] Lambert and John have been connected directly to several of these collections, and I have argued that Manasses had a hand in compiling the small collection of canons containing elements of *Sinemuriensis* in Reims, Bibliothèque municipale, 15, in addition to commissioning the complete copy of Burchard's *Decretum* found in Reims, Bibliothèque municipale, 673. While Fowler-Magerl's model usefully links infrastructure and texts, clerical networks like the one studied here—dense, overlapping, fraternal, semi-autonomous—generated powerful solidarities predicated on shared ideas about the law and shared political agendas.

As a final observation, one problem with the idea of reform is that it obscures the fact that historical events are often driven by highly personal, idiosyncratic, even whimsical aims. To suggest that bishops undertook reform initiatives purely in service to abstract ideals and oblivious to concrete political and personal motives, is surely misguided. We must replace the master narrative of reform with regional narratives, analogous to the 'horizontal' model of legal development proposed by Greta Austin in this volume.[95] The resulting account will surely be more complicated, indeed messy, but that, of course, is the essence of History.

---

92 Celia Applegate, "A Europe of Regions: Reflections on the Historiography of Sub-National Places in Modern Times," *The American Historical Review* 104:4 (1999), 1157–82.

93 Linda Fowler-Magerl, "The Collection and Transmission of Canon Law along the Northern Section of the Via Francigena in the Eleventh and Twelfth Centuries," in *Bishops, Texts and the Use of Canon Law around 1100: Essays in the Honour of Martin Brett*, ed. Bruce Clark Brasington and Kathleen G. Cushing, Church, Faith and Culture in the Middle Ages (Aldershot, 2008), pp. 129–39.

94 Lotte Kéry, *Canonical Collections of the Early Middle Ages (ca. 400–1140): A Bibliographical Guide to the Manuscripts and Literature*, History of Medieval Canon Law (Washington, D.C., 1999), pp. 203–04, 262–63, 279.

95 See Austin's chapter in this volume.

6 Acknowledgment

I would like to extend my sincere thanks to Andreas Thier and Christof Rolker, the organizers of the 2014 Zurich colloquium on new approaches to canon law, for their kind invitation to present this work; to Claudia Zey for her response to the initial paper; to the anonymous reviewer for his/her suggestions; and to Enrico Veneziani, for sharing references and his doctoral dissertation with me.

CHAPTER 5

The Role of Hagiography in the Development of Canon Law in the Reform Era

Tatsushi Genka

1 Introduction[1]

In his "Un tournant de l'histoire du droit 1060–1140," Paul Fournier argued that the pontificate of Gregory VII and that of Urban II marked two distinct stages in the history of canon law: while the former is characterized by its efforts to identify the texts that represent the authentic tradition and to eliminate those that oppose it, the latter shows more flexible attitudes in this regard. The champions of the new stage of history, says Fournier, are Bernold of Konstanz and Ivo of Chartres, whose methods of interpretation, which consist of principles of hermeneutics as well as a hierarchy of texts, reflect the flexibility towards the tradition that characterizes the pontificate of Urban II.[2]

1 The present article is a revised version of the paper read at the conference "New Discourses in Canon Law Research" organized by Professor Andreas Thier (Zurich) and Professor Christof Rolker (Bamberg). I would like to thank them for inviting me to the conference and for their hostpitality. I am also grateful to Professor Mathias Schmoeckel (Bonn), Professor Peter Landau (Munich), Dr Martin Brett (Cambridge), Professor Bruce Clark Brasington (Canyon) and Professor Greta Austin (Tacoma) for their valuable comments and supports. I would like to note with gratitude that this article was originally conceived as a part of my research project "Juristic Personality in the High Middle Ages" funded by Tokyo Marine Kagami Foundation (Tokyo).

2 Paul Fournier, "Un tournant de l'histoire du droit 1060–1140," *Nouvelle revue historique du droit français et étranger* 41 (1917), 129–80, at p. 130: "L'évolution dont il s'agit s'est produite successivement sur deux terrains. D'abord, au temps de Grégoire VII (1073–1085), les esprits sont surtout préoccupés de la critique des textes canonique adimits plus ou moirns généralement dans l'Église, et de l'introduction de textes, témoignages du passé, que l'on fait sortir de l'ombre où ils sont demeurés. Puis, à l'époque d'Urbain II (1088–1099), on fut amené par les circonstances à rechercher une méthode conduisant à la synthèse par la conciliation des textes. Ainsi l'œvre du pontificat de Grégoire VII concerne surtout la rénovation des textes canoniques; celle du pontificat d'Urbain II a trait à la méthode d'interprétation de ces textes."

 | DOI:10.1163/9789004394384_007

This view of Fournier's did not go unchallenged, most notably by Stephan Kuttner in his study on Urban II and the doctrine of interpretation[3] and by Martin Brett in his study on the canonical collections attributed to Ivo.[4] Kuttner attacked Fournier's assumption that a version of Urban's letter (JL 5383) found in the *Collectio Britannica* was evidence of Urban's contribution to the later developments of hermeneutics. Kuttner argued that the direction of influence was in fact the other way round.[5] Brett, on the other hand, called Fournier's dating of the Ivonian collections into question by re-examining in detail formal as well as material sources of the collections used by Fournier to date and attribute them to Ivo.[6] They posed serious questions to some fundamental assumptions of Fournier's theses. But it was Christof Rolker's studies on Ivo that have brought us changes that should properly be called drastic. The most notable example is that Ivo's authorship of the *Panormia* is now seriously in question. But, more importantly, his way of thinking has now come to be interpreted not in isolation but in the context of the whole Ivonian corpus. As a result, the famous *Prologus*, for example, is now thought to represent Ivo as a pastor who seeks practical solutions for the problems his flock faced, rather than Ivo as a scholar who seeks to reconcile conflicting traditions. That is to say, this famous text is now placed in the pastoral setting of *cura animarum* rather than in the academic milieu of a cathedral school.[7]

As regards Bernold, the advances in research in the last decades have not been as spectacular as those concerning Ivo, but there still have been some notable ones. Fournier's thesis of the two-stage development of canon law is based on the assumption that *De fontibus iuris ecclesiastici*, in which Bernold identifies the sources of canon law and formulates a theory of hierarchy of texts as well as hermeneutic principles of reconciling conflicting texts, was written

3 Stephan Kuttner, "Urban II and the Doctrine of Interpretation: A Turning Point?," *Studia Gratiana* 15 (1972), 55–85; repr. in idem, *The History of Ideas and Doctrines of Canon Law in the Middle Ages*, 2nd ed., Variorum Collected Studies Series 113 (London, 1992), no. IV.

4 Martin Brett, "Urban II and the Collections Attributed to Ivo of Chartres," in *Proceedings of the Eighth International Congress of Medieval Canon Law: San Diego, University of California at La Jolla, 21–27 August 1988*, ed. Stanley Chodorow, MIC Subsidia 9 (Vatican City, 1992), pp. 27–46.

5 Kuttner, "Urban II" (see above, n. 3), p. 58. For a cautious attempt of attenuating Kuttner's conclusion see Robert Somerville, *Pope Urban II, the* Collectio Britannica *and the Council of Melfi (1089)* (Oxford 1996), pp. 104–15. For a careful treatment of the same subject rather in favour of Urban's authorship see Christof Rolker, *Canon Law and the Letters of Ivo of Chartres*, Cambridge Studies in Medieval Life and Thought, Fourth Series 76 (Cambridge, 2010), pp. 95–97.

6 Brett, "Urban II" (see above, n. 4), passim.

7 Rolker, *Canon Law* (see above, n. 5).

around 1091 during the reign of Urban II.[8] It was this assumption that was to be challenged. On the basis of the issues and arguments common to *De fontibus iuris ecclesiastici* and *Apologeticus*, one of the polemical writings of Bernold's which can safely be dated around 1076, Doris Stöckly and Detlev Jasper argued that the two works had been written in the same period, that is, around 1076 in the pontificate of Gregory VII.[9] The new dating of *De fontibus iuris ecclesiastici* has an important consequence. It means that Bernold's hermeneutic principles and the theory of hierarchy of texts were both conceived at the same time in a circumstance different from the one Fournier had in mind. This should be a serious challenge to his fundamental assumption of the two-stage development of canon law. Bernold, too, called for a reinterpretation.

In my article "Hierarchie der Texte, Hierarchie der Autoritäten," I argued that the hierarchy of texts conceived by Bernold was not an interpretive method of dealing with conflicting texts but an expression of his idea of the structural organization of the church. By making the authority of the conciliar canons, both universal and regional, derive ultimately from the papacy, Bernold tried to solve a problem inherent in the church, i.e. the tension between the papal primacy on the one hand and the autonomy and collegiality of the bishops on the other, that is at the same time the conflict between those texts issued by the papacy and those of the councils. Bernold's answer was a hierarchy of texts based upon derivation of authority, the point of which was to establish an objective order among the different but legitimate principles of the structural organization of the church. The hermeneutic principles of reconciling conflicting texts were conceived as an instrument to stabilize this order.[10]

Ivo now being interpreted quite differently from the way Fournier did, there is, if my argument based on the new dating of *De fontibus iuris ecclesiastici* is plausible, not much left of Fournier's two-stage development of canon law. We do need a new way of looking at the history of canon law of this period. In the present paper, as a part of preliminary work for a new narrative, I explore the backgrounds of Bernold's thoughts.

8 Fournier, "Un tournant" (see above, n. 1), p. 159: "J'incline à penser qu'il ne saurait être de beaucoup postérieur à 1091."

9 Bernold von Konstanz, *De excommunicatis vitandis, de reconciliatione lapsorum et de fontibus iuris ecclesiastici* (*libellus X*), ed. Doris Stöckly and Detlev Jasper, MGH Fontes iuris 15 (Hanover, 2000), p. 46.

10 Tatsushi Genka, "Hierarchie der Texte, Hierarchie der Autoritäten. Zur Hierarchie der Rechtsquellen bei Gratian," *Zeitschrift der Savigny-Stiftung für Rechtsgeschichte, kanonistische Abteilung* 95 (2009), 101–27.

2 Question

As mentioned previously, Bernold made the authority of the councils and their canons, both universal and regional, derive ultimately from the papacy. In this way Bernold established a hierarchical relationship between them. Apparently Bernold regarded a mere assertion of primacy based on Matthew 16:18–19 as insufficient for establishing a hierarchy of texts. It should be noted, however, that a relationship in which one authority derives from the other does not in itself inevitably lead to a hierarchical relationship in the church. To take an obvious example, in the preface to the third book of his *De trinitate*, Augustine says:

> […] the Son is not inferior to the Father because the latter sent (the former) and the former was sent (by the latter), and the Holy Spirit is not inferior to the Father and the Son because it is written in the Gospel that the Holy Spirit was sent by the Father and the Son […].[11]

Without going into the intricacies of the doctrine, it will suffice to point out that, while there may be a natural inclination to see a hierarchical relationship in derivation of authority (in this case between 'sending' and 'being sent'), Augustine deliberately avoids such a conclusion. He confirms both individuality and equality of the Divine Persons. Deriving one authority from the other and conceiving a hierarchical relationship between them are two distinct ways of thinking independent of each other. Bernold, therefore, acted on certain premises when he combined them. The question is what his premises are.

If we look for examples closer to Bernold's time, we find a similar way of thinking to that of Bernold's in a letter of Peter Damian's to Hildebrand (the later Pope Gregory VII) written in 1059 (Letter 65).[12] In this letter, the cardinal bishop of Ostia, a man born and raised in Ravenna, informs the archdeacon of the Roman church of the incident which took place in Milan when he visited the city as a legate of Pope Nicholas II. In order to persuade the Milanese dissidents to obey the Roman church, Peter Damian reminded them, in addition to the Damasian doctrine of the Roman supremacy as found in the *Decretum Gelasianum*, of the martyrs of Milan who consecrated the city

11 *Sancti Aurelii Augustini De trinitate libri xv*, ed. William J. Mountain with the help of Frater Glorie, CCSL 50 (Turnhout, 1968), pp. 128–9, lines 49–52: "[…] non ideo minorem patre filium quia ille misit, hic missus est, nec ideo minorem utroque spiritum sanctum quia et ab illo et ab illo missus in euangelio legitur […]."

12 *Die Briefe des Petrus Damiani* 2, ed. Kurt Reindel, MGH Die Briefe der deutschen Kaiserzeit 4 (Munich, 1988), pp. 228–47.

by their blood: They were, says Peter Damian, disciples of St Paul and Linus, himself a disciple and successor of St Peter on the Roman see.[13] To establish a hierarchical relationship between the church of Rome and that of Milan, Peter Damian appeals not only to the Roman primacy based on Matthew 16:18–19 but also to the fact that the martyrs of one church were sent (thus derived) from the other. There is an apparent similarity between Bernold and Peter Damian in their respective ways of thinking. This is not to say that Peter Damian's Letter 65 is the only case in which a similar way of thinking can be observed, nor that Bernold knew the letter and was influenced by it when he wrote *De fontibus iuris ecclesiastici*, although the possibility is not precluded. But there is enough similarity to make a comparison worthwhile.[14]

The present paper tries to understand Bernold's hierarchical principle by comparing it with Peter Damian's Letter 65, more precisely, by asking how the latter infers a hierarchical relationship from the fact that one authority derives from the other, and how it relates to canon law. For this purpose, I draw upon Peter Damian's sermons preached on the feast of Apollinaris, the patron saint of Ravenna, between 1044 and 1046.[15] In these sermons Peter Damian describes the relationship between the church of Ravenna and that of Rome in the same way as in Letter 65, but, as will be shown presently, from the opposite viewpoint. Then, as these sermons are an interpretation of the *Passio* of Apollinaris of Ravenna (BHL 623),[16] I draw on, in addition to the *Passio* itself, another interpretation of the *Passio*, the vita of Apollinaris found in the *Liber Pontificalis ecclesie Ravennatis* written by Agnellus of Ravenna in the 830s and the 840s.[17] I use this text from the Carolingian period for its heuristic value,

13 See below III-3.

14 For a similar approach compare the magisterial treatment of John Joseph Ryan, *Saint Peter Damiani and his Canonical Sources: A Preliminary Study in the Antecedents of the Gregorian Reform*, Pontifical Institute of Medieval Studies. Studies and Texts 2 (Toronto, 1956), pp. 144–47.

15 *Sancti Petri Damiani sermones*, ed. Giovanni Lucchesi, CCCM 57 (Turnhout, 1983), pp. 180–83. For dating of these sermons see Hans Peter Laqua, *Traditionen und Leitbilder bei dem Ravennater Reformer Petrus Damiani 1042–1052*, Münstersche Mittelalter-Schriften 30 (Munich, 1976), pp. 174–208.

16 For the text of the *Passio* see AA SS Iulii v (Antwerp, 1727), pp. 344–45. See also "Spicilegium Ravennatis Historiae sive Monumenta Historica ad Ecclesiam et Urbem Ravennatem spectantia," in *Rerum Italicarum Scriptores* 1/2, ed. Ludovico A. Muratori (Milan, 1725), pp. 529–30.

17 For the text of the vita see *Agnelli Ravennatis Liber pontificalis ecclesiae Ravennatis*, ed. Deborah M. Deliyannis, CCCM 199 (Turnhout, 2006), pp. 147–48. See also Agnellus von Ravenna, *Liber pontificalis / Bischofsbuch*, 1, ed. and tr. Claudia Nauerth, Fontes Christiani 21/1 (Freiburg, Basel, Vienna, Barcelona, Rome, and New York, 1996), pp. 94, 96; *Codex pontificalis ecclesiae Ravennatis*, 1, ed. Alessandro Testi-Rasponi, Rerum Italicarum

i.e. in order to elucidate the characteristics of Peter Damian's interpretation of the same material. In order to find out how it relates to canon law, I draw on another letter of Peter Damian's, which was written in 1062 to Cunibertus, the bishop of Turin (Letter 112).[18]

In the following, I first describe the *Passio* and Agnellus' vita from the viewpoint of Apollinaris' relationship with St Peter, the so-called apostolic succession (III-1). Then I describe two of Peter Damian's sermons preached on the feast of St Apollinaris and compare them with the *Passio* and Agnellus' vita (III-2). On the basis of this comparison I examine Peter Damian's arguments in Letter 65 (III-3). In order to elucidate how his arguments relate to canon law, I draw on the letter of 1062 (III-4) and analyse its contents, before I come back to Bernold (III-5, IV).

3 Derivation of Authority as a Constitutive Principle of the Church

3.1 *The* Passio *of Apollinaris of Ravenna* (BHL *623*) *and Agnellus' Interpretation*

As mentioned above with an example taken from Augustine's *De trinitate*, the fact that one authority derives from the other does not entail a hierarchical relationship between them. The same principle applies to the Legend or the *Passio* of Apollinaris, a disciple of St Peter and the founding bishop of the church of Ravenna.[19]

Scriptores n.s. 2/3 (Bologna, 1924), pp. 21–8; *Agnelli qui et Andreas Liber pontificalis ecclesiae Ravennatis*, ed. Oswald Holder-Egger, MGH SS rer. Lang. 1 (Hanover, 1878), pp. 265–391, here pp. 280–81; AA SS Iulii v (Antwerp, 1727), pp. 350–51. For an English translation with a commentary see Agnellus of Ravenna, *The Book of Pontiffs of the Church of Ravenna*, tr. Deborah M. Deliyannis (Washington, D.C., 2004).

18 *Die Briefe des Petrus Damiani 3*, ed. Kurt Reindel, MGH Die Briefe der deutschen Kaiserzeit 4 (Munich, 1989), pp. 258–88. Compare Ryan's discussion on this letter in Ryan, *Saint Peter Damiani* (see above, n. 14), pp. 140–41.

19 For Apollinaris as the first bishop of Ravenna see Giorgio Orioli, "I vescovi di Ravenna: note di cronologia e di storia," *Bollettino della badia greca di Grottaferrata* 32 (1978), 45–67, here at pp. 46–51. For a useful comparison with other regions see Herrick's studies on Northern France in the early Middle Ages: Samantha Kahn Herrick, *Imagining the Sacred Past: Hagiography and Power in Early Normandy* (Cambridge and London, 2007); eadem, "Studying Apostolic Hagiography: The Case of Fronto of Périgueux, Disciple of Christ," *Speculum* 85 (2010), 235–70; eadem, "Le pouvoir du passé apostolique," in *Hagiographie, idéologie et politique au Moyen Âge en Occident: actes du colloque international du Centre d'Études supérieures de Civilisation médiévale de Poitiers 11–14 semptembre 2008*, ed. Edina Bozóky (Turnhout, 2012), pp. 129–38.

The *Passio* of Apollinaris is thought to have taken its shape sometime between the late 5th and the mid-7th century (666 at the latest).[20] The vulgate version as is known today is thought to have been a product of the struggle of the church of Ravenna for autocephaly at the end of this period.[21] The gist of the passages concerning the relationship of Apollinaris with St Peter, the so-called apostolic succession, is as follows:

1. St Peter came to Rome from Antioch in the reign of Emperor Claudius with many faithful who served him. He preached to the Jewish community

20 While Zattoni and Lanzoni argue for 7th century, Mazzotti argues for 6th century, at least in an earlier recension, and Orioli for an even earlier date. Girolamo Zattoni, "La data della 'Passio S. Apollinaris' di Ravenna'," in idem, *Scritti storici e ravennati*, ed. Mario Mazzotti (Ravenna, 1975), pp. 113–28 (first published in *Atti della Reale Accademia delle Scienze di Torino* 39 (1904), 364–78); Francesco Lanzoni, "Le fonti della leggenda di Sant Apollinare di Ravenna," *Atti e memorie della reale deputazione di storia patria per le provincie di Romagna, Serie 4* 5 (1914–15), 111–76; Mario Mazzotti, "Per una nuova datazione della 'Passio S. Apollinaris'," *Studi romagnoli* 3 (1952), 123–29; Giorgio Orioli, "Osservazioni sulla data della Passio S. Apollinaris di Ravenna," *Bollettino della badia greca di Grottaferrata* 32 (1978), 67–75; idem, "La Vita sancti Apolenaris di Ravenna e gli antecedenti storici dell'organizzazione ecclesiastica ravennate," *Apollinaris* 59 (1986), 251–67.

21 See Hans Reinhard Seeliger, "Apollinaris," in *Lexikon für Theologie und Kirche*, 1, 3rd ed. (Freiburg, Basel, and Vienna, 1993), pp. 828–29: "Der Kult ist mit der im 5. Jh. überall einsetzenden Verehrung der Gründerbischöfe in Verbindung zu bringen. [...] Reflex der Autokephaliebestrebungen des Exarchats von Ravenna ist die *Passio* des 7. Jh. (BHL 623), die Apollinaris mit dem hl. Petrus in Verbindung bringt." See also Jean-Charles Picard, *Le souvenir des évêques: sépultures, listes épiscopales et culte des évêques en Italie du Nord des origines au Xe siècle*, Bibliothèque des écoles françaises d'Athènes et de Rome 268 (Rome, 1988), p. 658: "L'entreprise de solenisation du culte des évêques locaux est complétée au VIIe siècle par la réalisation d'un nouveau monument, mais un monument littéraire cette fois, la Passio S. Apollinaris." Ibid., n. 266: "[...] Seul M. Mazzotti s'est séparé de G. Zattoni pour proposer d'attribuer la Passio à l'époque de Maximianus; il n'existe pas d'argument de fait en faveur d'une telle anticipation, qui me paraît brusquer l'évolution des ravennates vers l'autocéphalie. On n'entend pas parler de la Passio pendant le siècle qui précède la concession de l'autocéphalie, et en particulier dans la correspondance de Grégoire le Grand; même si l'argument *a silentio* n'est jamais décisif, constatons au moins que cela n'incite pas à suivre M. Mazzotti." For a more nuanced view in line with Mazzotti see Giovanni Lucchesi, "Apollinare," in *Bibliotheca sanctorum*, 2 (Rome, 1962), pp. 239–42, at p. 241: "Oggi, però, si torna volentieri ad una sua [the *Passio*, TG] almeno parziale rivalutazione, sia per la data, che è stata anticipata di un secolo (almeno per una sua primitiva redazione conosciuta anche dal Liber Pontificalis di Agnello ravennate), sia per alcuni elementi degni di fede che vi si ravvisano." For a concise summary of the debate see Meliyannis, *Liber pontificalis* (see above, n. 17), pp. 39–40, n. 70; Paolo Tomea, *Tradizione apostolica e coscienza critica a Milano nel medioevo: la leggenda di san Barnaba* (Milan, 1994), pp. 11–12, n. 22; Laqua, *Traditionen* (see above, n. 15), p. 189, n. 144 and p. 197, n. 164.

in Rome, to which he said he himself belonged, about Jesus Christ and his deeds and miracles performed in Israel. He won many converts, even among non-Jewish Romans.[22]

2. After a long time, St Peter told his disciple Apollinaris in the form of a rhetorical question that the latter, having already learnt everything about the deeds of Jesus Christ, did not need to stay with him any longer. Conferring on Apollinaris 'spiritus sanctus' as well as 'pontificatus', St Peter prayed for him with an imposition of a hand and sent him to Ravenna with a kiss.[23]

3. After having left Rome for Ravenna, Apollinaris performed two miracles. The first occasion came when he stayed with Erenaeus who lived not far from the city. Having made a sign of the cross and prayed "God, you are not restricted to a particular locality but ubiquitous" ("Deus, qui non localiter, sed ubique es"), asking Him to open not only the bodily but also spiritual eyes of the gentiles around him, Apollinaris healed the blind son of Erenaeus. Everyone present witnessed the event, and subsequently they were baptized.[24]

---

22 AA SS (see above, n. 16), pp. 344–45 §1: "1. In diebus Claudii caesaris veniens Petrus apostolus Jesu Christi Nazareni ab Antiochia in urbem Romam [plurimos ad Dominum convertit] et multi cum eo Christiani administrantes ei, Romam venerunt; qui statim ad synagogam Hebraeorum ascendentes [innotuerunt et] dedit eis notitiam Petrus dicens, quod et ipse Hebraeus esset, et a Judaea propter fratrum caritatem advenisset. Cum vero per multos dies sermocinaretur cum Judaeis, introducebat de nomine Jesu, quod vere Dei esset filius, qui salvum fecit omne genus humanum, indicans illis, quantas operationes, et virtutes in Israel fecisset secundum propheticas voces. Multi vero ex Judaeis, agentes poenitentiam pro ignorantia sua, credebant in Jesum, praedicante Petro. Non solum [autem] Judaei, sed etiam Romani, suscipientes verbum, gavisi sunt, quod visitatione visitasset Deus genus humanum, mittens filium suum, renovare mundum; et credentes in Jesum baptizabantur."

23 Ibid., p. 345, § 2: "2. Post multum vero temporis ait beatus Petrus apostolus Apollinari discipulo suo: Quid sedes nobiscum? Ecce eruditus es de omnibus, quae fecit Jesus, surge, et accipe Spiritum sanctum, simulque pontificatum, et perge ad urbem, quae vocatur Ravennantium; multitudo enim populi illic moratur: praedica eis de nomine Jesu, et ne formidaveris; constat enim apud te, quod vere sit Dei filius, qui mortuis vitam reddidit, et aegris intulit verbo medicinam. Et post multa dans orationem beatus Petrus [benedixit eum] et ponens manum super caput ejus, ait ei: Mittat Dominus noster Jesus Christus angelum suum, qui praeparet iter tuum, et quae postulaveris annuat; et osculans eum, emisit a se."

24 Ibid., p. 345, § 3: "3. Cumque pervenisset beatus Apollinaris non longe ab urbe Ravenna, mansit apud quemdam militem Astaticum, nomine Herenaeum, cui indicans, unde advenisset, aut quid ageret, ait ad eum ille miles: Hospes, filius meus excaecatus est, sed si qua virtus est praedicationis tuae, adhibe medicinam, ut videat, et sequar Deum tuum credens in eum. Quem puerum beatus Apollinaris alacriter ad se perduci jussit.

4. Apollinaris performed his second miracle inside the city when he healed the wife of the *tribunus militum* of Ravenna. After having been informed by Erenaeus of the healing performed by Apollinaris and of his being apparently a Greek rather than a Roman, the *tribunus militum* secretly invited him to his house in the city. Apollinaris, having prayed God to work with him just as He had worked with St Peter his teacher, entered the house and, in front of the *tribunus militum* and his *milites*, healed the *matrona* who had been unable to leave her bed for so many years. Subsequently the *tribunus militum* and his wife, together with many others, were baptized.[25]

Interpreting or adapting the *Passio*, Agnellus wrote a shorter but in part more detailed account of the vita of Apollinaris in his *Liber Pontificalis* of the church of Ravenna.[26] The book itself, which betrays a strong anti-Roman sentiment,

---

Videntes cuncti, qui aderant, nihil aliud Apollinaris, quam signum Crucis super oculos caeci faciens dixit: Deus, qui non localiter, sed ubique es, tu intromitte cognitionem Filii tui Domini nostri Jesu Christi in istam civitatem, ut non solum istos oculos corporales illumines, sed etiam interiores oculos gentilium commorantium in loco isto aperias, ut celeriter agnoscentes Jesum Christum filium, suum [Dominum] esse Deum [convertantur, ut] locus mihi praedicationis tribuatur cum magno effectu. Expletis his sermonibus, vidit caecus, et provolutus pedibus beati Apollinaris una cum parentibus suis, credentes Christo baptizati sunt in fluvio non longe ab urbe Ravenna."

25 Ibid., p. 345, §§ 4–6: "4. Matrona vero cuiusdam tribuni militum nomine Tecla per annos plurimos gravissima tenebatur infirmitate, quam nullus medicorum poterat erigere. Factum est ut miles Christianus adstaret ante tribunum, et orta fabula, tribunus de conjuge infirma ait miles: Est apud me quidam peregrinus provecta aetate, qui etiam filium meum, absque ullo medicamine inluminavit, si permittis illum videre, mox convalescit. Ait ei tribunus: Et hic unde advenit? Qui respondit: Ab urbe Roma. Tribunus dixit: Ergo Romanus genere est? Respondit: Nescio. Plus tamen Graecus esse videtur. Dicit ei tribunus: Secrete perduc eum in domum meam, ut cognoscam vera esse, quae dicis. Cumque ingressus fuisset urbem Ravennam Apollinaris, circumsignans se dixit: 5. Deus, qui operaris cum Petro magistro meo, operare et mecum, ut clarificetur nomen tuum, et fiat voluntas tua. Et ingressus domum tribuni, est officiosissime susceptus; [...] Tribunus ait: Veniant principes, ut cognoscamus virtutem Jesu. Cumque adstarent, ait tribunus: Ecce mulier mea lecto tenetur infirma annis plurimis, cui omnis medicina contraria extitit; si qua enim virtus est in te, operare. 6. Cui Apollinaris respondit: Aperiat Deus oculos cordis vestri, ut videntes mirabilia eius, credatis Jesum Deum. Tunc adprehendens manum mulieris ait: Surge [...] Statim surgens mulier [surrexit] descendit sana de lectulo [...] Interea ipse tribunus cum uxore [sua] et filiis, et familia sua credentes in Jesum, baptizati sunt; sed et multi alii ex paganis, qui interfuerunt, perceperunt fidem Jesu Christi."

26 For Agnellus' sources see Deliyannis, *Liber pontificalis* (see above, n. 17), pp. 20–52, for the vita especially pp. 39–43.

was meant to be the Ravennate equivalent of the Roman *Liber Pontificalis*.[27] The gist of the relevant passages is as follows:

1. Apollinaris was born in Antioch and had a profound knowledge (*heruditus*) of both Greek and Latin literature. He was a disciple of St Peter and came to Rome with him.[28]

2–1. After a long time, St Peter ordained Apollinaris a bishop (of Ravenna), conferring on him 'spiritum sanctum' through imposition of a hand and blessing him with a kiss.[29]

2–2. When Apollinaris left Rome, St Peter accompanied him on his way to Ravenna. As they prayed outside Rome, at the place where a chapel ('monasterium') called 'Ad Ianuculum' was to be dedicated to the apostle, St Peter performed the first miracle. Then, as they slept at night where another chapel called 'Ad Ulmum' was to be dedicated, again, to St Peter, the apostle performed the second miracle. The next day St Peter left Apollinaris and returned to Rome.[30]

3. Having separated from St Peter, Apollinaris began to perform miracles himself. He first healed the blind son of Erenaeus outside Ravenna.[31]

4. Then he performed many miracles inside the city.[32]

---

27 For Agnellus' tendencies see, in addition to the literature cited in n. 17, Joaquín Martínez Pizarro, *Writing Ravenna. The Liber Pontificalis of Andreas Agnellus* (Ann Arbor, 1995), pp. 9–65. For the relation of the *Liber Pontificalis* with the Roman *Liber Pontificalis* see Deborah M. Deliyannis, "The Liber Pontificalis of the Church of Ravenna: Its Relation with its Roman Model," in *Liber, Gesta, histoire: écrire l'histoire des évêques et des papes, de l'Antiquité au XXIe siècle: actes du colloque international organisé au Centre d'Études Médiévales d'Auxerre les 25, 26 et 27 juin 2007*, ed. François Bougard and Michel Sot (Turnhout, 2009), pp. 283–95.

28 Deliyannis, *Liber pontificalis* (see above, n. 17), p. 148, lines 2–4: "Sanctus Apolenaris, natione Antiochenus, Graecis et Latinis literis eruditus, apostoli Petri discipulus, et cum eo in urbem Romam peruenit."

29 Ibid., lines 5–7: "Qui post plurimum tempus eum pontificem ordinavit atque per impositionem manus spiritum sanctum tribuit et osculum illi dedit [...]."

30 Ibid., lines 7–15: "[...] et ab urbe Roma quasi terdenos milliarios communiter cum eo uenit, in quo situm est monasterium beati Petri quod uocatur ad Ianuculum. Ibi Christi apostolus orauit, et ubi genus posuit, lapis mollis apparuit, ut cera ab igne, et in modum eius lapis genu concauus est. Et ad aliud monasterium ipsius apostoli, quod uocatur ad Vlmum, in ipsa nocte pariter sopiti sunt, et apparent fossae in illo lapide, ubi caput uel terga atque nates et crura tenuerunt, usque in hunc diem. Et post Rauennam eum direxit."

31 Ibid., lines 16–18: "Et ipse beatissimus, antequam in urbem Rauennam ingrederetur, Herenei filium caecum illuminauit, Hereneus quippe 'pacificus' intelligitur [...]."

32 Ibid., lines 18–19: "[...] et intrinsecus huius ciuitatis plurimas peregit uirtutes [...]."

For the *Passio* as well as Agnellus, the authority of Apollinaris is predicated on his relationship with St Peter. This, however, does not seem to entail Apollinaris' subordination to the apostle. Both the *Passio* and Agnellus have Apollinaris become, even if not equal to St Peter, at least independent and autonomous as an apostolic successor.

In the *Passio*, in order to heal the son of Erenaeus who lives not far from Ravenna, Apollinaris prays to God who is omnipresent and not restricted to a particular locality, without mentioning the apostle. Then, when it comes to heal the wife of the *tribunus militum* inside the city, he again prays God to work with him just as He worked with St Peter his teacher.[33] The second prayer shows Apollinaris' close relationship with St Peter. Read in the light of Ravenna's struggle for autocephaly, however, Apollinaris seems to be depicted as claiming the same authority as that of the apostle rather than as showing obedience to him. Apollinaris' relationship with St Peter, it is true, could be interpreted in different ways, e.g. as an assertion against other churches than Rome.[34] However, it has to be admitted that, while such interpretations may not be precluded, the *Passio* did indeed play an important role in the struggle for autocephaly.

Interpreting the *Passio*, Agnellus omits Apollinaris' prayers. But he adds some topographical details of Apollinaris' journey, which, combined with the miracles, accentuate his independence and autonomy (2–2).[35] A quick comparison makes this point clear. In the *Passio*, St Peter does not perform any miracles nor does he accompany Apollinaris on his way to Ravenna. The succession is completed in Rome. For Agnellus, on the other hand, the

33 AA SS 32 (see above, n. 16), 345 §3: "Deus, qui non localiter, sed ubique es […]." Ibid., §5: "Deus, qui operaris cum Petro magistro meo, operare et mecum, ut clarificetur nomen tuum, et fiat voluntas tua."

34 See Lucchesi (see above, n. 21), p. 241: "Anche il motivo della missione petrina, sebbene storicamente inammissibile, è stato in certo modo rivalutato, in quanto non è difficile trovarne tracce in epoca anteriore alla lotta per l'autocefalia, come, per es., nello stesso Liber Pontificalis romano (ed., Duchesne, I, 323), se non addirittura in tutte quelle fonti ravennati del VI sec., nelle quali il vescovo è chiamato 'vir apostolicus' (ma tale espressione, in quel secolo ed anche prima, è usata comunemente per ogni vescovo, senza riguardo alla fondazione apostolica o meno della sua Chiesa). Anzi, un analogo richiamo allo stesso apostolo Pietro in una polemica del Crisologo con la giurisdizione milanese (Serm., 175), ed, insieme, il fatto che furono detti discepoli di s. Pietro anche i protovescovi di Arles e di Aquileia (chiese erette a metropoli ai danni di Milano, come Ravenna), farebbero supporre quella leggenda originata da mire antimilanesi ben più antiche del 666 e di ben altro ambiente che Ravenna. In conclusione, la Passio sancti Apollinaris, più che inventare, avrebbe ampliati temi preesistenti, del VI ed anche del V sec."

35 See Testi-Rasponi, *Codex pontificalis* (see above, n. 17), p. 22.

succession seems to consist of a series of interconnected events, completed step by step in correspondence with the territorial relations of the two cities: St Peter, having conferred 'spiritus sanctus' and 'pontificatus' on Apollinaris, accompanied him on his way to Ravenna. Outside Rome, at two places where chapels 'Ad Ianuculum' and 'Ad Ulmum'[36] were to be dedicated to St Peter, the apostle performed the first two miracles. Then, St Peter having returned to Rome, Apollinaris began to perform miracles in his turn, first outside Ravenna, then finally in the city itself. It is significant that the succession was completed outside Rome after St Peter had returned home. In the light of Agnellus' anti-Roman sentiment, this separation, which seems to be reflected onto the territorial relations of the two cities,[37] highlights Apollinaris' independence and autonomy as an apostolic successor just as those of the Roman see.

3.2 *The* Passio *of Apollinaris in Peter Damian's Sermons 31 and 30*

The idea that the authority of the church of Ravenna was predicated on Apollinaris' succession to St Peter was well known in the eleventh century when Peter Damian preached his sermons on the feast of Apollinaris between 1044 and 1046.[38] In those sermons he repeatedly reminds his audience ('fratres carissimi') of the *Passio* and St Peter's blessing of Apollinaris.

The Sermon 31 is explicit in this regard.[39] Having praised Antioch, Rome and Ravenna for Apollinaris, to which he is son, disciple and patron respectively, and also having extolled the missionary success of Apollinaris in Ravenna,[40]

36 See ibid., n. 8: "Pel primo di essi è evidente che egli considerava il nome Ad genuculum derivato dalla miracolosa impressione delle ginocchia; quanto all'altro Ad ulmum nulla ci è noto. Potrebbe darsi che si trattasse del San Pietro Ad ulmum di Viterbo, tanto più che nell'VIII e IX secolo la strada più battuta per recarsi da Roma a Ravenna era ancora la via Cassia." Testi-Rasponi concedes, however, that it is impossible to identify the precise location of *Ad Ulmum*.

37 Ibid.: "Queste notizie [St Peter's miracles performed at two monasteria, TG], che mancano nelle precedenti fonti, non ci rappresentano altro che il tentativo fatto da Agnello di riattaccare alle memorie dei due monasteria Ad genuculum e Ad ulmum la leggenda delle relazioni fra l'apostolo Pietro e il protovescovo ravennate." For the relations between hagiography and territory in other regions, see Herricks studies on Northern France cited in n. 19.

38 Laqua, *Traditionen* (see above, n. 15), pp. 174–208.

39 Lucchesi, *Sermones* (see above, n. 15), pp. 180–83. For a magisterial treatment of this sermon see Laqua, *Traditionen* (n. 15), pp. 176–95, esp. pp. 184–95. Laqua dates the sermon to 1044.

40 Lucchesi, *Sermones* (see above, n. 15), p. 180, lines 9–25: "Gaudeat Antiochia, quae talem meruit gignere filium; exultet Roma, quae talem potuit habere disciplum: praecipue urbs Rauenna, quae tantum meruit referre patronum. Quae enim daemonum antea delubrum, per hunc caelestium senatorum facta est capitolium. [...] Iuste ergo egregia illa metropolis

Peter Damian says Ravenna has received such a high status from the highest see of Rome that the former is properly called daughter, while the latter is her mother; Ravenna possesses everything in the disciple what Rome does in the heavenly holder of the keys, and what the apostle confers on Rome, that confers the apostolic martyr ('apostolicus martyr') on Ravenna.[41] Then, calling both Constantinople and Ravenna 'secunda Roma', he compares these cities and exalts Ravenna over Constantinople: While Constantinople received Roman citizens from Rome and is 'secunda Roma' in a physical sense, Ravenna received a martyr from Rome and is thus 'secunda Roma' in a spiritual sense.[42] Then he praises God for having conferred so much on Ravenna as to be called 'suppar' to Rome.[43]

The same way of thinking is observed in the Sermon 30 preached two years later.[44] Interpreting the kiss with which St Peter blessed Apollinaris, Peter Damian points out that it is exactly the way a Patriarch of the Old Testament blessed his successor.[45] He then asks his audience to infer from this both 'apostolica dignitas' and 'patriarchalis sublimitas' of Apollinaris, who was consecrated by the apostle in the same manner as an ancient Patriarch consecrated his successor.[46] He concludes his sermon saying that, if one who

---

de beati Apolenaris festiuitate specialiter gaudet, per quem, olim profana et rustica, facta est nunc sacerdotalis et regia."

41 Ibid., p. 180, lines 25–28: "Cui [Ravenna, TG] cum romanis arcibus adeo communis est dignitas, ut illa mater, ista dicatur congrue filia. Quod enim illa in caelesti clauigero, hoc totum ista possidet in discipulo; et quod illi praerogat apostolus, hoc etiam isti martyr apostolicus."

42 Ibid., pp. 180–81, lines 28–35: "Si enim Constantinopolitana ciuitas, quia romanos in se transtulit ciues, secunda Roma est nuncupata, quanto magis haec, quae tantum principem de Roma suscepit, secunda Roma est appellanda? Numquidnam gloriosius est suscipere Quirites de romana curia, quam habere martyrem de romana ecclesia? Ex ea igitur parte qua Roma carnalis est, carnalem genuit; ex ea uero qua spiritalis est, spiritalem ex se filium procreauit."

43 Ibid., p. 181, lines 36–40: "Quod autem tantum ciuitati illi tribuimus, ut Romae supparem esse dicamus, ad laudem Dei referimus, non fauores hominum affectamus. Nam ornatus habitationis decus est habitantis, et honor militis gloria est imperatoris."

44 Ibid., pp. 172–78. For a detailed discussion of this sermon see Laqua, *Traditionen* (see above, n. 15), pp. 200–07. Laqua dates this sermon to 1046 (ibid., pp. 206–07).

45 Lucchesi, *Sermones* (see above, n. 15), p. 176, lines 168–73: "Illud etiam praetereundum non est, quod beatus apostolus osculans discipulum emisit eum a se. Hoc antiquorum patrum consuetudo recolitur, et in nouo iam saeculo ueterum patriarcharum antiquitas reparatur. Ecce Ysaac iterum filium osculatur; ecce Iacob iterum benedicitur, et patriarcha a patriarcha ex authenticae traditionis ordine consecratur."

46 Ibid., p. 177, lines 183–89: "Hinc, fratres, hinc rogo colligite beati Apolenaris quanta sit celsitudo, qui ut apostolus ad arcem pontificatus eligitur, ut patriarcha solempniter ordinatur. Qui et ab illo et non diuerso modo prouehitur a quo et apostoli promouentur.

suffered for the truth is called martyr, the one who not only suffered but also was chosen by the apostle for martyrdom should rightly be called 'apostolicus martyr'.[47]

The title 'apostolicus martyr' constantly used in the sermon together with 'apostolica dignitas' and 'patriarchalis sublimitas' reminds the audience of the epithet of the bishop of Rome 'apostolicus'.[48] The exaltation of Apollinaris in this manner, it is true, serves primarily as an exhortation for his audience to imitate the saint in their battles against sins and vices; these sermons are, therefore, of moral character.[49] Interpreting the *Passio*, however, he constantly refers to the apostolic status of Ravenna which is even higher than that of Constantinople and very close ('suppar') to Rome. The sermons, therefore, have ecclesiological dimensions as well. Compared from this viewpoint with the *Passio* and Agnellus, they show marked differences in their respective ways of thinking.

The most apparent difference is the nature of Apollinaris' relationship with St Peter. Peter Damian, the *Passio* and Agnellus all agree that Apollinaris' authority is predicated on St Peter's blessing. However, while the *Passio* and Agnellus put emphasis on the independence and autonomy of the successor, which are achieved by separating from St Peter in time and space, the sermons of Peter Damian ignore this aspect of the legend completely. The initial relationship of the founding bishop with St Peter is directly linked to the present authority of Ravenna, and the audience is repeatedly reminded of the relation with Rome as the source from which Ravenna constantly derives its present authority. The epithet 'apostolic' appears to be used by Peter Damian to denote this relationship. Furthermore, in addition to *magister* and *discipulus*, the relational terms used also by the *Passio* and Agnellus, Peter Damian uses *mater* and *filia* as their equivalents, the relational terms with a strong connotation of authority of the mother over the daughter.[50] It is important to note that in

---

Videtur ergo in illo et apostolica dignitas et patriarchalis sublimitas, quia et apostolico ore prouehitur et patriarchali solempnitate consecratur."

47 Ibid., p. 177, lines 189–93: "Vnde fit ut, cum ceteri qui pro testimonio ueritatis supplicia passi sunt, martyres nuncupentur; hic, quia non solum passus, sed etiam ad martyrium ab apostolo tam nobiliter est electus, apostolicus martyr iure dicatur."

48 See Laqua, *Traditionen* (see above, n. 15), pp. 203–06.

49 Lucchesi, *Sermones* (see above, n. 15), p. 188, line 111: "ad exemplum imitationis"; ibid., p. 190, lines 195–96: "Sed quia ad aedificationem uestram, dilectissimi, huius tam praecipuae uirtutis exemplum ponere uolumus [...]." Compare Laqua, *Traditionen* (see above, n. 15), pp. 205–07.

50 Compare Ernst Dassmann, *Kirchengeschichte*, 1, 3rd ed. (Stuttgart, 2012), p. 161: "Das Bild von der Kirche als Mutter prägt dagegen stark die westliche Ekklesiologie [...] Das von der nordafrikanischen Theologie entfaltete Bild von der Mutter Kirche hat in

the same sermon Peter Damian describes Ravenna as 'suppar' to Rome, nearly equal, but not equal. His interpretation is purely of hierarchical character, even if it exalts Ravenna towards Rome.

3.3 *Peter Damian's Letter 65 (1059)*

The same way of thinking as in the sermons can be observed in his letter to Hildebrand written 15 years later in 1059 (Letter 65). Peter Damian just makes his arguments from the opposite viewpoint.

In the letter he mentions Hildebrand's request, which he neglected, to search through the 'decreta' or 'gesta' of the Roman Pontiffs so as to assemble into a collection those excerpts that contain anything specifically belonging to the authority of the apostolic see, before he describes the incident he encountered in Milan, to which he was sent as a legate of Nicholas II, as if God gave him an opportunity to understand the importance of Hildebrand's request.[51] According to Peter Damian, some Milanese clergy and lay people ('populus') asserted that the church of St Ambrose should not be subjected to the laws of the Roman church ('legibus Romanis') and no right to judge or to decide in that see belonged to the Roman Pontiff.[52] After having explained to

---

der westlichen Kirche weitergewirkt; es entsprach der römischen Betonung von Recht und Ordnung, und die paternale Struktur des Amtes legte eine maternale Ergänzung in der Ekklesiologie nahe. *Mater et magistra*, nicht *virgo et sponsa*, hat noch Johannes XXIII. seine Kirchenenzyklika genannt. Es drückt das abendländische Verständnis von Kirche aus, vor allem im Hinblick auf das normgebende Lehramt." See also Yves Congar's preface to Karl Delahaye, *Ecclesia Mater chez les pères des trois premiers siècles: pour un renouvellement de la pastorale d'aujourd'hui* (Paris, 1964), pp. 7–32, here at 9–10. Peter Damian applies the notion 'mater', which implied the authority of the Church over the faithul, to the relations among the churches, just as he applies in Letter 65 the notion 'caput', which originally meant Jesus Christ, to the Roman Church. See Reindel, *Briefe 2* (see above, n. 12), p. 229, lines 4–10.

51 Reindel, *Briefe 2* (see above, n. 12), p. 229, line 10 to p. 230, line 3: "Hoc tu suptiliter, ut et alia multa perpendens, frequenter a me karitate, quae superat omnia, postulasti, ut Romanorum pontificum decreta vel gesta percurrens quicquid apostolicae sedis auctoritati spetialiter competere videretur, hinc inde curiosus excerperem, atque in parvi voluminis unionem nova compilationis arte conflarem. Hanc itaque tuae petitionis instantiam cum ego neglegens floctipenderem, magisque superstitioni quam necessitati obnoxiam iudicarem, divinitus, ut reor, actum est, ut Mediolanensem urben beatissimi Nicholai papae legatione functus adirem." For 'gesta' and 'parvi voluminis unionem nova compilationis arte' see ibid. nn. 7 and 8. Erdmann interprets 'gesta' as 'Akten': Carl Erdmann, "Gesta Romanae ecclesiae contra Hildebrandum," *Zeitschrift der Savigny-Stiftung für Rechtsgeschichte, kanonistische Abteilung* 26 (1937), 433–36.

52 Ibid., pp. 230–36, at p. 231, lines 5–7: "[...] non debere Ambrosianam aecclesiam Romanis legibus subiacere, nullumque iudicandi vel disponendi ius Romono pontifici in illa sede competere."

Hildebrand how he persuaded the Milanese dissidents of the supremacy of Rome, Peter Damian confesses that he now recognizes the importance of the knowledge of the special status ('privilegium')[53] of the Roman church, and praises Hildebrand for his foresight.[54] In the rest of the letter he explains how, after having regained control of the situation, he handled the cases of clerical abuse in Milan.[55]

To persuade the Milanese dissidents, Peter Damian employed two arguments. The first one is based on an interpretation of Matthew 16:18–19 found in the *Decretum Gelasianum*.[56] Peter Damian begins by posing a rhetorical question if there is any province throughout the world found to be outside the jurisdiction of the one whose decision binds or loosens even the heaven itself.[57] He then points out that, while the other ecclesiastical institutions are all of human origin, the Roman church was founded by Jesus Christ himself and thus enjoys the special status ('privilegium') and the authority of the divine founder.[58] He concludes from this that anyone who violates the special status ('privilegium') of the Roman Church commits a heresy and thus becomes a heretic, because anyone who acts against the mother of the faith, i.e. the Roman church, acts

53 For 'privilegium' see Pietro Palazzini, *Il diritto strumento di riforma ecclesiastica in S. Pier Damiani* (Rome, 1956), 16–21; Orazio Condorelli, "S. Pier Damiani e il diritto della Chiesa nella societas christiana," in *Pier Damiani l'eremita, il teologo, il riformatore (1007–2007): atti del xxix Convegno del Centro Studi e Ricerche Antica Provincia Ecclesiastica Ravennate, Faenza-Ravenna, 20–23 settembre 2007*, ed. M. Tagliaferri (Bologna, 2009), pp. 325–63, at pp. 327–34.

54 Reindel, *Briefe 2* (see above, n. 12), p. 236, lines 5–9: "His itaque rationibus de praerogativa et principatu sedis apostolicae redditis populus omnino benivolus redditur, et executurum se, quicquid iniungerem, unanimiter pollicetur. Tunc nimirum liquido persensi, in aecclesiasticis causis quantum Romanae aecclesiae nosse privilegium valeat, quamque hoc sancta tua prudentia non otiose deposcat."

55 Ibid., pp. 236–47.

56 For the sources of Peter Damian's arguments see Ryan, *Saint Peter Damiani* (see above, n. 14), pp. 59–67.

57 Reindel, *Briefe 2* (see above, n. 12), p. 232, line 14 to p. 233, line 1: "Quae autem provintia per omnia regna terrarum ab eius ditione extranea reperitur, cuius arbitrio ipsum quoque coelum et ligatur et solvitur."

58 Ibid., p. 233, lines 1–11: "Omnes autem sive patriarchivi cuiuslibet apicem, sive metropoleon primatus, aut episcopatuum cathedras, vel aecclesiarum cuiuscumque ordinis dignitates, sive rex, sive imperator, sive cuiuslibet conditionis homo purus instituit, et prout voluntas aut facultas erat, spetialium sibi praerogativarum iura praefixit: Romanam autem aecclesiam solus ille fundavit et super petram fidei mox nascentis erexit, qui beato vitae aeternae clavigero terreni simul et coelestis imperii iura commisit. Non ergo quaelibet terrena sententia, sed illud verbum, per quod constructum est coelum et terra, per quod denique omnia condita sunt elementa, Romanam fundavit aecclesiam. Illius certe privilegio fungitur, illius auctoritate fulcitur."

against the faith and becomes a recalcitrant ('contumax') against the one who made the Roman church preeminent among the churches.[59]

The second argument concerns in concreto the relationship between the two churches. Peter Damian begins by reminding the Milanese that St Peter and St Paul, just as they consecrated Rome with their own blood, won Milan to the Christian faith through their disciples martyred in the city, i.e. Nazarius, who was baptized by St Peter's successor Linus, and Celsus.[60] Peter Damian further points out that the holy martyrs Protasius and Gervasius were disciples of St Paul, as the apostle himself testified to St Ambrose (i.e. in his dream)[61]; therefore, just as the Savior sent two disciples, so did the apostles send those duos to the city as preachers of the sacred faith.[62] Peter Damian concludes from this that the church of Rome is the mother, while the church of St Ambrose is the daughter, and this relationship is not at all a novelty but the order of things of old, as one can see from the fact that St Ambrose, being unable to cope with the nicholaitism in the city, sought support from the apostolic see.[63] Encouraging the Milanese dissidents to convince themselves by letting those

59 Ibid., p. 233, line 11 to p. 234, line 6: "Unde non dubium, quia quisquis cuilibet aecclesiae ius suum detrahit, iniustitiam facit, qui autem Romane [*sic*] aecclesiae privilegium ab ipso summo omnium aecclesiarum capite traditum auferre conatur, hic proculdubio in heresim labitur, et cum ille notetur iniustus, hic est dicendus hereticus. Fidem quippe violat, qui adversus illam agit, que mater est fidei, et illi contumax invenitur, qui eam cunctis aecclesiis praetulisse cognoscitur."

60 Ibid., p. 234, lines 8–14: "[...] non debet ignorare sancta vestra devotio, quia beati apostolorum principes Petrus et Paulus, sicut per suum sanguinem Romanam aecclesiam consecrarunt, ita mox inter ipsa nascentis fidei rudimenta hanc Mediolanensem aecclesiam per suos discipulos lucrati sunt Christo, Nazarius quippe martyr insignis, sicut scripturae testantur, Petri baptisma a Lino eius successore suscepit, qui postmodum cum beato Celso in hac sancta urbe martyrio coronatus est." For Nazarius and Celsus (BHL 6039) see Cécile Lanéry, "Hagiographie d'Italie (300–550), I: les Passions latines composées en Italie," in *CC Hagiographies 5* (Turnhout, 2010), pp. 264–72.

61 Ibid., p. 234, lines 14–16: "Sancti vero martires Protasius atque Gervasius beatum Paulum apostolum magistrum ac praeceptorem habuisse noscuntur, sicut beato Ambrosio et ipse testatur." See ibid. n. 29. For Protasius and Gervasius (BHL 3514) see Lanéry, "Hagiographie d'Italie" (see above, n. 60), pp. 61–68.

62 Ibid., p. 235, lines 1–4: "Sicut ergo salvator noster binos ante fatiem suam discipulos misit, ita quodammodo uterque sanctus apostolus ex magisterio suo in hanc urbem praedicatores sanctae fidei geminos destinavit."

63 Ibid., p. 235, lines 5–11: "Cum ergo vestrae salutis auctores ex Romanae aecclesiae prodierint disciplina, consequens est iuxta aequitatis ordinem, ut aecclesia Romana mater, Ambrosiana sit filia. Ut autem hic ordo inter utramque Ambrosianam videlicet et apostolicam sedem non noviter oriri, sed antiquitus tenuisse non dubitetur, beatus Ambrosius cum hanc Nicolaitarum sordem ad multorum foetere pernitiem in hac urbe doleret, eamque per se solus coercere non posset, sedis apostolicae mox quaesivit auxilium [...]."

they trust examine their own records, Peter Damian asks them to accept the teaching and the apostolic faith of the mother instead of resisting the truth and harassing her crudely.[64]

In the second argument Peter Damian uses the idea of apostolic succession in order to establish a hierarchical relationship between Rome and Milan. This relationship is expressed in the relational terms 'mater' and 'filia' as in the sermon on Apollinaris. It is significant that Peter Damian then returns to Hildebrand's request of a small compilation of excerpts from decreta or 'gesta' pertaining to the special status ('privilegium') of the Roman church, even if he did not fulfil the archdeacon's wish.[65] For Peter Damian appears to have become aware of the importance of giving a normative expression to the hierarchical order he established between individual churches.

3.4 *Peter Damian's Letter 112 (1064)*

The classical example of Peter Damian's achievement in this regard is his letter to Cunibertus, the bishop of Turin, written in 1064 (Letter 112).[66] In this long polemical letter Peter Damian reprimands the bishop for permitting clerics of his church to be married regardless of their respective ranks in the holy order. He tries to make his case by quoting many authoritative texts. In the course of his argumentation he refers to a council of Tribur ('concilium Triburiense'), whose name he vaguely remembers. It was brought up against him by his opponents of the church of Lodi ('Laudensis aecclesia') to support

64 Ibid., p. 235, line 14 to p. 236, line 4: "Scrutamini itaque et scripturas vestras, per quos vultis, diligenter inquirite, et si non potestis apud vosmetipsos invenire, quod loquimur, mendacii arguite, si autem potestis, nolite veritati resistere, nolite matrem vestram crudeliter inpugnare, sed ex cuius uberibus lac suxistis apostolicae fidei, eius semper gaudete solidis doctrinae coelestis dapibus recreari."—A similar argument can be found e.g. in *Petri Damiani Vita beati Romualdi*, ed. Giovanni Tabacco, Fonti per la storia d'Italia 94 (Rome, 1957), p. 75, lines 9–18: "Inter ceteros autem, precipue seculares clericos qui per peccuniam ordinati fuerant, durissima severitate corripiebat, et eos, nisi ordinem sponte desererent, omnino damnabiles et hereticos asserebat. Qui novam rem audientes, occidere illum moliti sunt. Per totam namque illam monarchiam usque ad Romualdi tempora, vulgata consuetudine, vix quisquam noverat symoniacam heresem esse peccatum. Qui dixit eis: 'Canonum mihi libros afferte, et utrum vera sint que dico, vestris attestantibus paginis comprobate.' Quibus itaque diligenter inspectis, et crimen agnoscunt et errata deplangunt." For Peter Damian's hagiographical works see Pierluigi Licciardello, "Agiografia latina dell'Italia centrale, 950–1130," in *CC Hagiographies 5* (Turnhout, 2010), pp. 447–729, at pp. 454–83; Umberto Longo, *Come angeli in terra: Pier Damiani, la santità e la riforma del secolo XI* (Viella, 2012).

65 See above, n. 54.

66 Reindel, *Briefe 3* (see above, n. 18), pp. 258–88. See Ryan, *Saint Peter Damiani* (see above, n. 14), pp. 140–01.

their argument for clerical marriage.[67] Peter Damian's reply was that the so-called council of Tribur, even if it was called 'council', would not be accepted by him, if it did not agree with the decrees of the Roman Pontiffs.[68] He says that 'adinventiones hominum' are different from the decisions given by the Holy Spirit, and that those who do not hesitate to go against the sacred canons undoubtedly offend the Holy Spirit by whom those canons are promulgated.[69]

Peter Damian may seem to eliminate a conciliar canon by using a hierarchy of texts as an interpretive tool. But a closer look reveals that the real issue is whether a decision derives (ultimately) from the Holy Spirit or it is just a human invention. It is, therefore, a question of how to discern the authentic tradition, not that of validity of an otherwise authentic canon. In other words, the Holy Spirit was given by Jesus Christ to the apostles and by the apostles to their disciples and so on. The authentic canons are those that belong to this line of succession, while the 'adinventiones hominum', which remind the reader of Letter 65 of the argument based on the *Decretum Gelasianum*,[70] are those born outside this pedigree. The agreement with decrees of the Roman Pontiffs is the hallmark of the authenticity.[71] In its essence, therefore, Peter Damian's argument in Letter 112 is the same as that of Letter 65: He applied the 'mater'/'filia'-relationship to canon law.

3.5 *Peter Damian and Bernold: A Comparison*

The agreement with the Roman Church as the hallmark of authenticity had been well known to the church long before Peter Damian.[72] He just applied

67 Ibid., p. 266, line 23 to p. 267, line 4: "Aliquando cum me Laudensis aecclesiae tauri pingues armata conspiratione vallarent, ac furioso strepitu vituli multi tumultuantes infrenderent, tanquam ructum fellis in os meum evomuere dicentes: Habemus auctoritatem Triburiensis, si tamen ego nomen teneo, concilii, quae promotis ad aecclesiasticum ordinem ineundi coniugii tribuat facultatem."

68 Ibid., p. 267, lines 4–6: "Concilium, inquam, vestrum, quodcunque vultis, nomen optineat, sed a me non recipitur, si decretis Romanorum pontificum non concordat."

69 Ibid., p. 267, lines 9–12: "Distant enim adinventiones hominum a sententiis, quae prolatae sunt per Spiritum sanctum, et qui sacris canonibus repugnare non metuunt, ipsum proculdubio spiritum, a quo promulgantur, offendunt."

70 See above, n. 54.

71 For the principle of non-contradiction as a criterium of authenticity in canon law see Stephan Kuttner, "Liber Canonicus: A Note on the *Dictatus Papae* c. 17," *Studi Gregoriani* 2 (1947), 387–401 (reprinted with retractationes in idem, *The History of Ideas and Doctrines of Canon Law in the Middle Ages*, 2nd ed., Variorum Collected Studies Series 113 (London, 1992), no. II. For Peter Damian in particular see Ryan, *Saint Peter Damiani* (see above, n. 13), pp. 139–41.

72 See e.g. Robert B. Eno, "The Work of Optatus as a Turning Point in the African Ecclesiology," *The Thomist* 37 (1973), 668–85; idem, "The Significance of the List of Roman Bishops in the Anti-Donatist Polemic," *Vigiliae Christianae* 47 (1993), 158–69.

it to canon law. The point is rather that he turned the relationship in which one authority derived from the other into a hierarchial one. In this sense he deserves to be regarded as a precursor of Bernold's. But while Peter Damian just eliminated those texts that he regarded as inauthentic, Bernold, in his *De fontibus iuris ecclesiastici*, employs the same idea in different ways, i.e. to identify the authentic texts which constitute the body of canon law[73] and to establish a hierarchical relationship among them.[74]

The first point is especially visible in his treatment of the fifty *capitula* of the *Canones apostolorum*.[75] According to Bernold there are people who have doubts about their authenticity on the grounds that they are not found among the canons of the apostolic synods.[76] Bernold argues that many things have been received from the apostles that are not always found among the synods of the apostles.[77] Besides, each apostle has the authority to give normative instructions just as the Roman pontiffs do.[78] We should, says Bernold, reject the opinion wrongly held by some people and trust the testimonies of apostolic men, i.e. Roman pontiffs, who vouch for almost all of those capitula, saying here and there in their decrees that they were established by the apostles.[79] These holy fathers were men who would rather die for the truth

73 Bernold, *De fontibus*, ed. Stöckly and Jasper (see above, n. 9), p. 120, lines 3–5: "Ecclesiasticarum regularum institutiones partim ab ipsis apostolis accepimus, partim a Romanis pontificibus, partim ab aliis sanctis patribus, quorum tamen iudicia Romani pontifices firmaverunt."

74 Genka, "Hierarchie" (see above, n. 10), 116–22.

75 Bernold, *De fontibus*, ed. Stöckly and Jasper (see above, n. 9), p. 122, lines 18–19: "Preter hec autem L capitula inveniuntur, que canones apostolorum inscribuntur […]." Bernold's comments on the *Canones apostolorum* have antecedents in much earlier prefaces to canonical collections. Compare Robert Somerville and Bruce Clark Brasington, *Prefaces to Canon Law Books in Latin Christianity: Selected Translations, 500–1245* (New Haven and London, 1998), pp. 11, 20, 47, 56, 57.

76 Bernold, *De fontibus*, ed. Stöckly and Jasper (see above, n. 9), p. 122, lines 19–20: "[…] quibus tamen quidam difficile credunt, qui in praedictis apostolorum synodis nihil de his commemoratum inveniunt."

77 Ibid., p. 123, lines 1–2: "Sed plurima sunt, que ex apostolica institutione accepimus, que tamen in illis nequaquam invenimus."

78 Ibid., p. 123, lines 2–5: "Nec utique necesse fuit, ut apostoli omnia communiter instituerent, cum et singillatim talia instituere possent, sicut etiam Romani pontifices ex eorum auctoritate adhuc facere solent."

79 Ibid., p. 123, lines 5–8: "Ergo postposita quorundam inconsiderata opinione, nos magis apostolicorum virorum, Romanorum utique pontificum, adtestationi credamus, qui singula pene capitula eorundem canonum apostolos instituisse sparsim in decretis suis testificantur."

than lie for their lives.[80] Therefore, so concludes Bernold, we have to trust their testimonies lest we should be regarded as less trustful of the Holy Spirit who no doubt made them testify.[81] As to the *De libris recipiendis et non recipiendis* attributed to Gelasius which lists the book called *De canonibus apostolorum* among the Greek apocryphal writings, Bernold assumes that the book listed by Gelasius either did not contain those capitula accepted by the fathers or, if it did, contained some errors which were carefully eliminated when translated into Latin, just as Jerome is known to have done when he translated Origen.[82]

For Bernold as well as for Peter Damian, the Holy Spirit is the ultimate author of the canons.[83] But Peter Damian employed this idea just to deny the authenticity of the texts that do not agree with papal decrees. Bernold's argument is the other way round. In the course of identifying the authentic texts, he recognizes the authenticity, which is otherwise questionable, so long as the texts are recognized by papal decrees, saying that it was the Holy Spirit who made them testify. It is, however, not just a matter of direction of their respective ways of thinking. The very interest of Bernold's in identifying the corpus of authentic texts led him to elaborate on the internal structure of the corpus, i.e. to develop a theory of hierarchy of texts as an expression of the hierarchical order of the church. It also enabled him, even if incidentally, to prevent the authority in canon law from including everyone who received the Holy Spirit, although we have to wait for Gratian for a theoretical solution of the problem caused by the tension between office and grace.[84]

---

80 Ibid., p. 124, lines 2: "[…] qui magis pro veritate mori quam vel pro vita mentiri delegerunt."

81 Ibid., p. 124, lines 3–5: "Horum igitur testimoniis et nos necessario credimus, ne ipsi sancto spiritui minus credere iudicemur, cuius instinctu ipsos talia testificatos fore non dubitamus."

82 Ibid., p. 124, lines 5–12: "Sciendum autem, quod beatus Gelasius papa librum, qui de canonibus apostolorum apud Grecos inscribitur, pro apocrifo deputavit […]. Fortasse liber ille de capitulis, que sancti patres receperunt, nihil dicit, aut si dicit, nonnihil mendosum annectit: quod tamen sollercia catholici interpretis prudenter nobis in Latino subtraxit, sicut beatus Ieronimus, cum transferret Origenem, sepe fecisse monstratur."

83 Bernold states this idea explicitly when he justifies his method of interpretation. See Bernold, *De fontibus*, ed. Stöckly and Jasper (see above, n. 9), p. 180, lines 6–9: "Nam ipsi sancto spiritui magnam iniuriam irrogare videmur, si illa, que ipse per sanctos patres instituisse legitur, quasi contraria et ideo contempnenda interpretari non veremur."

84 Genka, "Hierarchie" (see above, n. 10), passim. Compare Robert Somerville, "Canon Law, Inspired Law, and Papal Authority," in *Neti'ot Le David: Jubilee Volume for David Weiss Halivini*, ed. Yakov Elman, Ephraim Bezalel Halivni, Zvi Arie Steinfeld (Jerusalem, 2004), pp. 119–34.

4 Conclusion

Before Bernold, Peter Damian turned the relationship in which one authority derives from the other into a hierarchical one, and combined it with the idea that the Holy Spirit is the ultimate author of the canons. It was this way of thinking that underlay Bernold's thought. When Bernold identified the corpus of authentic texts and developed a theory of their hierarchy as an expression of the structural organization of the church, with principles of interpretation[85] as a means to stabilize it, canon law began its development as a constitutive element of the church in the high Middle Ages. What Fournier thought had been achieved over two distinct periods, the one represented by Gregory VII and the other by Urban II, was in fact an achievement of the former, for which hagiography played an important role. If Urban's pontificate is still to be regarded as the second stage of the development of canon law in the Reform era, new criteria have to be established. It is also important to bear in mind that at the root of such developments we may find elements which we do not usually call 'legal'.

85 For Peter Damian as a precursor of Bernold's as regards principles of interpretation see Ryan, *Saint Peter Damiani* (see above, n. 14), pp. 143–47.

CHAPTER 6

Of Scholasticism and Canon Law: Narratives Old and New

John C. Wei

One of the oldest and most popular narratives concerning the relationship of scholasticism, i.e., the intellectual culture of the high and late medieval schools and universities, to the development of canon law in the twelfth century is a story about how a 'great' theologian (Peter Abelard) composed a 'great' book (the *Sic et non*) that expounded a 'great' idea (the scholastic method for reconciling contradictory authorities), which a 'great' jurist (Gratian) then applied to canon law in his own 'great' work (the *Concordia discordantium canonum* or *Decretum*). Both the appeal and the weakness of this narrative lie in its simplicity. Like intellectual history more generally, medieval intellectual history, including medieval legal history, has long loved to focus on great thinkers and their great books and great ideas. Yet, as is now widely recognized, history and important historical developments seldom involve just the thoughts and actions of 'great' men. 'Lesser' thinkers, anonymous works, and more mundane ideas also frequently play a significant role, as do philological accidents and developments in material culture and technology.

This article explores the history of the aforementioned narrative (henceforth the 'old narrative') and submits it to critical evaluation. Part I traces the origins of the old narrative and an early variation upon it. Part II then discusses developments that call the old narrative into question. The paper concludes with some thoughts on what a new narrative on the relationship between scholasticism and the development of canon law should provide.

1 The Origins of the Old Narrative

The old narrative of the relationship between scholasticism and canon law developed in two stages. The first stage, the rediscovery of the *Sic et non* around the 1830s, was the work of a French philosopher and historian of philosophy,

 | DOI:10.1163/9789004394384_008

Victor Cousin (1792–1867).[1] The second stage, the linking of the *Sic et non* to Gratian in the 1880s, was the work of Austrian medievalists, particularly Friedrich Thaner (1839–1915).[2]

1.1 *The Rediscovery of the* Sic et non

Sometime before 1836, Victor Cousin rediscovered Abelard's *Sic et non.*[3] Previous scholars had known about this work from a letter written by William of Saint-Thierry to St Bernard of Clairvaux, as well as the reports of early modern French authors.[4] However, scholars had never had access to the text or studied it in detail before.

Cousin's interpretation of the *Sic et non* made it foundational to the development of medieval theology. For Cousin, the essence of scholasticism lay in its method: the application of dialectic to theology.[5] Cousin found the *Sic et non* significant for providing an early explanation of the scholastics' method.[6] While the body of the *Sic et non* simply collects and arranges conflicting texts on a wide variety of theological subjects, the prologue to the *Sic et non* sets forth interpretative principles and rules for reconciling these contradictions. The prologue, for example, notes that conflicts between authorities may be due to textual issues (e.g., a text may be apocryphal, corrupted, or poorly translated), literary issues (e.g., retractation of an issue by an author, citation of an opposing opinion), linguistic reasons (e.g., poetic usage), or moral or historical circumstances (e.g., whether a text is intended as a precept or merely a counsel), among other reasons.[7] In Cousin's opinion, the *Sic et non* was the earliest extant theological work by Abelard, dating to

1 On Cousin, see John Marenbon, "Victor Cousin," in *Medieval Scholarship: Biographical Studies on the Formation of a Discipline*, 3: *Philosophy and the Arts*, ed. Helen Damico (New York, 2000), pp. 13–22.

2 On Thaner, see Heinrich Singer, "Friedrich Thaner," *Zeitschrift der Savigny-Stiftung für Rechtsgeschichte, kanonistische Abteilung* 6 (1916), V–XI.

3 Peter Abelard, *Sic et non*, ed. Victor Cousin, *Ouvrages inédits d'Abélard* (Paris, 1836), pp. 1–169. The modern critical edition is Peter Abelard, *Sic et non: A Critical Edition*, ed. Blanche B. Boyer and Richard McKeon (Chicago, 1976).

4 For the details, see the discussion by Cousin, *Ouvrages inédits* (see above, n. 3), pp. CLXXXIV–CLXXXV.

5 See ibid., pp. III–IV.

6 Ibid., p. CXCVI: "un monument précieux de la première application de sa méthode théologique."

7 For a more detailed discussion of the hermeneutical principles in the prologue to the *Sic et non* and their purpose, see Antonio Crocco, "Le cinque regole ermeneutiche del Sic et non," *Rivista critica di storia della filosofia* 34 (1979), 452–58; Cornelia Rizek-Pfister, "Die hermeneutischen Prinzipien in Abaelards Sic et non," *Freiburger Zeitschrift für Philosophie und Theologie* 47 (2000), 484–501; Guillaume Bady, "Le prologue du *Sic et non* d'Abélard," in

before the Council of Soissons in 1121.[8] Later scholastics may or may not have read the prologue to the *Sic et non*, but they continued to employ its method for reconciling contradictory authorities and in that sense were, according to Cousin, Abelard's heirs. Cousin writes:

> Malgré ses erreurs et les anathèmes de deux conciles, sa [i.e., Abelard's] périlleuse mais féconde méthode est devenue la méthode universelle de la théologie scolastique. Les erreurs s'effacèrent, et la méthode resta, comme une conquête de l'esprit d'indépendance. Pierre le Lombard est le fondateur reconnu de la théologie scolastique; or, Pierre le Lombard est un élève direct d'Abélard, et l'héritier sinon de sa doctrine, au moins de sa méthode épurée et perfectionnée: le *Sic et Non* est l'antécédent du livre des *Sentences*.[9]

Cousin's views about the *Sic et non*'s purpose and significance found widespread acceptance, even though they arguably stemmed more from patriotic feeling than rational analysis.[10] For Cousin, Abelard was to the Middle Ages what Descartes was to modernity: the founder of his era's philosophy.[11] Cousin was proud that both of these giants were Frenchman, and he delighted in being able to find parallels between them. Cousin explicitly notes that both Abelard and Descartes came from the same region of France, Brittany.[12] And he describes both thinkers as possessing similar temperaments:

> confiance dans leurs forces et le mépris de leurs adversaires, plus de conséquence que de solidité dans leurs opinions, plus de sagacité

Les réceptions des Pères de l'Église au Moyen Âge: le devenir de la tradition ecclésiale, ed. Rainer Berndt and Michel Fédou, 2 vols (Münster, 2013), 2:727–42, at pp. 727–30.

8 Cousin, *Ouvrages inédits* (see above, n. 3), pp. CXCIV–CXCVI. But see Georg Stephan Lindenkohl, *De Petri Abaelardi libro Sic et non commentatio* (Marburg, 1851), pp. 21–34, who provides a detailed critique of Cousin's dating. Today it is widely accepted that the earliest version of the *Sic et non* dates to shortly after the Council of Soissons. See Constant Mews, "On dating the works of Peter Abelard," *Archives d'histoire doctrinale et littéraire du Moyen Âge* 52 (1985), 73–134, at p. 131.

9 Cousin, *Ouvrages inédits* (see above, n. 3), p. CC.

10 See Marenbon, "Victor Cousin" (see above, n. 1), p. 19: "Cousin came to Abelard in part for patriotic reasons. Abelard extended the French tradition of thought back five hundred years before Pascal, and Cousin was proud to be able to declare that it was France that had given Europe both the founder of Scholasticism—Abelard—and Descartes, the founder of modern philosophy."

11 Cousin, *Ouvrages inédits* (see above, n. 3), pp. IV–V.

12 Ibid., p. IV.

> que d'étendue, plus de vigueur dans la trempe de l'esprit et du caractère que d'élévation ou de profondeur dans la pensée, plus d'invention que de sens commun; abondants dans leur sens propre plutôt que s'élevant à la raison universelle, opiniâtres, aventureux, novateurs, révolutionnaires.[13]

A further parallel that Cousin does not explicitly note but which appears to have influenced his interpretation of Abelard in general and of the *Sic et non* in particular was the role of doubt in each thinker's thought. Descartes famously began his *Meditations* by employing a methodological scepticism, Cartesian doubt.[14] Doubt, Cousin emphasizes, occupies a similar place in the theological method set forth in the *Sic et non*. While the body of the work seems at first glance to be nothing more than a compilation of contradictory authorities, it is in fact a construction of theological problems and antinomies that condemns the spirit to a provisional, 'salutary doubt', that helps the reader come to better solutions.[15] The prologue, moreover, proclaims doubt to be the true key of wisdom.[16] Abelard and Descartes thus resemble each other not only in their background and temperaments, but even in their methods.

1.2 *The* Sic et non *in Canon Law*

In the 1880s, scholars began to adapt and apply Cousin's views on the *Sic et non* to the development of canon law. The Austrian medievalist Heinrich Denifle appears to have been the first to propose that the *Sic et non* influenced Gratian,[17] but only with his countryman Friedrich Thaner did someone actually attempt to prove this hypothesis.[18] In a lecture first delivered in 1886 but not published until 1900, where it appeared in expanded form as *Abälard und das canonische Recht*, Thaner argued that the *Sic et non* exercised a direct influence on Gratian. Thaner laid great weight on the numerous dicta in which

---

13 Ibid., p. v.

14 The bibliography is vast. A good starting point is Janet Broughton, *Descartes's Method of Doubt* (Princeton, 2002).

15 Cousin, *Ouvrages inédits* (see above, n. 3), p. CLXXXIX: "Au premier coup-d'oeil, c'est donc ici une pure compilation d'autorités contraires; mais, en réalité, c'est une construction de problèmes et d'antinomies théologiques puissamment établis, qui condamnent l'esprit à un doute salutaire, le prémunissent contre le danger de toute solution étroite et précipitée, et le préparent à des solutions meilleures."

16 Ibid., pp. CXCIII–CXCIV.

17 Heinrich Denifle, "Die Sentenzen Abälards und die Bearbeitungen seiner Theologia vor Mitte des 12. Jahrhunderts," *Archiv für Litteratur- und Kirchengeschichte des Mittelalters* 1 (1885), 402–621, at pp. 619–20.

18 Friedrich Thaner, *Abälard und das canonische Recht; Die Persönlichkeit in der Eheschliessung, Zwei Festreden* (Graz, 1900), pp. 5–29.

Gratian harmonized apparently contradictory texts by distinguishing between multiple senses of the same word, a technique Abelard had discussed in the *Sic et non*. Earlier canonists like Ivo of Chartres and Alger of Liège, by contrast, had generally employed other harmonization techniques like distinguishing between interpretations according to the rigor of the law and interpretations according to mercy.[19] As further evidence that Abelard had influenced Gratian, Thaner pointed to evidence that the *Sic et non* was known to contemporaries and disciples of Gratian active in Italy.[20]

Particularly because of Thaner, the view that Abelard influenced Gratian found widespread acceptance among later scholars, including Paul Fournier,[21] who incorporated the old narrative into what Christof Rolker has called the 'standard model' for the development of law and learning in the eleventh and twelfth centuries.[22] Fournier viewed the political and ecclesiastical history of this period, particularly the Investiture Controversy, as the main force behind contemporary developments in legal thought and education. According to Fournier, the papal reform movement inspired not only the incorporation of new texts (e.g., long-ignored canons, patristic authorities, Roman law) into the canonical tradition, but also the development of new methods for reconciling contradictory authorities. Fournier painted Ivo of Chartres as the link between the old narrative and his standard model: Gratian took his method from Abelard, among the theologians,[23] but both Gratian and Abelard also drew upon Ivo[24] and Ivo in turn was inspired to develop his hermeneutics by the reform pope Urban II.[25]

19 On these older harmonization techniques, see Christof Rolker, *Canon Law and the Letters of Ivo of Chartres*, Cambridge Studies in Medieval Life and Thought, Fourth Series 76 (Cambridge, 2010), pp. 165–71; Bruce Clark Brasington, *Ways of Mercy: The Prologue of Ivo of Chartres: Edition and Analysis*, Vita regularis. Editionen 2 (Münster, 2004); Christoph H.F. Meyer, *Die Distinktionstechnik in der Kanonistik des 12. Jahrhunderts. Ein Beitrag zur Wissenschaftsgeschichte des Hochmittelalters*, Mediaevalia Lovaniensia. Studia 29 (Leuven, 2000), pp. 129–43; Robert Kretzschmar, *Alger von Lüttichs Traktat 'De misericordia et iustitia'. Ein kanonistischer Konkordanzversuch aus der Zeit des Investiturstreits: Untersuchungen und Edition*, Quellen und Forschungen zum Recht im Mittelalter 2 (Sigmaringen, 1985).

20 Thaner, *Abälard und das canonische Recht* (see above, n. 18), p. 24.

21 See Paul Fournier, "Un tournant de l'histoire du droit 1060–1140," *Nouvelle revue historique de droit français et étranger* 41 (1917), 129–80, at p. 167 and n. 3; repr. in idem, *Mélanges de droit canonique*, ed. Theo Kölzer, 2 vols (Aalen, 1983), 2:373–424.

22 See Rolker, *Canon Law* (see above, n. 19), pp. 292–302.

23 Fournier, "Un tournant" (see above, n. 21) p. 167 and n. 3.

24 Ibid., p. 166.

25 Ibid., pp. 155–58.

Only two scholars I am aware of rejected the old narrative outright. One was Martin Grabmann, who in his *Geschichte der scholastischen Methode* argues that there is no need to posit Gratian's knowledge of the *Sic et non*, since older canonistic works suffice to explain Gratian's method.[26] The other critic was another Austrian, Franz Bliemetzrieder, who in 1932 proposed a great man variation to the old narrative.[27] An enthusiastic investigator of the writings connected with Anselm of Laon that Grabmann had unearthed in the 1900s,[28] but often a rather mediocre scholar,[29] Bliemetzrieder argued that the link between scholasticism and canon law should be sought not in Abelard but rather in Anselm of Laon.[30] As evidence for this hypothesis, Bliemetzrieder pointed mainly to parallels between the *Decretum* and a sentence collection that he had edited under the title of the *Sententiae Anselmi*, but which he and everyone else later recognized was in fact the product of one of Anselm's students.[31]

Bliemetzrieder's thesis never gained much acceptance. In 1934, just two years after Bliemetzrieder proposed his variation to the old narrative, Stephan Kuttner published an article critiquing Bliemetzrieder's arguments and showing that the parallels on which Bliemetzrieder had based his thesis were all vague and inconclusive. Closer parallels, Kuttner demonstrated, existed between the *Decretum* and the works of both Abelard and Hugh of Saint-Victor.[32] While it was certainly not impossible for Gratian to have been Anselm's disciple, Bliemetzrieder had provided no real evidence in support.

---

26 Martin Grabmann, *Die Geschichte der scholastischen Methode. Nach den gedruckten und ungedruckten Quellen*, 2 vols (Freiburg, 1909–11), 2:213–17.

27 Franz Bliemetzrieder, "Gratian und die Schule Anselms von Laon," *Archiv für katholisches Kirchenrecht* 112 (1932), 37–63.

28 Grabmann, *Geschichte der scholastischen Methode* (see above, n. 26), 2:141–51.

29 See, e.g. André Wilmart, "Une rédaction française des Sentences dites d'Anselme de Laon," *Recherches de théologie ancienne et médiévale* 11 (1939), 119–44, at pp. 120–21; Cédric Giraud, *Per verba magistri: Anselme de Laon et son école au XII*[e] *siècle*, Bibliothèque d'histoire culturelle du Moyen Âge 8 (Turnhout, 2010), pp. 367–68.

30 Bliemetzrieder, "Gratian und die Schule Anselms von Laon" (see above, n. 27). Anselm of Laon should not be confused with his more famous contemporary Anselm of Bec/Canterbury, the philosopher and theologian now famed for his ontological argument for the existence of God and satisfaction theory of Christ's atonement.

31 On the authorship of the so-called *Sententiae Anselmi*, now generally referred to after its incipit as *Principium et causa*, see Cédric Giraud, "Le recueil de sentences de l'école de Laon *Principium et causa*: un cas de pluri-attribution," in *Parva pro magnis munera: études de littérature tardo-antique et médiévale offertes à François Dolbeau par ses élèves*, ed. Monique Goullet, Instrumenta patristica et mediaevalia 51 (Turnhout, 2009), pp. 245–69.

32 Stephan Kuttner, "Zur Frage der theologischen Vorlagen Gratians," *Zeitschrift der Savigny-Stiftung für Rechtsgeschichte, kanonistische Abteilung* 23 (1934), 243–68; repr. in idem,

2 Problems with the Old Narrative

In the decades since Denifle, Thaner, and the Bliemetzrieder-Kuttner exchange, approaches to intellectual history have broadened considerably. While plenty of scholarship continues to focus on 'great' men, 'great' books, and 'great' ideas, scholars now largely also recognize the need to look at 'not-so-great' men and even not-men, 'not-so-great' books, 'not-so-great' ideas, philological research, and the various ways in which material culture and technology affect intellectual culture. The more nuanced understandings that have resulted from these new approaches highlight the inadequacies of the old narrative and demonstrate the need for a broader approach to the relationship between scholasticism and the development of canon law, one that moves beyond 'great' theologians, 'great' jurists, and 'great' ideas.

2.1 *Beyond 'Great' Theologians*

Since the 1880s, scholars have repeatedly identified the *Sic et non* as the link between scholasticism and canon law. However, little evidence exists to back up this claim. First, contrary to what some have argued, Abelard did not invent the scholastic method for harmonizing contradictory texts himself. Anselm of Laon had already employed it before him, if not to the same extent, and even Anselm may not have been the originator of the scholastic method.[33] So the mere fact that Gratian resolved contradictions by distinguishing between different senses of the same word does not suffice to prove that Abelard and/or the *Sic et non* influenced Gratian, whether directly or indirectly.

Second, there exists no solid textual evidence that Gratian—or at least Anders Winroth's Gratian 1, the author of the first recension of the *Decretum*—knew the *Sic et non* either.[34] As is now well known, the *Decretum* exists in multiple recensions that likely stem from multiple authors.[35] The first recension appears to have been completed sometime in or after 1139; the second recension with the exception of the tract *De consecratione* was finished sometime after the first recension and before 1150; and the second recension, inclusive of *De consecratione*, dates to sometime after the completion of the

Gratian and the Schools of Law, 1140–1234, Varioum Collected Studies Series 185 (London, 1983), no. III.

33 See Anselm's letter to Heribrand, ed. Odon Lottin, *Psychologie et morale aux XIIe et XIIIe siècles*, 5: *L'école d'Anselme de Laon et de Guillaume de Champeaux* (Gembloux, 1959), pp. 175–77.

34 Anders Winroth, *The Making of Gratian's Decretum*, Cambridge Studies in Medieval Life and Thought, Fourth Series 49 (Cambridge, 2000).

35 Ibid., esp. pp. 175–92.

second-recension distinctions and *causae*, but not to after 1158.[36] The *Sic et non* seems to have been a formal source for *De consecratione*,[37] but not the first- or second-recension distinctions and *causae*. The sole evidence that the *Sic et non* was used at all in the compilation of the rest of the *Decretum* is a series of texts from C. 15, q. 1, d.a.c. 1 that Tatsushi Genka has drawn attention to.[38] But these parallels between the *Sic et non* and the *Decretum*, I would argue, should be discounted as evidence that Gratian used the *Sic et non* and knew its prologue, both on the basis of the omissions and variants noted by Genka and because a version of the texts closer to Gratian's exists in the *Sententiae Sidonis*. While the *Sententiae Sidonis* postdates the *Decretum* and thus could not have been Gratian's formal source, textual affinities with the *Decretum* suggest either that both the *Sententiae Sidonis* and the *Decretum* employed the same unknown florilegium of theological texts, which was not the *Sic et non*, or that both the *Sententiae Sidonis* and the *Decretum* drew on an unknown florilegium dependent on the *Sic et non*.[39]

In contrast to the paucity of evidence linking Gratian to Abelard, there exists a wealth of textual evidence connecting Gratian to various anonymous texts generally associated with the school of Laon. Titus Lenherr has shown that Gratian drew upon early forms of what became the *Glossa ordinaria* to the Bible.[40] Atria Larson has provided further evidence that Gratian used the *Glossa ordinaria*.[41] And I have studied various sentence collections generally classified as belonging to the school of Laon (*Ut autem hoc evidenter* and *Baptizato homine*, which generally circulated together with or as part of

---

36 See John C. Wei, *Gratian the Theologian*, Studies in Medieval and Early Modern Canon Law 13 (Washington, D.C., 2016), pp. 24–26 and 277–80.

37 Peter Landau, "Gratian und die Sententiae Magistri A.," in *Aus Archiven und Bibliotheken. Festschrift für Raymund Kottje zum 65. Geburtstag*, ed. Hubert Mordek (Frankfurt, 1992), pp. 311–26, at pp. 317–18 and 326; repr. in idem, *Kanones und Dekretalen: Beiträge zur Geschichte der Quellen des kanonischen Rechts* (Goldbach, 1997), pp. 161*–76*, at pp. 167*–68* and 176*; John C. Wei, "Peter Abaelard and the *Collectio sancte Genoveve*," *Zeitschrift der Savigny-Stiftung für Rechtsgeschichte, kanonistische Abteilung* 94 (2008), 21–37, at pp. 35–37.

38 Tatsushi Genka, "Zur textlichen Grundlage der Imputationslehre Gratians," *Bulletin of Medieval Canon Law*, n.s. 25 (2002–03), 40–81.

39 See the appendix.

40 Titus Lenherr, "Die *Glossa ordinaria* zur Bibel als Quelle von Gratians Dekret. Ein (neuer) Anfang," *Bulletin of Medieval Canon Law*, n.s. 24 (2000), 97–129.

41 Atria Ann Larson, "The Influence of the School of Laon on Gratian: The Usage of the *Glossa ordinaria* and Anselmian *Sententiae* in *De penitentia* (*Decretum* C.33 Q.3)," *Mediaeval Studies* 72 (2010), 197–244; eadem, *Master of Penance: Gratian and the Development of Penitential Thought and Law in the Twelfth Century*, Studies in Medieval and Early Modern Canon Law 11 (Washington, D.C., 2014), pp. 271–97.

the sentence collection *Deus itaque summe*) that appear to have been used in the composition of the tract *De penitentia*.[42] None of these works explains the scholastic method for reconciling contradictory texts in the way that the prologue to the *Sic et non* does. But each one employs this method and applies it to topics that Gratian examines in the *Decretum*.

Both the *Glossa ordinaria* and the sentence collections that Gratian employed are generally attributed to the school of Laon. One would therefore, I think, be justified in asserting that Anselm of Laon influenced Gratian, at least indirectly, since works belonging to or associated with the school of Laon were part of Gratian's 'library', i.e., the collection of texts he had at his disposal. But I would hesitate to claim that Gratian was himself a disciple of Anselm or in some sense a member of the school of Laon.[43] There is no evidence that Gratian was familiar with Anselm's *sententiae*, i.e., Anselm's theological dicta, which circulated in contemporary florilegia and were at times discussed in sentence collections.[44] The *Glossa ordinaria* was simply a reference work, which, despite its attribution to Anselm by some later writers, may have been mostly or entirely the work of students and collaborators, and which theologians of all persuasions drew upon and used.[45] And far from defending

42 John C. Wei, "Penitential Theology in Gratian's *Decretum*: Critique and Criticism of the Treatise *Baptizato homine*," *Zeitschrift der Savigny-Stiftung für Rechtsgeschichte, kanonistische Abteilung* 95 (2009), 78–100; idem, "Gratian and the School of Laon," *Traditio* 64 (2009), 279–322; idem, "The Sentence Collection *Deus non habet initium uel terminum* and its Reworking, *Deus itaque summe atque ineffabiliter bonus*," *Mediaeval Studies* 73 (2011), 1–118; idem, "A Twelfth-Century Treatise on Charity: The Tract 'Vt autem hoc euidenter' of the Sentence Collection *Deus itaque summe atque ineffabiliter bonus*," *Mediaeval Studies* 74 (2012), 1–50; idem, *Gratian the Theologian* (see above, n. 36). pp. 148–85.

43 As was done by Bliemetzrieder, "Gratian und die Schule Anselms von Laon" (see above, n. 27) and, more recently, by Larson, "Influence of the School of Laon" and eadem, *Master of Penance* (see above, n. 41).

44 Larson, "Influence of the School of Laon" and eadem, *Master of Penance* (see above, n. 41) shows that there are doctrinal parallels between Gratian and Anselm's *sententiae*. But as these same doctrines are found in the patristic texts on which Anselm's teachings are based, it is unclear to what extent any of these doctrines can be considered 'Anselmian'. See my reservations about Larson's arguments in John C. Wei, "The Importance and Influence of Gratian's *De penitentia*," *Zeits Zeitschrift der Savigny-Stiftung für Rechtsgeschichte, kanonistische Abteilung* 101 (2015), 373–88, at pp. 376–78.

45 On the authorship of the *Glossa ordinaria*, see Alexander Andrée, "Laon Revisited: Master Anselm and the Creation of a Theological School in the Twelfth Century," *The Journal of Medieval Latin* 22 (2012), 257–81, at pp. 269–75, esp. p. 274: "there is no doubt that Anselm was *associated* with the glossing of Scripture; but jumping from that to the claim that he produced the Gloss on any particular book is quite a large leap. We just do not know in what precise way he was involved." See also idem, "Anselm of Laon Unveiled: The *Glosae*

positions espoused by works belonging to the school of Laon, Gratian in fact rejects several of them in *De penitentia*.[46]

Older historiography was fond of organizing theologians and theological literature into schools,[47] so much so that scholars sometimes seem to have regarded their work as complete once they had decided on an appropriate classification. However, if we abandon the great man perspective on intellectual history, then assigning Gratian to a theological school fades in importance. What matters is not whether Gratian was in fact the pupil of such and such a master, but rather which teachings and works influenced Gratian, how they did so, and why.

2.2 *Beyond 'Great' Jurists*

The old narrative's focus on Gratian is bound up with the idea that the *Decretum* constitutes a turning point in legal history, which in many ways it does. But as more recent research has emphasized, the *Decretum* did not change the study or practice of canon law overnight. Pre-Gratian canonical collections continued to be studied and used,[48] not least of all to expand and supplement the *Decretum*.[49] And under Gratian's successors and students both the *Decretum*'s scope and its jurisprudence continued to evolve,[50] most notably through the increasing assimilation of Roman law.[51]

The jurists responsible for these developments were often theologians in their own right, or at least were or may have been familiar with various scholastic theological texts. Thaner and other scholars supportive of the old narrative,

---

super Iohannem and the Origins of the *Glossa ordinaria* on the Bible," *Mediaeval Studies* 73 (2011), 217–40.

46 See Wei, *Gratian the Theologian* (see above, n. 36), pp. 148–85.

47 A prime example is Artur Michael Landgraf, *Introduction à l'histoire de la littérature théologique de la scolastique naissante*, trans. Louis-B. Geiger (Montreal, 1973).

48 See the other contributions in this volume and the literature cited therein.

49 See, e.g. Rudolf Weigand, "Burchardauszüge in Dekrethandschriften und ihre Verwendung bei Rufin und als Paleae im Dekret Gratians," *Archiv für katholisches Kirchenrecht* 158 (1989), 429–51.

50 See John C. Wei, "The Later Development of Gratian's *Decretum*," in *Proceedings of the Fourteenth International Congress of Medieval Canon Law, Toronto, 5–11 August 2012*, ed. Joseph W. Goering et al., MIC Subsidia 15 (Vatican City, 2016), pp. 149–61.

51 On Roman law in the *Decretum*, see Winroth, *Making of Gratian's Decretum* (see above, n. 34), pp. 146–74; idem, "Roman Law in Gratian and the *Panormia*," in *Bishops, Texts and the Use of Canon Law around 1100: Essays in the Honour of Martin Brett*, ed. Bruce Clark Brasington and Kathleen G. Cushing, Church, Faith and Culture in the Middle Ages (Aldershot, 2008), pp. 183–90. On the Romanization of canon law, see Pierre Legendre, *La pénétration du droit romain dans le droit canonique classique de Gratien à Innocent IV, 1140–1254* (Paris, 1964).

for instance, have frequently noted that Masters Omnebene and Roland not only commented on the *Decretum*, but also composed theological sentence collections heavily dependent on Abelard's works.[52] To give another example, the decretist Gandulph who authored various glosses to the *Decretum* may well be the same person as the Master Gandulph of Bologna who abbreviated and reworked Peter Lombard's *Four Books of Sentences*.[53] Other decretists, like the author of *Reverentia sacrorum canonum*, appear to have known and drawn upon the Lombard's *Four Books of Sentences* and other scholastic texts in compiling their legal works.[54]

Yet, despite scholarly awareness of these twelfth-century jurist-theologians, their significance for the relationship between scholasticism and the development of canon law has remained largely unexplored. Thaner and other legal historians who have noted Omnebene and Roland's theological activity have generally looked at it only within the confines of the old narrative, as additional evidence that Abelard influenced Gratian. If Gratian's immediate students were disciples of Abelard, so the argument runs, then Gratian must have been one as well. The theological activity of other jurist-theologians has often received not even this amount of attention. The case of Master Vacarius is the exception that proves the rule.[55]

These shortcomings should be rectified. Post-Gratian jurists did more than just refine a programme set in place by the 'father of the science of canon

52 See, e.g. Thaner, *Abälard und das canonische Recht* (see above, n. 17), p. 24; Thomas Bouquillon, "The University of Paris," *The Catholic University Bulletin* 1 (1895), 349–69, at p. 360. Master Roland is now known not to be the same person as Roland Bandinelli/Pope Alexander III (1159–81). See John T. Noonan, "Who was Rolandus?," in *Law, Church, and Society: Essays in Honor of Stephan Kuttner*, ed. Kenneth Pennington and Robert Somerville (Philadelphia, 1977), pp. 21–48; Rudolf Weigand, "Magister Rolandus und Papst Alexander III.," *Archiv für katholisches Kirchenrecht* 149 (1980), 3–44; repr. in idem, *Glossatoren des Dekrets Gratians* (Goldbach, 1997), pp. 73*–114*.

53 On Gandulph the decretist, see Rudolf Weigand, "The Development of the *Glossa ordinaria* to the *Decretum*," in *The History of Medieval Canon Law in the Classical Period, 1140–1234: From Gratian to the Decretals of Pope Gregory IX*, ed. Wilfried Hartmann and Kenneth Pennington, History of Medieval Canon Law (Washington, D.C., 2008), pp. 55–97, at pp. 73–74; idem, "Gandulphusglossen zum Dekret Gratians," *Bulletin of Medieval Canon Law*, n.s. 7 (1977), 15–48. On Gandulph the theologian, see Gandulph of Bologna, *Sententiarum libri quattuor*, ed. Johannes de Walter (Vienna, 1924).

54 See, e.g. *Summa 'Reverentia sacrorum canonum'*, ed. John C. Wei, MIC Corpus glossatorum 9 (Vatican City, 2018), p. 200, lines 7–8 (= *Summa* ad C. 1, q. 1, c. 59) and the apparatus thereto.

55 See Jason Taliadoros, *Law and Theology in Twelfth-Century England: The Works of Master Vacarius (c. 1115/20–c. 1200)*, Disputatio 10 (Turnhout, 2006); idem, "Synthesizing the Legal and Theological Thought of Master Vacarius," *Zeitschrift der Savigny-Stiftung für Rechtsgeschichte, kanonistische Abteilung* 95 (2009), 48–77.

law'.[56] They also contributed substantively to the development of law and legal method. It would be useful to understand the role that scholasticism played in the development of these jurists' legal thinking and how it compared to and differed from the influence of scholasticism on Gratian.

2.3 *Beyond 'Great' Ideas*

The old narrative focused on the scholastic method for reconciling contradictory authorities as scholasticism's great contribution to the development of canon law. But this focus is too narrow and, furthermore, unnecessary if the *Sic et non* is not the link between scholasticism and canon law that Thaner and others supposed. For the medieval schools contributed to the development of canon law in other key ways as well, ways that were perhaps no less important, even if arguably less 'brilliant'.

These other contributions naturally include doctrinal developments in areas where theology and canon law overlapped, e.g., penance, marriage.[57] But they also encompassed habits of thought and intellectual practice cultivated and formed in the medieval schools. While further research needs to be done into these issues, there is reason to think that scholasticism's non-doctrinal contributions to the development of canon law include at least the following:

1. The interweaving of authorities and commentary. Alger of Liège, of course, did this as well in his *De misericordia et iustitia*.[58] But theological sentence collections like *Deus itaque summe* were another genre that adopted this approach, and which provided a model for Gratian and his successors.[59]
2. The idea of compiling a *Glossa ordinaria* to authoritative legal texts. Over the course of the twelfth and thirteenth centuries, the scholastic theologians of northern France compiled what became standard gloss apparatuses to each book of the Bible.[60] Beginning in the 1150s, the medieval canonists did the same for the *Decretum*.[61]

---

56 Stephan Kuttner, "The Father of the Science of Canon Law," *The Jurist* 1 (1941), 2–19.

57 See, e.g. Nicholas M. Häring, "The Interaction between Canon Law and Sacramental Theology in the Twelfth Century," in *Proceedings of the Fourth International Congress of Medieval Canon Law, Toronto, 21–25 August 1972*, ed. Stephan Kuttner, MIC Subsidia 5 (Vatican City, 1976), pp. 483–93.

58 See Kretzschmar, *Alger von Lüttichs Traktat* (see above, n. 19).

59 See Wei, "The Sentence Collection *Deus non habet*" (see above, n. 42).

60 See Beryl Smalley, *The Study of the Bible in the Middle Ages*, 3rd ed. (Oxford, 1983); Alexander Andrée, *Gilbertus Universalis: Glossa ordinaria in Lamentationes Ieremie prophete: prothemata et liber I: A Critical Edition with an Introduction and a Translation* (Stockholm, 2005); Andrée, "Laon Revisited" (see above, n. 45); Lesley Smith, *The Glossa ordinaria: The Making of a Medieval Bible Commentary* (Leiden, 2009).

61 See Weigand, "Development of the *Glossa ordinaria*" (see above, n. 53).

3. New literary genres. Both scholasticism and canon law developed new literary genres.[62] Some of these, like the *quaestiones*, were the same in both disciplines, and their development appears to have been closely related.[63]

3 Conclusion

The old narrative concerning the relationship between scholasticism and canon law is not only incorrect as a matter of history; it is also overly narrow and in many ways misguided. The old narrative focused on 'great' men and their 'great' books and 'great' ideas. A new narrative should adopt a considerably broader perspective.

First, it should abandon the preoccupation with categorizing Gratian (and other jurists) according to theological schools. Scholars should continue to investigate the theological education of medieval jurists. But where explicit sources on the subject are lacking (as is the case with Gratian), the focus should be on how these jurists interacted with and transformed their sources rather than speculation on who they may or may not have met or studied with.

Second, a new narrative should abandon the fixation with turning points and teleological storytelling embodied by the 'great' man, 'great' book, and 'great' idea approaches to history. Instead, a new narrative should devote more attention to the incremental steps by which legal thought and education were transformed in the twelfth century and the myriad connections between scholasticism and canon law that made this transformation possible. To that end, a new narrative should adopt a wider timeframe and devote greater attention to thinkers who came after Gratian. Particularly promising in this regard might be an examination of jurists who were or may have been theologians, such as Omnebene, Roland, and Gandulph.

Third, a new narrative should look beyond the scholastic method and even beyond the doctrines of the scholastics to the various other ways in which the schools of theology transformed intellectual practices and modes

62 See generally Stephan Kuttner, *Repertorium der Kanonistik. Prodromus corporis Glossarum*, Studi e testi 71 (Vatican City, 1937); Kenneth Pennington and Wolfgang P. Müller, "The Decretists: The Italian School," in *The History of Medieval Canon Law in the Classical Period: From Gratian to the Decretals of Pope Gregory IX*, ed. Wilfried Hartmann and Kenneth Pennington, History of Medieval Canon Law (Washington, D.C., 2008), pp. 121–73, at pp. 160–72.

63 Kuttner, *Repertorium der Kanonistik* (see above, n. 62), p. 243: "Das Quaestionenverfahren, im Unterricht disputatorisch geübt, weist enge Beziehungen zur scholastischen Methode in der Theologie auf."

of thinking. To what extent were similar developments in the schools of law due to the influence of the scholastics? To what extent were they independent developments? Much more research in this area is needed.

A new narrative along these lines will inevitably be more complicated than the old narrative. But such a narrative should also prove to be more interesting and fruitful. Such a narrative will not ignore Abelard, Gratian, or their books and ideas, but rather strive to place them in their larger historical context and to give other, hitherto neglected actors, works, and activities the credit they should be due.

4 Appendix: Gratian, the *Sic et non*, and the *Sententiae Sidonis*

In his study of C. 15, q. 1, Tatsushi Genka identified four authorities not found in any of Gratian's known formal sources but present in the *Sic et non* (= SN).[64] These extracts, which stem from Augustine, are all cited in C. 15, q. 1, d.a.c. 1 and already appear in the first recension of the *Decretum*, where they are found in close proximity and in roughly the same order as in the *Sic et non*. Following Genka, I shall term these authorities 'Texts 1–4'. Genka's examination of these authorities reveals numerous variants between the *Sic et non* and Gratian. The lack of other possible candidates for Gratian's formal source, however, leads Genka to suggest that Gratian used the *Sic et non* in conjunction with a copy of Augustine's *Retractationes* in composing C. 15, q. 1, d.a.c. 1, although Genka does not exclude the possibility that Gratian employed an unknown *florilegium* dependent on the *Sic et non* or one of the *Sic et non*'s formal sources.[65] Here

64 Genka, "Zur textlichen Grundlage" (see above, n. 38). In addition to consulting Fr = *Decretum magistri Gratiani*, ed. Emil Friedberg (Leipzig, 1879), Genka collated the following manuscripts: Aa = Admont, Stiftsbibliothek, 43; Bi = Biberach, Spitalarchiv, 3515; Cd = Cambridge, Mass., Harvard Law Library 64; Cg = Cambridge, Gonville and Caius, 6/6; Florence, Biblioteca Nazionale Centrale, Conv. Soppr. A.1.402; Hk = Heiligenkreuz, Stiftsbibliothek 44; Hl = Heiligenkreuz, Stiftsbibliothek 43; In = Innsbruck, Universitäts- und Landesbibliothek Tirol, 90; Ka = Cologne, Dombibliothek 127; Kb = Cologne, Dombibliothek 128; Mc = Munich, Bayerische Staatsbibliothek, Clm 4505; Munich, Bayerische Staatsbibliothek, Clm 13004; Munich, Bayerische Staatsbibliothek, Clm 28161; Mz = Mainz, Stadtbibliothek, II.204; Pk = Paris, Bibliothèque nationale de France, lat. 3890; Sa = Salzburg, Stiftsbibliothek Erzabtei Sankt Peter, a.XII.9; Sb = Salzburg, Stiftsbibliothek Erzabtei Sankt Peter, a.XI.9; Sg = St Gall, Stiftsbibliothek, 673; Tr = Trier, Stadtbibliothek, 906 (1141).

65 Genka, "Zur textlichen Grundlage" (see above, n. 38), p. 73: "Aus diesem Befund ergibt sich, dass das Florilegium, das zwischen Augustin und Gratian liegt, mit SN identisch oder auf jeden Fall mit SN eng verwandt ist. Es gibt aber immer noch drei Möglichkeiten. A. Die Benutzung von SN, womöglich in einer unbekannten Fassung, B. Das Vorhandensein einer gemeinsamen Quelle, C. Die Benutzung eines von SN abhängigen Florilegiums.

I would like to present evidence that Gratian's formal source was more likely a *florilegium* dependent on *Sic et non* or one of the *Sic et non*'s formal sources.

As it turns out, Texts 1–4 are also found in the *Sententiae Sidonis*, a sentence collection that probably postdates Gratian. According to its prologue, the *Sententiae Sidonis* is an expanded version of the *excerptiones* of an otherwise unknown Master Ubaldus.[66] Ubaldo/Baldo was a relatively common name in northern and central Italy in the twelfth century, so it is possible that Master Ubaldus was Italian and that the *Sententiae Sidonis* which made use of his work was compiled in Italy, although Vat. lat. 1345, the sole manuscript containing this work, was likely copied in the Holy Land.[67] Whatever the provenance of the *Sententiae Sidonis*, it seems clear that the earliest readers of Vat. lat. 1345 were French, since French translations of Latin words appear occasionally in the margins (e.g., fol. 172v, 'eschaupe' for 'tergiuersatio').[68]

The *Sententiae Sidonis* took its material from a variety of formal sources, most notably the Pseudo-Ivonian *Panormia*,[69] the *Summa sententiarum*,[70] and the sentence collection *Deus itaque summe*.[71] The *Sic et non* may have been among the *Sententiae Sidonis*'s sources as well. In several instances, the *Sententiae Sidonis* contains fuller inscriptions than the *Summa sententiarum* and actual quotations where the *Summa sententiarum* provides just paraphrases. This fact led Artur Michael Landgraf to argue against Paul Fournier, Martin Grabmann, and Joseph de Ghellinck that the *Sententiae Sidonis* depends not upon the

---

Da die Grenzen zwischen A und C so fließend ist, lassen die Möglichkeiten sich auf A reduzieren, und wenn Abelard die *fontes materiales* selbst benutzt hätte, dann könnte man vielleicht auf SN schließen. Jedoch muß ich die Frage offen lassen."

66 *Sententiae Sidonis*, prologus (Vatican City, Biblioteca Apostolica Vaticana, Vat. lat. 1345, fol. 4r), ed. Paul Fournier, "Les collections canoniques attribuées à Yves de Chartres," *Bibliothèque de École des Chartes* 57 (1896), 645–98 and *Bibliothèque de École des Chartes* 58 (1897), 26–77, 293–326, 410–44, and 622–76, at p. 665: "Hoc igitur diligenter considerans, o socii, licet multis sim impeditus occupationibus, tam lectionibus quam aliis undique progredientibus, pro quibus uideatur me huic operi uacare non posse, tamen et rogatui uestro libenter satisfacere uolens ad id perficiendum animum applicui, presertim cum magister Ubaldus excerptiones suas inciperet, ac expletis duobus quaternionibus nescio si posset, nobis tantum amplius dare minime uellet, et hac occasione commotus magis ad hoc intendere uolui."

67 Anneliese Maier, "Die Handschriften der *Ecclesia Sidonensis*," *Manuscripta* 11 (1967), 39–45; repr. in eadem, *Ausgehendes Mittelalter*, ed. Agostino Paravicini Bagliani, 3 vols (Rome, 1964–77), 3:281–8.

68 Stephan Kuttner and Reinhard Elze, *A Catalogue of Canon and Roman Law Manuscripts in the Vatican Library*, 1: *Codices Vaticani latini 541–2299*, Studi e testi 322 (Vatican City, 1986), pp. 98–100.

69 On the collection, see Rolker, *Canon Law* (see above, n. 19), pp. 123–26 and 248–89.

70 PL 176:41–174.

71 On this source, see Wei, "Sentence Collection *Deus non habet*" and idem, "A Twelfth-Century Treatise" (see above, n. 42 for both articles).

Summa sententiarum, but rather upon a common source.[72] As Damien van den Eynde notes, however, Landgraf's explanation raises an insurmountable difficulty.[73] Studies of the *Summa sententiarum* have shown that the author often paraphrased and abbreviated the authorities and treatises which he incorporated into his work. Unlike the author of the *Sententiae Sidonis*, he never copied his sources slavishly. Yet, if one assumes that the *Summa sententiarum* depends upon the *Sententiae Sidonis* or that both depend upon a common source, then one must argue that the author of the *Summa sententiarum* did just that whenever both works contain parallel passages. The same logic, moreover, would lead one to conclude that the treatise *De coniugio* of Walter of Mortagne (1136–1139/41),[74] which became attached to the *Summa sententiarum* soon after the latter work was completed, likewise depends upon the *Sententiae Sidonis*, since there too the *Sententiae Sidonis* occasionally contains fuller inscriptions and quotations.[75] These difficulties are easily solved, however, if one assumes that the author of the *Sententiae Sidonis* expanded the quotations in the *Summa sententiarum* and Walter of Mortagne's *De coniugio* (which he likely possessed together in the same manuscript) to make them more precise.

72 Artur Michael Landgraf, "Die Summa Sententiarum und die Summe des Cod. Vat. lat. 1345," *Recherches de théologie ancienne et médiévale* 11 (1939), 260–70; Fournier, "Collections canoniques" (see above, n. 66), pp. 664–72; Paul Fournier, with the collaboration of Gabriel Le Bras, *L'histoire de collections canoniques en Occident depuis les Fausses Décrétales jusqu'au Décret de Gratien*, 2 vols (Paris, 1931–32), 2:344–47; Grabmann, *Geschichte der scholastischen Methode* (see above, n. 26), 2:301–09; Joseph de Ghellinck, *Le mouvement théologique au XII siècle, sa préparation lointaine avant et autour de Pierre Lombard, ses rapports avec les initiatives des canonistes: études, recherches et document*, Museum Lessianum. Section Historique 10, 2nd ed. (Bruges, 1948), pp. 124 and 463.

73 Damien van den Eynde, "William of Saint-Thierry and the Author of the *Summa Sententiarum*," *Franciscan Studies* 10 (1950), 241–56.

74 For the dating of Walter's *De coniugio*, see Hans Zeimentz, *Ehe nach der Lehre der Frühscholastik. Eine moralgeschichtliche Untersuchung zur Anthropologie und Theologie der Ehe in der Schule Anselms von Laon und Wilhelms von Champeaux, bei Hugo von St. Viktor, Walter von Mortagne und Petrus Lombardus* (Düsseldorf, 1973), pp. 253 and 274.

75 Van den Eynde, "Summa sententiarum" (see above, n. 73), p. 141: "Les rapports des *Sententiae Sidonis* avec le traité de Gautier de Mortagne ne diffèrent guère de celles qui les relient à la *Summa Sententiarum*. Par exemple, la réference *Augustinus de bono nuptiarum*, par laquelle débute dans les *Sententiae Sidonis* le second des passages cités, se réduit dans le text de Gautier aux simples mots *dicit Augustinus*. Si A. Langraf avait eu connaissance de cette particularité, en aurait-il conclu, comme il le fit pour la *Summa Sententiarum*, que le traité *De coniugio* de Gautier de Mortagne dépend soit des *Sententiae Sidonis* soit d'une somme théologique qui aurait servi de source commune? On peut en douter. Pour ma part, je préfère penser que l'auteur des *Sententiae Sidonis* avait à sa disposition un exemplaire de la *Summa Sententiarum*, avec, en appendice, le traité de Gautier sur le mariage."

Van den Eynde's argument becomes even more convincing when one notes that, in the example cited by Landgraf, the compiler of the *Sententiae Sidonins* provides fuller inscriptions and/or citations only for those authorities found in his other known formal sources and that the information he provides never exceeds the data provided in these collections (see Table 6.1; an asterisk denotes entries where the *Sententiae Sidonis* contains more accurate inscriptions than the *Summa sententiarum*). When these collections provide the exact work and chapter, the *Sententiae Sidonis* does as well (e.g., *Sententiae Sidonis* 14.88). When these collections provide only the name of a work, then the *Sententiae Sidonis* does likewise (e.g., *Sententiae Sidonis* 14.98, which expands the 'Item Augustinus' of the *Summa sententiarum* to the 'Item Augustinus contra mendacium' found in the *Panormia*).

TABLE 6.1 Parallels in the inscriptions of the *Sententiae Sidonis* and its formal sources

Sententiae Sidonis	*Summa sentiarum*[a]	*Panormia*	*Sic et non*[b]
14.84	4.5 (122D)		
14.85		8.124	
14.86		8.126.1	
14.87		8.125a	
*14.88	4.5 (122D)		Prologue, p. 99.235
14.89	4.5 (122D)		
*14.90	4.5 (122D)		Prologue, p. 99.236–38
*14.91	4.5 (122D–123A)	8.129	
14.92			
14.93	4.5 (123A)		
14.94	4.5 (123A)		
14.95	4.5 (123A)		
14.96	4.5 (123AB)		
*14.97	4.5 (123B)	8.133a	
*14.98	4.5 (123BC)	8.125	
*14.99	4.5 (123C)	8.128	
*14.100	4.5 (123C)	8.130a	
*14.101		8.131	
14.102	4.5 (123CD)		
*14.103	4.5 (123D)	8.130b	
14.104		8.134	

a The numbers in parentheses are references to the column number in PL 176.
b The page and line numbers are to the edition by Boyer and McKeon (see above, n. 3).

TABLE 6.2 Texts 1–4 in the *Sententiae Sidonis*, Gratian's *Decretum*, and the *Sic et non*

Sententiae Sidonis	**Gratian**	***Sic et non***
7.68	C. 15, q. 1, Text 2	145.4
7.69	C. 15, q. 1, Text 3	145.6
7.70	C. 15, q. 1, Text 1	145.8
7.71	C. 15, q. 1, Text 4	145.9

In the *Sententiae Sidonis*, Texts 1–4 appear in the order found in the *Sic et non* rather than the order found in the *Decretum* (see Table 6.2), but in a version intermediate between the *Decretum* and the *Sic et non*. The other seven items from SN 145, which are not found in Gratian, are likewise missing from the *Sententiae Sidonis*.

A close examination of the textual variants shows that the *Sententiae Sidonis* contains Texts 1–4 in a version intermediate between Gratian's *Decretum* and the *Sic et non*. In what follows, I provide first a transcription of the relevant portion of the *Sententiae Sidonis* and then an analysis of the variants. Angle brackets ['<...>'] enclose text present in Gratian's *Decretum* or the *Sic et non*, but absent from the *Sententiae Sidonis*. Parentheses ['(...)'] enclose text that is illegible in the *Sententiae Sidonis*. The presence of variant readings in Gratian's *Decretum* and/or the *Sic et non* is indicated by the use of bold or italics. In the comparative tables that follow, '*deest*' indicates that a word or phrase is not present, while '*idem*' indicates that the reading is identical to that of the *Sententiae Sidonis*.

***Sententiae Sidonis* 7.68 = C. 15, q. 1, d.a.c. 1, Text 2 = SN 145.4**
Idem[76] de uera religione.

<**Nunc**> usque adeo peccatum uoluntarium malum est, ut **nullomodo sit peccatum si non fit uoluntarium**. Et hoc quidem **ita** manifestum est, ut nulla hinc doctorum paucitas, nulla indoctorum turba dissentiat. Quare aut negandum est pecatta committi, aut fatendum est **cum uoluntate** committi.

Text 2 bears the same inscription and is of the same length in the *Decretum*, the *Sic et non*, and the *Sententiae Sidonis*. The *Decretum* and the *Sententiae Sidonis* provide the same readings for variants 1 and 4, which do not appear in any extant manuscript of the *Sic et non*. For variants 2 and 4, on the other hand,

76 Idem = Augustinus.

TABLE 6.3 Variants in Text 2 in the *Sententiae Sidonis*, Gratian's *Decretum*, and the *Sic et non*

	***Sententiae Sidonis* 7.68**	**C. 15, q. 1, d.a.c. 1, Text 2**	***Sic et non* 145.4**
1	*deest*	*deest*	Nunc
2	nullomodo sit peccatum si non fit uoluntarium	nisi sit uoluntarium nullomodo sit peccatum	nullomodo sit peccatum si non sit uoluntarium
3	ita	adeo	*idem*
4	cum uoluntate	*idem*	uoluntate

TABLE 6.4 Variants in Text 3 in the *Sententiae Sidonis*, Gratian's *Decretum*, and the *Sic et non*

	***Sententiae Sidonis* 7.69**	**C. 15, q. 1, d.a.c. 1, Text 3**	***Sic et non* 145.6**
1	*deest*	*deest*	inquam
2	Diffinitio	distinctio	*idem*
3	Discutiatur	executiatur	*idem*
4	quippe illud	illud quippe	*idem*
5	non quod etiam	*idem*	non etiam
6	Quia	*idem*	que
7	uel a	*idem*	a
8	omnimodo	omnino	*idem*
9	Possint	*idem*	possunt
10	sine uoluntate committi	non uoluntaria dici	*idem*
11	Quoniam ... hereditarium	*deest*	*idem*
12	*deest*	*deest*	ut nullomodo sit peccatum si non sit uoluntarium

the *Sententiae Sidonis* agrees with the *Sic et non* rather than the *Decretum*. (We can disregard 'fit' rather than 'sit' in variant 2 as a copyist error.) Five manuscripts studied by Genka—Bi, Mk, Mz, Pk, and Tr—contain the reading found in the *Sic et non* rather than the variant found in most manuscripts of the *Decretum*.

***Sententiae Sidonis* 7.69 = C. 15, q. 1, d.a.c. 1, Text 3 = SN 145.6**
De libro I. retractacionum (*add. in marg.*).

Usque adeo <**inquam**> peccatum uoluntarium malum est, ut nullomodo sit peccatum si non sit uoluntarium. Potest uideri falsa hec **diffinitio**. Sed si diligenter **discutiatur**, inuenitur uerissima. Peccatum **quippe illud** cogitandum est, quod tantummodo peccatum est, **non quod etiam** pena peccati. Quamuis (et) illa que non (immerito) non uoluntaria peccata dicuntur, **quia uel a** nescientibus uel coactis perpetrantur, non **omnimodo possint sine (uolu) ntate committi.** *Quoniam et ille qui* [...] *hereditarium.*

The *Sententiae Sidonis* contains almost the whole of SN 145.6: only the last phrase has been omitted. The inscription, which is lacking in the text, has been supplied by a later hand. The *Sententiae Sidonis* and the *Decretum* contain the same readings for variants 1, 5–7, and 9, while the *Sententiae Sidonis* agrees with the *Sic et non* for the remaining variants.

Sententiae Sidonis 7.70 = C. 15, q. 1, d.a.c. 1, Text 1 = SN 145.8
In eodem.

Itemque alio loco ipsam uoluntatem diffiniui dicens: Voluntas est animi motus **cogente nullo** <**ad**> aliquid uel non **amittendum** uel adipiscendum. Quod **propterea** dictum est **ut hac diffinitione uolens a nolente discerneretur** ***et*** *sic ut ad illos referretur intentio qui primi in paradyso fecerunt humano generi originem mali, nullo cogente,* ***hoc est libera uoluntate peccando*** *quia et scientes contra preceptum fecerunt et* ***ille*** *temptator suasit* ***ut hoc fieret*** *non coegit.*

TABLE 6.5 Variants in Text 1 in the *Sententiae Sidonis*, Gratian's *Decretum*, and the *Sic et non*

	Sententiae Sidonis 7.70	C. 15, q. 1, d.a.c. 1, Text 1	*Sic et non* 145.8
1	Itemque ... ipsam	*deest*	*deest*
2	uoluntatem ... dicens	*deest*	*idem*
3	uoluntas est	Est enim uoluntas	*idem*
4	cogente nullo	*deest*	*idem*
5	*deest*	ad	ad
6	Amittendum	Imitandum	admittendum
7	propterea	*idem*	*deest*
8	ut ... discerneretur et	ut ... discerneretur	*deest*
9	hoc est libera uoluntate peccando	*deest*	peccando hoc est libera uoluntate
10	ille	*deest*	*deest*
11	ut hoc fieret	*deest*	*deest*

TABLE 6.6 Variants in Text 4 in the *Sententiae Sidonis*, Gratian's *Decretum*, and the *Sic et non*

	Sententiae Sidonis **7.71**	**C. 15, q. 1, d.a.c. 1, Text 4**	***Sic et non*** **145.9**
1	Itemque	*deest*	*deest*
2	qua	quam	*idem*
3	*deest*	*deest*	et
4	est	*deest*	*deest*

The *Sententiae Sidonis* contains a longer text than the *Decretum*, but a shorter one than the *Sic et non*. For variants 2–4 and 6, the *Sententiae Sidonis* contains the same reading as the *Sic et non*. Variant 5, the omission of 'ad', is clearly due to scribal error. Variant 9 is a simple case of transposition. Variants 1, 7, 8, 10, and 11 are readings found in the material source, but left out of the *Sic et non* by Abelard.[77] Since variants 7 and 8 also appear in the *Decretum*, it seems likely that the compiler of the formal source rather than the compiler of the *Sententiae Sidonis* was responsible for correcting SN 145.8 through a comparison with the material source.

Sententiae Sidonis **7.71 = C. 15, q. 1, d.a.c. 1, Text 4 = SN 145.9**
In eodem.

Itemque diffinitio peccati **qua** diximus peccatum est uoluntas retinendi uel consequendi quod iusticia uetat, <et> unde liberum est abstinere, propterea uerum est, quia id diffinitum est, quod tantummodo pecatum est, non quod etiam pena peccati **est**.

The length and extent of Text 4 is the same in the *Sententiae Sidonis* and the *Decretum*, while the *Sic et non* contains a much longer text. Variant 1 is a connecting phrase found in Augustine's *Retractationes*, but omitted from the *Sic et non*.[78] Variant 2 is insignificant and most likely due to a copyist error, even though, as Genka observes,

77 Augustine, *Retractationes* 1.15.3, ed. Almut Mutzenbecher, CCSL 57 (Turnhout, 1984), pp. 46.47–47.54.

78 Augustine, *Retractationes* 1.15.4, ed. Mutzenbecher, p. 47.71.

> fast alle Gratianhandschriften (Bi, Cd, Cg, Fd, Fr, Hk, Hl, In, Ka, Kb, Mc, Me, Mk, Mz, Pk, Sa (Sb), Tr) statt *qua* die Lesart *quam* [haben, JCW], die auch in zwei SN-Handschriften (Einsiedeln, Stiftsbibliothek 300 und Avranches, Bibliothèque Municipale 12) vorkommt.[79]

Variant 3, the omission of 'et', occurs in both the *Sententiae Sidonis* and the *Decretum*. Variant 4 is probably due to the editorial activity of the compiler of the *Sententiae Sidonis*.

There are only three possible scenarios that can account for the agreement of the *Sententiae Sidonis* sometimes with the *Sic et non*, at other times with the *Decretum*, and on still other occasions with the material source. First, the same *florilegium* was a source for the *Sententiae Sidonis*, the *Sic et non*, and Gratian, but Abelard modified his text in many places. Second, the same *florilegium*—one dependent on the *Sic et non* and collated against Augustine's *Retractationes*—was employed in the composition of both the *Sententiae Sidonis* and the *Decretum*. Third, the compiler of the *Sententiae Sidonis* made direct use of Augustine's *Retractationes*, the *Sic et non* (or a collection dependent on the *Sic et non*), and Gratian's *Decretum*, choosing to excerpt only those authorities present in the *Decretum* and ordering them in the sequence found in the *Sic et non*, yet taking three of the texts directly from a copy of Augustine's *Retractationes*. The complexity of this last scenario makes it sufficiently implausible that we should probably rule it out entirely.

Two other authorities, which Genka terms Text 5 (= c. 3) and Text 6 (= d.p.c. 3), are contained in the other two *dicta* of the first-recension C. 15, q. 1.[80] Text 5 is found in SN 106.30, the *Collectio canonum* of Anselm of Lucca 11.153, and the Ivonian *Decretum* 1.130, while Text 6 does not appear in any known canonical collection. Neither of these texts is found in the *Sententiae Sidonis*. Genka suggests that Text 5 derives from the *Sic et non*. It seems more plausible, however, that Text 5 and Text 6 derive from the same source (and hence that Text 5 does not derive from the SN), since the material source for both texts is Fulgentius of Ruspe's *De fide ad Petrum*. The absence of these two texts from the *Sententiae Sidonis* thus in no way argues against the view either that the *Sententiae Sidonis*, the *Sic et non*, and Gratian all drew upon a common source or that the *Sententiae Sidonis* incorporates a *florilegium* dependent on the *Sic et non* and used in the composition of the first-recension *Decretum*.

79 Genka, "Zur textlichen Grundlage" (see above, n. 38), p. 72.

80 All the manuscripts examined by Friedberg and Genka present C. 15, q. 1, c. 3 as a part of d.p.c. 2 rather than as a separate canon.

CHAPTER 7

The *Decretum* of Gratian: A Janus-Faced Collection

Stephan Dusil

1 Introduction

Gratian is considered to be a turning point in the history of canon law, as he marks the watershed between the learned law of the late Middle Ages and the other, 'non-learned', more intuitive use of canon law of the early and high Middle Ages. Gratian represents the shift between the collectors of normative texts and the erudite interpretation of these texts. Once, he was even named the 'father of the science of canon law'.[1] Therefore, it is not surprising that Gratian has been in the focus of historical research for a long time: whereas some scholars tried to unravel the mysteries of his life, locating him as a Camaldolese monk in Bologna or placing him as a bishop to Chiusi in central Italy,[2] others focussed on his *Concordantia discordantium canonum*, briefly known as the *Decretum Gratiani*, in order to learn more about the theory of canon law in the middle of the twelfth century.[3] The discovery of at least two versions of the *Decretum Gratiani* some twenty years ago gave a tremendous boost to the analysis of this piece of literature: researchers have now been able to scrutinize the making of this seminal œuvre and to study from up close how Gratian pieced texts, rubrics and commentaries together.[4] At the same time,

1 Stephan Kuttner, "The Father of the Science of Canon Law," *The Jurist* 1 (1941), 2–19.

2 John T. Noonan, "Gratian Slept Here: The Changing Identity of the Father of the Systematic Study of Canon Law," *Traditio* 35 (1979), 145–72; Anders Winroth, "Where Gratian Slept: The Life and Death of the Father of Canon Law," *Zeitschrift der Savigny-Stiftung für Rechtsgeschichte, kanonistische Abteilung* 99 (2013), 105–28.

3 As an introduction to Gratian see Peter Landau, "Gratian and the *Decretum Gratiani*," in *The History of Medieval Canon Law in the Classical Period: From Gratian to the Decretals of Pope Gregory IX*, ed. Wilfried Hartmann and Kenneth Pennington, History of Medieval Canon Law (Washington, D.C., 2008), pp. 22–54.

4 Anders Winroth, "The Two Recensions of Gratian's Decretum," *Zeitschrift der Savigny-Stiftung für Rechtsgeschichte, kanonistische Abteilung* 83 (1997), 22–31; idem, *The Making of Gratian's Decretum*, Cambridge Studies in Medieval Life and Thought, Fourth Series 49 (Cambridge, 2000). An overview of the current state of scholarship is provided by Melodie Harris Eichbauer, "Gratian's Decretum and the Changing Historiographical Landscape," *History Compass* 11:12 (2013), 1111–25. The theory of the two versions was confirmed several times; see, for instance, Jean Werckmeister, "Les deux versions du 'de matrimonio' de Gratien," *Revue de droit canonique* 48 (1998), 301–15; Rudolf Weigand, "Causa 25 des Dekrets

 | DOI:10.1163/9789004394384_009

the discovery of the two versions has raised new questions,[5] and it especially sparked a debate on who the author of the *Decretum* was. Commonly, the authors are just named 'Gratian 1' and 'Gratian 2' to indicate that both worked with—more or less—subtle differences which led to the conclusion that Gratian 1 was a "pastor with a strong interest in law; Gratian 2 was a professional jurist."[6] The question, however, remains open as to whether 'Gratian 2' just adopted a different perspective as an older man or whether the first version was transformed into the second version by a different master. Secure ground in this question can possibly never be reached and it is not the aim of this paper to envisage such an audacious endeavour. Nonetheless, the question of how the authors of both versions worked will be tackled from another and seemingly new perspective, namely the perspective of 'knowledge'.

'Knowledge' is a pivotal term that has been successfully used in humanities in the last decade. Knowledge was by some historians understood as the social

---

und die Arbeitsweise Gratians," in *Grundlagen des Rechts. Festschrift für Peter Landau*, ed. Richard H. Helmholz et al., Rechts- und Staatswissenschaftliche Veröffentlichungen der Görres-Gesellschaft N. F. 91 (Paderborn, Munich, Vienna, and Zurich, 2000), pp. 277–90; Mary E. Sommar, "Gratian's Causa VII and the Multiple Recension Theories," *Bulletin of Medieval Canon Law*, n.s. 24 (2000), 78–96.

5 A consensus has not been reached about the question of a "Ur-Gratian" which might be transmitted in a single manuscript (St Gall, Stiftsbibliothek, 673). The stance of Carlos Larrainzar, "El borrador de la 'Concordia' de Graziano: Sankt Gallen, Stiftsbibliothek MS 673 (= Sg)," *Ius Ecclesiae* 11 (1999), 593–666 has been heavily discussed. Up to the present day, it remains under discussion whether this text represents the very first version of Gratian's *Decretum*, an abbreviation of the second version mixed with elements of the first, or even the *reportatio* of a medieval lecture on canon law, but this question will not be in the focus of this paper. Larrainzar's stance was rather supported, for instance, by Kenneth Pennington, "Gratian, Causa 19, and the Birth of Canonical Jurisprudence," in *Panta rei: studi dedicati a Manlio Bellomo*, ed. Orazio Condorelli, 5 vols (Rome, 2004), 4:339–55; and it was critically assessed by Anders Winroth, "Recent Work on the Making of Gratian's Decretum," *Bulletin of Medieval Canon Law*, n.s. 26 (2004–06), 1–29, esp. pp. 11–21; John C. Wei, "A Reconsideration of St Gall, Stiftsbibliothek 673 (Sg) in Light of the Sources of Distinctions 5–7 of the De penitentia," *Bulletin of Medieval Canon Law*, n.s. 27 (2007), 141–80; Titus Lenherr, "Die vier Fassungen von C. 3 q. 1 d.p.c. 6 im Decretum Gratiani. Zugleich ein Einblick in die neueste Diskussion um das Werden von Gratians Dekret," *Archiv für Katholisches Kirchenrecht* 169 (2000), 353–81, p. 377 and also idem, "Ist die Handschrift 673 der St. Galler Stiftsbibliothek (Sg) der Entwurf zu Gratians Dekret? Versuch einer Antwort aus Beobachtungen an D. 31 und D. 32," available at http://www.mgh-bibliothek.de/dokumente/a/a117039.pdf (last access 2018 July 13).

6 See Anders Winroth, "Marital Consent in Gratian's Decretum," in *Readers, Texts and Compilers in the Earlier Middle Ages: Studies in Medieval Canon Law in Honour of Linda Fowler-Magerl*, ed. Martin Brett and Kathleen G. Cushing, Church, Faith and Culture in the Medieval West (Aldershot, 2009), pp. 111–21, here at p. 121, and Winroth, *Making of Gratian's Decretum* (see above, n. 4), pp. 175–92.

product of a society, a creation to understand and to interpret reality; others tried to contrast knowledge-based societies with prior societies in order to grasp the fundamental 'knowledge' shift that emerged in the 19th and 20th centuries.[7] Even jurists tried to implement knowledge in their research by scrutinizing the 'knowledge of the state' and by analysing the knowledge to understand the functioning of (early) modern administrations.[8] Despite its success in other disciplines, legal historians have never applied this concept to legal sources, including medieval canon law.[9]

The idea, however, to understand canonical collections as repositories of ecclesiastical knowledge that provided the readers with normative rules is not too far-fetched.[10] The *Decretum* of Burchard of Worms, the *Diversorum patrum sententie*, also known as *Collection in 74 Titles*, and Deusdedit's *Collectio canonum*, just to name a few of these canonical collections, can be seen as repositories of normative texts. And they reflect a certain perspective of their compilers: Burchard's *Decretum* mirrors the episcopal structure of the church around 1000; the *Collection in 74 Titles* presents an anti-episcopal and pro-monastic point of view from between 1050 and 1070, and Deusdedit's compilation echoes the idea of a pronounced papacy.[11] But the compilers

---

7 Achim Landwehr, "Diskurs—Macht—Wissen. Perspektiven einer Kulturgeschichte des Politischen," *Archiv für Kulturgeschichte* 85 (2003), 71–117; *Geschichte(n) der Wirklichkeit. Beiträge zur Sozial- und Kulturgeschichte des Wissens*, ed. Achim Landwehr, Documenta Augustana 11 (Augsburg, 2002); Nico Stehr, "Wissensgesellschaften," in *Handbuch der Kulturwissenschaften*, 3: *Themen und Tendenzen*, ed. Friedrich Jaeger and Jörn Rüsen (Stuttgart and Weimar, 2004), pp. 34–49.

8 Michael Stolleis, "Der lernfähige und lernende Staat," in *Wissenskulturen. Über die Erzeugung und Weitergabe von Wissen*, ed. Johannes Fried and Michael Stolleis (Frankfurt and New York, 2009), pp. 58–78; *Das Wissen des Staates. Geschichte, Theorie, Praxis*, ed. Peter Collin and Thomas Horstmann (Baden-Baden, 2004).

9 The contribution by Christoph H.F. Meyer, "Ordnung durch Ordnen. Die Erfassung und Gestaltung des hochmittelalterlichen Kirchenrechts im Spiegel von Texten, Begriffen und Institutionen," in *Ordnungskonfigurationen im hohen Mittelalter*, ed. Bernd Schneidmüller and Stefan Weinfurter, Vorträge und Forschungen 64 (Sigmaringen, 2006), pp. 303–411 analyses the systematization of canon law until the twelfth century, but it does not consider the term 'knowledge'; nor does Rainer Maria Kiesow, *Das Alphabet des Rechts* (Frankfurt, 2004), define 'knowledge'.

10 Andreas Thier, "Dynamische Schriftlichkeit. Zur Normbildung in den vorgratianischen Kanonessammlungen," *Zeitschrift der Savigny-Stiftung für Rechtsgeschichte, kanonistische Abteilung* 93 (2007), 1–33.

11 Greta Austin, *Shaping Church Law around the Year 1000: The* Decretum *of Burchard of Worms*, Church, Faith and Culture in the Medieval West (Aldershot, 2009); Christof Rolker, "The Collection in Seventy-Four Titles: A Monastic Canon Law Collection from Eleventh-Century France," in *Readers, Texts and Compilers in the Earlier Middle Ages: Studies in Medieval Canon Law in Honour of Linda Fowler-Magerl*, ed. Martin Brett and

of these collections not only gathered older material, they also created new knowledge by selecting and combining the older material into new collections: Burchard altered the wording and varied the rubrics to highlight the importance of bishops, but he also generated a new legal problem for the church to tackle by dedicating a complete book to incest; the compiler of the *Collection in 74 Titles* rephrased Pseudo-Isidorian canons and even merged independently appearing sentences in order to shape new legal ideas; and Deusdedit used the refined technique of a *capitulatio* to extend the meaning of texts.[12] All of these authors used, more or less frankly, the early medieval methods of selecting, rephrasing, altering, shortening, rubricating, structuring, or even forging in order to create texts that supported their view of the world. In doing so, they altered older and created new knowledge.[13]

This process did not stop at the end of the eleventh or at the beginning of the twelfth century. Gratian, for instance, formulated a new understanding of normative texts in his attempt to harmonize conflicting rules, and so did the later decretists and decretalists in their glosses, *summae, casus, notabilia* and collections of decretals. No doubt, the methodological approaches changed from a 'word-by-word analysis' into a sophisticated interpretation of older texts, but the phenomenon—the supplanting, transformation and creation of knowledge—remained the same.[14]

The redactive layers of Gratian's *Decretum* allows us to have a closer look at legal knowledge and its presentation in both versions and to compare them in order to illuminate the approach of its two 'authors'. This study focuses on the example of clerical celibacy which was addressed by the 'Gratians' in their first *Distinctiones*-part. It is aimed at demonstrating the different attitudes

---

Kathleen G. Cushing, Church, Faith and Culture in the Medieval West (Aldershot, 2009), pp. 59–72; Stephan Dusil, *Wissensordnungen des Rechts im Wandel. Päpstlicher Jurisdiktionsprimat und Zölibat zwischen 1000 und 1215*, Mediaevalia Lovaniensia 47 (Leuven, 2018), pp. 79–117.

12 The example of Burchard is given by Christof Rolker, "The Hot and the Cold Language: Incest Discourses in the Twelfth and Thirteenth Centuries," in *Proceedings of the Fourteenth International Congress of Medieval Canon Law, Toronto, 5–11 August 2012*, ed. Joseph W. Goering et al., MIC Subsidia 15 (Vatican City, 2016), pp. 651–65, esp. pp. 657–60. On the other examples see Dusil, *Wissensordnungen* (see above, n. 11), pp. 117–66.

13 See Dusil, *Wissensordnungen* (see above, n. 11), esp. pp. 162–6.

14 It was Peter Landau, "Gefälschtes Recht in den Rechtssammlungen bis Gratian," in *Fälschungen im Mittelalter. Internationaler Kongreß der Monumenta Germaniae Historica, München, 16.–19. September 1986*, 2: *Gefälschte Rechtstexte. Der bestrafte Fälscher*, Schriften der Monumenta Germaniae historica 33/2 (Hanover, 1988), pp. 11–49, at p. 49 who stated very pointedly: "Der Erfolg des Decretum Gratiani zeigte sich nicht zuletzt darin, daß der Fälscher nicht mehr gebraucht wurde, damit das Recht seine Ordnungsaufgaben erfüllten konnte; an seine Stelle trat der geschulte Jurist."

towards legal knowledge: whereas Gratian 1 drafted a concise treatise in order to introduce the reader to legal argumentation, Gratian 2 compiled a book reminiscent of an older canonical collection in order to provide a repository of normative knowledge.

2 Clerical Celibacy in the Two Versions of Gratian's *Decretum*

Clerical celibacy was a much discussed topic around 1100. Together with simony and the investiture of clerics, it was one of the most hotly debated issues in the second half of the eleventh century, during the so-called Gregorian Reform. The church, driven by the papacy, strove to enforce the continence of major clerics. To the major order belonged (sub)deacons, priests, and bishops who were all forbidden from being sexually active after being ordained, although their already existing marriages remained valid due to the sacramental character of such a union. It was strictly forbidden, however, to enter into a new marriage once having received major orders.[15]

Newly promulgated conciliar decisions and papal decretals drew on the older legislation of late Antiquity and the early Middle Ages; nonetheless, the frequency with which the prohibitions were repeated increased dramatically: Pope Leo IX (1049–1054), Pope Nicholas II (1059–1061), and Pope Gregory VII (1073–1085) all ruled on clerical continence, and even went beyond the older rules, as they tried to stop incontinent priests from celebrating the Holy Service and prohibited the faithful from attending the masses they

15 Literature on celibacy is abundant; see for instance Martin Boelens, *Die Klerikerehe in der Gesetzgebung der Kirche unter besonderer Berücksichtigung der Strafe. Eine rechtsgeschichtliche Untersuchung von den Anfängen der Kirche bis zum Jahre 1139* (Paderborn, 1968); Roger Gryson, *Les origines du célibat ecclésiastique du premier au septième siècle*, Recherches et synthèses, section d'histoire 2 (Gembloux, 1970); Filippo Liotta, *La continenza dei chierici nel pensiero canonistico classico da Graziano a Gregorio IX*, Quaderni di "Studi Senesi" 24 (Milan, 1971); Christian Cochini, *Apostolic Origins of Priestly Celibacy* (San Francisco, 1990); Roman Cholij, *Clerical Celibacy in East and West* (Herefordshire, 1989); Georg Denzler, *Die Geschichte des Zölibats* (Freiburg, Basel, and Vienna, 1993); Alfons Maria Stickler, *Der Klerikerzölibat. Seine Entwicklungsgeschichte und seine theologischen Grundlagen* (Abensberg, 1993); *Medieval Purity and Piety: Essays on Medieval Clerical Celibacy and Religious Reform*, ed. Michael Frassetto (New York and London, 1998); Richard M. Price, "Zölibat. II. Kirchengeschichtlich," in *Theologische Realenzyklopädie*, 36 vols (Berlin, 1976–2004), 36:722–39; William E. Phipps, *Clerical Celibacy. The Heritage* (New York and London, 2004); Helen Parish, *Clerical Celibacy in the West: c. 1100–1700*, Catholic Christendom 1300–1700 (Farnham, 2010).

celebrated.[16] Gregory VII, in particular, vigorously strove to implement these rules in daily church life: for instance, he released the faithful in Konstanz from an oath sworn to the local bishop, and forced other bishops to fight the incontinence of clerics by threating to depose them.[17] Even though the rules on continence were already established in older decisions, their vehement enforcement in the eleventh century marks an unprecedented development. The rule-making against unchaste clerics came to a preliminary end in 1139 when the Second Lateran Council not only prohibited marriages that followed an ordination, but also declared these marriages invalid.[18] This decision later

16 On Pope Leo IX see Boelens, *Klerikerehe*, pp. 120–21, 125, 135–37 and Anne Llewellyn Barstow, *Married Priests and the Reforming Papacy: The Eleventh-Century Debates*, Texts and Studies in Religion 12 (New York and Toronto, 1982), pp. 49–56. See the conciliar decision of Pope Nicholas II (*Vigilantia universalis*, c. 3, JL 4405, 4406), ed. Ludwig Weiland, MGH Const. 1, pp. 546–48 (no. 384), here at p. 547: "Ut nullus missam audiat presbyteri, quem scit concubinam indubitanter habere aut subintroductam mulierem. Unde etiam ipsa sancta synodus hoc capitulum sub excommunicatione statuit, dicens: Quicunque sacerdotum, diaconorum, subdiaconorum post constitutum beatae memoriae predecessoris nostri sanctissimi Leonis papae de castitate clericorum, concubinam palam duxerit vel ductam non reliquerit, ex parte omnipotentis Dei auctoritate beatorum apostolorum Petri et Pauli precipimus et omnino contradicimus, ut missam non cantet neque evangelium vel epistolam ad missam legat, neque in presbyterio ad divina officia cum iis qui praefatae constitutioni obędientes fuerint maneat, neque partem ab aecclesia suscipiat, quousque a nobis sententia super huiusmodi Deo concedente procedat."

17 On Gregory VII see Uta-Renate Blumenthal, "Pope Gregory VII and the Prohibition of Nicolaitism," in *Medieval Purity and Piety* (see above, n. 15), pp. 239–67 and Herbert E.J. Cowdrey, "Pope Gregory VII and the Chastity of the Clergy," ibid., pp. 269–302. The example of the bishop of Konstanz is mentioned by Helmut Maurer, "Die Konstanzer Bürgerschaft im Investiturstreit," in *Investiturstreit und Reichsverfassung*, ed. Josef Fleckenstein, Vorträge und Forschungen 17 (Sigmaringen, 1973), pp. 363–71, at p. 366. On the threat of Gregory VII to depose bishops see the decision of the Roman synod (1078 November 10, c. 12 / 28), ed. Erich Caspar, MGH Epp. sel. 2/1, pp. 400–06 (no. 6.5b), here at pp. 405–06: "Si quis episcopus fornicationem presbyterorum diaconorum seu subdiaconorum vel crimen incestus in sua parroechia precibus vel pretio interveniente consenserit vel commissum sibique compertum auctoritate sui officii non inpugnaverit, ab officio suspendatur."

18 Second Lateran Council, 1139, c. 7 in *Conciliorum Oecumenicorum Decreta*, ed. Giuseppe Alberigo et al., 3rd ed. (Bologna, 1973), p. 198 / COGD II/1, 106): "Ad haec praedecessorum nostrorum Gregorii VII, Urbani et Paschalis Romanorum pontificum vestigiis inhaerentes, praecipimus ut nullus missas eorum audiat, quos uxores vel concubinas habere cognoverit. Ut autem lex continentiae et Deo placens munditia in ecclesiasticis personis et sacris ordinibus dilatetur, statuimus quatenus episcopi presbyteri diaconi subdiaconi regulares canonici et monachi atque conversi professi, qui sanctum transgredientes propositum uxores sibi copulare praesumpserint, separentur. Huiusmodi namque copulationem, quam contra ecclesiasticam regulam constat esse contractam, matrimonium non esse censemus." The decision of the Second Lateran Council is based

became the cornerstone for the characterization of the ordination as diriment impediment.[19]

Chastity played a crucial role in the first part of the *Decretum Gratiani*, the so-called *distinctions*-part. The masterplan of Gratian 1 in these *distinctiones* was aimed at explaining the requirements for a consecration with aid of the letter of Paul to Timothy. The apostle Paul had given a description of how an ideal bishop should be, namely temperate, self-controlled, respectable, hospitable, able to teach, not a drunkard, not quarrelsome—and 'husband of one wife' ('unius uxoris vir').[20] These requirements were used by Gratian to structure this first part. It is in D. 26 to D. 34 that Gratian scrutinizes the meaning of 'unius uxoris vir'. The way in which the two versions of the *Decretum* deal with the continence of higher clerics in this section points to their different approaches to legal knowledge.

2.1 *The First Version of the* Decretum

The first version of the *Decretum Gratiani* (composed between 1120 and 1140[21]) starts with the explanation of 'husband of one wife' in D. 26. Gratian's first concern is bigamy, whereby he meant the subsequent marriage of a clergy candidate who had already been married.[22] Men in a second marriage as well as those married to widows, Gratian asserted, were not allowed to be ordained (D. 26). Then, he moved on to the understanding of this Pauline expression as referring to the continence of priests. Gratian 1 demonstrated that clerics ought to profess continence before their ordination (D. 27, c. 1 to D. 27, d.p.c. 1) and keep this continence afterwards (D. 28 to 32). Otherwise, they were threatened with removal from office and loss of benefices.[23] In this part, Gratian also touched upon some topics which were more loosely related to continence. He raised the

on the Council of Pisa in 1135, as printed in *Sacrorum conciliorum nova et amplissima collectio*, ed. Giovanni D. Mansi, 31 vols (Venice, 1758–78), 19:487–92, here at cols 489–90.

19 See, for instance, Stickler, *Klerikerzölibat* (see above, n. 15), p. 34.

20 1 Tim 3.

21 The precise dating of the versions remains under discussion: whereas some espouse a late date for the first version (namely 1139 or later), other prefer an early date, possibly as early as 1120. The question is of lesser importance for this paper. On this discussion see Eichbauer, "Gratian's Decretum" (see above, n. 4), pp. 1115–16. The second version is unanimously dated to the 1140s.

22 A preliminary edition of the first version of the *Decretum* is now available online at https://sites.google.com/a/yale.edu/decretumgratiani/home (last access 2018 July 13). A list of canons was previously published by Anders Winroth, *The Making of Gratian's Decretum*, Cambridge Studies in Medieval Life and Thought, Fourth Series 49 (Cambridge, 2000), pp. 197–227.

23 Gratian touched upon celibacy again in D. 81, c. 6 and D. 84, c. 3, the so-called 'epilogue'.

question of whether a marriage entered into *after* a vow of chastity was valid or not, and answered this question by distinguishing between 'votum simplex' and 'votum solemne'. Only the latter nullified the subsequent marriage.[24] He also discussed with whom a cleric may live together lest he was endangered by carnal desire;[25] and, furthermore, explained that continence did not mean that a cleric was no longer responsible for his wife and his children (since the marriage remained valid!), but that he was obliged to maintain them.[26] Finally, Gratian 1 drew on more recent legislation to compile his *Decretum* and added the decretal by Pope Alexander II according to which all faithful should eschew the Holy Service of incontinent priests.[27] In sum, the first version of the *Decretum* reflects the normative rules of the first half of the twelfth century rather accurately. Clerics in minor orders were allowed to marry and to have intercourse, whereas clerics in higher orders (starting with the subdeaconate) needed to abstain from their wives, although their marriages remained valid.

The path to reach this result, however, was winding. Gratian 1 faced a diverse tradition of canons, some prohibiting any sexual activity, some allowing deacons and priests to be married and to have intercourse, and some distinguishing between subdeacons and deacons on the one hand and priests and bishops on the other. Gratian did not conceal these different legal traditions, but presented them frankly and tried to reconcile them. How did he do this?

D. 28, to start with, is a pivotal example of the dialectic *sic et non*-method used by Gratian to reconcile conflicting canons.[28] He first presented different canons to prove the assertion that even subdeacons needed to swear an oath of chastity (D. 28, c. 1, c. 6, c. 7, and d.p.c. 7), before introducing seemingly contradictory canons. The Council of Ankara (314), for instance, granted deacons the possibility of reserving the right of a later marriage; and the conciliar decision of Neocaesarea (today Niksar, Turkey; 314/325) punished the incontinent priest, but not the incontinent (sub)deacon (D. 28, c. 8, c. 9).[29]

24 D. 27, cc. 2–9.

25 D. 32, cc. 16–18.

26 D. 31, cc. 10 and 11.

27 D. 32, c. 6.

28 See, for instance, John F. McCarthy, "The Genius of Concord in Gratian's *Decree*," *Ephemerides Iuris Canonici* 19 (1963), 105–51 and 259–95.

29 D. 28, c. 8: "Diaconi non prohibeantur a ministerio pro nuptiis, si in ordinatione dicunt, se continere non posse. // Diaconi quicumque ordinantur, si in ipsa ordinatione protestati sunt, dicentes, se uelle habere uxores, nec posse se continere, hi, si postea ad nuptias uenerint, maneant in ministerio, propterea quod his licentiam dederit episcopus. Quicumque sane tacuerint, et susceperint manus inpositionem professi continentiam, si postea ad nuptias conuenerint, a ministerio cessare debent."; D. 28, c. 9: "Presbiter ducens

After gathering further contradictory canons, Gratian 1 presented his solution: both the council of Neocaesarea and Ankara are to be understood *ex tempore* as well as *ex loco* (D. 28, d.p.c. 13). First, they were peculiar to early Christianity as chastity had not yet been introduced ("ex tempore, quia nondum introducta erat continentia ministrorum altaris"), and, second, they belonged to the councils of the Eastern Church in which a vow of chastity was unknown ("ex loco quia utraque sinodus orientalis est, et orientalis ecclesia non suscipit generale votum castitatis"). Having resolved this first difficulty, Gratian 1 complicated this issue by proposing that the canonical rules anathematized not only the priests who despised their wives, but also the faithful who disregarded the Holy Service of a married priest.[30] Obviously, these assertions—taken from the *Canones apostolorum* and the Council of Gangra—blatantly contradicted the required chastity of higher clerics and the recent papal legislation.

The methodological approach used by Gratian 1 to tackle these contradictory traditions is set out in D. 29 where he called upon 'Isidore' to limit the scope of canons: "Sed notandum est, quod secundum Ysidorum pleraque capitula ex causa, et loco, et tempore, consideranda sunt."[31] Knowledge of the cause, the time, and the place of a canon's origin was necessary to fully understand its meaning and legal scope as a normative text, Gratian's Isidore programmatically stated. These so-called circumstances allowed a precise interpretation of each canon. Although the origin of this statement must remain untold,[32] its function is clear: it serves as the starting point for an in-depth analysis of the diverse traditions of chastity.

Gratian 1 started his analysis of contradictory canons by reminding the reader that the *Canones Apostolorum* and the decision of the Council of Gangra must be read with regard to cause—and here he meant the circumstances that led to the making of the rule—and time.[33] To this end, he shed light on

---

uxorem, ab ordine deponatur / Item ex Concilio Neocesariensi. [c. 1]. // Presbiter si uxorem duxerit, ab ordine illum deponi debere. Quod si fornicatus fuerit, uel adulterium commiserit, extra ecclesiam abici et ad penitentiam inter laicos redigi oportet."

30 D. 28, c. 14: "Si quis docuerit, sacerdotem sub obtentu religionis propriam uxorem contempnere, anathema sit."; D. 28, c. 15: "Si quis discernit presbiterum coniugatum, tanquam occasione nuptiarum quod offere non debeat, et ab eius oblatione ideo abstinet, anathema sit."

31 D. 29, d.p.c. 1.

32 On D. 29 and esp. D. 29, c. 1 see Peter Landau, "Apokryphe Isidoriana bei Gratian," in *Vita Religiosa im Mittelalter. Festschrift für Kaspar Elm zum 70. Geburtstag*, ed. Franz J. Felten and Nikolas Jaspert, Berliner Historische Studien 31, Ordensstudien 13 (Berlin, 1999), pp. 837–44; Dusil, *Wissensordnungen* (see above, n. 11), pp. 400–4.

33 On the structure, see Lenherr, "Handschrift 673" (see above, n. 5).

the background of these two rules: the cause for the canons, Gratian stated, was Manichaeism whose followers despised marriages ("causa fuit heresis Manicheorum, que coniugium detestabatur"; D. 30, d.p.c. 1); and the time was one in which the continence of clerics had not yet been instituted ("tempus quia nondum erat institutum, ut sacerdotes continentiam servarent"; D. 31, d.p.c. 1). Afterwards, Gratian 1 took up the idea of the place ('locus') in order to limit the applicability of certain canons. He expounded that a canon of the Quinisext Council (691/692) can be understood as a specific rule made for the Eastern Church, as the Eastern Church has never forced clerics to a chaste life ("hoc autem ex loco intelligendum est. Orientalis enim ecclesia [...] votum castitatis in ministris altaris non suscepit"; D. 31, d.p.c. 13; see D. 28, d.p.c. 13).[34] Gratian repeated this pattern of argumentation throughout the D. 28 to D. 32. The circumstances of cause, time, and place helped him to show that the more lenient rules were no longer adequate for the Western Church of the twelfth century and to underpin the stricter rules of the Western Church. The decisions of the Councils of Gangra and Ankara and of the Quinisext Synode were either outdated, historical rules, or foreign, belonging to the Eastern Church; in any case, they were not applicable in the Western Church.

In his dense discussion of chastity, Gratian not only offered an interpretation of canons according to their circumstances, but also a thorough word-for-word analysis. The canon that prompted Gratian to reflect on the wording, was the aforementioned decision of the Council of Gangra according to which wives were not to be despised by their husbands-clerics (D. 28, c. 14).[35] The canon could also be interpreted in a different way, stated Gratian later (D. 31, d.p.c. 9), since the wife, who should not be condemned by the priest, was not necessarily married *after*, but could also be married *before* the ordination. Such a verbatim interpretation led Gratian to conclude that clerics ought to take care of their wives and support them and their children even after ordination; sexual intercourse, however, remained forbidden for all clerics in higher orders ("necessaria subministrare, debita vero reddere non valent"; D. 31, d.p.c. 11).

Provisionally, we can state that the section of the *Decretum* on chastity consists of a thorough analysis of divergent ecclesiastical traditions whose canons are interpreted according to the circumstances of cause, time, and place, in addition to verbatim interpretations. The observation that D. 27 to D. 32 form one unit is underlined by the lack of any partition, since the

34 On the Quinisext Council see Heinz Ohme, *Concilium Quinisextum / Das Konzil Quinisextum, griechisch-deutsch*, Fontes Christiani 82 (Turnhout, 2006), esp. pp. 137–47 and Cholij, *Clerical Celibacy* (see above, n. 15).

35 D. 28, c. 14 (see above, n. 30).

manuscripts of the first version (nor the early of the second version) do not carry the later division into distinctions.[36] Gratian intended this section to be a single unit.

The way that Gratian 1 worked comes more fully into view if one takes into consideration the structure of the collection which formed the basis for Gratian's first version. D. 31 and D. 32 are heavily based on the *Panormia*, a popular canonical collection that was compiled between 1094 and 1116/18, most likely around 1115 in Northern France.[37] Chastity is addressed in canons 84 to 115 of its third book. A closer look at this part of the *Panormia* reveals its division into three units. The compiler started with the observation that both churches, the Eastern and the Western, have different traditions ("Aliter se habet orientalium traditio ecclesiarum, aliter huius sancte romane ecclesie", c. 84).[38] The ensuing canons present these different legal traditions, since the more lenient rules of the Eastern Church (cc. 85–88) were confronted with the stricter rules of the Western Church (cc. 89–115). The first canon, *Aliter se habet*, serves therefore as an interpretative guideline for this part: the different place of the origin of these canons explains the different treatment of sexuality. But this is the only hint offered by the compiler of the *Panormia* of how to reconcile the conflicting rules. He did not interpret the canons individually, disclose a consistent solution for their harmonization, or make the rather rudimentary dialect structure (*sic et non*) explicit.

How did Gratian 1 realign the canons of the *Panormia*? One need to distinguish between D. 31 and D. 32: not many changes can be found in the latter whose second part follows the line of thought of the *Panormia* rather closely (D. 32, cc. 9–18; the first part, namely D. 32 cc. 1–8, is heavily based on

36 See Franz Gillmann, "Rührt die Distinktioneneinteilung des ersten und des dritten Dekretteils von Gratian selbst her?," *Archiv für Katholisches Kirchenrecht* 112 (1932), 504–33, esp. pp. 519–21. The standard edition by Friedberg is in this regard misleading and presents the text in a fragmented manner. See Figure 8.1.

37 On the dating of the *Panormia* see Christof Rolker, *Canon Law and the Letters of Ivo of Chartres*, Cambridge Studies in Medieval Life and Thought, Fourth Series 76 (Cambridge, 2010), pp. 272–84. A provisional edition of the *Panormia* by Martin Brett and Bruce Brasington is available at http://ivo-of-chartres.github.io/panormia.html (last access 2018 July 13). A brief introduction and a list of manuscripts is provided by Linda Fowler-Magerl, *Clavis Canonum: Selected Canon Law Collections before 1140: Access with Data Processing*, MGH Hilfsmittel 21 (Munich, 2005), pp. 198–202 and Lotte Kéry, *Canonical Collections of the Early Middle Ages (ca. 400–1140): A Bibliographical Guide to the Manuscripts and Literature*, History of Medieval Canon law (Washington, D.C., 1999), pp. 253–60.

38 *Panormia* 3.84: "Aliter se habet orientalium traditio ecclesiarum, aliter huius sancte Romane ecclesie. Nam eorum sacerdotes, presbiteri scilicet, diaconi atque subdiaconi, matrimonio copulantur. Istius autem ecclesie vel occidentalium, nullus sacerdotum a subdiaconis usque ad episcopum licentiam habet coniugium sortiendi."

excerpts from the *Tripartita*).[39] In contrast to D. 32, Gratian fundamentally realigned the material he used from the Panormia in D. 31. Instead of the simple *sic et non*-structure of his source, he discussed the canons individually and declared them as rulings related to time, place, and cause respectively, and, most importantly, he turned the *Panormia* upside down. The starting canon, *Aliter se habet* (c. 84), became the last canon in D. 31 as c. 14, thereby changing its function: whereas the canon served as methodological programme in the *Panormia*, Gratian used it only to foster the *ex loco*-interpretation that stands next to the *ex tempore* and the *ex causa*-interpretations. In contrast to the compiler of the *Panormia*, who worked only with the *ex loco*-circumstance, Gratian 1 had three circumstances at hand which offered a wider range of interpretations. In addition to this, his own the interpretative guideline was explicitly offered in D. 29, where he referred to the programme by Isidore. One can therefore conclude that Gratian 1 substantially developed and expanded what was presented by the compiler of the *Panormia*; briefly, Gratian 1 made explicit what was previously implicitly presented.

TABLE 7.1 Formal sources of D. 31 and D. 32 of Gratian's *Decretum*

D. 31, c. 1	*Panormia* c. 3.89
D. 31, c. 2	*Panormia* c. 3.92
D. 31, c. 3	*Panormia* c. 3.93
D. 31, c. 4	*Panormia* c. 3.94
D. 31, c. 5	only second version
D. 31, c. 6	*Panormia* c. 3.95
D. 31, c. 7	*Panormia* c. 3.96
D. 31, c. 8	unkown source
D. 31, c. 9	unkown source
D. 31, c. 10	*Panormia* c. 3.106 or *Tripartia* c. 1.43.10
D. 31, c. 11	*Panormia* c. 3.115
D. 31, c. 12	*Panormia* c. 3.85
D. 31, c. 13	*Panormia* c. 3.86
D. 31, c. 14	*Panormia* c. 3.84
D. 32, c. 1	*Polycarpus* c. 4.32.28
D. 32, c. 2	*Palea*
D. 32, c. 3	*Tripartita* c. 1.55.87
D. 32, c. 4	*Tripartita* c. 1.62.45

39 See table 8.1.

TABLE 7.1 (*cont.*)

D. 32, c. 5	only second version
D. 32, c. 6a	*Tripartita* c. 1.66.2.3
D. 32, c. 6b	only second version
D. 32, c. 7	*Tripartita* c. 2.11.2
D. 32, c. 8	*Tripartita* c. 2.17.11
D. 32, c. 9	*Panormia* c. 3.99
D. 32, c. 10	*Panormia* c. 3.101
D. 32, c. 11	*Panormia* c. 3.103
D. 32, c. 12	*Panormia* c. 3.104
D. 32, c. 13	*Panormia* c. 3.105
D. 32, c. 14	*Panormia* c. 3.107
D. 32, c. 15	*Panormia* c. 3.110
D. 32, c. 16	*Panormia* c. 3.112
D. 32, c. 17	*Palea*
D. 32, c. 18	*Panormia* c. 3.114
D. 32, c. 19	only second version

Table of the *fontes formales* of D. 31 and D. 32 of the first version of Gratian's *Decretum*[40]

In sum, we can state that the first version of Gratian 1 is a rather lean, to-the-point treatise in which he discussed the divergent legal traditions of the Eastern and Western churches. In contrast to the *Panormia,* he disclosed the contradictions and revealed the discrepancies explicitly. He tried to reconcile the contradictory legal opinions by explaining the background of the canons and their original motive ('causa') as well as time ('tempus') and place ('locus') of their origin. The knowledge that Gratian 1 revealed in the first version reflects the common knowledge of continence in the early twelfth century; its presentation, however, is in comparison to older collections such as the *Panormia* groundbreakingly new.

40 This table is based on Lenherr, "Handschrift 673" (see above, n. 5).

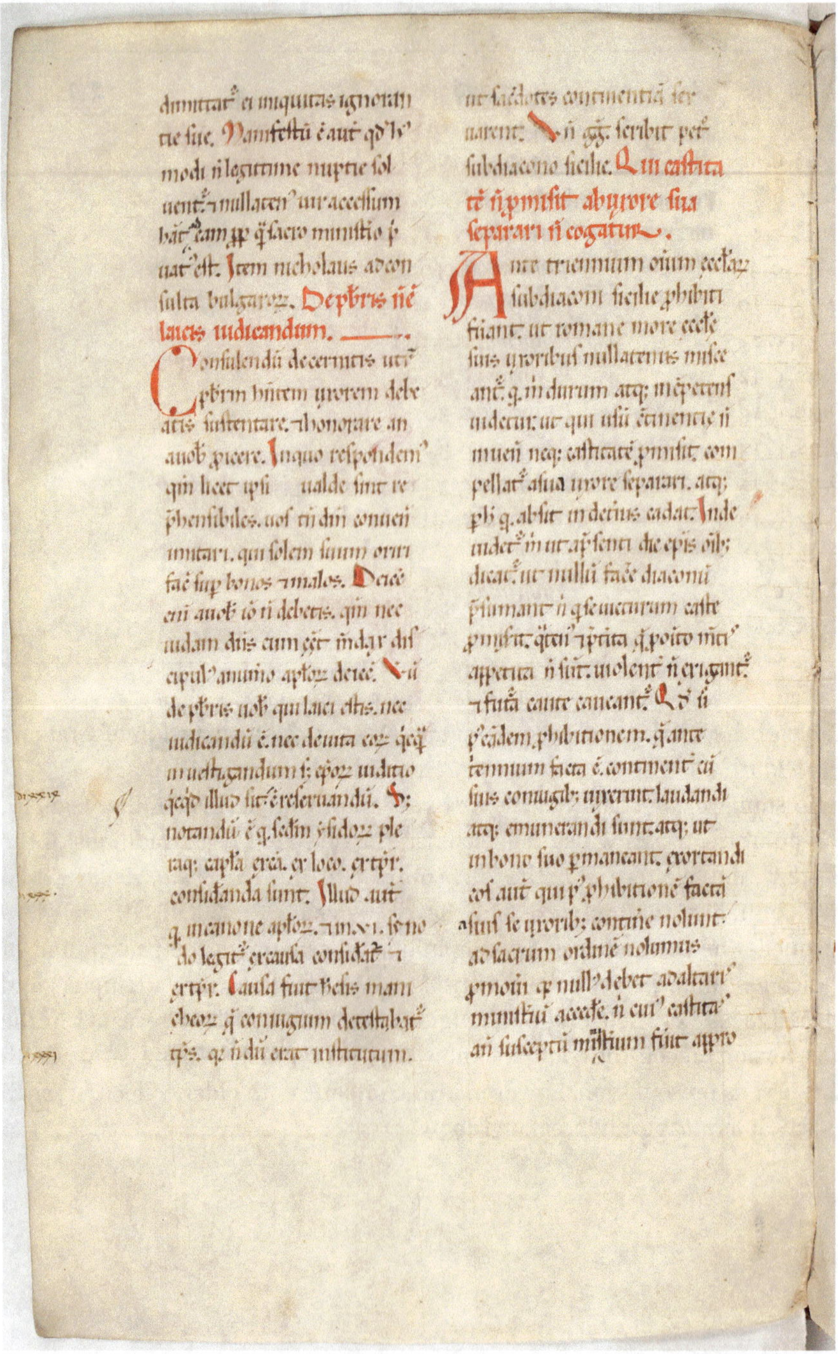

FIGURE 8.1 Paris, Bibliothèque nationale, nouvelles acquisitions françaises 1761, fol. 29v: manuscript of the first recension. The image shows the later D. 29; the *Distinctiones* were later added in margin.

2.2 *The Second Version of the* Decretum

Gratian 2 heavily reworked Gratian 1's section on the chastity of clerics: he added canons, doubled existing ones, and even incorporated a long chain of seventeen new canons. Thereby, Gratian 2 effectively destroyed the explanation of the methodology by Gratian 1 in D. 29 and D. 30, where he distinguished normative texts according to cause, time, and place. What did Gratian 2 do?

The amended version of D. 29 aligns somewhat with the structure of Gratian 1, since Gratian 2 added three canons to back up the methodological statement of Isidore; the first, an—obviously—pseudo-Isidorian canon, reiterated almost verbatim the statement of Gratian 1,[41] the second, a canon attributed to Gregory that reads: "Regule sanctorum patrum pro tempore, loco et persona negotio instante necessitate tradite sunt."[42] In contrast to the first two canons, the third canon was an authentic excerpt from St Jerome. Jerome had explained in the prologue to his commentary on the letter to the Ephesians that writings have—according to the diversity of time, places, and people—different causes, arguments and origins.[43] In his revised D. 29, therefore, Gratian 2 underlined with further, though (at least partly) suspect authorities the methodological programme set out by Gratian 1.

The ensuing D. 30, however, was substantially re-worked. Gratian 2 was prompted by the reference of Gratian 1 to the heresy of Manichaeism to add a chain of seventeen canons in which he reported the decisions of the council of Gangra that fought the Manichaean teachings on marriage, conventions, and alimentation. In short, he inflated a brief remark on the *causa* to the divagating and verbose later D. 30. This interpolation interrupts the line of thought of Gratian 1 and goes off-topic, from chastity to the heresies of a minor group in early Christianity.[44]

In contrast to D. 30, D. 31 remained mostly intact.[45] In D. 32, however, Gratian 2 succumbed once again to the temptation to discuss whether the sacraments of heretics were valid or not, a debate he associatively linked with

---

41 On D. 29, c. 1 see Landau, "Apokryphe Isidoriana" (see above, n. 32) and Dusil, *Wissensordnungen* (see above, n. 1), pp, 400–4.

42 This canon was presumably excerpted from the *Collection in Three Books* as *fons formalis* (c. 2.34.22), although it is also transmitted in the collection Bb of Anselm of Lucca. See *Anselmi episcopi Lucensis collectio canonum una cum collectione minore*, ed. Friedrich Thaner (Innsbruck 1906–15), p. 222 n. ad c. 3.50 and *Collectio canonum trium librorum*, 2: *Liber III*, ed. Joseph Motta, MIC Corpus collectionum 8/2 (Vatican City, 2008), p. 449. The *fons materialis*, however, remains unknown. The chapter was partly described as *capitulum incertum* of Gregory I (JE † 1944), partly ascribed to the time of Gregory VII (see Landau, "Apokryphe Isidoriana" (see above, n. 32), p. 839 n. 9).

43 Jerome, *In epistolam ad Ephesios*, ed. PL 26:439–554, here at 440C–441A.

44 D. 30, d.p.c. 1 (starting with "sicut etiam quorundam") to c. 17.

45 The only exception is the short reference in D. 31, d.p.c. 11 ("hinc et illud—require infra").

the prohibition to attend the Service of married priests.[46] The importance of this prohibition to Gratian 2 is evidenced by his doubling of the proscription. The canon taken up by Gratian 1 was based on the decisions of a council under the guidance of Pope Alexander II (D. 32, c. 6), who repeated the older ruling by Nicholas II (D. 32, c. 5).[47] *Nullus missam audiat* admonished, therefore, the faithful twice.

Gratian 2 not only reworked D. 26–43, but also a later section, namely C. 27, q. 1.[48] Here, he updated the *Decretum* with the more recent legislation of the Second Lateran Council in 1139, adding the decision according to which marriages of higher clerics, entered into after the ordination, are invalid. It was this formulation of the Second Lateran Council that was later called a diriment impediment and formed a pillar of clerical chastity.[49] The place chosen for this addition seems appropriate as the question of whether the vow forms an impediment is at the heart of C. 27, even though this question had already been touched upon in D. 27, d.p.c. 1 to c. 9. Distinctio 27, however, remained a stub.

In sum, Gratian 2 continued qua content along the lines of Gratian 1; only his inclusion of the decision of the Second Lateran Council marks a new aspect in the discussion of clerical celibacy. Qua presentation, however, Gratian 2 destroyed the compelling presentation of the first version: he doubled canons, joined new texts, and interrupted the line of thought by adding canons which were more loosely related to the topic. In doing so, he extended the first version with associatively linked discussions but also fundamentally changed the way in which legal knowledge was presented.

3 Conclusion

Years ago, the French canonist Jean Gaudemet analysed the presentation of celibacy in Gratian's *Decretum* and was surprised, almost disappointed, by the confusing and even fuzzy argumentation that the master Gratian had offered:

---

46 In D. 32, new are: c. 5, the discussion on sacraments in c. 6 ("Verum principia harum auctoritatum—ad penitentiam prouocantur") and also c. 19. D. 32, c. 2 and c. 17 are *paleae*, see Jürgen Buchner, *Die Paleae im Dekret Gratians. Untersuchung ihrer Echtheit*, Pontificum Athenaeum Antonianum 127 (Rome, 2000), p. 319.

47 D. 32, c. 5 and c. 6; on these canons, see above n. 16.

48 Gratian 2, however, dit not elaborate on the epilogue; he just included D. 84, c. 3 that enforced bishops, priests, and deacons to live chastely, but not subdeacons.

49 Stephan Dusil, "The Emerging Jurisprudence, the Second Lateran Council of 1139 and the Development of Canonical Impediments," in *The Use of Canon Law in Ecclesiastical Administration, 1000–1234*, ed. Melodie Harris Eichbauer and Danica Summerlin, Medieval Law and its Practice (Leiden, 2018), questioning the importance of this canon in the later Jurisprudence, pp. 140–158.

> Soucieux de donner beaucoup de textes, Gratien a peut-être été quelque peu dérouté par leurs divergences. Les *dicta* auraient pu lui offrir l'occasion de classer les solutions et de proposer des choix. Le Maître ne s'y guère employé.[50]

Gaudemet described an observation that is also at the heart of this paper, but it became clear that Gratian 1 is not to blame for all these divergences, but Gratian 2. In a similar vein, Gratian 2 was characterized as "plus prolixe" and someone "qui n'hésite pas à se perdre [...] dans toutes sortes de digressions", whereas the first version was "plus incisive, moins verbeuse, plus convaincante."[51] Other scholars underlined these findings by presenting further instances of how distorted the arguments of the first version became in the second version.[52]

Although the original purpose of Gratian's *Decretum* must remain shadowy, it seems to be widely accepted that it was born out of a classroom atmosphere, designed as a teaching tool aimed at introducing curious young men to the tradition of these normative texts.[53] Presumably, the *Decretum* was written for 'theological readers' rather than lawyers, since it is observed that Gratian 1 was more a (penitential) theologian than a lawyer.[54] If this is true, it is not very surprising that Gratian 1 presents a rather lean and concise text on the

---

50 Jean Gaudemet, "Gratien et le célibat ecclésiastique," *Studia Gratiana* 13 (1967), 339–69, p. 368.

51 Jean Werckmeister, "Les deux versions" (see anove, n. 4), p. 311: "Probablement faut-il parler de deux auteurs: le premier Gratien, auteur de la version courte, qui a le sens de la concision et qui répond avec clarté aux questions posées. Le second (qui pourrait être collectif), plus prolixe et qui n"hésite pas à se perdre (et à égarer le lecteur) dans toutes sortes de digressions." Similarly, p. 306: "Globalement, la version courte, du fait même de sa plus grande cursivité, est plus incisive, moins verbeuse, plus convaincante."

52 See, for instance, José M. Viejo-Ximénez, "'Concordia' y 'Decretum' del maestro Graciano: in memoriam Rudolf Weigand," *Ius canonicum* 39 (1999), 333–57, esp. p. 340.

53 On the classrom atmosphere see Atria Ann Larson, *Master of Penance: Gratian and the Development of Penitential Thought and Law in the Twelfth Century*, Studies in Medieval and Early Modern Canon Law 11 (Washington, D.C., 2014), pp. 297–312; Christoph H.F. Meyer, *Die Distinktionstechnik in der Kanonistik des 12. Jahrhunderts. Ein Beitrag zur Wissenschaftsgeschichte des Hochmittelalters*, Mediaevalia Lovaniensia. Studia 29 (Leuven, 2000), p. 165; and Kenneth Pennington and Wolfgang P. Müller, "The Decretists: The Italian School," in *The History of Medieval Canon Law in the Classical Period: From Gratian to the Decretals of Pope Gregory IX*, ed. Wilfried Hartmann and Kenneth Pennington, History of Medieval Canon Law (Washington, D.C., 2008), pp. 121–73, who state at p. 121: "The *Decretum* began as a book for teaching, and it remained a text for the classroom."

54 On Gratian as penitential theologian see John C. Wei, *Gratian the Theologian*, Studies in Medieval and Early Modern Canon Law 13 (Washington, D.C., 2016). It remains doubtful whether the distinction in theologians and lawyers is useful before the end of the twelfth century, see Larson, *Master of Penance* (see above, n. 53), p. 490.

interpretation of law, especially since the discussion on chastity is the first place where Gratian discloses his methodological approach and where the reader encounters his methodology in practice. This might be the reason why Gratian dwelled on the argumentative foundations of chastity to such a great extent. It therefore seems—although this is impossible to prove—that this part had not only the function to present the debate on celibacy, but also to demonstrate how to argue convincingly and to harmonize seemingly incompatible canons. The discussion of chastity has therefore a central function in his book.

But what is the purpose of the longer, second version? Although a definitive answer to this question cannot be reached, the distortions and digressions lead to the idea that collecting normative texts was more important than the concise presentation and interpretation of the canons themselves. Canonical collections of the pre-Gratian era were—more or less—thematically structured, and offered a bulk of texts to the readers. It was up to the readers to find the appropriate text and to make use of it; the canonical collections stored knowledge rather than offering any guidance in the interpretation and thus the application of this knowledge.[55] The presentation of normative texts in Gratian 2 is reminiscent of this older presentation of legal knowledge: Gratian 2 added loosely related canons, overshadowed the line of thought, and disturbed the cogent discussion on the sexual behaviour of clerics. In contrast to Gratian 2, Gratian 1 raised questions, proved positions with statements, explained canons, reconciled the canonical tradition, and joined canons into a rather compelling treatise on celibacy.

The presentation of legal knowledge in the *Decretum* of Gratian is, therefore, twofold: in its first version, it is an introduction to the interpretation of normative texts; in its second version, it is a repository of normative texts that was to be interpreted elsewhere, namely in glosses and *summae*. In this way, the *Decretum* of Gratian appears Janus-faced, at the same time pointing the way to the interpretatorial future and looking back to the repositories of canonical knowledge.

---

55 On canonical collections see Paul Fournier, with the collaboration of Gabriel Le Bras, *Histoire des collections canoniques en Occident dépuis les Fausses Décrétales jusqu'au Décret de Gratien*, 2 vols (Paris, 1931–32); Gérard Fransen, *Les collections canoniques*, Typologie des sources du moyen âge occidental 10 (Turnhout, 1973); idem, *Les collections canoniques*, Typologie des sources du moyen âge occidental, Mise à jour du fascicule n° 10 (Turnhout, 1985); Kéry, *Canonical Collections* (see above, n. 37); Fowler-Magerl, *Clavis Canonum* (see above, n. 37).

CHAPTER 8

Using the 'Old Law' in Twelfth-Century Decretal Collections

Danica Summerlin

The years surrounding 1140 represent one of the most repeatedly-observed breaks in the history of canon law.* Scholars focus, by and large, on collections compiled either before or after 1140 although there are as always exceptions who focus more broadly on the period 1100 to 1250. Nevertheless, the idea that 1140 marked the end of something old and the beginning of something new remains fundamental to narratives of legal change in the Middle Ages. From the nineteenth century to the present, the pivot for this moment of change has been the appearance and dissemination of Gratian's *Decretum*, in one of its many versions. Gratian's collection and its effects have been referred to as critical to understanding how and why law changed. With a renewed interest in earlier collections evident over the last thirty years now is the time to ask how the later-twelfth century collections can be assimilated into the new narrative that is appearing following Anders Winroth's shake-up of work on Gratian in the mid-1990s.[1]

Most of the studies in this volume have looked at the period leading up to 1140, or have taken a broader, more general approach. Instead, I want to ask a very specific question: how significant was the change that affected the sources of canonical collections compiled in the period 1140 to 1234? To adopt a cliché, any chosen end-point has to be accompanied by a subsequent beginning, and a fundamental part of any argument positing Gratian as a critical pivot and the end of an old era presupposes that what followed was something new and different. That idea of Gratian as a major turning point, and in particular the catalyst for fundamental change, rests on a mixture of different rationales

* In this article, twelfth-century decretals are quoted by their numbers in Jaffé's *Regesta* and the Holtzmann-Kartei; if the decretal in question is not found there, this is indicated by 'JL –' and 'WH –', respectively.

The Holtzmann-Kartei is available online at http://www.kuttner-institute.jura.uni-muenchen.de/holtzmann_formular.htm. I would also like to thank the Leverhulme Trust and the British Academy for their support in funding the research that underpins this study.

1 Anders Winroth, *The Making of Gratian's Decretum*, Cambridge Studies in Medieval Life and Thought, Fourth Series 49 (Cambridge, 2000).

 | DOI:10.1163/9789004394384_010

and reasonings. The most succinct, enunciated by Landau, noted three fundamental reasons for the importance of the *Decretum Gratiani*: its ability to witness the depth and quality of contemporary intellectual horizons, the role that the *Decretum* played in distinguishing canon law in Latin Christendom from its eastern relative, and the *longue durée* of a collection which directly shaped a legal tradition. By using *dicta* and dialectic, Gratian contributed to the formation of 'a new legal science'.[2] In this, and implicitly, Landau was building on a simpler point: that the *Decretum* came to be quickly incorporated into the teaching curriculum of the schools, as shown by the speed with which glosses and *summae* appeared, and thus shaped the thought of the men who used it. Charles Duggan also saw the *Decretum*'s importance in terms of its eventual influence. In contrast to Landau, however, and perhaps influenced by a general distaste for Whig history present in post-war Anglophone academia, Duggan was more interested in the after-effects of the *Decretum*'s appearance. He stressed that "the academic success of Gratian's compendium [...] created the conditions for, and encouraged the emergence of, the so-called 'new law' ('ius novum'), based on current papal decisions and conciliar decrees."[3] Duggan and Landau, however, also show a more fundamental disjuncture: trained in law, Landau's argument builds on a *longue durée* interpretation of legal history, while Duggan, who was interested particularly in medieval English history, focussed on different aspects of the *Decretum*'s story.[4]

This study takes an unashamedly historical focus in investigating one of the after-effects of the *Decretum*'s popularity, and in particular the one which has received the most attention and, according to much traditional scholarship, had the greatest impact: the upsurge in the importance of papal decretals in medieval canon law, and the appearance of the decretal collections. It asks whether these presented something new and innovative in the context of

2 Peter Landau, "Gratian and the *Decretum Gratiani*," in *The History of Medieval Canon Law in the Classical Period: From Gratian to the Decretals of Pope Gregory IX*, ed. Wilfried Hartmann and Kenneth Pennington, History of Medieval Canon Law (Washington, D.C., 2008), pp. 22–54, at pp. 53–54.

3 Charles Duggan, "Decretal Collections from Gratian's *Decretum* to the *Compilationes antiquae*: The Making of the New Case Law," in *The History of Medieval Canon Law in the Classical Period: From Gratian to the Decretals of Pope Gregory IX*, ed. Wilfried Hartmann and Kenneth Pennington, History of Medieval Canon Law (Washington, D.C., 2008), pp. 246–92, at p. 247.

4 Something similar can be said for the debates surrounding marriage law under Alexander III, summarized for example in Charles Donahue, "Johannes Faventinus on Marriage," in *Medieval Church Law and the Origins of the Western Legal Tradition: A Tribute to Kenneth Pennington*, ed. Wolfgang P. Müller and Mary E. Sommar (Washington, D.C., 2006), pp. 179–97, at p. 195.

earlier canon law. All too often, the framing of this question leaves much to be desired: Charles Duggan, who used the term 'new law' ('ius novum') frequently, never explained where it came from and precisely why it became so critical, although he did at least make his definition clear. The first, and inevitably longest, section therefore focusses on the historiographical interpretations of the later-twelfth century collections, and particularly upon the process by which they came to be seen, by scholars of canon law and more broadly, as representing an entirely new formulation of law that appeared only after the widespread dissemination of the *Decretum* from 1140. The second segment looks at the decretal collections' development, before finally moving on to a broad analysis of the collections *en masse*, using them to investigate how far collections known to have been compiled after *c.*1140 were composed principally of later texts. As the starting point for a longer and more detailed investigation, it is necessarily brief yet wide-ranging; nevertheless, it hopefully represents a step toward a new appraisal of later-twelfth century canonical collections.

1 Gratian as a Pivot, and the Appearance of the Decretal Collections after *c.*1160

It is fairly well established that texts formalised in the years before 1140 continued to be used in the years that followed. Aside from the *Decretum* itself, which contained thousands of earlier texts, other collections continued to be seen as useful: many of the *paleae* added into later-twelfth century copies were taken directly or indirectly from Burchard of Worms' *Decretum*, while at least one copy of Burchard was copied after 1150.[5] Around a third of surviving *Panormia* manuscripts were copied after the mid-twelfth century, and some

5 On the *paleae*, see Rudolf Weigand, "Zusätzliche 'Paleae' in fünf Dekrethandschriften. Domenico Maffei zum 65. Geburtstag gewidmet," *Zeitschrift der Savigny-Stiftung für Rechtsgeschichte, kanonistische Abteilung* 78 (1992), 62–120; Rudolf Weigand, "Versuch einer neuen, differenzierten Liste der Paleae und Dubletten im Dekret Gratians," in *Life, Law and Letters: Historical Studies in Honour of Antonio García y García*, ed. Peter Linehan, Studia Gratiana 29 (Rome, 1998), pp. 883–99 with a list at pp. 897–99; most recently, Jürgen Buchner, *Die Paleae im Dekret Gratians. Untersuchung ihrer Echtheit*, Pontificum Athenaeum Antonianum 127 (Rome, 2000); for Reims, Bibliothèque municipale, 674 see most recently Peter Landau, "Die Dekretsumme 'Tractaturus Magister' und die Kanonistik in Reims in der zweiten Hälfte des 12. Jahrhunderts," *Zeitschrift der Savigny-Stiftung für Rechtsgeschichte, kanonistische Abteilung* 100 (2014), 132–52.

of these have gloss references to Gratian.[6] In studies on the twelfth-century decretal collections, however, references to these earlier texts are limited. Peter Landau demonstrated how certain decretal collections and some of the *summae* borrow extensively from earlier collections, but his studies remain brief introductions to the problem.[7] As only two decretal collections have been edited since the publication of Holtzmann's notes in 1982 and the intervening period has seen a deepening of interest in canon law before 1140, the earlier absence of serviceable editions of pre-Gratian collections provides one explanation for this lacuna.[8] Yet the very point of interest about the decretal collections, their extensive use of 'new' law, has had a greater effect. It counts against detailed studies of the collections' pre-Gratian content, because the main focus relates to ideas of papal government. Even in Landau's seminal article on the pre-Gratian contents of the decretal collections, there is a sense of surprise around the inclusion of the earlier texts, as if they have no place in the newer law.

---

6 The best evidence for this remains the analysis undertaken by Martin Brett, available in his "Table of Panormia MSS," at https://ivo-of-chartres.github.io/panormia/mslist.pdf, with date/revision stamp 2014–06–03/b8a41.

7 Peter Landau, "Vorgratianische Kanonessammlungen bei Dekretisten und in frühen Dekretalensammlungen," in *Proceedings of the Eighth International Congress of Medieval Canon Law, San Diego, University of California at La Jolla, 21–27 August 1988*, ed. Stanley Chodorow, MIC Subsidia 9 (Vatican City, 1992), pp. 93–116, at pp. 99–108.

8 The results of Holtzmann's years of research were published in 1979 by Christopher and Mary Cheney; this remains the best introduction to most of the collections: Walther Holtzmann, *Studies in the Collections of Twelfth-Century Decretals*, ed., rev., and trans. Christopher R. Cheney and Mary G. Cheney, MIC Corpus collectionum 3 (Vatican City, 1979) [henceforth cited as Holtzmann-Cheney]; the additional two collections are the *Francofurtana*, in *Die Collectio Francofurtana. Eine französische Decretalensammlung. Analyse beruhend auf Vorarbeiten von Walther Holtzmann†*, ed. Peter Landau and Gisela Drossbach, MIC Corpus collectionum 9 (Vatican City, 2007) and the *Cheltenhamensis*, in *Die Collectio Cheltenhamensis. Eine englische Decretalensammlung. Analyse beruhend auf Vorarbeiten von Walther Holtzmann†*, ed. Gisela Drossbach, MIC Corpus collectionum 10 (Vatican City, 2014). In contrast, the intervening period has seen advances in the study of earlier texts, including Brett's, Brasington's and others' Ivo site, available (at 30 May 2015), at https://ivo-of-chartres.github.io, and Linda Fowler-Magerl's indispensible *Clavis Canonum: Selected Canon Law Collections before 1140: Access with Data Processing*, MGH Hilfsmittel 21 (Munich, 2005); the *Clavis* database is also available at http://www.mgh.de/ext/clavis/. Professor Gisela Drossbach is in the process of completing a *Regesta Decretalium* and has studied a number of other collections in some detail, with analyses of others forthcoming including the *Collectio Petrihusensis* and its sister collection, the *Cottoniana*; see also her recent "Die Collectio Victorina prima—Dekretalenrecht in Saint-Victor," in *Diligens scrutator sacri eloquii. Beiträge zur Exegese- und Theologiegeschichte des Mittelalters. Festgabe für Rainer Berndt SJ zum 65. Geburtstag*, ed. Hanns Peter Neuheuser, Ralf M.W. Stammberger, and Matthias M. Tischler, Archa verbi. Subsidia 14 (Münster, 2016), pp. 349–64.

The nomenclature surrounding the decretal collections provides an additional and more compelling explanation for overlooking their earlier contents, however. Although the Psuedo-Isidorian forgeries have frequently been referred to the 'False Decretals', for historians of canon law the decretal collections are a specific sub-set of canonical collections compiled during the so-called 'classical' period of canon law, which ran from *c.*1140 to *c.*1234.[9] Walther Holtzmann noted 62 such collections in the 1960s, and the number has since risen.[10] Their defining feature is presented as the relatively high proportion of recent papal letters incorporated into the contents: almost the entire collection, in the example of the 'Worcester' collection compiled in southern England in the 1180s, where only three out of 274 chapters were not letters written by Alexander III.[11]

The term 'decretal collection', although used widely by Holtzmann, was not coined by him. Instead, it was popularised by the publication, in 1913, of Heinrich Singer's analysis of the *Collectiones Compendiensis, Sangermanensis* and *Abrincensis*, all of which he referred to as 'decretal collections'.[12] Ever since, it has become widely employed as the catch-all term for the canonical collections compiled in the late-twelfth century. An unfortunate consequence is that scholars have followed, if not unquestioningly, then nevertheless without much consideration. In his *Repertorium*, Stephan Kuttner accepted the distinction between pre-Gratian and 'decretal' collections; despite noting that the decretal collections did contain other material, he believed the term to be appropriate.[13] More recently, Charles Duggan rarely, if ever, looked to the earlier material present in the decretal collections. There are explanations for

9 For a list, see Holtzmann-Cheney (see above, n. 8), pp. xx–xxxi; see also Gérard Fransen, *Les décrétales et les collections de décrétales*, Typologie des sources du moyen âge occidental 2 (Turnhout, 1972).

10 Holtzmann-Cheney (see above, n. 8), p. xxxii.

11 London, British Library, Royal 10.A.ii, fols 5–62; Hans-Eberhard Lohmann, "Die Collectio Wigorniensis (Collectio Londoniensis regia). Ein Beitrag zur Quellengeschichte des kanonischen Rechts im 12. Jahrhundert," *Zeitschrift der Savigny-Stiftung für Rechtsgeschichte, kanonistische Abteilung* 22 (1933), 36–187, at pp. 42, 161.

12 Heinrich Singer, *Neue Beiträge über die Dekretalensammlungen vor und nach Bernhard von Pavia*, Sitzungsberichte der kaiserlichen Akademie der Wissenschaften, Wien, philosophisch-historische Klasse 171 (Vienna, 1913); reviewed favourably by Friedrich Heyer, "Rezension: Heinrich Singer, Neue Beiträge über die Dekretalensammlungen vor und nach Bernhard von Pavia," *Zeitschrift der Savigny-Stiftung für Rechtsgeschichte, kanonistische Abteilung* 3 (1913), 615–42.

13 Stephan Kuttner, *Repertorium der Kanonistik. Prodromus corporis Glossarum*, Studi e testi 71 (Vatican City, 1937), p. 272; see also Walther Holtzmann, "Über eine Ausgabe der päpstlichen Dekretalen des 12. Jahrhunderts," *Nachrichten von der Akademie der Wissenschaften in Göttingen, philologisch-historische Klasse* 24 (1945), 15–36, at p. 18.

this oversight: Duggan's primary interest was the English collections, which contain a lower proportion of earlier material, and his focus the contribution made by papal letters to the broader field of medieval history, rather than assessing the development of law.[14] At the same time, Duggan was bound into a particular way of conceiving 'new law': in his own words, it was "defined in recent conciliar legislation and, still more significantly, in papal decretal letters addressed to many thousands of recipients throughout Latin Christendom."[15] Decretal collections were the vehicles of that new law, and as a result any earlier texts they included could be overlooked.

Such a narrow view of the collections is, however, comparatively recent and markedly different to earlier perceptions. In the late-nineteenth century works of Schulte and Friedberg, only the *Liber extra* is consistently referred to as a decretal collection.[16] Even Friedberg's analysis of nine collections, all of which are now referred to as decretal collections, used the term 'collections of canons' ('Canones-Sammlungen') in its title, rather than the more specific 'Dekretalensammlungen' employed by Singer. Not all nineteenth-century historians shunned such explicit terminology: while Friedberg later called it a 'collectio canonum', when Richter published the first commentary on the *Lipsiensis* collection he referred to it as a decretal collection.[17] Overall, however, in work published in the nineteenth century there is a happy absence of any implicit presumption that the collections which post-dated Gratian only contained papal decretals, an approach which to this day affects the dating of earlier collections.[18]

---

14 E.g. Charles Duggan, *Twelfth-Century Decretal Collections and their Importance in English History* (London, 1965) and see also the articles reprinted in idem, *Decretals and the Creation of the 'New Law' in the Twelfth Century: Judges, Judgements, Equity and Law*, Variorum Collected Studies Series 607 (Aldershot, 1998). As an example, even the article "Decretal Letters to Hungary" (ibid., article no. v) emerges from his interest in the English collections, in this case specifically *Petrihusensis* and *Cottoniana*: Charles Duggan, "Decretal Letters to Hungary," *Folia Theologica* 3 (1992), 5–31, at p. 6.

15 Charles Duggan, "Papal Judges Delegate and the Making of the 'New Law' in the Twelfth Century," in *Cultures of Power: Lordship, Status, and Process in Twelfth-Century Europe*, ed. Thomas N. Bisson (Philadephia, 1995), pp. 172–99, at p. 173.

16 Johann Friedrich von Schulte, *Die Geschichte der Quellen und Literatur des canonischen Rechts von Gratian bis auf die Gegenwart*, 3 vols (Stuttgart, 1875; repr. Clark, N.J., 2000); *Quinque compilationes antiquae, nec non Collectio canonum Lipsiensis*, ed. Emil Friedberg (Leipzig, 1882; repr. Graz 1956); *Die Canones-Sammlungen zwischen Gratian und Bernhard von Pavia*, ed. Emil Friedberg (Leipzig, 1897; repr. Graz, 1957).

17 Emil Ludwig Richter, *De inedita decretalium collectione Lipsiensi* (Leipzig, 1836).

18 See for example the fact that most collections contained in Lotte Kéry, *Canonical Collections of the Early Middle Ages (ca. 400–1140): A Bibliographical Guide to the*

A major problem with the later-twelfth century decretal collections is therefore in part their definition. Decretal collections are, as the name suggests, collections of decretals, which are letters sent by the pope that have legal relevance—because they are contained in a decretal or other canonical collection.[19] While most of the letters are obviously legally significant—to give one example, *Sicut dignum est* which explained *Si quis suadente*[20]—a number of 'decretals' in the collections were in fact sections of larger letters that may have possessed no great legal innovation, including the fragment of a tithe privilege that made its way into a number of collections including Bernard of Pavia's *Breviarium extravagantium*.[21] Equally, many letters which were *responsa*, i.e. responses to questions on legal matters, or represent disputes and cases were never incorporated into the legal collections. At least one immense collection of letters, those of Henry, archbishop of Reims, found in Arras, Bibliothèque municipale, 964 and published by Martène and Durand, is a collection of letters of use to the archbishop.[22] While not necessarily possessing its own peculiar legal importance, a number of its letters found their way into later collections such as *Brugensis*; moreover, the letters in the Arras manuscript demonstrate the quotidian processes of ecclesiastical government, if not at the absolute highest levels, then at the most locally significant ones.[23] Meanwhile,

Manuscripts and Literature, History of Medieval Canon Law (Washington, D.C., 1998), are dated to pre-1140 on the basis that they would not have been compiled after.

19 Fransen, *Les décrétales* (see above, n. 9), pp. 7, 12, comments on the 'custom' to refer to all letters in canonical collections as decretals, but see also Duggan, "Decretal Collections" (see above, n. 3), pp. 246–47.

20 JL 12180 [WH 929]; see also Katherine Christensen, "The 'Lost' Papal Gloss on *Si quis suadente* (C. 17, q. 4, c. 29): John of Salisbury and the Canonical Tradition in the Twelfth Century," *Bulletin of Medieval Canon Law*, n.s. 18 (1988), 1–11; Richard H. Helmholz, "*Si quis suadente*: Theory and Practice," in *Proceedings of the Seventh International Congress of Medieval Canon Law, Cambridge, 23–27 July 1984*, ed. Peter Linehan, MIC Subsidia 8 (Vatican City, 1988), pp. 425–38.

21 JL 14173 [WH 895]: *1 Comp*. 3.26.12, where its source is given as "Item ex privilegio Alex.".

22 Arras, Bibliothèque municipale, 964; Edmund Martène and Ursine Durand, *Veterum scriptorum et monumentorum historicorum, dogmaticorum, moralium amplissima collectio*, 9 vols (Paris, 1724–33), 2:622–1011. Ludwig Falkenstein, "Alexandre III et Henri de France: conformités et conflits," in *L'église de France et la papauté (Xe–XIIIe siècle) / Die französische Kirche und das Papsttum*, ed. Ralf Große, Studien und Dokumente zur Gallia Pontificia 1 (Bonn, 1993), pp. 103–76, at pp. 104–05 summarizes the contents of the manuscript and gives an account of the historiography.

23 For *Brugensis*, see Ludwig Falkenstein, "Zur Entstehungsort und Redaktor der Collectio Brugensis," in *Proceedings of the Eighth International Congress of Medieval Canon Law, San Diego, University of California at La Jolla, 21–27 August 1988*, ed. Stanley Chodorow, MIC Subsidia 9 (Vatican City, 1992), pp. 117–51, at p. 124 for the link to Arras, Bibliothèque municipale, 964, where he gives further literature.

the *Belverensis* decretal collection is found within a collection of the letters of Gilbert Foliot, and the collection named *Fontanensis* by Holtzmann is preserved in the cartulary of Fountains Abbey.[24] From the perspective of using canon law to understand ecclesiastical government, ignoring these other sources of legal argumentation is a critical oversight even though they contributed little to the 'development' of the 'new law' in the twelfth century. Within that context they represent unfinished tangents in canon law studies, but to only perceive them as such ignores the reality that they must have served a particular purpose, even if that purpose is now elusive.

By limiting the definition of a decretal and focussing solely on the decretal collections, the variety and scope of later-twelfth century law is therefore often overlooked. Given the importance of the system of direct papal law-making that the collections represent, an investigation of its formulation is sensible, but it has to be seen in its broader context. At the same time as the decretal collections were being compiled, for example, canonists were creating abbreviations and alternative versions of the *Decretum Gratiani*. Omnebene's *Abbreviatio decretorum* survives in nine manuscripts, more than any single version of a pre-*Compilatio prima* decretal collection, and equal to the number of surviving complete manuscripts of the largest family.[25] Rather than presenting a straightforward shortening of the *Decretum*, however, Omnebene changed some of its structure; other compilers of abbreviations added canons and excerpts from the *summae*.[26] Laborans, a cardinal in Alexander III's curia with legal training, even compiled a *Transformatio decretorum* in around

24 Duggan, *Decretal collections* (see above, n. 14), pp. 71–73; Holtzmann-Cheney (see above, n. 8), pp. 100–15 with an analysis on 103–15; Peter Landau, "Die *Collectio Fontanensis*: A Decretal Collection of the Twelfth Century for an English Cistercian Abbey," in *Law as Profession and Practice in Medieval Europe: Essays in Honor of James A. Brundage*, ed. Kenneth Pennington and Melodie Harris Eichbauer (Aldershot, 2011), pp. 187–204, at pp. 190–92.

25 On Omnebene, see Kenneth Pennington and Wolfgang P. Müller, "The Decretists: The Italian School," in *The History of Medieval Canon Law in the Classical Period: From Gratian to the Decretals of Pope Gregory IX*, ed. Wilfried Hartmann and Kenneth Pennington, History of Medieval Canon Law (Washington, D.C., 2008), pp. 121–73, at p. 124, and the literature therein. The family in question is *Bambergensis*, see the analysis by Walter Deeters, *Die Bambergensisgruppe der Dekretalensammlungen des 12. Jahrhunderts* (Bonn, 1954).

26 See Pennington and Müller, "The Decretists," pp. 123–25, which includes a summary of and references to the earlier literature; on the abbreviations themselves, see e.g. Alfred Beyer, *Lokale Abbreviationen des Dekret Gratiani. Analyse und Vergleich der Dekretabbreviationen "Omnes leges aut divine" (Bamberg), "Humanum genus duobus regitur" (Pommersfelden), und "De his qui intra claustra monasterii consistunt" (Lichtenthal, Baden-Baden)*, Bamberger theologische Studien 6 (Frankfurt and New York, 1998). More recently on the

1182.[27] It combined selected contents of the *Decretum* with decretals and tens of other texts in two parts that bear little resemblance to either recension of Gratian's compilation, but had a very limited circulation: only one known manuscript survives, believed to be Laborans' autograph.[28] As well as those drastic alterations to its structure, the addition of the *paleae* in some texts demonstrates the gradual enlargement of the *Decretum*.[29] To put it bluntly, until later in the period, the vitality and innovation connected with twelfth-century canon law did not become limited to the collectors of decretals and, in any case, the strict terminology employed within studies of canon law all to easily, and often accidentally, creates an inflexible paradigm in which these nuances are obscured.

The work of Walther Holtzmann, who did more than any other person since Friedberg to advance the study and understanding of later-twelfth century canonical collections, provides a salutory example. Despite being highly aware of the presence of earlier texts in collections including *Lipsiensis* and the *Breviarium*, Holtzmann rarely took them into account in his analyses of the collections. On at least one occasion he refused to refer to a gathering of such texts as a true collection, despite the fact that it preceded two sections of a decretal collection now recognized as being highly important, *Dunelmensis I*.[30] In this instance, neither Charles Duggan nor the Cheneys had much sympathy with his approach.[31] A key reason for this was Holtzmann's more

subject of abbreviations, see Atria Ann Larson, "An *abbreviatio* of the First Recension of Gratian's *Decretum* in Munich?," *Bulletin of Medieval Canon Law*, n.s. 29 (2011–12), 51–118.

27 von Schulte, *Quellen und Literatur* (see above, n. 16), 1:148–49; Johannes Brixius, *Die Mitglieder des Kardinalkollegiums von 1130–1181* (Berlin, 1912), pp. 63–64; Kuttner, *Repertorium* (see above, n. 13), pp. 267–68; Norbert Martin, "Die 'Compilatio decretorum' des Kardinal Laborans," in *Proceedings of the Sixth International Congress of Medieval Canon Law, Berkeley, California, 28 July–2 August 1980*, ed. Stephan Kuttner and Kenneth Pennington, MIC Subsidia 7 (Vatican City, 1985), pp. 125–38, at p. 125; Stefan Weiß, *Die Urkunden der päpstlichen Legaten von Leo IX. bis Coelestin III. (1049–1198)*, Beihefte zu J.F. Böhmer, Regesta Imperii 13 (Cologne, 1995), pp. 269–70.

28 Norbert Martin, *Die Compilatio Decretorum des Kardinals Laborans. Eine Umarbeitung des Gratianischen Dekrets aus dem 12. Jahrhunderts* (Heidelberg, 1985), summarized in idem, "Die 'Compilatio Decretorum'" (see above, n. 27).

29 Marked '*palea*' and with square brackets in Friedberg's edition; see for example the copy of the *Decretum* in Salzburg, Stiftsbibliothek Erzabtei Sankt Peter, a.XI.9, in which a number of texts are written into the margins. For the *paleae* in general, see Weigand, "Zusätzliche 'Paleae' in fünf Dekrethandschriften" (see above, n. 5).

30 See the Cheneys' editorial comment in Holtzmann-Cheney (see above, n. 8), p. 75.

31 Charles Duggan, "A Durham Canonical Manuscript of the Late-Twelfth Century," *Studies in Church History* 2 (1965), 179–85; Duggan, *Twelfth-Century Decretal Collections* (see above, n. 14), pp. 78–79, deals extensively with the collection.

legalistic definition of a collection: he wanted an underlying organising principle that underpinned the gathering of the texts. Where such a principle was absent, he purposefully overlooked the accumulation of canonistic material. In contrast, the importance of florilegia and farraginous collections, particularly for understanding the relationships between earlier medieval canonical collections, has become increasingly apparent in the work of Linda Fowler-Magerl and others; using similar techniques for the later period seems an increasingly sensible way of proceeding.[32]

As limiting as Holtzmann's focus on collections which fulfilled his specific criteria, and emanating from a similar perspective, was Kuttner's overwhelming interest in only those *Dekretanhänge*—the appendices of canonical texts sometimes found in *Decretum* manuscripts—which contained recent papal decretals. A case in point is Paris, Bibliothèque nationale, lat. 15001. The main content of the second half of this manuscript is a copy of *Quoniam egestas*, a *Decretum* abbreviation that dates to the 1150s or 1160s.[33] There is also a short canonical collection, a handful of decretals and the canons of the 1163 council of Tours. Despite the fact that the collection must have been copied out after 1148, as it incorporates a canon from Eugenius III's council at Reims, Kuttner only mentioned the abbreviation, the three decretals and the later conciliar canons in his *Repertorium*, overlooking the rest of the manuscript's canonical contents. His focus is understandable given that in the 1930s, scholars were less aware of the variety, number, and sophistication of the earlier collections, presenting them instead as means to an end: the creation of the *Decretum* and papal codifications of law. Since that time, however, huge advances made in

32 Linda Fowler-Magerl, "The Collection and Transmission of Canon Law along the Northern Section of the Via Francigena in the Eleventh and Twelfth Centuries," in *Bishops, Texts and the Use of Canon Law around 1100: Essays in the Honour of Martin Brett*, ed. Bruce Clark Brasington and Kathleen G. Cushing, Church, Faith and Culture in the Middle Ages (Aldershot, 2008), pp. 129–39, e.g. at pp. 131–32, which defines a farrago as "an accumulation of canon law material with no apparent internal order," before describing some examples from northern France.

33 The canonical material is Paris, Bibliothèque nationale de France, lat. 15001, fols 121va–246va. The collection is fols 122v–123v, 125r–126v. Kuttner mentions three decretals on fol. 122 and the canons of Tours on fol. 237ra–va in Kuttner, *Repertorium* (see above, n. 13), pp. 286–87, but see also Stephan Kuttner, "The 'Extravagantes' of the *Decretum* in Biberach," *Bulletin of Medieval Canon Law*, n.s. 3 (1973), 61–71, at p. 67. On the *Abbreviatio Quoniam egestas*, see Kuttner, *Repertorium* (see above, n. 13), p. 263; Rudolf Weigand, "Die Dekretabbreviatio 'Quoniam Egestas' und ihre Glossen," in *Fides et ius. Festschrift für Georg May am 65. Geburtstag*, ed. Winfried Aymans, Anna Egler, and Joseph Listl (Regensburg, 1991), pp. 249–65 and for a description of the Paris manuscript in particular at p. 251.

understanding earlier collections and the increasing awareness that earlier manuscripts continued to be copied make such an approach less amenable.

2 Decretals and Decretal Collections

Despite the advances toward a more nuanced understanding of the continued role of earlier texts in the century or so after Gratian, the outline development of the decretal collections remains essentially unchanged since the time of Kuttner and Holtzmann. It presents a procession of collections from simple to most sophisticated: first came *Dekretanhänge*, then primitive decretal collections, then systematic decretal collections, and finally the *Breviarium extravagantium* of Bernard of Pavia, completed by 1191 in five books, each divided into multiple titles.[34] Such a progression is highly teleological; it also presupposes that the urge to expand collections such as Gratian took the same form in all areas of Europe. In fact, the only area where the story of the collections has significantly changed concerns the greater awareness of the role played by clerics and collectors working outside of Italy. Despite the predominance of English decretals in the collections, Holtzmann posited an Italian, or more specifically Bolognese, origin for many of the sophisticated works of canon law, especially the *Appendix*.[35] Kuttner and Rathbone first announced the existence of a strong Anglo-Norman school of canon lawyers, to which a Rhenish school around Cologne has now also been added.[36] Charles Duggan also emphasised the strength of decretals' connection with England, noting that somewhere around half of those contained in the collections

34 The best recent example of this is found in Duggan, "Decretal Collections" (see above, n. 3), pp. 253–87.

35 Holtzmann-Cheney (see above, n. 8), esp. pp. 117–18, which although a commentary by the Cheneys points to Holtzmann's general outlook.

36 Stephan Kuttner and Eleanor Rathbone, "Anglo-Norman Canonists of the Twelfth Century," *Traditio* 7 (1949–51), 279–358, and more recently Rudolf Weigand, "The Transmontane Decretists," in *The History of Medieval Canon Law in the Classical Period: From Gratian to the Decretals of Pope Gregory IX*, ed. Wilfried Hartmann and Kenneth Pennington, History of Medieval Canon Law (Washington, D.C., 2008), pp. 174–210, who nevertheless asserts in his opening sentences that "the title underlines the author's conviction that the Bolognese school set the standard for the academic study of canon law". See also Peter Landau, "Die Kölner Kanonistik des 12. Jahrhunderts. Ein Höhepunkt der europäischen Rechtswissenschaft," in *Vortrag vor dem Rheinischen Verein für Rechtsgeschichte e. V. in Köln am 27. Mai 2008*, ed. Dieter Strauch, Kölner Rechtsgeschichtliche Vorträge 1 (Cologne, 2008), pp. 1–39 and idem, "Die Entstehung der systematischen Dekretalensammlungen und die europäische Kanonistik der 12. Jahrhunderts," *Zeitschrift der Savigny-Stiftung für Rechtsgeschichte, kanonistische Abteilung* 65 (1979), 120–48, at p. 133.

were sent to English recipients and commenting on the importance of both Worcester and Exeter in the compilation of key early collections.[37] Limiting the systematic collections to Italy is no longer possible; in fact, aside from a few descendants of the *Bambergensis* group and the *Breviarium*, the opposite is true even when, as in the case of the *Collectio Francofurtana*, the collection contains both pre- and post-Gratian texts.[38] The result is a greater awareness of the role played by different centres of canon law, mostly those in Tours and the Capetian heartlands around Paris including Reims and Sens, while the focus for the early years of the decretal collections remains the English material that became such a significant proportion.[39]

To move on to a more detailed investigation of the evidence, rather than simply the historiography, the twelfth-century decretal collections have been closely tied with the growth of the 'papal monarchy' via their extensive use of new, papal law. Their importance thus rests on the fact that they represent the first time that recent precedents had more authority than their earlier counterparts, and that letters were considered more or as authoritative as conciliar canons, in contrast to the general impulse toward conservatism perceived in medieval society. In the Treatise on Laws (*Decretum*, D. 1–20), Gratian devoted an entire *distinctio* to the authority of papal decretals ending with the conclusion that "decretals are equal in law to conciliar canons."[40] Over the course of the twelfth century, the definition of a 'decretal' became a critical part of the commentaries on Gratian, expanding over the period. While Paucapalea limited his discussion on D. 19 to a few lines, the anonymous author

---

37 Duggan pointed to Exeter as a possible locale for a core collection of decretals now only visible implicitly through the *Alcobacensis prima* manuscript: Charles Duggan, "Decretals of Alexander III to England," in *Miscellanea Rolando Bandinelli, Papa Alessandro III*, ed. Filippo Liotta (Siena, 1986), pp. 87–151, at pp. 90–93; in the same article on p. 93 he comments in more depth on the existence of a 'Worcester" selection.

38 *Die Collectio Francofurtana*, ed. Landau and Drossbach (see above, n. 8); see also Gisela Drossbach, "Decretals and the Schools? The *Collectio Francofurtana*," *Bulletin of Medieval Canon Law*, n.s. 24 (2000), 65–77; the only collections which now have an unchallenged Italian provenance are *Parisiensis II* (Paris, Bibliothèque nationale de France, lat. 1566, fols 1r–54v), *Lipsiensis* (Leipzig, Universitätsbibliothek 975, fols 116–53), and the *Breviarium*.

39 Although John Wei and, now, Gisela Drossbach are suggesting also the potential for northern-French origins of the early decretal collections, e.g. John C. Wei, "Gratian's *Decretum* in France and Halberstadt," in *Rechtshandschriften des deutschen Mittelalters. Produktionsorte und Importwege*, ed. Patrizia Carmassi and Gisela Drossbach, Wolfenbütteler Mittelalter-Studien 29 (Wiesbaden, 2015), pp. 363–83, esp. pp. 375–80, 382; idem, "The Later Development of Gratian's *Decretum*," in *Proceedings of the Fourteenth International Congress of Medieval Canon Law, Toronto, 5–11 August 2012*, ed. Joseph W. Goering et al., MIC Subsidia 15 (Vatican City, 2016), pp. 149–61, at pp. 155–56.

40 Gratian, *Decretum*, D. 20, d.a.c. 1.

the *Summa Parisiensis* took some care over his discussion, and Huguccio, writing in *c.*1190, even more.[41] Charles Duggan and Jacoba Hanenburg both took great time and joy in explaining how decretals were something new and different, chasing their definitions across the *summae* of the twelfth century, but both also overlooked the fact that decretals had been employed in earlier collections including most notably the Pseudo-Isidorian forgeries. Duggan even expressed surprise that the early canonists took such a long time to understand fully the implications of Gratian's discussion, seeing it as an automatic change that could not be stopped.[42]

Nevertheless, the critical reference to 'new law' is in the preface to Bernard of Pavia's *Breviarium extravagantium*, finished sometime between 1189 and 1191 while he was provost of Pavia. Here, Bernard wrote that he had "compiled *extravagantia* from the old and the new law under titles."[43] He expanded slightly in the preface to his *Summa decretalium*, written later in the 1190s to explain the contents of his collection, saying

> the book was titled *extravagantia*; for the most part [they are] decretals [...] the subject matter is made up of decretals and certain useful provisions which Gratian left out—saving fruit new and old for us—in the corpus of canons, in the register of Gregory, and in Burchard [the Brocards].[44]

41 *Die Summa des Paucapalea über das Decretum Gratiani*, ed. Johann Friedrich von Schulte (Giessen, 1890), p. 20; *The Summa Parisiensis on the Decretum Gratiani*, ed. Terence McLaughlin (Toronto, 1952), pp. 20–22; Huguccio, *Summa Decretorum, Tom. I: Dist. 1–20*, ed. Oldřich Přerovský, MIC Corpus collectionum 6 (Vatican City, 2006), pp. 296–328. The increasing complexity of the commentaries is simply, if crudely, demonstrated by the increasing size of their printed editions.

42 Duggan, *Twelfth-Century Decretal Collections* (see above, n. 14), pp. 27–39; critiqued in Jacoba Hanenburg, "Decretals and Decretal Collections in the Second Half of the Twelfth Century," *Tijdschrift voor Rechtsgeschiednis* 34 (1966), 552–99 at great length, but in this case esp. pp. 552–85.

43 Robert Somerville and Bruce Clark Brasington, *Prefaces to Canon Law Books in Latin Christianity: Selected Translations, 500–1245* (New Haven and London, 1998), p. 231; *Quinque Compilationes*, ed. Friedberg (see above, n. 16), p. 1: "Ego B. Papiensis prepositus extrauagantia de ueteri nouoque iure sub titulis compilaui". Although Bernard is one of the better-known canonists, that does not say much: for a relatively recent biography, see the relevant sections in *The History of Medieval Canon Law in the Classical Period: From Gratian to the Decretals of Pope Gregory IX*, ed. Wilfried Hartmann and Kenneth Pennington, History of Medieval Canon Law (Washington, D.C., 2008).

44 *Prefaces*, trans. Somerville and Brasington (see above, n. 43), p. 232; *Bernardi Papiensis Faventini episcopi Summa decretalium*, ed. Theodor Laspeyres (Regensburg 1860; repr. Graz, 1956). According to the edition, Bernard refers to the sections as 'Brocardo', translated by Somerville and Brasington to mean 'Burchard'.

These two clauses, in two different books, are the key to the idea that the 'new law' was the law of the decretals, and in particular the biblical allusion to 'fruit new and old for us' (Song of Songs 7:13).

Bernard gives no definition of the dividing line which differentiated the new law from the old, however; nor is there any reference to whether new law was considered more authoritative than its elder sibling. Although the success of the *Liber extra* has led to the term 'extravagantes' referring mostly to decretals, in the twelfth century it seems to have been used to refer more broadly to any text taken from neither the *Decretum* nor a pre-existing collection of canon law such as Burchard. Decretals taken from the collections were one source of additional texts; equally, in their *summae* Rufinus and Simon of Bisignano used Burchard as well as a source. At C. 2, q. 6, c. 19, in fact, Simon referred to both Burchard and a collection of *extravagantes*. He employed Burchard as a foil to Gratian, referring obliquely to Burchard 1.68, *Item placuit*, then commenting that Gratian "seems to contradict" it; eventually, he came to the conclusion that "this canon cannot be used in this situation, saving the Master's peace."[45] Later on in the same section of his commentary, he pointed to three letters "in Extra."[46] Rufinus, writing slightly earlier than Simon, also employed various other texts not incorporated into Gratian in his commentary, including some taken from Burchard.[47] Compared to Simon, however, Rufinus used Burchard much more than he referred to recent decretals. Only two appeared in the *summa*: Adrian IV's *Nobis in eminenti*, sent to the abbot of Pontigny in 1155, and Innocent II's *Quotiens frater*, sent to a series of Italian bishops at some point between 1138 and 1142.[48] Singer accepted the tens of Burchard references without much comment.[49] There is a strong temptation here to reinforce the idea of the 'new law' slowly moving from England toward Italy: Peter Landau has recently argued that Simon was writing north of the Alps, whereas Rufinus' principle geographical attachment remains Bologna; equally, however, Simon wrote around fifteen years after Rufinus, and the explanation could be as

45 Simon of Bisignano, *Summa* to C. 2, q. 6, c. 19, ed. Pier V. Aimone-Braida, *Summa in Decretum Simonis Bisinianensis*, MIC Corpus glossatorum 8 (Vatican City, 2014), p. 133; Burchard of Worms, *Decretum* 1.68.

46 Simon of Bisignano, *Summa* to C. 2, q. 6, c. 19, ed. Aimone (see above, n. 45), pp. 133–34: "ut in extra c. Super eo quod" = JL 13162 [WH 649–650]; "ut in extra c. Cum sacrosancta" = JL 12020 [WH –]; "ut in Extra c. Sicut Romana ecclesia" = JL 12293 [WH 944a].

47 For a summary, see *Die Summa decretorum des Magisters Rufinus*, ed. Heinrich Singer (Paderborn, 1902), pp. cvi–cx, which gives a resumé of all the other texts employed by Rufinus in his *Summa*.

48 Adrian IV, *Nobis in eminenti* = JL 10444 [WH 664]; Innocent II, *Quotiens frater* = JL 8289 [WH 842].

49 Rufinus, *Summa*, ed. Singer (see above, n. 47), pp. cii–cvi.

simple as there was a greater selection of decretals available and relevant at the time.[50]

Although he gives no indication as to the authority inherent in individual texts, there is certainly a sense of time in Bernard's collection. Broadly speaking, the titles of the *Breviarium* are arranged chronologically, starting with older texts before moving toward more recent ones. It is difficult to decide whether this is a side-effect of the editorial decision by which the collection was gathered together, or whether it was a more deliberate process on Bernard's part. To take three examples, in *1 Comp.* 1.15, *De offitio archidiaconi*, there are only five chapters.[51] The first three, including two taken from the corresponding title in *Parisiensis II*, all bear inscriptions that date them earlier than the year 1000. One is an extract from a letter of Gregory the Great; another purports to be "ex libro Romani ordinis", and the third from a council at Toledo. The final two chapters in the collection, by way of contrast, are both decretals of Alexander III.[52] In this instance, both 1.15.2 and 1.15.3 were in *Parisiensis II*, while the others were added from other sources. The general distinction between earlier and later sources is evident, if a little murkier, in *1 Comp.* 5.1 and 5.2. The early chapters of both these titles contain a selection of earlier material, followed by decretals of Alexander III and Lucius III, but in both a single chapter is inserted later in the title. In 5.1, for example, the first nine chapters, the equivalent of *2 Par.* 27.1–27.6 with one lacuna and four additions, are followed by *2 Par.* 27.7, a section of Alexander III's decretal *Licet preter solitum*. After that extract falls a chapter taken from Augustine, with two more letters from Alexander added at the end of the title, neither of which were included in *2 Par.*[53] Similarly, in *1 Comp.* 5.2, a text attributed to Deusdedit sits in the midst of a section of Alexandrine decretals, at 5.2.16.[54] In a similar fashion to the earlier title, this chapter falls in the additions to *2 Par.* 26,

50 Peter Landau, "Simon von Bisignano, Sikard von Cremona und die Mainzer Kanonistik der Barbarossazeit: Zur Biographie des Simon von Bisignano und zur Forschungsgeschichte," *Bulletin of Medieval Canon Law*, n.s. 28 (2008), 119–44, at pp. 136–38.

51 *Quinque Compilationes*, ed. Friedberg (see above, n. 16), p. 6.

52 *1 Comp.* 1.15.4: Alexander III, *Cum satis sit*, to the archdeacon of Ely = JL 13898 [WH 301]; *1 Comp.* 1.15.5: Alexander III, *Archidiaconis de ecclesiastica*, to the bishop of Worcester = JL 13166 [WH 92].

53 *Quinque Compilationes*, ed. Friedberg (see above, n. 16), pp. 53–54.The two additional decretals are Alexander III, *Cum Petrus*, to a bishop elect in Italy = JL 11338 [WH 292], and Alexander III, *Ex parte tua*, to Roger, bishop of Worcester = JL 11872 [WH 468].

54 *Quinque Compilationes*, ed. Friedberg (see above, n. 16), pp. 54–55; *1 Comp.* 5,2,1–6 all bear early inscriptions.

De symoniachis.[55] Again, the first seven chapters present a rejigged formulation of the earlier collection, with Alexander's council at Tours coming last (instead of fourth), just prior to a canon from the later council at the Lateran and the papal letters. Regardless of the addition of the Deusdedit canon, the rearrangement of these chapters suggests that some concern was taken over the organisation of these texts, with the subsequent structure presenting earlier texts first and following them with more recent extracts.

When he compiled his collection, Bernard obviously re-arranged some sections. Although by no means fool-proof, as a general rule—and for example in 5.2—where he did rearrange extracts taken from *Parisiensis II*, the earlier material falls at the beginning of each title. The pontificate of Innocent II seems to represent the cut-off point for this distinction, with the letters of Innocent and his successors appearing by and large after the earlier material. In fact, in terms of the juxtaposition between 'old' and 'new' law, the correlation of dates here is rather too tempting: in around 1140, the first recension of the *Decretum* had begun to circulate, and it could well be that Bernard, aware of this development, chose to use the *Decretum* as his dividing line.

There is an alternative, however, to continuing the idea that Gratian was the critical pivot. Away from the scholarly charged question of the growth of papal power, the medieval 'old law' could have been perceived as Old Testament law—and, helpfully, 15 extracts taken from the books of Exodus and Leviticus appear in the *Breviarium*.[56] Equally, when Bernard talks of 'decretals' in his explanation of the collections' contents, there is no automatic limitation on when those decretals were sent. After the letters of Alexander III, the most copious source in the *Breviarium* is the Register of Gregory the Great with 71 letters, while in total around a third of the chapters in the *Breviarium* were ascribed to a pre-Gratianic origin, or 315 chapters out of 920.[57] A blank reading of Bernard's text, with modern knowledge and understanding of the events that occurred after its appearance and particularly the promulgation of the *Liber extra*, could imply that the 'old' law is pre-Gratian, and the 'new' post-Gratian, but Bernard's own writings do not provide any such explanation. Removing

55 *Canones-Sammlungen*, ed. Friedberg (see above, n. 16), p. 36; Paris, Bibliothèque nationale de France, lat. 1566, fols 12v–13v.

56 Peter Landau, "Alttestamentliches Recht in der 'Compilatio Prima' und sein Einfluss auf das kanonische Recht," *Studia Gratiana* 20 (1976), 111–33, at p. 114.

57 *Quinque Compilationes*, ed. Friedberg (see above, n. 16), passim; the important point details are the inscriptions given in the collection, rather than necessarily the known original source of the extracts. For a number of these, the inscription may well be mistaken, but the accurate source is of considerably lesser interest than the source that was believed to have been used.

the modern perception does not automatically challenge the definition. But it does leave open the possibility that Bernard's reference to the 'old law' was referring to that biblical law rather than the laws of men, and that the 'new law' to which he referred was in fact the remainder of the canons and decretals that he collected together in his *Breviarium*, regardless of the date they were written.

3 Decretal Collections' Contents and 'New Law'

The final focus is the contents of other collections and whether they represent a concerted effort on the part of the compilers to gather together only newer law. Given the complexity of the collections, it is difficult to find one answer to such a broad, dogmatic, question. To begin with, the collections have different formats: some are stand-alone collections that have survived in manuscripts with a variety of other material, while others are part of larger accumulations of canonical material; some are lawyers' handbooks, written in scrawling hands that verge on the barely-legible, while others are beautiful display manuscripts. London, British Library, Royal 10.B.iv, for example, contains the early English 'Canterbury' collection alongside other legal materials, including at least one *ordo*.[58] Others are reminiscent of appendices: Erlangen, Universitätsbibliothek, 342 sees a systematic collection falling after a copy of Gratian's *Decretum*; other examples of a similar phenomenon include London, British Library, Arundel 490, and Bernkastel-Kues, Hospitalbibliothek, 229, where earlier collections are appended to copies of the *Decretum* and an abbreviation respectively, while the *Fontanensis* and *Belverensis* collections are incorporated into manuscripts containing non-canonical accumulations.[59] Even when they are divided into subject-based titles, most of the early decretal collections are higgledy-piggledy collections of material. They are not deliberately chronologically organized. Equally, these collections were not drawn up using the idiosyncratic structure

58 London, British Library, Royal 10.B.iv, various; see Linda Fowler-Magerl, *Ordo iudiciorum vel ordo iudiciarius*, Ius Commune Sonderheft 19 (Frankfurt, 1984), pp. 273–89 and 297–300 give two separate *ordines* found in the London manuscript.

59 Erlangen, Universitätsbibliothek, 342, fols 291ra–306va = *Erlangensis*, following a copy of Gratian with the *Ordinaturus Magister* gloss apparatus. London, British Library, Arundel 490, fols 210–21, see Kuttner, *Repertorium* (see above, n. 13), p. 281, Walther Holtzmann, "*Collectio Eberbacensis*," *Zeitschrift der Savigny-Stiftung für Rechtsgeschichte, kanonistische Abteilung* 17 (1928), 548–55. Bernkastel-Kues, Hospitalbibliothek, 229, fols 67r–123v, see Kuttner, *Repertorium* (see above, n. 13), p. 291, Holtzmann-Cheney (see above, n. 8), pp. 66–74.

of dialectic employed in the *Decretum* and, with the important exception of the *Francofurtana*, rarely used dicta or lengthy rubrics to convey the opinions of their compiler.[60] Compared with the great systematic collections like the *Panormia* or the *Decretum* of either Ivo or Burchard, these collections are also small. The three collections titled *Decretum*, so that of Burchard, Ivo, and Gratian, incorporated 1,785, 3,760, and 3,945 extracts respectively.[61] In contrast, the largest of the late-twelfth century decretal collections, the *Breviarium*, has 920 extracts. Most of the 'primitive' collections, including *Berolinensis I*, have between 100 and 200 chapters; in some cases, as in the *Dunelmensis* and *Fontanensis* collections, that total is made up of three smaller collections, each with around 50–60 texts.[62]

The collections have also been subjected to implicit manipulation, in part a result of the focus on the recent papal letters amongst their contents. To re-adjust that manipulation gives some intriguing results. In 1234, when the *Liber extra* was promulgated, it contained sections from 599 of the 13,700 or so letters known to have been sent in the years between 1143 and 1198, meaning that four and a half per cent of the letters sent at the time were incorporated into its contents.[63] In total, Holtzmann estimated that just over 1,050 discrete letters were incorporated into the collections in one state or another, meaning that slightly less than eight per cent of contemporary letters known to have been sent were included in the collections. At the same time, the *Liber extra* contains 60 letters taken from the Register of Gregory the Great, presumably via the *Breviarium*—or about seven per cent of the enregistered letters, so those which are known and which would have been known in the twelfth

60 *Die Collectio Francofurtana*, ed. Landau and Drossbach (see above, n. 8), xxi, c. 13 = 174, for one example.

61 For Burchard, see Fowler-Magerl, *Clavis canonum* (see above, n. 8), passim; for Ivo, see Brett's lists available at https://ivo-of-chartres.github.io/decretum.html, with date stamp of 2014–06–03; for Gratian, see Winroth, *Making of Gratian's Decretum* (see above, n. 1), p. 122.

62 For the analysis of *Berolinensis I*, which has 126 chapters, see Josef Juncker, "Die *Collectio Berolinensis*. Ein Beitrag zur Geschichte des kanonischen Rechts im ausgehenden zwölften Jahrhundert," *Zeitschrift der Savigny-Stiftung für Rechtsgeschichte, kanonistische Abteilung* 44 (1924), 284–426, with an analysis on pp. 348–407, including the canons of the 1179 Lateran council; for *Dunelmensis* see above, n. 31 and below n. 81; for *Fontanensis*, see n. 24 above.

63 *Corpus iuris canonici*, ed. Emil Friedberg, 2 vols (Leipzig, 1879–81), 2:xii–xiv; for projected numbers of papal letters, see Rudolf Hiestand, "Die Leistungsfähigkeit der päpstlichen Kanzlei im 12. Jahrhundert mit einem Blick auf den lateinischen Osten," in *Papsturkunde und europäisches Urkundenwesen. Studien zu ihrer formalen und rechtlichen Kohärenz vom 11. bis 15. Jahrhundert*, ed. Peter Herde und Hermann Jakobs, Archiv für Diplomatik. Beiheft 7 (Cologne, 1999), pp. 1–26, at p. 23.

century, when Gregory's *Register* became a widely read source again.[64] Despite its date, therefore, the *Liber extra* contained a similar proportion of Gregory's surviving letters as of did recent papal decretals, a fact that becomes even more stark when the extent of the loss suffered by the twelfth-century letters is taken into account. Far more letters were sent than have survived, meaning that the proportion of letters considered to have enough legal value to be included in the collections was much lower. 22 per cent (184 in total) of Gregory's registered letters, plus eight apocrypha, had already been incorporated into the *Decretum* in its second form, meaning that just shy of a third of Gregory's letters were included in the two principal contemporary canonical collections that would eventually form the *Corpus Iuris Canonici*.

Statistically, therefore, while Gregory's letters represent a small proportion of the *Extra*, the collection represents a comparatively large proportion of Gregory's letters for one which is supposed to represent 'new law'. Such a statistical comparison is at best inexact, particularly as the absence of surviving twelfth-century registers makes it difficult to know which sort of documents were enregistered, and why.[65] Nevertheless, it can be assumed that during the processes of compiling the Register an amount of pre-selection would have taken place; the known contents seem to suggest that the Registers were weighted toward letters perceived to have a significance or long-term impact. Even taking these caveats into account, the brutal point is that up-ending the approach can significantly change the perspective on these late-twelfth century collections. In this case, it was not just recent papal decretals in which the clerics were interested, but ancient ones too, and the proportion of the letters included in the collections becomes important.

So where does that leave the 'new law'? There is clearly something different about certain of the English collections. The 'Worcester' collection mentioned above clearly preferred decretals, as shown in the title rubrics, and recent conciliar provisions, including the canons promulgated at Tours in 1163 and the Lateran in 1179, are absent from the collection.[66] In fact, it contains only two excerpts from conciliar canons, both of which were misattributed to

64 *Corpus iuris canonici*, ed. Friedberg, 2:xii.

65 For some of the literature, see e.g. Uta-Renate Blumenthal, "Papal Registers in the Twelfth Century," in *Proceedings of the Seventh International Congress of Medieval Canon Law, Cambridge, 23–27 July 1984*, ed. Peter Linehan, MIC Subsidia 8 (Vatican City, 1988), pp. 137–51; Kenneth Pennington, "Epistolae Alexandrinae: A Collection of Pope Alexander III's Letters," in *Miscellanea Rolando Bandinelli, Papa Alessandro III*, ed. Filippo Liotta (Siena, 1986), pp. 337–53.

66 Lohmann, "*Collectio Wigorniensis*" (see above, n. 11); e.g. London, British Library, Royal 10.A.ii, fol. 5ra, which states "here begin the decretal letters of Alexander III [...]".

letters of Alexander III; one is from the early years of the Church, and one much later.[67] Furthermore, there is only one chapter containing pre-Gratian material, and that is a confusing hotchpotch of extracts from multiple sources present in a number of early collections.[68] The extent of the absence of this non-decretal material, especially when combined with the clear statement that the titles contained the "decretal letters of Alexander III", suggests that it was intentional. Other early English collections, including *Cantuariensis*, one of Holtzmann's 'English' family, also consist almost entirely of decretals, while only 17 chapters of the 579 in the *Appendix concilii Lateranensis* decretal collection date from before 1100.[69]

67 Christopher N.L. Brooke, "The Canons of English Church Council in the Early Decretal Collections," *Traditio* 13 (1957), 471–81, at p. 478, and *Wig*. 2.13(f).

68 One chapter, *Wig*. 2.13, appears in a bizarre form whereby it is pulled together from ten discrete sections, from a variety of sources and including their own inscriptions: 2.13(a) and 2.13(b) to the archbishop of York; 2.13(c) "from a privilege of pope Adrian"; 2.13(d) "Pope Paschal II"; 2.13(e) "as St Gregory said"; 2.13(f) "Item, from the council of Mainz"; 2.13(g) "Item Pope Gregory"; 2.13(h) "Item Paschal II"; 2.13(i) lacks and inscription; and 2.13(k) "Item from a privilege of Pope Alexander". A similar chapter appears as *Wigorniensis altera* c. 10 and *Belverensis* c. 11, see Duggan, *Twelfth-Century Decretal Collections* (see above, n. 14), pp. 154, 156 and e.g. London, British Library, Royal 11.B.ii, fol. 100r–v, while in *Parisiensis I* it appears as separate but consecutive canons: see *Canones-Sammlungen*, ed. Friedberg (see above, n. 16), p. 53 and Paris, Bibliothèque nationale de France, lat. 1596, fols 12v–13v, where Friedberg and Holtzmann's dissection of the canons mostly holds true. However, one section, consisting of *1 Par*. cc. 12–13, lacks the line break characteristic to differentiating between canons in the collection, which goes some way toward suggesting how the accumulation could have occurred, as well as opening up interesting questions surrounding the relationship between *Parisiensis I* and the early English collections. However, for the current purpose the important point is that the chapter begins with an inscription to the archbishop of York, suggesting that the compiler of *Wigorniensis* perceived it as a decretal rather than as a miscellany canon.

69 On *Cantuariensis*, see Duggan, *Twelfth-Century Decretal Collections* (see above, n. 14), pp. 162–71; the only two chapters which are not taken from recent papal decretals are *Cant*. 1.26, *Videtur nobis*, purporting to be a letter of an unidentifiable Pope Celestine to the bishop of Florence, and which ultimately formed part of both the *Decretum* as a *palea* at C. 34, q. 6, c. 2 and the *Extra* at 4.18.3, and *Cant*. 3.14, which is c. 1 from Alexander III's 1163 council at Tours, *Maioribus ecclesie beneficiis*, on which see also Robert Somerville, *Pope Alexander III and the Council of Tours (1163)* (Berkeley, 1977), p. 49 and for the canonistic transmission pp. 43–48. For the Appendix, see the vague analysis in *Canones-Sammlungen*, ed. Friedberg (see above, n. 16), pp. 63–84; Peter Landau, "Studien zur Appendix und den Glossen in frühen systematischen Dekretalensammlungen," *Bulletin of Medieval Canon Law*, n.s. 9 (1979), 1–21, at pp. 1–5; Duggan, "Decretal Collections" (see above, n. 3), pp. 277–70. The chapters in question are 6.5: "Idem ex concilio Africano," 6.27: "Idem Benedictus papa," 13.9: "Idem Gregorius," 13.15: "Idem Johannes papa," 17.7: "Idem ex registro Gregorii," 31.6.2: "Ex decretis Gelasii pape cap. 2," 38.5: "Item gloriosus Clemens in lib. Stromatum," 38.6: "Item Gregorius Syracusano episcopo," 43.2: "Item papa Leo tertius,"

Yet other collections show a much more limited proclivity to such new law. The continued reference back to earlier texts as late as the collections of the 1170s is highly interesting, but it is also critical to the narrative of the late-twelfth century collections as, in their most successful incarnations, they too incorporated such early texts. The *Francofurtana*, a systematic collection that survives in four manuscripts, contained 132 pre-Gratian texts in its most basic version, with a further 143 texts appearing with no inscription, but which seem to pre-date the 1140s.[70] Overall, around one third of the *Francofurtana*'s contents pre-dated Gratian. Although some collections of the *Bambergensis* group contain comparatively few pre-Gratian texts, several contain a much larger proportion. *Lipsiensis*, for example, contained 148 pre-Gratian extracts, equating to just over twenty per cent of its contents.[71] In fact, of the systematic collections, the one which seems to have been most limited in its circulation was, in fact, the one which had the lowest proportion of non-decretal material. The *Appendix concilii Lateranensis* survives today in three manuscripts, although a fourth, now lost, copy also existed in the sixteenth century; it was used mostly, if not exclusively, in England.[72] In contrast, the most successful of the late-twelfth century collections, the *Breviarium*, used non-decretal material for a third of its contents yet survives in well over a hundred manuscripts.[73]

The variety of locations for these later-twelfth century collections within their manuscripts has already been noted, particularly with reference to the English collections. For the primitive collections, the location of the collection changes between English material and that from the continent. The majority

43.4: "Item Gregorius Augustino Anglorum episcopo," 43.5: "Item ex concilio Maguntiensi, cap. primo," 44.1: "Item Gregorius Augustino Anglorum episcopo," 45.8: "Idem ex concilio Triburiensi", 48.2: "Idem Gregorius universis episcopis," 49.10: "Ex decretis Hormisde pape," with an additional chapter given no inscription at 38.7, all available in *Concilia omnia, tam generalia quam particularia* [...], ed. Pierre Crabbe, 2nd ed., 2 vols (Cologne, 1551) and in later collections to Mansi.

70 *Die Collectio Francofurtana*, ed. Landau and Drossbach (see above, n. 8), passim; Kuttner, *Repertorium* (see above, n. 13), pp. 295–96.

71 Leipzig, Universitätsbibliothek, 975, fols 116–53; see also Kuttner, *Repertorium* (see above, n. 13), p. 292; *Quinque Compilationes*, ed. Friedberg (see above, n. 16), pp. 189–208.

72 Although the *Appendix* made it to Tours, where it was used in the compilation of *Ur-Bambergensis*: Landau, "Die Entstehung" (see above, n. 27), p. 129 on *App.* and then pp. 134–35; but see Kuttner and Rathbone, "Anglo-Norman Canonists" (see above, n. 36), pp. 283–84 on the use of the *Appendix* solely amongst the Anglo-Norman school of canonists.

73 Gérard Fransen, "La tradition manuscrite de la 'Compilatio Prima'," in *Proceedings of the Second International Congress of Medieval Canon Law, Boston College, 12–16 August 1963*, ed. Stephan Kuttner and J. Joseph Ryan, MIC Subsidia 1 (Vatican City, 1965), pp. 56–62, at p. 56.

of the 'English' decretal collections appear in manuscripts which contain *legalia* or selections of material but not the *Decretum*. The *Cantuariensis* manuscript, for example, also contains an interesting *ordo* analysed by Fowler-Magerl. The exceptions are the *Dunelmensis* manuscript, which includes a copy of Gratian, and the *Roffensis* manuscript, where the collection falls after the *Dekretabbreviatio* of Omnebene.[74] In contrast, all five of the collections in Holtzmann's 'Italian' group are found in either a full or abbreviated Gratian manuscripts.[75] Most of the *Dekretanhänge* are continental in origin and most of these contain a high proportion of earlier material: the majority of texts in the *Dekretanhang* of Heiligenkreuz, Stiftsbibliothek, 44 were not decretals.[76] While in England, these collections may have been something else entirely, on the continent they were still viewed very much as the texts which wandered outside of Gratian. While Gratian remains the cut-off point, that seems to have been because of its general use rather than because there was a marked difference between the laws.

In fact, the distinction between the 'English' collections and those of the Continent carries over into the sender of some of the letters. While a majority of Alexander III's surviving decretals were sent to English recipients, the reverse is true of earlier papal letters. Individual letters are not found infrequently in the early *Dekretanhänge* or the proto-collections, and these tend to be (although are not limited to) letters of Eugenius III and Adrian IV. Honorius II's *Inherentes* can be found at the end of a number of *Decretum* manuscripts, including in Verona, Biblioteca Capitolare, 184.[77] All but one of the letters of Eugenius III to survive in the decretal collections were sent to continental recipients, and most of those were Italian.[78] A majority of the decretals of Adrian IV which entered

74 Durham, Cathedral and Chapter Library, C.III.1, fols 8va–18va, with intermissions; London, British Library, Royal 10.C.iv, fols 137v–154.

75 Berlin, Staatsbibliothek, Phill. 1742 (*Decretum* followed by *Collectio Berolinensis I*); Douai, Bibliothèque municipale, 590 (*Decretum* with fragmentary *Collectio Duacensis* in the flyleaves); Milan, Archivio capitolare di S. Ambrogio, M.54 (*Decretum*, followed by *Collectio Ambrosiana*); Sankt Florian, Stiftsbibliothek, III.5 (*Decretum* with *Collectio Florianensis* following); Bernkastel-Kues, Hospitalbibliothek, 229 (*Decretum* abbreviation followed by *Collectio Cusana*), although note the potential links between Holtzmann's 'Italian' group and northern France outlined in Wei, "Later Development" (see above, n. 39), pp. 155–56.

76 Rudolf Weigand, "Die Dekretanhänge in den Handschriften Heiligenkreuz 44, Pommersfelden 142 and München 28175," *Bulletin of Medieval Canon Law*, n.s. 13 (1983), 1–25, at pp. 3–8.

77 Verona, Biblioteca Capitolare, CLXXXIV (164), fol. 254rb.

78 The letters of Eugenius III in the collections or elsewhere are JL – [WH 332] to Uberto, archbishop of Milan; JL 8963 [WH 415] to 'A', bishop of Florence; JL 9653 [WH 545] to the bishops of Aix-en-Provence, Maguelonne, and Nîmes; JL 9506 [WH 560] to a cardinal

the later-twelfth century collections had French recipients.[79] The volume of decretals is a degree of magnitude lower, only 12 and 10 compared to over 700 Alexandrine letters, but it is still a significant point especially given that, as yet, there is no satisfactory answer as to why England became such a hotspot for canon law in the twelfth century. Since Duggan was primarily interested in the role of the decretal collections in English history, it is unfair to criticize him for not looking at the continental collections, but his disinclination to examine that material does over-emphasise the role of the English collections at the expense of others which employed different sources.

The point that I want to make here is that simply because the English material is so prevalent in the collections does not mean that only in England were recent papal decretals viewed as important legal texts, and in particular that England was not the only centre for engaging with and developing law in the period between 1140 and 1234. French and Italian clerics were also copying out letters sent to their territories too, albeit on a different scale. Equally, most of the *Dekretanhänge* identified by Kuttner seem to have non-English provenances. Troyes, Médiathèque du Grand Troyes, Fonds ancien 103, for example, has a handful of decretals in its flyleaves; the manuscript was probably Cistercian.[80] Two of these, one sent to Reims and one sent to Sens, also appear at the end of *Wigorniensis altera*, the oldest extant collection according to Duggan.[81] Elsewhere, the presence of a decretal sent to Treviso in the first section of the tripartite *Dunelmensis* collection demonstrates that the interest

priest 'G' and the bishop of 'Aretino'; JL 9659 [WH 595] to the clerics of Urbino and a priest 'Esculapius'; JL 14216 [WH 603] to the chapter of Bordeaux; JL 9654 [WH 625] to Master Omnebene and Arditius, subdeacon of the Roman church; JL – [WH 752] to the abbot of Saint-Denis; JL – [WH 943] to the cardinal deacon of Sant'Eustachio; JL 9667 [WH 1011] to the bishop of Padua; JL 9656 [WH 1015] to Conrad, vicar and clerk of the Romans; and JL – [WH 656*], to G., bishop of Bologna. The exception is JL 8959 [WH 736] to Jocelin, bishop of Salisbury.

79 JL – [WH 353*] = Adrian IV to the bishop of Châlons-sur-Marne (Châlons-en-Champagne); JL – [WH 366] = Adrian IV to the archbishop of Sens and the bishop of Auxerre; JL 10445 [WH 344] = Adrian IV to Everard, archbishop of Salzburg; JL 10444 [WH 664] = Adrian IV to Adam, prior of Pontigny; JL 10062 [WH 1049] = Adrian IV to the archbishop of Tours; JL – [WH 454] = Adrian IV to the bishop of Città di Castello; JL – [WH 533*] = Adrian IV to an unknown recipient; JL 10459 [WH 735] = Adrian IV to the monks of Astino. The exception is JL 11660 [WH 134] = Adrian IV to the archbishop of Canterbury.

80 Troyes, Médiathèque du Grand Troyes (olim Bibliothèque municipale), Fonds ancien 103, flyleaves; Duggan, "Decretal Collections" (see above, n. 3), p. 255.

81 London, British Library, Royal 11.B.ii, see Duggan, "Decretal Collections" (see above, n. 3), pp. 257–58 for literature.

in decretals was not the sole preserve of English clerics.[82] It is one of only two Alexandrine texts in that first section, which otherwise strongly resembles a *Dekretanhang* of the type appended to Innsbruck 80.[83] In fact, Holtzmann hypothesized that the entire first section of *Dunelmensis* was extra-English—most probably Italian—in origin, in part on the basis that the decretal to Treviso survives nowhere else. The most likely explanation for its inclusion in the Durham collection, whose later sections were heavily influenced by English material, is that it formed part of an Italian *Dekretanhang* that was later expanded somewhere in England, before making its way to Durham.

4 Conclusions

A critical argument behind the compilation of the decretal collections is that they were gathered together because local clerics were increasingly focussed on new law. Unfortunately, while some clerics clearly did have such a focus, others looked elsewhere. Saying that the amount of earlier material in the late-twelfth century collections was lower because such a large proportion was included in Gratian is one thing and is most likely accurate; arguing that the decretal collections themselves were conscious choices to rely purely on recent papal precedent is another. For one thing, outside of *Wigorniensis* it is rarely true. Some clerics were explicitly against the widespread use of decretals, so it should come as no surprise that the canonical collections compiled in the later-twelfth century reflect their views as well as the perspectives of those who did prioritise decretals. Taking into account the earlier contents of the collections, or even just switching the emphasis of any statistical or numerical comparison, gives a different perspective on the role played by these later twelfth century collections in the legal environment of the later-twelfth century.

By the time of the *Liber extra* in 1234, papal letters were of great importance in ecclesiastical government, while the study of and interaction with canon law was a sophisticated enterprise. Nevertheless, the collections that preceded the *Extra* were not purely 'decretal' collections and it makes more sense to

82 Durham, Cathedral and Chapter Library, C.III.1, fols 5v–18r; Holtzmann-Cheney (see above, n. 8), pp. 75–99; Duggan, *Twelfth-Century Decretal Collections* (see above, n. 14), pp. 78–79; the decretal to Treviso is *1 Dun.* 50, JL – [WH 417], and the other Alexandrine text in that early section is JL 13792/14190/14202 [WH 84], sent by Alexander III but in this case with an inscription to Alexander II rather than his later successor.

83 Innsbruck, Universitäts- und Landesbibliothek Tirol, 80, fols 273–77; an amount of the material here is in fact in common with one of the Durham collections: Kuttner, *Repertorium* (see above, n. 13), p. 286.

consider them within the sphere of earlier collections of canon law rather than necessarily as a distinct and new creation, important purely because they represented some thing novel. The two broadest areas here, which may help to understand the importance of letters in the twelfth century, are research in the broader field of letter collections and the continued interest, amongst scholars of eleventh-century canon law, in the florilegia and farraginous collections which, in fact, the early decretal collections mimic. The distinctions between and within the decretal collections have helped scholars to understand the connections and differences between the collections. But the strict definitional archetype they perpetuate can veil the realities of late-twelfth century canon law. Regardless of where the collections originated, the most successful in the long-term were those which combined decretal and earlier material, particularly in the case of the *Breviarium*.

In the later-twelfth century, 'new law' was something that was not yet tangible: there was no *Liber extra* to hold up as a gold standard. Ultimately, for there to be a 'new law' the old had to be widely accepted, a process which took decades. Understanding the contribution made by canonists later in the twelfth century to that process means going beyond the basic distinctions all too often drawn between terms and focussing as much on the continuities in legal practice and legal collections as on the differences that began to appear.

Canon Law before Gratian: A Bibliographical Appendix

Christof Rolker

1 Canon Law before Gratian: A Select Bibliography

The following list a selection of works which are of particular importance for the field, from shorter overviews (e.g. the articles by Clarke, Rennie/Taliadoros, and Reynolds) to highly specialised studies. Preference has been given to recent work, mainly (but not exclusively so) written in English. Apart from the *Histoire*, two works deserve special mention: Fowler-Magerl's *Clavis canonum* (and the database of the same name, available online at www.clavis.mgh.de) and Kéry's bibliography are indispensable for anyone interested in the field; they are the first port of call both for basic information on any given pre-Gratian collection and for specialized research on them. It is hoped that scholarship in the field will, alongside the 'new narrative', provide for updated versions of these tools of research; information on this on-going project is to be found at www.clavis.mgh.de, too.

Austin, Greta, "The Bishop and the Law of the Church, 900–1050," in *The Bishop Reformed: Studies in Episcopal Culture and Power in the Central Middle Ages (900–1215)*, ed. John Ott and Anna Trumbore (Aldershot, 2007), pp. 39–56.

Austin, Greta, *Shaping Church Law around the Year 1000: The* Decretum *of Burchard of Worms*, Church, Faith and Culture in the Medieval West (Aldershot, 2009).

Berman, Harold Joseph, *Law and Revolution: The Formation of the Western Legal Tradition* (Cambridge, Mass. and London, 1983).

Blumenthal, Uta-Renate, *Papal Reform and Canon Law in the 11th and 12th Centuries*, Variorum Collected Studies Series 618 (Aldershot, 1998).

Brasington, Bruce Clark, *Ways of Mercy: The Prologue of Ivo of Chartres: Edition and Analysis*, Vita regularis. Editionen 2 (Münster, 2004).

Brett, Martin, "Urban II and the Collections Attributed to Ivo of Chartres," in *Proceedings of the Eighth International Congress of Medieval Canon Law, San Diego, University of California at La Jolla, 21–27 August 1988*, ed. Stanley Chodorow, MIC Subsidia 9 (Vatican City, 1992), pp. 27–46.

Brett, Martin, "Canon Law and Litigation: The Century before Gratian," in *Medieval Ecclesiastical Studies in Honour of Dorothy M. Owen*, ed. Michael J. Franklin and Christopher Harper-Bill, Studies in the History of Medieval Religion 7 (Woodbridge, 1995), pp. 21–40.

 | DOI:10.1163/9789004394384_011

Brett, Martin, "Creeping up on the *Panormia*," in *Grundlagen des Rechts. Festschrift für Peter Landau*, ed. Richard H. Helmholz, Paul Mikat, Jörg Müller, and Michael Stolleis, Rechts- und Staatswissenschaftliche Veröffentlichungen der Görres-Gesellschaft N.F. 91 (Paderborn, Munich, Vienna, and Zurich, 2000), pp. 205–70.

Brett, Martin, "Editions, Manuscripts and Readers in Some Pre-Gratian Collections," in *Ritual, Text and Law: Studies in Medieval Canon Law and Liturgy Presented to Roger E. Reynolds*, ed. Richard F. Gyug and Kathleen Grace Cushing, Church, Faith, and Culture in the Medieval West (Aldershot, 2004), pp. 205–44.

Brett, Martin, "Finding the Law: The Sources of Canonical Authority before Gratian," in *Law before Gratian: Law in Western Europe c. 500–1100*, ed. Per Andersen, Mia Münster-Swendsen and Helle Vogt, Proceedings of the Carlsberg Academy Conference on Medieval Legal History 3 (Copenhagen, 2007), pp. 51–72.

Brett, Martin, "Editing Canon Law Collections between Burchard and Gratian," in *Proceedings of the Twelfth International Congress of Medieval Canon Law, Washington, D.C., 1–7 August 2004*, ed. Uta-Renate Blumenthal, Kenneth Pennington and Atria Ann Larson, MIC Subsidia 13 (Vatican City, 2008), pp. 89–107.

Clarke, Peter D., "Canon Law," in *Routledge History of Medieval Christianity, 1050–1500*, ed. Robert N. Swanson (Abingdon and New York, 2015), pp. 77–90.

Conrat (Cohn), Max, *Geschichte der Quellen und Literatur des Römischen Rechts im frühen Mittelalter* (Leipzig, 1891).

Cushing, Kathleen Grace, *Papacy and Law in the Gregorian Revolution: The Canonistic Work of Anselm of Lucca*, Oxford Historical Monographs (Oxford, 1998).

Cushing, Kathleen Grace, *Reform and the Papacy in the Eleventh Century: Spirituality and Social Change*, Manchester Medieval Studies (Manchester and New York, 2005).

Cushing, Kathleen Grace, "Law, Penance, and the 'Gregorian' Reform: The Case of Padua, Biblioteca del Seminario Vescovile MS 529," in *Canon Law, Religion and Politics: Liber Amicorum Robert Somerville*, ed. Uta-Renate Bluwmenthal, Anders Winroth and Peter Landau (Washington, D.C., 2012), pp. 28–40.

Dusil, Stephan, *Wissensordnungen des Rechts im Wandel. Päpstlicher Jurisdiktionsprimat und Zölibat zwischen 1000 und 1215*, Mediaevalia Lovaniensia 47 (Leuven, 2018).

Eichbauer, Melodie Harris, "From Gratian's *Concordia discordantium canonum* to Gratian's *Decretum*: The Evolution from Teaching Text to Comprehensive Code of Canon Law" (PhD thesis, Washington, D.C., 2010).

Fournier, Paul, "Les collections attribuées à Yves de Chartres," *Bibliothèque de l'École des Chartes* 57 (1896), 645–98, *Bibliothèque de l'École des Chartes* 58 (1897), 26–77, 293–326, 410–44 and 624–76; repr. in idem, *Mélanges de droit canonique*, ed. Theo Kölzer, 2 vols (Aalen, 1983), 1:451–678.

Fournier, Paul, "Le Décret de Burchard de Worms: ses caractères, son influence," *Revue d'histoire ecclésiastique* 12 (1911), 451–73 and 670–701; repr. in idem. *Mélanges de droit canonique*, ed. Theo Kölzer, 2 vols (Aalen, 1983), 1:393–447.

Fournier, Paul, "Un tournant de l'histoire du droit 1060–1140," *Nouvelle revue historique de droit français et étranger* 40 (1917), 129–80; repr. in idem, *Mélanges de droit canonique*, ed. Theo Kölzer, 2 vols (Aalen, 1983), 2:373–424.

Fournier, Paul, with the collaboration of Gabriel Le Bras, *Histoire des collections canoniques en Occident dépuis les Fausses Décrétales jusqu'au Décret de Gratien*, 2 vols (Paris, 1931–32; repr. Aalen, 1972).

Fowler-Magerl, Linda, "Fine Distinctions and the Transmission of Texts," *Zeitschrift der Savigny-Stiftung für Rechtsgeschichte, kanonistische Abteilung* 83 (1997), 146–86.

Fowler-Magerl, Linda, "The Use of the Letters of Pope Gregory I in Northeastern France and Lorraine before 1100," in *"Ins Wasser geworfen und Ozeane durchquert". Festschrift für Knut Wolfgang Nörr*, ed. Mario Ascheri, Friedrich Ebel, Martin Heckel, Antonio Padoa-Schioppa, Wolfgang Pöggeler, Filippo Ranieri and Wilhelm Rütten (Cologne, 2003), pp. 237–60.

Fowler-Magerl, Linda, *Clavis Canonum: Selected Canon Law Collections before 1140: Access with Data Processing*, MGH Hilfsmittel 21 (Munich, 2005).

Fowler-Magerl, Linda, "The Collection and Transmission of Canon Law along the Northern Section of the Via Francigena in the Eleventh and Twelfth Centuries," in *Bishops, Texts and the Use of Canon Law around 1100: Essays in the Honour of Martin Brett*, ed. Bruce Clark Brasington and Kathleen Grace Cushing, Church, Faith and Culture in the Middle Ages (Aldershot, 2008), pp. 129–39.

Fransen, Gérard, *Les collections canoniques*, Typologie des sources du moyen âge occidental 10 (Turnhout, 1973).

Fransen, Gérard, *Les collections canoniques*, Typologie des sources du moyen âge occidental, mise à jour du fascicule n° 10, (Turnhout, 1985).

Fransen, Gérard, "Le Décret de Burchard de Worms: valeur du texte de l'édition: essai de classement des manuscrits," *Zeitschrift der Savigny-Stiftung für Rechtsgeschichte, kanonistische Abteilung* 63 (1977), 1–19.

Fransen, Gérard, *Canones et quaestiones: évolution des doctrines et système du droit canonique*, ed. Antonio García y García, Bibliotheca eruditorum 25, 3 vols (Goldbach, 2002).

Fuhrmann, Horst, "Über den Reformgeist der 74-Titel-Sammlung (Diversorum patrum sententiae)," in: *Festschrift für Hermann Heimpel*, 3 vols, Veröffentlichungen des Max-Planck-Instituts für Geschichte 36 (Göttingen 1972), 2:1101–20.

Fuhrmann, Horst, *Einfluß und Verbreitung der Pseudoisidorischen Fälschungen. Von ihrem Auftauchen bis in die neuere Zeit*, 3 vols, Schriften der Monumenta Germaniae historica 24 (Stuttgart, 1972–74).

Fuhrmann, Horst, "The Pseudo-Isidorian Forgeries", in Detlev Jasper and Horst Fuhrmann, *Papal Letters in the Early Middle Ages*, History of Medieval Canon Law (Washington, D.C., 2001), pp. 135–95.

Genka, Tatsushi, "Zur textlichen Grundlage der Imputationslehre Gratians," *Bulletin of Medieval Canon Law*, n.s. 26 (2006), 40–81.

Genka, Tatsushi, "Hierarchie der Texte, Hierarchie der Autoritäten. Zur Hierarchie der Rechtsquellen bei Gratian," *Zeitschrift der Savigny-Stiftung für Rechtsgeschichte, kanonistische Abteilung* 95 (2009), 101–27.

Gilchrist, John T., "Was There a Gregorian Reform Movement in the Eleventh Century?," *Study Sessions of the Canadian Catholic Historical Association* 37 (1970), 1–10; repr. in idem *Canon Law in the Age of Reform, 11th–12th Century*, Variorum Collected Studies Series 406 (Aldershot, 1993), no. VII.

Gilchrist, John T., "The Reception of Pope Gregory VII into the Canon Law (1073–1141)," *Zeitschrift der Savigny-Stiftung für Rechtsgeschichte, kanonistische Abteilung* 90 (1973), 34–82 and 97 (1980), 192–229; repr. in idem *Canon Law in the Age of Reform, 11th–12th Century*, Variorum Collected Studies Series 406 (Aldershot, 1993), nos VIII–IX.

Giraud, Cédric, *"Per verba magistri": Anselme de Laon et son école au XIIe siècle*, Bibliothèque d'histoire culturelle du Moyen Âge 8 (Turnhout, 2010).

Hartmann, Wilfried, *Kirche und Kirchenrecht um 900. Die Bedeutung der spätkarolingischen Zeit für Tradition und Innovation im kirchlichen Recht*, Schriften der Monumenta Germaniae historica 58 (Hanover, 2008).

Hoffmann, Hartmut, and Pokorny, Rudolf, *Das Dekret des Bischofs Burchard von Worms. Textstufen—Frühe Verbreitung—Vorlagen*, MGH Hilfsmittel 12 (Munich, 1991).

Jasper, Detlev, "Burchards Dekret in der Sicht der Gregorianer," in *Bischof Burchard von Worms, 1000–1025*, ed. Wilfried Hartmann, Quellen und Abhandlungen zur mittelrheinischen Kirchengeschichte 100 (Mainz, 2000).

Jasper, Detlev, "The Beginning of the Decretal Tradition: Papal Letters from the Origin of the Genre through the Pontificate of Stephen V", in Detlev Jasper and Horst Fuhrmann, *Papal Letters in the Early Middle Ages*, History of Medieval Canon Law (Washington, D.C., 2001), pp. 1–133.

Kéry, Lotte, *Canonical Collections of the Early Middle Ages (ca. 400–1140): A Bibliographical Guide to the Manuscripts and Literature*, History of Medieval Canon law (Washington, D.C., 1999).

Kéry, Lotte, *Gottesfurcht und irdische Strafe. Der Beitrag des mittelalterlichen Kirchenrechts zur Entstehung des öffentlichen Strafrechts* (Cologne, Weimar, and Vienna, 2006).

Kuttner, Stephan, *Harmony from Dissonance: An Interpretation of Medieval Canon Law* (The Wimmer Lecture 10, Latrobe, Penn., 1960).

Kuttner, Stephan, "Urban II and the Doctrine of Interpretation: A Turning Point?," *Studia Gratiana* 15 (1972), 55–85; repr. in idem, *The History of Ideas and Doctrines of Canon Law in the Middle Ages*, 2nd ed., Variorum Collected Studies Series 113 (London, 1992), no. IV.

Kuttner, Stephan, "The Revival of Jurisprudence," in *Renaissance and Renewal in the Twelfth Century*, ed. Robert Benson and Giles Constable (Boston, 1982), pp. 299–323; repr. in idem, *Studies in the History of Medieval Canon Law*, Variorum Collected Studies Series 325 (Aldershot, 1990), no. III.

Landau, Peter, "Erweiterte Fassungen der Kanonessammlung des Anselm von Lucca aus dem 12. Jahrhundert," in *Sant'Anselmo, Mantova e la lotta per le investiture: atti di convegno internazionale di studi (Mantova 23–24–25 Maggio 1986)*, ed. Paolo Golinelli (Bologna, 1987), pp. 323–37.

Landau, Peter, "Gefälschtes Recht in den Rechtssammlungen bis Gratian," in *Fälschungen im Mittelalter. Internationaler Kongreß der Monumenta Germaniae Historica, München, 16.–19. September 1986, 2: Gefälschte Rechtstexte. Der bestrafte Fälscher*, Schriften der Monumenta Germaniae historica 33/2 (Hanover, 1988), pp. 11–49.

Landau, Peter, "Vorgratianische Kanonessammlungen bei Dekretisten und in frühen Dekretalensammlungen," in *Proceedings of the Eighth International Congress of Medieval Canon Law, San Diego, University of California at La Jolla, 21–27 August 1988*, ed. Stanley Chodorow, MIC Subsidia 9 (Vatican City, 1992), pp. 93–116.

Landau, Peter, "Gratian and the *Decretum Gratiani*," in *The History of Medieval Canon Law in the Classical Period: From Gratian to the Decretals of Pope Gregory IX*, ed. Wilfried Hartmann and Kenneth Pennington, History of Medieval Canon Law (Washington, D.C., 2008), pp. 22–54.

Landau, Peter, "Die Dekretsumme 'Tractaturus Magister' und die Kanonistik in Reims in der zweiten Hälfte des 12. Jahrhunderts," *Zeitschrift der Savigny-Stiftung für Rechtsgeschichte, kanonistische Abteilung* 100 (2014), 132–52.

Larson, Atria Ann, *Master of Penance: Gratian and the Development of Penitential Thought and Law in the Twelfth Century*, Studies in Medieval and Early Modern Canon Law 11 (Washington, D.C., 2014).

Lenherr, Titus, "Die 'Glossa Ordinaria' zur Bibel als Quelle von Gratians Dekret," *Bulletin of Medieval Canon Law*, n.s. 24 (2000), 97–129.

Lenherr, Titus, "Die Vier Fassungen von C. 3 q. 1 d.p.c. 6 im Decretum Gratiani. Zugleich ein Einblick in die neueste Diskussion um das Werden von Gratians Dekret," *Archiv für katholisches Kirchenrecht* 169 (2000), 353–81.

Maassen, Friedrich, *Geschichte der Quellen und der Literatur des Canonischen Rechts im Abendlande bis zum Ausgange des Mittelalters, 1: Die Rechtssammlungen bis zur Mitte des 9. Jahrhunderts* (Graz, 1870) [all published].

Meyer, Christoph H.F., *Die Distinktionstechnik in der Kanonistik des 12. Jahrhunderts. Ein Beitrag zur Wissenschaftsgeschichte des Hochmittelalters*, Mediaevalia Lovaniensia. Studia 29 (Leuven, 2000).

Mordek, Hubert, "Kanonistik und Gregorianische Reform. Marginalien zu einem nicht-marginalen Thema," in *Reich und Kirche vor dem Investiturstreit. Vorträge beim wissenschaftlichen Kolloquium aus Anlaß des 80. Geburtstags von Gerd Tellenbach*, ed. Karl Schmid (Sigmaringen, 1985), pp. 65–82.

Mostert, Marco, *The Political Theology of Abbo of Fleury: A Study of the Ideas about Society and Law of the 10th-Century Monastic Reform Movement*, Middeleeuwse studies en bronnen 2 (Hilversum, 1987).

Ott, John Stephens, *Bishops, Authority and Community in Northwestern Europe, c. 1050–1150*, Cambridge Studies in Medieval Life and Thought, Fourth Series 102 (Cambridge, 2015).

Rennie, Kriston R., and Taliadoros, Jason, "Why Study Medieval Canon Law?," *History Compass* 12:2 (2014), 133–49.

Reynolds, Roger E., *Studies on Medieval Liturgical and Legal Manuscripts from Spain and Italy*, Variorum Collected Studies Series 927 (Aldershot, 2009).

Reynolds, Roger E., "The Influence of Eastern Patristic Fathers on the Canonical Collections of South Italy in the Eleventh and Early Twelfth Centuries," in *Canon Law, Religion and Politics: Liber Amicorum Robert Somerville*, ed. Uta-Renate Blumenthal, Anders Winroth and Peter Landau (Washington, D.C., 2012), pp. 75–106.

Reynolds, Roger E., "Law, Canon: To Gratian", in *Dictionary of the Middle Ages*, 7 (New York, 1986), pp. 395–413.

Rolker, Christof, "The *Collection in Seventy-Four Titles*: A Monastic Canon Law Collection from Eleventh-Century France," in *Readers, Texts and Compilers in the Earlier Middle Ages: Studies in Medieval Canon Law in Honour of Linda Fowler-Magerl*, ed. Martin Brett and Kathleen Grace Cushing, Church, Faith and Culture in the Medieval West (Aldershot, 2009), pp. 59–72.

Rolker, Christof, *Canon Law and the Letters of Ivo of Chartres*, Cambridge Studies in Medieval Life and Thought, Fourth Series 76 (Cambridge, 2010).

Ryan, John Joseph, *Saint Peter Damiani and his Canonical Sources: A Preliminary Study in the Antecedents of the Gregorian Reform* Pontifical Institute of Medieval Studies. Studies and Texts 2 (Toronto, 1956).

von Schulte, Johann Friedrich, *Die Geschichte der Quellen und Literatur des canonischen Rechts*, 3 vols (Stuttgart, 1875; repr. Clark, N.J., 2000).

Somerville, Robert, *Papacy, Councils, and Canon Law in the 11th–12th Centuries*, Variorum Collected Studies Series 312 (Aldershot, 1990).

Somerville, Robert, *Pope Urban II's Council of Piacenza* (Oxford, 2011).

Somerville, Robert, and Brasington, Bruce Clark, *Prefaces to Canon Law Books in Latin Christianity: Selected Translations, 500–1245* (New Haven and London, 1998).

Somerville, Robert, in collaboration with Stephan Kuttner, *Pope Urban II, the* Collectio Britannica, *and the Council of Melfi (1089)* (Oxford, 1996).

Thier, Andreas, "Dynamische Schriftlichkeit. Zur Normbildung in den vorgratianischen Kanonessammlungen," *Zeitschrift der Savigny-Stiftung für Rechtsgeschichte, kanonistische Abteilung* 124 (2007), 1–33.

Thier, Andreas, *Hierarchie und Autonomie. Regelungstraditionen der Bischofsbestellung in der Geschichte des kirchlichen Wahlrechts*, Recht im ersten Jahrtausend 1 (Frankfurt, 2011).

Wei, John C., "Gratian and the School of Laon," *Traditio* 64 (2009), 279–322.

Wei, John C., "The Sentence Collection *Deus non habet initium uel terminum* and its Reworking, *Deus itaque summe atque ineffabiliter bonus*," *Mediaeval Studies* 74 (2012), 1–118.

Wei, John C., "A Twelfth-Century Treatise on Charity: The Tract 'Vt autem hoc euidenter' of the Sentence Collection *Deus itaque summe atque ineffabiliter bonus*," *Mediaeval Studies* 72 (2012), 1–50.

Wei, John C., *Gratian the Theologian*, Studies in Medieval and Early Modern Canon Law 13 (Washington, D.C., 2016).

Winroth, Anders, *The Making of Gratian's Decretum*, Cambridge Studies in Medieval Life and Thought, Fourth Series 49 (Cambridge, 2000).

2 Bibliography

The following bibliography contains complete bibliographical information for the sources and literature quoted in the preceedings chapters.

Primary Sources

Agnellus of Ravenna, *Liber pontificalis ecclesiae Ravennatis*, ed. Oswald Holder-Egger, MGH SS rer. Lang. 1 (Hanover, 1878), pp. 265–391.

Agnellus of Ravenna, *Codex pontificalis ecclesiae Ravennatis*, 1, ed. Alessandro Testi-Rasponi, Rerum Italicarum Scriptores n.s. 2/3 (Bologna, 1924).

Agnellus of Ravenna, *Liber pontificalis / Bischofsbuch*, 1, ed. and tr. Claudia Nauerth, Fontes Christiani 21/1 (Freiburg, Basel, Vienna, Barcelona, Rome, and New York, 1996).

Agnellus of Ravenna, *The Book of Pontiffs of the Church of Ravenna*, tr. Deborah M. Deliyannis (Washington, D.C., 2004).

Agnellus of Ravenna, *Liber pontificalis ecclesiae Ravennatis*, ed. Deborah M. Deliyannis, CCCM 199 (Turnhout, 2006).

Anselmi episcopi Lucensis collectio canonum una cum collectione minore, ed. Friedrich Thaner, 2 in 1 vol (Innsbruck, 1906–15).

Augustine, *De Trinitate libri XV*, ed. William J. Mountain with the help of Frater Glorie, CCSL 50, 2 vols (Turnhout, 1968).

Augustine, *Retractationes*, ed. Almut Mutzenbecher, CCSL 57 (Turnhout, 1984).

Bernard of Pavia, *Summa decretalium: ad librorum manuscriptorum fidem, cum aliis eiusdem scriptoris anecdotis*, ed. Ernst Adolph Theodor Laspeyres (Regensburg, 1860).

Bernard of Pavia, *Breviarium extravagantium*, in *Quinque compilationes antiquae, nec non Collectio canonum Lipsiensis*, ed. Emil Friedberg (Leipzig, 1882; repr. Graz, 1956), pp. 1–66.

Bernold of Konstanz, *De excommunicatis vitandis, de reconciliatione lapsorum et de fontibus iuris ecclesiastici* (*Libellus X*), ed. Doris Stöckly and Detlev Jasper, MGH Fontes iuris 15 (Hanover, 2000).

Burchard of Worms, *Decretorum libri XX* [...]. *Ergänzter Neudruck der* Editio princeps *Köln 1548*, ed. Gérard Fransen and Theo Kölzer (Aalen, 1992).

Die Canones-Sammlungen zwischen Gratian und Bernhard von Pavia, ed. Johann Friedrich von Schulte (Leipzig, 1897).

Collectio canonum trium librorum, ed. Giuseppe Motta, MIC Corpus collectionum 8, 2 vols (Vatican City, 2005–08).

Die Collectio Cheltenhamensis. Eine englische Decretalensammlung. Analyse beruhend auf Vorarbeiten von Walther Holtzmann†, ed. Gisela Drossbach, MIC Corpus collectionum 10 (Vatican City, 2014).

Die Collectio Francofurtana. Eine französische Decretalensammlung. Analyse beruhend auf Vorarbeiten von Walther Holtzmann†, ed. Peter Landau and Gisela Drossbach, MIC Corpus collectionum 9 (Vatican City, 2007).

Concilia omnia, tam generalia quam particularia [...], ed. Pierre Crabbe, 2nd ed., 2 vols (Cologne, 1551).

Conciliorum oecumenicorum decreta, ed. Giuseppe Alberigo et al. (Bologna, 1973); with an English translation by Norman P. Tanner, *Decrees of the ecumenical councils*, 2 vols (London, 1990).

Concilium Quinisextum / Das Konzil Quinisextum, griechisch-deutsch, ed. and tr. Heinz Ohme (Turnhout, 2006).

Decretales Pseudo-Isidorianae et Capitula Angilramni, ed. Paul Hinschius (Leipzig, 1863).

Decretalium collectiones / Decretales Gregorii, ed. Emil Friedberg, Corpus iuris canonici 2 (Leipzig, 1881; repr. Graz, 1956).

Diuersorum patrum sententie siue Collectio in LXXIV titulos digesta, ed. John T. Gilchrist, 2 vols, MIC Corpus collectionum 1 (Vatican City, 1973); English tr. by John T. Gilchrist, *The Collection in Seventy-Four Titles: A Canon Law Manual of the Gregorian Reform*, Mediaeval Sources in Translation 22 (Toronto, 1980).

Gandulph of Bologna, *Sententiarum libri quattuor*, ed. Johannes de Walter (Vienna, 1924).

Gilbertus Universalis, *Glossa Ordinaria in Lamentationes Ieremie Prophete, Prothemata et Liber I*, ed. and tr. Alexander Andrée (Stockholm, 2005).

Gratian, *Decretum magistri Gratiani*, ed. Emil Friedberg, Corpus Iuris Canonici 1 (Leipzig, 1879; repr. Graz, 1956).

Huguccio, *Summa Decretorum*, ed. Oldřich Přerovský, MIC Corpus collectionum 6 (Vatican City, 2006).

Ivo of Chartres, *Prologus*, ed. Bruce Clark Brasington, *Ways of Mercy: The Prologue of Ivo of Chartres: Edition and Analysis*, Vita regularis. Editionen 2 (Münster, 2004), pp. 115–42.

Die Konzilsordines des Früh- und Hochmittelalters, ed. Herbert Schneider, MGH Ordines de celebrando concilio (Hanover, 1996).

Lambert of Arras, *Le registre de Lambert, évêque d'Arras (1093–1115)*, ed. and trans. Claire Giordanengo, Sources d'histoire médiévale 34 (Paris, 2007).

Liber canonum diuersorum sanctorum patrum sive Collectio in CLXXXIII titulos digesta, ed. Giuseppe Motta, MIC Corpus collectionum 7 (Vatican City, 1988).

Lodovico Antonio Muratori, *Spicilegium Ravennatis historiae sive monumenta historica ad ecclesiam et urbem Ravennatem spectantia* (Milan, 1725).

Paucapalea, *Die Summa des Paucapalea über das Decretum Gratiani*, ed. Johann Friedrich von Schulte (Giessen, 1890).

Peter Abelard, *Sic et non: ouvrages inédits d'Abélard*, ed. Victor Cousin (Paris, 1836).

Peter Abelard, *Sic et non: A Critical Edition*, ed. Blanche Beatrice Boyer and Richard Peter McKeon (Chicago and London, 1977).

Peter Damian, *Vita beati Romualdi*, ed. Giovanni Tabacco (Rome, 1957).

Peter Abelard, *Sancti Petri Damiani Sermones*, CCCM 57, ed. Giovanni Lucchesi (Turnhout, 1983).

Peter Abelard, *Die Briefe des Petrus Damiani*, ed. Kurt Reindel, MGH Briefe der deutschen Kaiserzeit 4, 4 vols (Munich, 1983–93).

Regino of Prüm, *Libri duo de synodalibus causis et disciplinis ecclesiasticis*, ed. Friedrich Wilhelm Hermann Wasserschleben (Leipzig, 1840).

Le registre de l'officialité de Cerisy, ed. Gustave Dupont (Caen, 1880).

Rufin, *Die Summa decretorum des Magisters Rufinus*, ed. Heinrich Singer (Paderborn, 1902).

Sacrorum conciliorum nova et amplissima collectio, ed. Giovanni Domenico Mansi, 31 vols (Venice, 1758–78).

Simon of Bisignano, *Summa in Decretum*, ed. Pier V. Aimone-Braida, MIC Corpus glossatorum 8 (Vatican City, 2014).

Robert Somerville and Bruce Clark Brasington, *Prefaces to Canon Law Books in Latin Christianity: Selected Translations, 500–1245* (New Haven and London, 1998).

The Summa Parisiensis on the Decretum Gratiani, ed. Terence P. McLaughlin (Toronto, 1952).

Summma 'Reverentia sacrorum canonum', ed. John C. Wei, MIC Corpus glossatorum 9 (Vatican City, 2018).

Veterum scriptorum et monumentorum historicorum, dogmaticorum, moralium amplissima collectio, ed. Edmond Martène and Ursin Durand, 9 vols (Paris, 1724–33).

Secondary Literature

Andrée, Alexander, "Anselm of Laon Unveiled: The *Glosae super Iohannem* and the Origins of the *Glossa ordinaria* on the Bible," *Mediaeval Studies* 73 (2011), 217–40.

Andrée, Alexander, "Laon Revisited: Master Anselm and the Creation of a Theological School in the Twelfth Century," *The Journal of Medieval Latin* 22 (2012), 257–81.

Applegate, Celia, "A Europe of Regions: Reflections on the Historiography of Sub-National Places in Modern Times," *The American Historical Review* 104:4 (1999), 1157–82.

Audebert, Myriam Soria, *La crosse brisée: des évêques agressés dans une Église en conflits (royaume de France, fin X^e–début XIIIe siècle)*, Culture et société médiévales 6 (Turnhout, 2005).

Austin, Greta, "Canon Law in the Long Tenth Century, 900–1050," in *Cambridge Companion to Medieval Canon Law*, ed. Anders Winroth and John C. Wei (Cambridge, forthcoming).

Austin, Greta, "The Bishop and the Law of the Church, 900–1050," in *The Bishop Reformed: Studies in Episcopal Culture and Power in the Central Middle Ages (900–1215)*, ed. John Ott and Anna Trumbore Jones (Aldershot, 2007), pp. 39–56.

Austin, Greta, *Shaping Church Law around the Year 1000: The* Decretum *of Burchard of Worms*, Church, Faith and Culture in the Medieval West (Aldershot, 2009).

Bady, Guillaume, "Le prologue du *Sic et non* d'Abélard," in *Les réceptions des Pères de l'Église au Moyen Âge: le devenir de la tradition ecclésiale*, ed. Rainer Berndt and Michel Fédou, 2 vols (Münster, 2013), 2:727–42.

Ballerini, Pietro, and Ballerini, Girolamo, "De antiquis tum editis tum ineditis collectionibus et collectoribus canonum ad Gratianum usque," in *Sancti Leonis Magni Romani pontificis opera*, ed. iidem (Venice, 1757), pp. i–cccxx.

Barstow, Anne Llewellyn, *Married Priests and the Reforming Papacy: The Eleventh-Century Debates*, Texts and Studies in Religion 12 (New York and Toronto, 1982).

Basdevant-Gaudemet, Brigitte, and Domingo, Rafael, "Paul Fournier," in *Great Christian Jurists in French History*, ed. Olivier Descamps and Rafael Domingo (Cambridge, 2019), forthcoming.

Becker, Alfons, *Studien zum Investiturproblem in Frankreich. Papsttum, Königtum und Episkopat im Zeitalter der gregorianischen Kirchenreform (1049–1119)*, Schriften der Universität des Saarlandes (Saarbrücken, 1955).

Becker, Alfons, *Papst Urban II. (1088–1099)*, 3 vols, Schriften der Monumenta Germaniae historica 19 (Stuttgart, 1964–2012).

Berardi, Carlo Sebastiano, *De variis sacrorum canonum collectionibus ante Gratianum* (Turin, 1752).

Berman, Harold Joseph, *Law and Revolution: The Formation of the Western Legal Tradition* (Cambridge, Mass. and London, 1983).

Berman, Harold Joseph, *Faith and Order: The Reconciliation of Law and Religion*, Emory University Studies in Law and Religion 3 (Atlanta, 1993).

Beyer, Alfred, *Lokale Abbreviationen des Decretum Gratiani. Analyse und Vergleich der Dekretabbreviationen "Omnes leges aut divine" (Bamberg), "Humanum genus duobus regitur" (Pommersfelden) und "De his qui intra claustra monasterii consistunt" (Lichtenthal, Baden-Baden)*, Bamberger theologische Studien 6 (Frankfurt and New York, 1998).

Bliemetzrieder, Franz Plazidus, "Gratian und die Schule Anselms von Laon," *Archiv für katholisches Kirchenrecht* 112 (1932), 37–63.

Blumenthal, Uta-Renate, *The Early Councils of Pope Paschalis II 1100–1110*, Pontifical Institute of Medieval Studies. Studies and Texts 43 (Toronto, 1978).

Blumenthal, Uta-Renate, "Papal Registers in the Twelfth Century," in *Proceedings of the Seventh International Congress of Medieval Canon Law, Cambridge, 23–27 July 1984*, ed. Peter Linehan, MIC Subsidia 8 (Vatican City, 1988), pp. 137–51.

Blumenthal, Uta-Renate, "Pope Gregory VII and the Prohibition of Nicolaitism," in *Medieval Purity and Piety: Essays on Medieval Clerical Celibacy and Religious Reform*, ed. Michael Frassetto (New York and London, 1998), pp. 239–67.

Boelens, Martin, *Die Klerikerehe in der Gesetzgebung der Kirche* (Paderborn, 1968).

Bouquillon, Thomas, "The University of Paris," *The Catholic University Bulletin* 1 (1895), 349–69.

Bournazel, Éric, *Le gouvernement capétien au XIIe siècle, 1108–1180: structures sociales et mutations institutionnelles*, Publications de la Faculté de droit et des sciences économiques de Limoges 2 (Paris, 1975).

Brasington, Bruce Clark, *Ways of Mercy: The Prologue of Ivo of Chartres: Edition and Analysis*, Vita regularis. Editionen 2 (Münster, 2004).

Brasington, Bruce Clark, *Order in the Court: Medieval Procedural Treatises in Translation*, Medieval Law and its Practice 21 (Leiden, 2016).

Bresslau, Harry, "Bemerkungen zu den Papstbriefen der Britischen Sammlung," *Neues Archiv der Gesellschaft für ältere deutsche Geschichtskunde* 15 (1890), 189–93.

Brett, Martin, "Urban II and the Collections Attributed to Ivo of Chartres," in *Proceedings of the Eighth International Congress of Medieval Canon Law, San Diego, University of California at La Jolla, 21–27 August 1988*, ed. Stanley Chodorow, MIC Subsidia 9 (Vatican City, 1992), pp. 27–46.

Brett, Martin, "Creeping up on the *Panormia*," in *Grundlagen des Rechts. Festschrift für Peter Landau*, ed. Richard H. Helmholz, Paul Mikat, Jörg Müller, and Michael Stolleis, Rechts- und Staatswissenschaftliche Veröffentlichungen der Görres-Gesellschaft N.F. 91 (Paderborn, Munich, Vienna, and Zurich, 2000), pp. 205–70.

Brett, Martin, "Editions, Manuscripts and Readers in Some Pre-Gratian Collections," in *Ritual, Text and Law: Studies in Medieval Canon Law and Liturgy Presented to Roger E. Reynolds*, ed. Richard F. Gyug and Kathleen Grace Cushing, Church, Faith, and Culture in the Medieval West (Aldershot, 2004), pp. 205–44.

Brett, Martin, "Finding the Law: The Sources of Canonical Authority before Gratian," in *Law before Gratian: Law in Western Europe c. 500–1100*, ed. Per Andersen, Mia Münster-Swendsen and Helle Vogt, Proceedings of the Carlsberg Academy Conference on Medieval Legal History 3 (Copenhagen, 2007), pp. 51–72.

Brixius, Johannes, *Die Mitglieder des Kardinalkollegiums von 1130–1181* (Berlin, 1912).

Brooke, Christopher Nugent Lawrence, "The Canons of English Church Council in the Early Decretal Collections," *Traditio* 13 (1957), 471–81.

Broughton, Janet, *Descartes's Method of Doubt* (Princeton, 2002).

Brown, Warren C., and Gorecki, Piotr, "What Conflict Means: The Making of Medieval Conflict Studies in the United States, 1970–2000," in *Conflict in Medieval Europe*, ed. iidem (Aldershot and Burlington), pp. 1–35

Brundage, James A., *Medieval Canon Law*, The Medieval World (London and New York, 1995).

Buchner, Jürgen, *Die Paleae im Dekret Gratians. Untersuchung ihrer Echtheit*, Pontificum Athenaeum Antonianum 127 (Rome, 2000).

Capitani, Ovidio, "Esiste un'età gregoriana? Considerazioni sulle tendenze di una storiografia medievistica," *Rivista di storia e letteratura religiosa* 1 (1965), 454–81.

Capitani, Ovidio,, "'Ecclesia romana' e riforma: 'utilitas' in Gregorio VII," in *Chiesa, diritto e ordinamento della 'Societas Christiana' nei secoli XI e XII: atti della nona settimana internazionale di studio Mendola, 28 agosto–2 settembre 1983* (Milan, 1986), pp. 26–66.

Cholij, Roman, *Clerical Celibacy in East and West* (Herefordshire, 1989).

Christensen, Katherine, "The 'Lost' Papal Gloss on *Si quis suadente* (C.17 q.4 c. 29): John of Salisbury and the Canonical Tradition in the Twelfth Century," *Bulletin of Medieval Canon Law*, n.s. 18 (1988), 1–11.

Clarke, Peter D., "Canon Law," in *Routledge History of Medieval Christianity, 1050–1500*, ed. Robert N. Swanson (Abingdon and New York, 2015), pp. 77–90.

Cochini, Christian, *Apostolic Origins of Priestly Celibacy* (San Francisco, 1990).

Condorelli, Orazio, "S. Pier Damiani e il diritto della Chiesa nella societas christiana," in *Pier Damiani l'eremita, il teologo, il riformatore (1007–2007): atti del xxix Convegno del Centro Studi e Ricerche Antica Provincia Ecclesiastica Ravennate, Faenza-Ravenna, 20–23 settembre 2007*, ed. M. Tagliaferri (Bologna, 2009), pp. 325–63.

Congar, Yves, "Quelques expressions traditionnelles du service chrétien," in *L'épiscopat et l'Église universelle*, ed. idem and Bernard-Dominique Dupuy, Unam Sanctam 39 (Paris, 1962), pp. 101–32.

Congar, Yves, "Préface", in Karl Delahaye, *Ecclesia Mater chez les pères des trois premiers siècles: pour un renouvellement de la pastorale d'aujourd'hui* (Paris, 1964), pp. 7–32.

Conrat (Cohn), Max, *Geschichte der Quellen und Literatur des römischen Rechts im frühen Mittelalter* (Leipzig, 1891).

Cowdrey, Herbert Edward John, *Pope Gregory VII, 1073–1085* (Oxford, 1998).

Cowdrey, Herbert Edward John, "Pope Gregory VII and the Chastity of the Clergy," in *Medieval Purity and Piety: Essays on Medieval Clerical Celibacy and Religious Reform*, ed. Michael Frassetto (New York and London, 1998), pp. 239–302.

Crocco, Antonio, "Le cinque regole ermeneutiche del Sic et non," *Rivista critica di storia della filosofia* 34 (1979), 452–458.

Cushing, Kathleen Grace, *Papacy and Law in the Gregorian Revolution: The Canonistic Work of Anselm of Lucca*, Oxford Historical Monographs (Oxford, 1998).

Cushing, Kathleen Grace, "Anselm of Lucca and Burchard of Worms: Re-Thinking the Sources of Anselm 11, *De Penitentia*," in *Ritual, Text and Law: Studies in Medieval Canon Law and Liturgy Presented to Roger E. Reynolds*, ed Kathleen Grace Cushing and Richard F. Gyug, Church, Faith, and Culture in the Medieval West (Aldershot, 2004), pp. 225–39.

Cushing, Kathleen Grace, *Reform and the Papacy in the Eleventh Century: Spirituality and Social Change*, Manchester Medieval Studies (Manchester and New York, 2005).

Cushing, Kathleen Grace, "Polemic or Handbook? Recension Bb of Anselm of Lucca's Collectio canonum," in *Bishops, Texts and the Use of Canon Law around 1100: Essays in the Honour of Martin Brett*, ed. Bruce Clark Brasington and Kathleen Grace Cushing, Church, Faith and Culture in the Middle Ages (Aldershot, 2008), pp. 69–77.

Cushing, Kathleen Grace, "'Intermediate' and Minor Collections: The Case of the *Collectio canonum Barberiniana*," in *Readers, Texts and Compilers in the Earlier Middle Ages: Studies in Medieval Canon Law in Honour of Linda Fowler-Magerl*, ed. Martin Brett and Kathleen Grace Cushing, Church, Faith and Culture in the Medieval West (Aldershot, 2009), pp. 73–86.

Cushing, Kathleen Grace, "Law, Penance, and the 'Gregorian' Reform: The Case of Padua, Biblioteca del Seminario Vescovile MS 529," in *Canon Law, Religion and Politics: Liber Amicorum Robert Somerville*, ed. Uta-Renate Bluwmenthal, Anders Winroth and Peter Landau (Washington, D.C., 2012), pp. 28–40.

Cushing, Kathleen Grace, "Monastic 'Centres' of Law? Some Evidence from Eleventh-Century Italy," in *From Learning to Love: Schools, Law and Pastoral Care in the Middle Ages*, ed. Tristan Sharp, Abigail Firey and Isabelle Cochelin (Toronto, 2017), pp. 315–26.

Dachowski, Elizabeth, *First Among Abbots: The Career of Abbo of Fleury* (Washington, D.C., 2008).

Dassmann, Ernst, *Kirchengeschichte*, 1, 3rd ed. (Stuttgart, 2012).

David, Pierre, "Un disciple d'Yves de Chartres en Pologne—Galon de Paris et le droit canonique," in *La Pologne au VIIe Congrès international des sciences historiques, Varsovie 1933*, 2 vols (Warsaw, 1933), 1:99–113.

de Ghellinck, Joseph, *Le mouvement théologique du XII siècle sa préparation lointaine avant et autour de Pierre Lombard, ses rapports avec les initiatives des canonistes: études, recherches et document*, Museum Lessianum. Section Historique 10, 2nd ed. (Bruges, 1948).

Deeters, Walter, *Die Bambergensisgruppe der Dekretalensammlungen des 12. Jahrhunderts* (Bonn, 1954).

Delahaye, Karl, *Ecclesia Mater chez les pères des trois premiers siècles: pour un renouvellement de la pastorale d'aujourd'hui* (Paris, 1964).

Deliyannis, Deborah M., "The Liber Pontificalis of the Church of Ravenna: Its Relation with its Roman Model," in *Liber, Gesta, histoire: écrire l'histoire des évêques et des papes, de l'Antiquité au XXIe siècle: actes du colloque international organisé au Centre d'Études Médiévales d'Auxerre les 25, 26 et 27 juin 2007*, ed. François Bougard and Michel Sot (Turnhout, 2009), pp. 283–95.

Demouy, Patrick, "Actes des archevêques de Reims d'Arnoul à Renaud II, 997–1139," 2 vols (thèse de doctorat, Université de Nancy II, 1982).

Denifle, Heinrich, "Die Sentenzen Abälards und die Bearbeitungen seiner Theologia vor Mitte des 12. Jahrhunderts," *Archiv für Litteratur- und Kirchengeschichte des Mittelalters* 1 (1885), 402–621.

Denzler, Georg, *Die Geschichte des Zölibats* (Freiburg, 1993).

Didion, Joan, *The White Album* (New York, 1979).

Donahue, Charles, "Johannes Faventinus on Marriage," in *Medieval Church Law and the Origins of the Western Legal Tradition: A Tribute to Kenneth Pennington*, ed. Wolfgang P. Müller and Mary E. Sommar (Washington, D.C., 2006), pp. 179–97.

Drossbach, Gisela, "Decretals and the Schools? The *Collectio Francofurtana*," *Bulletin of Medieval Canon Law*, n.s. 24 (2000), 65–77.

Drossbach, Gisela, "Die Collectio Victorina prima—Dekretalenrecht in Saint-Victor," in *Diligens scrutator sacri eloquii. Beiträge zur Exegese- und Theologiegeschichte des Mittelalters. Diligens scrutator sacri eloquii. Beiträge zur Exegese- und Theologiegeschichte des Mittelalters. Festgabe für Rainer Berndt SJ zum 65. Geburtstag*, ed. Hanns Peter Neuheuser, Ralf M.W. Stammberger, and Matthias M. Tischler, Archa verbi. Subsidia 14 (Münster, 2016), pp. 349–64.

Duggan, Charles, "A Durham Canonical Manuscript of the Late-Twelfth Century," *Studies in Church History* 2 (1965), 179–85.

Duggan, Charles, *Twelfth-Century Decretal Collections and their Importance in English History*, University of London Historical Studies 12 (London, 1965).

Duggan, Charles, "Decretals of Alexander III to England," in *Miscellanea Rolando Bandinelli, Papa Alessandro III*, ed. Filippo Liotta (Siena, 1986), pp. 87–151.

Duggan, Charles, "Papal Judges Delegate and the Making of the 'New Law' in the Twelfth Century," in *Cultures of Power: Lordship, Status, and Process in Twelfth-Century Europe*, ed. Thomas N. Bisson (Philadephia, 1995), pp. 172–99.

Duggan, Charles, "Decretal Letters to Hungary," *Folia Theologica* 3 (1992), 5–31; repr. in idem *Decretals and the Creation of the 'New Law' in the Twelfth Century: Judges, Judgements, Equity and Law*, Variorum Collected Studies Series 607 (Aldershot, 1998), no V.

Duggan, Charles, *Decretals and the Creation of the 'New Law' in the Twelfth Century: Judges, Judgements, Equity and Law*, Variorum Collected Studies Series 607 (Aldershot, 1998).

Duggan, Charles, "Decretal Collections from Gratian's *Decretum* to the *Compilationes antiquae*: The Making of the New Case Law," in *The History of Medieval Canon Law in the Classical Period: From Gratian to the Decretals of Pope Gregory IX*, ed. Wilfried Hartmann and Kenneth Pennington, History of Medieval Canon Law (Washington, D.C., 2008), pp. 246–92.

Dusil, Stephan, *Wissensordnungen des Rechts im Wandel. Päpstlicher Jurisdiktionsprimat und Zölibat zwischen 1000 und 1215*, Mediaevalia Lovaniensia 47 (Leuven, 2018).

Dusil, Stephan, "The Emerging Jurisprudence, the Second Lateran Council of 1139 and the Development of Canonical Impediments," in *The Use of Canon Law in Ecclesiastical Administration, 1000–1234*, ed. Melodie Harris Eichbauer and Danica Summerlin, Medieval Law and its Practice 26 (Leiden, 2019), forthcoming.

Duve, Thomas, "Law and Revolution—revisited," *Rechtsgeschichte—Legal History* 21 (2013), 156–59.

Eichbauer, Melodie Harris, "Gratian's Decretum and the Changing Historiographical Landscape," *History Compass* 11:12 (2013), 1111–25.

Eno, Robert B., "The Work of Optatus as a Turning Point in the African Ecclesiology," *The Thomist* 37 (1973), 668–85.

Eno, Robert B., "The Significance of the List of Roman Bishops in the Anti-Donatist Polemic," *Vigiliae Christianae* 47 (1993), 158–69.

Erdmann, Carl, "Gesta Romanae ecclesiae contra Hildebrandum," *Zeitschrift der Savigny-Stiftung für Rechtsgeschichte, kanonistische Abteilung* 26 (1937), 433–36.

Erdö, Péter, *Die Quellen des Kirchenrechts. Eine geschichtliche Einführung*, Adnotationes in ius canonicum 23 (Frankfurt, 2002).

Erdö, Péter, *Geschichte der Wissenschaft vom kanonischen Recht. Eine Einführung*, ed. Ludger Müller, Kirchenrechtliche Bibliothek 4 (Berlin and Münster, 2006).

Esmein, Adhémar, "La question des investitures dans les lettres d'Yves de Chartres," *Bibliothèque de l'École des Hautes-Études: sciences religieuses* 1 (1889), 139–178.

Esmein, Adhémar, *Le mariage en droit canonique: études sur l'histoire du droit canonique privé*, 2nd ed., 2 vols (Paris, 1929–35).

Ewald, Paul, "Die Papstbriefe der Brittischen Sammlung," *Neues Archiv* 5 (1880), 275–414 and 505–96.

Falchi, Gian Luigi, and Ferme, Brian Edwin, *Introduzione allo studio delle fonti dell'utrumque ius*, Studia et documenta. Sectio iuris romani et historiae iuris 3 (Vatican City, 2006).

Falkenstein, Ludwig, "Zur Entstehungsort und Redaktor der Collectio Brugensis," in *Proceedings of the Eighth International Congress of Medieval Canon Law, San Diego, University of California at La Jolla, 21–27 August 1988*, ed. Stanley Chodorow, MIC Subsidia 9 (Vatican City, 1992), pp. 117–51.

Falkenstein, Ludwig, "Alexandre III et Henri de France: conformités et conflits," in *L'église de France et la papauté (Xe–XIIIe siècle) / Die französische Kirche und das Papsttum*, ed. Ralf Große, Studien und Dokumente zur Gallia Pontificia 1 (Bonn, 1993), pp. 103–76.

Ferme, Brian Edwin, *Introduction to the History of the Sources of Canon Law: The Ancient Law up to the Decretum of Gratian*, Gratianus (Montréal, 2007).

Filotas, Bernadette, *Pagan Survival, Superstitions and Popular Cultures in Early Medieval Pastoral Literature* (Toronto, 2005).

Firey, Abigail A., "Canon Law in the Carolingian Era," in *The Cambridge Companion to Medieval Canon Law*, ed. Anders Winroth and John C. Wei (Cambridge, forthcoming).

Fliche, Augustin, *Études sur la polémique religieuse à l'époque de Grégoire VII* (Paris, 1916).

Fliche, Augustin, "[Review of:] Paul Fournier avec la collaboration de Gabriel Le Bras. Histoire des collections canoniques en Occident depuis les Fausses Décrétales jusqu'au Décret de Gratien," *Revue d'histoire de l'Église de France* 19 (1933), 219–26.

Fliche, Augustin, *La Réforme grégorienne*, 3 vols (Louvain and Paris, 1924–37).

Foreville, Raymonde, "The Synod of the Province of Rouen in the Eleventh and Twelfth Centuries," in *Church and Government in the Middle Ages: Essays Presented to C.R. Cheney on his 70th Birthday*, ed. Christopher Nugent Lawrence Brooke, David Edward Luscombe, G. H. Martin, and Dorothy M. Owen (Cambridge, 1976), pp. 19–39.

Fornasari, Giuseppe, "Collectio canonum Barberiniana," *Apollinaris* 36 (1963), 214–97.

Fournier, Paul, *Des collèges industriels dans l'Empire romain* (Paris, 1878).

Fournier, Paul, "Les conflits de juridiction entre l'église et le pouvoir séculier de 1180 à 1328," *Revue des questions historiques* 27 (1880), 432–64.

Fournier, Paul, *Les officialités au moyen-âge: étude sur l'organisation, la compétence et la procedure des tribunaux ecclésiastiques ordinaires en France, de 1180 à 1328* (Paris, 1880).

Fournier, Paul, "La question des fausses décrétales," *Nouvelle revue historique de droit français et étranger* 11 (1887), 70–104 and 12 (1888), 103–09; repr. in idem, *Mélanges de droit canonique*, ed. Theo Kölzer, 2 vols (Aalen, 1983), 1:23–64.

Fournier, Paul, "De l'origine des Fausses Décrétales," in *Congrès scientifique international des catholiques, tenu à Paris, Avril 1888*, 2 vols (Paris, 1888), 2.403–19; repr. in idem, *Mélanges de droit canonique*, ed. Theo Kölzer, 2 vols (Aalen, 1983), 1:65–88.

Fournier, Paul, "Une forme particulière des *Fausses Décrétales*, d'après un manuscrit de la Grande-Chartreuse," *Bibliothèque de l'École des Chartes* (1888), 325–49.

Fournier, Paul, "La collezione canonica del regesto di Farfa," *Archivio della Società Romana di Storia Patria* 17 (1894), 285–301; repr. in idem, *Mélanges de droit canonique*, ed. Theo Kölzer, 2 vols (Aalen, 1983), 2:685–701.

Fournier, Paul, "Le premier manuel canonique de la réforme du XIe siècle," *Mélanges d'archéologie et d'histoire de l'École* française *de Rome* 14 (1894), 147–223 and 285–90; repr. in idem, *Mélanges de droit canonique*, ed. Theo Kölzer, 2 vols (Aalen, 1983), 2:551–633.

Fournier, Paul, "Une collection canonique italienne du commencement du 12e siècle," *Annales de l'enseignement supérieur de Grenoble* 6 (1894), 343–438.

Fournier, Paul, "Les collections attribuées à Yves de Chartres," *Bibliothèque de l'École des Chartes* 57 (1896), 645–98, *Bibliothèque de l'École des Chartes* 58 (1897), 26–77, 293–326, 410–44, and 624–76; repr. in idem, *Mélanges de droit canonique*, ed. Theo Kölzer, 2 vols (Aalen, 1983), 1:451–678.

Fournier, Paul, "De quelques collections canoniques issues du *Décret* de Burchard," in *Mélanges Paul Fabre: études d'histoire du moyen âge* (Paris, 1902), pp. 189–214.

Fournier, Paul, "Études sur les fausses décrétales," *Revue d'histoire ecclésiastique* 7 (1906), 33–51, 301–16, 543–64, 761–84, and *Revue d'histoire ecclésiastique* 8 (1907), 19–56; repr. in idem, *Mélanges de droit canonique*, ed. Theo Kölzer, 2 vols (Aalen, 1983), 1:83–201.

Fournier, Paul, "Études critiques sur le Décret de Burchard de Worms," *Nouvelle revue historique de droit français et étranger* 34 (1910), 41–112, 213–221, 289–331, and 564–584; repr. in idem, *Mélanges de droit canonique*, ed. Theo Kölzer, 2 vols (Aalen, 1983), 2:247–391.

Fournier, Paul, "Le Décret de Burchard de Worms: ses caractères, son influence," *Revue d'histoire ecclésiastique* 12 (1911), 451–73 and 670–701; repr. in idem, *Mélanges de droit canonique*, ed. Theo Kölzer, 2 vols (Aalen, 1983), 1:393–447.

Fournier, Paul, "Un tournant de l'histoire du droit 1060–1140," *Nouvelle revue historique de droit français et étranger* 40 (1917), 129–80; repr. in idem, *Mélanges de droit canonique*, ed. Theo Kölzer, 2 vols (Aalen, 1983), 2:373–424.

Fournier, Paul, "Les collections canoniques romaines de l'époque de Grégoire VII," *Mémoires de l'Institut National de France, Académie des Inscriptions et Belles-Lettres* 41 (1918), 271–397; repr. in idem, *Mélanges de droit canonique*, ed. Theo Kölzer, 2 vols (Aalen, 1983), 2:425–550.

Fournier, Paul, "La collection canonique dite 'Collectio XII partium': étude sur un recueil canonique allemand du XIe siècle," *Revue d'histoire de l'Église de France* 17 (1921), 31–62 and 229–59; repr. in idem, *Mélanges de droit canonique*, ed. Theo Kölzer, 2 vols (Aalen, 1983), 2:751–813.

Fournier, Paul, "La collection canonique dite *Caesaraugustana*," *Nouvelle revue historique de droit français et étranger* 45 (1921), 53–79; repr. in idem, *Mélanges de droit canonique*, ed. Theo Kölzer, 2 vols (Aalen, 1983), 2:815–41.

Fournier, Paul, with the collaboration of Gabriel Le Bras, *Histoire des collections canoniques en Occident dépuis les Fausses Décrétales jusqu'au Décret de Gratien*, 2 vols (Paris, 1931–32; repr. Aalen, 1972).

Fowler-Magerl, Linda, *Ordo iudiciorum vel ordo iudiciarius. Begriff und Literaturgattung*, Ius commune. Sonderhefte 19 (Frankfurt, 1984).

Fowler-Magerl, Linda, "The Use of the Letters of Pope Gregory I in Northeastern France and Lorraine before 1100," in *"Ins Wasser geworfen und Ozeane durchquert". Festschrift für Knut Wolfgang Nörr*, ed. Mario Ascheri, Friedrich Ebel, Martin Heckel, Antonio Padoa-Schioppa, Wolfgang Pöggeler, Filippo Ranieri, and Wilhelm Rütten (Cologne, 2003), pp. 237–60.

Fowler-Magerl, Linda, *Clavis Canonum: Selected Canon Law Collections before 1140: Access with Data Processing*, MGH Hilfsmittel 21 (Munich, 2005).

Fowler-Magerl, Linda, "The Collection and Transmission of Canon Law along the Northern Section of the Via Francigena in the Eleventh and Twelfth Centuries," in *Bishops, Texts and the Use of Canon Law around 1100: Essays in the Honour of Martin Brett*, ed. Bruce Clark Brasington and Kathleen Grace Cushing, Church, Faith and Culture in the Middle Ages (Aldershot, 2008), pp. 129–39.

Fransen, Gérard, "La tradition manuscrite de la 'Compilatio Prima'," in *Proceedings of the Second International Congress of Medieval Canon Law, Boston College, 12–16 August 1963*, ed. Stephan Kuttner and J. Joseph Ryan, MIC Subsidia 1 (Vatican City, 1965), pp. 56–62,

Fransen, Gérard, *Les décrétales et les collections de décrétales*, Typologie des sources du Moyen Age occidental 2 (Turnhout, 1972).

Fransen, Gérard, "Le Décret de Burchard de Worms: valeur du texte de l'édition: essai de classement des manuscrits," *Zeitschrift der Savigny-Stiftung für Rechtsgeschichte, kanonistische Abteilung* 63 (1977), 1–19.

Fransen, Gérard, *Les collections canoniques*, Typologie des sources du moyen âge occidental, mise à jour du fascicule n° 10, Turnhout 1985.

Fransen, Gérard, "Le *Décret* de Burchard," in *Burchardi Wormatiensis ecclesiae episcopi decretorum libri XX ex consiliis et orthodoxorum patrum decretis, tum etiam diversarum nationum synodis seu loci communes congesti. Ergänzter Neudruck der Editio princeps Köln 1548*, ed. idem and Theo Kölzer (Aalen, 1992), pp. 25–42.

Fuhrmann, Horst, "Über den Reformgeist der 74-Titel-Sammlung (Diversorum patrum sententiae)," in: *Festschrift für Hermann Heimpel*, 3 vols, Veröffentlichungen des Max-Planck-Instituts für Geschichte 36 (Göttingen 1972), 2:1101–20.

Fuhrmann, Horst, *Einfluß und Verbreitung der Pseudoisidorischen Fälschungen. Von ihrem Auftauchen bis in die neuere Zeit*, 3 vols, Schriften der Monumenta Germaniae historica 24 (Stuttgart, 1972–74).

Fuhrmann, Horst, "The Pseudo-Isidorian Forgeries", in Detlev Jasper and Horst Fuhrmann, *Papal Letters in the Early Middle Ages*, History of Medieval Canon Law (Washington, D.C., 2001), pp. 135–95.

Gallandi, Andrea, *De vetustis canonum collectionibus dissertationum sylloge. Quibus virorum doctissimorum cura et studio elucubratis, de Iuris Ecclesiastici origine atque progressi luculenter differitur* (Venice, 1778).

García y García, Antonio, *Historia del derecho canónico: el primer milenio* (Salamanca, 1967).

Gaudemet, Jean, "Gratien et le célibat ecclésiastique," *Studia Gratiana* 13 (1967), 339–69.

Gaudemet, Jean, *Le gouvernement de l'Église à l'époque classique*, 2: *Le gouvernement local*, Histoire du droit et des institutions de l'Église en occident 8/2 (Paris, 1979).

Gaudemet, Jean, "Avant-propos," in Paul Fournier, *Mélanges de droit canonique*, ed. Theo Kölzer, 2 vols (Aalen, 1983), 1:5–11.

Gaudemet, Jean, *Église et cité: histoire du droit canonique* (Paris, 1994).

Genka, Tatsushi, "Zur textlichen Grundlage der Imputationslehre Gratians," *Bulletin of Medieval Canon Law*, n.s. 26 (2006), 40–81.

Genka, Tatsushi, "Hierarchie der Texte, Hierarchie der Autoritäten. Zur Hierarchie der Rechtsquellen bei Gratian," *Zeitschrift der Savigny-Stiftung für Rechtsgeschichte, kanonistische Abteilung* 95 (2009), 101–27.

Gilchrist, John T., "Was There a Gregorian Reform Movement in the Eleventh Century?," *Study Sessions of the Canadian Catholic Historical Association* 37 (1970), 1–10; repr. in idem *Canon Law in the Age of Reform, 11th–12th Century*, Variorum Collected Studies Series 406 (Aldershot, 1993), no. VII.

Gilchrist, John T., "The Reception of Pope Gregory VII into the Canon Law (1073–1141)," *Zeitschrift der Savigny-Stiftung für Rechtsgeschichte, kanonistische Abteilung* 90 (1973), 34–82 and 97 (1980), 192–229; repr. in idem *Canon Law in the Age of Reform, 11th–12th Century*, Variorum Collected Studies Series 406 (Aldershot, 1993), nos VIII–IX.

Gillmann, Franz,"Rührt die Distinktioneneinteilung des ersten und des dritten Dekretteils von Gratian selbst her?," *Archiv für Katholisches Kirchenrecht* 112 (1932), 504–33.

Giraud, Cédric, "Le recueil de sentences de l'école de Laon *Principium et causa*: un cas de pluri-attribution," in *Parva pro magnis munera: études de littérature tardo-antique et médiévale offertes à François Dolbeau par ses élèves*, ed. Monique Goullet, Instrumenta patristica et mediaevalia 51 (Turnhout, 2009), pp. 245–69.

Giraud, Cédric, *Per verba magistri: Anselme de Laon et son école au XIIe siècle*, Bibliothèque d'histoire culturelle du Moyen Âge 8 (Turnhout, 2010).

Grabmann, Martin, *Die Geschichte der scholastischen Methode. Nach den gedruckten und ungedruckten Quellen*, 2 vols (Freiburg, 1909–11).

Gryson, Roger, *Les origines du célibat ecclésiastique du premier au septième siècle*, Recherches et synthèses, section d'histoire 2 (Gembloux, 1970).

Guyotjeannin, Olivier, *Episcopus et comes: affirmation et déclin de la seigneurie épiscopale au nord du royaume de France (Beauvais-Noyon, X^e–début XIIIe siècle)* (Geneva, 1987).

Hanenburg, Jacoba, "Decretals and Decretal Collections in the Second Half of the Twelfth Century," *Tijdschrift voor Rechtsgeschiednis* 34 (1966), 552–99.

Häring, Nicholas M., "The Interaction between Canon Law and Sacramental Theology in the Twelfth Century," in *Proceedings of the Fourth International Congress of Medieval Canon Law, Toronto, 21–25 August 1972*, ed. Stephan Kuttner, MIC Subsidia 5 (Vatican City, 1976), pp. 483–93.

Hartmann, Wilfried, *Kirche und Kirchenrecht um 900. Die Bedeutung der spätkarolingischen Zeit für Tradition und Innovation im kirchlichen Recht*, Schriften der Monumenta Germaniae historica 58 (Hanover, 2008).

Harttung, Julius, "Beiträge zur Geschichte Heinrichs II.: Die Synode von Seligenstadt und Burchards Decretum," *Forschungen zur deutschen Geschichte* 16 (1876), 587–93.

Haskins, Charles Homer, *The Renaissance of the Twelfth Century* (Cambridge, Mass., 1927).

Hauck, Albert, *Kirchengeschichte Deutschlands*, 5 in 6 vols (Berlin, 1887–1920).

Hauck, Albert, "Ueber den liber decretorum Burchard's von Worms," *Berichte über die Verhandlungen der Königlich Sächsischen Gesellschaft der Wissenschaften zu Leipzig. Philologisch-historische Classe* 46 (1894), 65–86.

Helmholz, Richard H., "*Si quis suadente*: Theory and Practice," in *Proceedings of the Seventh International Congress of Medieval Canon Law, Cambridge, 23–27 July 1984*, ed. Peter Linehan, MIC Subsidia 8 (Vatican City, 1988), pp. 425–38.

Herrick, Samantha Kahn, *Imagining the Sacred Past: Hagiography and Power in Early Normandy* (Cambridge, Mass. and London, 2007).

Herrick, Samantha Kahn, "Studying Apostolic Hagiography: The Case of Fronto of Périgueux, Disciple of Christ," *Speculum* 85 (2010), 235–70.

Herrick, Samantha Kahn, "Le pouvoir du passé apostolique," in *Hagiographie, idéologie et politique au Moyen Âge en Occident: actes du colloque international du Centre d'Études supérieures de Civilisation médiévale de Poitiers 11–14 semptembre 2008*, ed. Edina Bozóky (Turnhout, 2012), pp. 129–38.

Hermann Hüffer, Joseph Julius A., *Beiträge zur Geschichte der Quellen des Kirchenrechts und des römischen Rechts im Mittelalter* (Münster, 1862).

Heyer, Friedrich, "Rezension: Heinrich Singer, Neue Beiträge über die Dekretalensammlungen vor und nach Bernhard von Pavia," *Zeitschrift der Savigny-Stiftung für Rechtsgeschichte, kanonistische Abteilung* 3 (1913), 615–42.

Hiestand, Rudolf, "Die Leistungsfähigkeit der päpstlichen Kanzlei im 12. Jahrhundert mit einem Blick auf den lateinischen Osten," in *Papsturkunde und europäisches*

Urkundenwesen. Studien zu ihrer formalen und rechtlichen Kohärenz vom 11. bis 15. Jahrhundert, ed. Peter Herde und Hermann Jakobs, Archiv für Diplomatik. Beiheft 7 (Cologne, 1999), pp. 1–26.

Hinschius, Paul, "De collectione decretalium et canonum Isidori Mercatoris," in *Decretales Pseudo-Isidorianae et Capitula Angilramni*, ed. idem (Leipzig, 1863), pp. xi–ccxxxviii.

Hoffmann, Hartmut, *Buchkunst und Königtum im ottonischen und frühsalischen Reich*, 2 vols, Schriften der Monumenta Germaniae historica 30 (Stuttgart, 1986).

Hoffmann, Hartmut, *Schreibschulen und Buchmalerei. Handschriften und Texte des 9.–11. Jahrhunderts*, Schriften der Monumenta Germaniae historica 65 (Hanover, 2012).

Hoffmann, Hartmut, and Pokorny, Rudolf, *Das Dekret des Bischofs Burchard von Worms. Textstufen—Frühe Verbreitung—Vorlagen*, MGH Hilfsmittel 12 (Munich, 1991).

Holtzmann, Walther, "Collectio Eberbacensis," *Zeitschrift der Savigny-Stiftung für Rechtsgeschichte, kanonistische Abteilung* 17 (1928), 549–55.

Holtzmann, Walther, *Über eine Ausgabe der päpstlichen Dekretalen des 12. Jahrhunderts*, Nachrichten der Akademie der Wissenschaften in Göttingen. Philologisch-historische Klasse. Jahrgang 1945 (Göttingen, 1945).

Holtzmann, Walther, *Studies in the Collections of Twelfth-Century Decretals*, ed., rev., and trans. Christopher R. Cheney and Mary G. Cheney, MIC Corpus collectionum 3 (Vatican City, 1979).

Howe, John, *Before the Gregorian Reform: The Latin Church at the Turn of the First Millennium* (Ithaca, N.Y., 2016).

Hüls, Rudolf, *Kardinäle, Klerus und Kirchen Roms*, Bibliothek des Deutschen Historischen Instituts in Rom 48 (Tübingen, 1977).

Imbart de La Tour, Pierre, *Les élections épiscopales dans l'église de France du IXe au XIIe siècle: étude sur la décadence du principe électif, 814–1150* (Paris, 1890).

Jasper, Detlev, "Burchards Dekret in der Sicht der Gregorianer," in *Bischof Burchard von Worms, 1000–1025*, ed. Wilfried Hartmann, Quellen und Abhandlungen zur mittelrheinischen Kirchengeschichte 100 (Mainz, 2000).

Juncker, Josef, "Die Collectio Berolinensis. Ein Beitrag zur Geschichte des kanonischen Rechts im ausgehenden zwölften Jahrhundert," *Zeitschrift der Savigny-Stiftung für Rechtsgeschichte, kanonistische Abteilung* 44 (1924), 284–426.

Kéry, Lotte, *Die Errichtung des Bistums Arras*, Francia. Beihefte 33 (Sigmaringen, 1994).

Kéry, Lotte, *Canonical Collections of the Early Middle Ages (ca. 400–1140): A Bibliographical Guide to the Manuscripts and Literature*, History of Medieval Canon law (Washington, D.C., 1999).

Kiesow, Rainer Maria, *Das Alphabet des Rechts* (Frankfurt, 2004).

Kretzschmar, Robert, *Alger von Lüttichs Traktat 'De misericordia et iustitia'. Ein kanonistischer Konkordanzversuch aus der Zeit des Investiturstreits: Untersuchungen und Edition*, Quellen und Forschungen zum Recht im Mittelalter 2 (Sigmaringen, 1985).

Kuttner, Stephan, "Zur Frage der theologischen Vorlagen Gratians," *Zeitschrift der Savigny-Stiftung für Rechtsgeschichte, kanonistische Abteilung* 54 (1934), 243–68; repr. in idem, *Gratian and the Schools of Law, 1140–1234*, Varioum Collected Studies Series 185 (London, 1983), no. III.

Kuttner, Stephan, *Repertorium der Kanonistik (1140–1234). Prodromus corporis glossarum*, Studi e testi 71 (Vatican City, 1937).

Kuttner, Stephan, "The Father of the Science of Canon Law," *The Jurist* 1 (1941), 2–19.

Kuttner, Stephan, "Liber Canonicus: A Note on the Dictatus Papae," *Studi Gregoriani* 2 (1947), 387–401; repr. with retractationes in idem, *The History of Ideas and Doctrines of Canon Law in the Middle Ages*, 2nd ed., Variorum Collected Studies Series 113 (London, 1992), no. II.

Kuttner, Stephan, "Urban II and the Doctrine of Interpretation: A Turning Point?," *Studia Gratiana* 15 (1972), 55–85; repr. with retractationes in idem, *The History of Ideas and Doctrines of Canon Law in the* Middle Ages, 2nd ed., Variorum Collected Studies Series 113 (London, 1992), no. IV.

Kuttner, Stephan, "The "Extravagantes" of the Decretum in Biberach," *Bulletin of Medieval Canon Law*, n.s. 3 (1973), 61–71; repr. in idem, *Medieval Councils, Decretals, and Collections of Canon Law*: Selected Essays 2nd ed., Variorum Collected Studies Series 113 ([Aldershot], 1992), no. V.

Kuttner, Stephan, "The Revival of Jurisprudence," in *Renaissance and Renewal in the Twelfth Century*, ed. Robert Benson and Giles Constable (Boston, 1982), pp. 299–323; repr. in idem, *Studies in the History of Medieval Canon Law*, Variorum Collected Studies Series 325 (Aldershot, 1990), no. III.

Kuttner, Stephan, and Elze, Reinhard, *A Catalogue of Canon and Roman Law Manuscripts in the Vatican Library*, 1: *Codices Vaticani latini 541–2299*, Studi e testi 322 (Vatican City, 1986).

Kuttner, Stephan, and Rathbone, Eleanor, "Anglo-Norman Canonists of the Twelfth Century: An Introductory Study," *Traditio* 7 (1951), 279–358.

Landau, Peter, "Alttestamentliches Recht in der 'Compilatio Prima' und sein Einfluß auf das kanonische Recht," *Studia Gratiana* 20 (1976), 111–34.

Landau, Peter, "Die Entstehung der systematischen Dekretalensammlungen und die europäische Kanonistik des 12. Jahrhunderts," *Zeitschrift der Savigny-Stiftung für Rechtsgeschichte, kanonistische Abteilung* 66 (1979), 120–48.

Landau, Peter, "Studien zur Appendix und den Glossen in frühen systematischen Dekretalensammlungen," *Bulletin of Medieval Canon Law*, n.s. 9 (1979), 1–21.

Landau, Peter, "Gefälschtes Recht in den Rechtssammlungen bis Gratian," in *Fälschungen im Mittelalter. Internationaler Kongreß der Monumenta Germaniae Historica, München, 16.–19. September 1986, 2: Gefälschte Rechtstexte. Der bestrafte*

Fälscher, Schriften der Monumenta Germaniae historica 33/2 (Hanover, 1988), pp. 11–49.

Landau, Peter, "Gratian und die *Sententiae Magistri A.*," in *Aus Archiven und Bibliotheken. Festschrift für Raymund Kottje zum 65. Geburtstag*, ed. Hubert Mordek, Freiburger Beiträge zur mittelalterlichen Geschichte. Studien und Texte 3 (Frankfurt, 1992), pp. 311–26.

Landau, Peter, "Vorgratianische Kanonessammlungen bei Dekretisten und in frühen Dekretalensammlungen," in *Proceedings of the Eighth International Congress of Medieval Canon Law, San Diego, University of California at La Jolla, 21–27 August 1988*, ed. Stanley Chodorow, MIC Subsidia 9 (Vatican City, 1992), pp. 93–116.

Landau, Peter, "Wandel und Kontinuität im kanonischen Recht bei Gratian," in *Sozialer Wandel im Mittelalter. Wahrnehmungsformen, Erklärungsmuster, Regelungsmechanismen*, ed. Jürgen Miethke and Klaus Schreiner (Sigmaringen, 1994), pp. 215–33.

Landau, Peter, "Burchard de Worms et Gratien: à propos des sources immédiates de Gratien," *Revue de Droit canonique* 48 (1998), 233–45.

Landau, Peter, "Apokryphe Isidoriana bei Gratian," in *Vita Religiosa im Mittelalter. Festschrift für Kaspar Elm zum 70. Geburtstag*, ed. Franz J. Felten and Nikolas Jaspert, Berliner Historische Studien 31, Ordensstudien 13 (Berlin, 1999), pp. 837–44.

Landau, Peter, "The Development of Law," in *The New Cambridge Medieval History, c. 1024–1098*, 4/1, ed. David Luscombe and Jonathan Riley-Smith (Cambridge, 2015), pp. 113–47.

Landau, Peter, "Die Kölner Kanonistik des 12. Jahrhunderts. Ein Höhepunkt der europäischen Rechtswissenschaft," in *Vortrag vor dem Rheinischen Verein für Rechtsgeschichte e. V. in Köln am 27. Mai 2008*, ed. Dieter Strauch, Kölner Rechtsgeschichtliche Vorträge 1 (Cologne, 2008), pp. 1–39.

Landau, Peter, "Gratian and the *Decretum Gratiani*," in *The History of Medieval Canon Law in the Classical Period: From Gratian to the Decretals of Pope Gregory IX*, ed. Wilfried Hartmann and Kenneth Pennington, History of Medieval Canon Law (Washington, D.C., 2008), pp. 22–54.

Landau, Peter, "Simon von Bisignano, Sikard von Cremona und die Mainzer Kanonistik der Barbarossazeit. Zur Biographie des Simon von Bisignano und zur Forschungsgeschichte," *Bulletin of Medieval Canon Law*, n.s. 28 (2008), 136–38.

Landau, Peter, "Die *Collectio Fontanensis*: A Decretal Collection of the Twelfth Century for an English Cistercian Abbey," in *Law as Profession and Practice in Medieval Europe: Essays in Honor of James A. Brundage*, ed. Kenneth Pennington and Melodie Harris Eichbauer (Aldershot, 2011), pp. 187–204.

Landau, Peter, "Die Dekretsumme 'Tractaturus Magister' und die Kanonistik in Reims in der zweiten Hälfte des 12. Jahrhunderts," *Zeitschrift der Savigny-Stiftung für Rechtsgeschichte, kanonistische Abteilung* 100 (2014), 132–52.

Landgraf, Artur Michael, "Die Summa Sententiarum und die Summe des Cod. Vat. lat. 1345," *Recherches de Théologie ancienne et médiévale* 11 (1939), 260–70.

Landgraf, Artur Michael, *Einführung in die Geschichte der theologischen Literatur der Frühscholastik, unter dem Gesichtspunkte der Schulenbildung* (Regensburg, 1948); French trans. by Louis-B. Geiger, *Introduction à l'histoire de la littérature théologique de la scolastique naissante* (Montreal, 1973).

Landwehr, Achim, "Diskurs—Macht—Wissen. Perspektiven einer Kulturgeschichte des Politischen," *Archiv für Kulturgeschichte* 85 (2003), 71–117.

Lanéry, Cécile, "Hagiographie d'Italie (300–550), I: les Passions latines composées en Italie," in *CC Hagiographies 5* (Turnhout, 2010), pp. 264–72.

Lanzoni, Francesco, "Le fonti della leggenda di Sant'Apollinare di Ravenna," *Atti e memorie della reale deputazione di storia patria per le provincie di Romagna* 5,4 (1914–15), 111–176.

Laqua, Hans Peter, *Traditionen und Leitbilder bei dem Ravennater Reformer Petrus Damiani 1042–1052*, Münstersche Mittelalter-Schriften 30 (Munich, 1976).

Larrainzar, Carlos, "El borrador de la 'Concordia' de Graziano: Sankt Gallen, Stiftsbibliothek MS 673 (= Sg)," *Ius Ecclesiae* 11 (1999), 593–666.

Larson, Atria Ann, "The Influence of the School of Laon on Gratian: The Usage of the Glossa ordinaria and Anselmian Sententiae in De penitentia (Decretum C.33 Q.3)," *Mediaeval Studies* 72 (2010), 197–244.

Larson, Atria Ann, "An *abbreviatio* of the First Recension of Gratian's *Decretum* in Munich?," *Bulletin of Medieval Canon Law*, n.s. 29 (2011–12), 51–118.

Larson, Atria Ann, *Master of Penance: Gratian and the Development of Penitential Thought and Law in the Twelfth Century*, Studies in Medieval and Early Modern Canon Law 11 (Washington, D.C., 2014).

Le Bras, Gabriel, "Le *Liber de misericordia et justitia* d'Alger de Liège," *Nouvelle revue historique de droit français et étranger* 45 (1921), 80–118.

Le Bras, Gabriel, "Alger de Liège et Gratien," *Revue des sciences philosophiques et théologiques* 20 (1931), 5–26.

Le Bras, Gabriel, "Paul Fournier et l'histoire de l'Église de France," *Revue d'histoire de l'Église de France* 21 (1935), 532–49.

Le Bras, Gabriel, *Prolégomènes*, Histoire du droit et des institutions de l'Eglise en Occident 1 (Paris, 1955).

Legendre, Pierre, *La pénétration du droit romain dans le droit canonique classique de Gratien à Innocent IV, 1140–1254* (Paris, 1964).

Lenherr, Titus, *Die Exkommunikations- und Depositionsgewalt der Häretiker bei Gratian und den Dekretisten bis zur Glossa ordinaria des Johannes Teutonicus*, Münchener theologische Studien. Kanonistische Abteilung 42 (St. Ottilien, 1987).

Lenherr, Titus, "Die 'Glossa ordinaria' zur Bibel als Quelle von Gratians Dekret," *Bulletin of medieval canon law* n.s. 24 (2000), 97–129.

Lenherr, Titus, "Die vier Fassungen von C. 3 q. 1 d.p.c. 6 im Decretum Gratiani. Zugleich ein Einblick in die neueste Diskussion um das Werden von Gratians Dekret," *Archiv für katholisches Kirchenrecht* 169 (2000), 353–81.

Lenherr, Titus, "Ist die Handschrift 673 der St. Galler Stiftsbibliothek (Sg) der Entwurf zu Gratians Dekret? Versuch einer Antwort aus Beobachtungen an D. 31 und D. 32," available at http://www.mgh-bibliothek.de/dokumente/a/a117039.pdf.

Licciardello, Pierluigi, "Agiografia latina dell'Italia centrale, 950–1130," in *CC Hagiographies* 5 (Turnhout, 2010), pp. 447–729.

Lindenkohl, Georg Stephan, *De Petri Abaelardi libro Sic et non commentatio* (Marburg, 1851).

Liotta, Filippo, *La continenza dei chierici nel pensiero canonistico classico da Graziano a Gregorio IX* (Milan, 1971).

Lohmann, Hans-Eberhard, "Die Collectio Wigorniensis (Collectio Londoniensis regia). Ein Beitrag zur Quellengeschichte des kanonischen Rechts im 12. Jahrhundert," *Zeitschrift der Savigny-Stiftung für Rechtsgeschichte, kanonistische Abteilung* 22 (1933), 36–187.

Longo, Umberto, *Come angeli in terra: Pier Damiani, la santità e la riforma del secolo XI* (Viella, 2012).

Lottin, Odon, *Psychologie et morale aux XIIe et XIIIe siècles*, 6 in 8 vols (Gembloux, 1948–60).

Lucchesi, Giovanni, "Apollinare," in *Bibliotheca sanctorum*, 2 (Rome, 1962), pp. 239–42.

Luchaire, Achille, *Louis VI le Gros: annales de sa vie et de son règne (1081–1137): avec une introduction historique* (Paris, 1890).

Maassen, Friedrich, *Geschichte der Quellen und der Literatur des canonischen Rechts im Abendlande bis zum Ausgange des Mittelalters*, 1: *Die Rechtssammlungen bis zur Mitte des 9. Jahrhunderts* (Graz, 1870). [all published]

Maier, Anneliese, "Die Handschriften der *Ecclesia Sidonensis*," *Manuscripta* 11 (1967), 39–45.

Marenbon, John, "Victor Cousin," in *Medieval Scholarship: Biographical Studies on the Formation of a Discipline*, 3: *Philosophy and the Arts*, ed. Helen Damico (New York, 2000), pp. 13–22.

Martin, Norbert, "Die 'Compilatio decretorum' des Kardinal Laborans," in *Proceedings of the Sixth International Congress of Medieval Canon Law, Berkeley, California, 28 July–2 August 1980*, ed. Stephan Kuttner and Kenneth Pennington, MIC Subsidia 7 (Vatican City, 1985), pp. 125–38.

Martin, Norbert, *Die Compilatio Decretorum des Kardinals Laborans. Eine Umarbeitung des Gratianischen Dekrets aus dem 12. Jahrhunderts* (Heidelberg, 1985).

Maurer, Helmut, "Die Konstanzer Bürgerschaft im Investiturstreit," in *Investiturstreit und Reichsverfassung*, ed. Josef Fleckenstein, Vorträge und Forschungen 17 (Sigmaringen, 1973), pp. 363–71.

Mazzotti, Mario, "Per una nuova datazione della 'Passio S. Apollinaris'," *Studi romagnoli* 3 (1952), 123–29.
McCarthy, John F., "The Genius of Concord in Gratian's Decree," *Ephemerides Iuris Canonici* 19 (1963), 105–51.
Megan, McLaughlin, *Sex, Gender, and Episcopal Authority in an Age Of Reform, 1000–1122* (Cambridge, 2010).
Melve, Leidulf, "Ecclesiastical reform in historiographical context," *History Compass* 13 (2015), 213–21.
Menu, Jules-René, "Le droit canon au onzième siecle: recherches et nouvelle étude critique sur les recueils de droit canon attribués à Yves de Chartres" (diss. theol., Paris, 1880).
Mews, Constant J., "On Dating the Works of Peter Abelard," *Archives d'histoire doctrinale et littéraire du moyen âge* 52 (1985), 73–134.
Meyer, Christoph H. F., *Die Distinktionstechnik in der Kanonistik des 12. Jahrhunderts. Ein Beitrag zur Wissenschaftsgeschichte des Hochmittelalters*, Mediaevalia Lovaniensia. Studia 29 (Leuven, 2000).
Meyer, Christoph H. F., "Ordnung durch Ordnen. Die Erfassung und Gestaltung des hochmittelalterlichen Kirchenrechts im Spiegel von Texten, Begriffen und Institutionen," in *Ordnungskonfigurationen im hohen Mittelalter*, ed. Bernd Schneidmüller and Stefan Weinfurter, Vorträge und Forschungen 64 (Ostfildern, 2006), pp. 304–411.
Meyer, Otto, "Überlieferung und Verbreitung des Dekrets des Bischofs Burchard von Worms," *Zeitschrift der Savigny-Stiftung für Rechtsgeschichte, kanonistische Abteilung* 24 (1935), 141–83.
Michelet, Jules, *Histoire de France* (Paris, 1855).
Miller, Maureen C., "The Crisis in the Investiture Crisis Narrative," *History Compass* 7 (2009), 1570–80.
Mirbt, Carl, *Die Publizistik im Zeitalter Gregors VII.* (Leipzig, 1894).
Mommsen, Theodor, "Bemerkungen zu den Papstbriefen der Britischen Sammlung," *Neues Archiv der Gesellschaft für ältere deutsche Geschichtskunde* 15 (1890), 187–88.
Monod, Bernard, "L'Église et l'État au XIIe siècle: l'élection épiscopale de Beauvais de 1100 à 1104: Étienne de Garlande et Galon," *Mémoires de la société academique du département de l'Oise* 19 (1904–06), 53–74.
Monod, Bernard, *Essai sur les rapports de Pascal II avec Philippe Ier (1099–1108)*, Bibliothèque de l'École des Hautes Études: Sciences historiques et philologiques 164 (Paris, 1907).
Moore, Robert Ian, *The Formation of a Persecuting Society: Power and Deviance in Western Europe, 950–1250* (Oxford, 1987).
Mordek, Hubert, "Handschriftenforschungen in Italien I. Zur Überlieferung des Dekrets des Bischofs von Worms," *Quellen und Forschungen aus Italienischen Archiven und Bibliotheken* 51 (1971), 626–51.

Morelle, Laurent, "La pratique épistolaire de Lambert, évêque d'Arras (1093–1115)," in *Regards sur la correspondance (de Cicéron à Armand Barbès)*, ed. Daniel-Odon Hurel (Rouen, 1996), pp. 37–57.

Morris, Colin, *The Papal Monarchy: The Western Church from 1050 to 1250*, Oxford History of the Christian Church (Oxford, 1989).

Mostert, Marco, *The Political Theology of Abbo of Fleury: A Study of the Ideas about Society and Law of the 10th-Century Monastic Reform Movement*, Middeleeuwse studies en bronnen 2 (Hilversum, 1987).

N. N., "Chronique et mélanges," *Thèses des élèves de l'École des chartes* 40 (1879), 132–35.

N. N., "Rapport sur l'École pratique des hautes études, 1885–1886," *Annuaires de l'École pratique des hautes études* (1885), 3–225.

Newman, William M., *Les seigneurs de Nesle en Picardie (XII*e*–XIII*e *siècle): leurs chartes et leur histoire: étude sur la noblesse régionale ecclésiastique et laïque*, Memoirs of the American Philosophical Society 91 (Philadelphia, Penn., 1971).

Nitzsch, Karl Wilhelm, *Ministerialität und Bürgerthum im 11. und 12. Jahrhundert* (Leipzig, 1859).

Noonan, John T., "Who was Rolandus?," in *Law, Church, and Society: Essays in Honor of Stephan Kuttner*, ed. Kenneth Pennington and Robert Somerville (Philadelphia, 1977), pp. 21–48.

Noonan, John T., "Gratian Slept Here: The Changing Identity of the Father of the Systematic Study of Canon Law," *Traditio* 35 (1979), 145–72.

Orioli, Giorgio, "I vescovi di Ravenna: note di cronologia e di storia," *Bollettino della badia greca di Grottaferrata* 32 (1978), 45–67.

Orioli, Giorgio, "Osservazioni sulla data della Passio S. Apollinaris di Ravenna," *Bollettino della badia greca di Grottaferrata* 32 (1978), 67–75.

Orioli, Giorgio, "La Vita sancti Apolenaris di Ravenna e gli antecedenti storici dell'organizzazione ecclesiastica ravennate," *Apollinaris* (1986), 251–67.

Ott, John Stephens, *Bishops, Authority and Community in Northwestern Europe, c. 1050–1150*, Cambridge Studies in Medieval Life and Thought: Fourth Series 102 (Cambridge, 2015).

Palazzini, Pietro, *Il diritto strumento di riforma ecclesiastica in S. Pier Damiani* (Rome, 1956).

Parish, Helen L., *Clerical Celibacy in the West, c. 1100–1700*, Catholic Christendom, 1300–1700 (Burlington, 2010).

Pennington, Kenneth, *Pope and Bishops: The Papal Monarchy in the Twelfth and Thirteenth Centuries*, (Philadelphia, Penn., 1984).

Pennington, Kenneth, "Gratian, Causa 19, and the Birth of Canonical Jurisprudence," in *Panta rei: studi dedicati a Manlio Bellomo*, ed. Orazio Condorelli, 5 vols (Rome, 2004), 4:339–55.

Pennington, Kenneth, "The 'Big Bang': Roman Law in the Early Twelfth Century," *Rivista internazionale del diritto commune* 18 (2007), 65–85.

Pennington, Kenneth, and Müller, Wolfgang P., "The Decretists: The Italian School," in *The History of Medieval Canon Law in the Classical Period: From Gratian to the Decretals of Pope Gregory IX*, ed. Wilfried Hartmann and Kenneth Pennington, History of Medieval Canon Law (Washington, D.C., 2008), pp. 121–73.

Phipps, William E., *Clerical Celibacy: The Heritage* (New York and London, 2004).

Picard, Jean-Charles, *Le souvenir des évêques: sépultures, listes épiscopales et culte des évêques en Italie du Nord des origines au Xe siècle* (Rome, 1988).

Pizarro, Joaquín Martínez, *Writing Ravenna: The Liber Pontificalis of Andreas Agnellus* (Ann Arbor, Mich., 1995).

Plöchl, Willibald M., *Geschichte des Kirchenrechts*, 3 in 5 vols (Vienna and Munich, 1960–70).

Pollock, Frederick, and Maitland, Frederic William, *The History of English Law before the Time of Edward I*, 2 vols (Cambridge, 1898).

Pontal, Odette, *Les conciles de la France capétienne jusqu'en 1215* (Paris, 1997).

Price, Richard M., "Zölibat. II. Kirchengeschichtlich," in *Theologische Realenzyklopädie*, 36 vols (Berlin, 1976–2004), 36:722–39.

Rennie, Kriston R., *Law and Practice in the Age of Reform: The Legatine Work of Hugh of Die (1073–1106)*, Medieval Church Studies 17 (Turnhout, 2010).

Rennie, Kriston R., and Taliadoros, Jason, "Why Study Medieval Canon Law?," *History Compass* 12 (2014), 133–49.

Reynolds, Roger E., "Penitentials in South and Central Italian Canon Law Manuscripts of the Tenth and Eleventh Centuries," *Early Medieval Europe* 14 (2006), 65–84.

Richter, Emil Ludwig, *Beiträge zur Kenntnis der Quellen des kanonischen Rechts* (Leipzig, 1834).

Richter, Emil Ludwig, *De inedita decretalium collectione Lipsiensi* (Leipzig, 1836).

Rizek-Pfister, Cornelia, "Die hermeneutischen Prinzipien in Abaelards Sic et non," *Freiburger Zeitschrift für Philosophie und Theologie* 47 (2000), 484–501.

Rolker, Christof, "The *Collection in Seventy-Four Titles*: A Monastic Canon Law Collection from Eleventh-Century France," in *Readers, Texts and Compilers in the Earlier Middle Ages: Studies in Medieval Canon Law in Honour of Linda Fowler-Magerl*, ed. Martin Brett and Kathleen Grace Cushing, Church, Faith and Culture in the Medieval West (Aldershot, 2009), pp. 59–72.

Rolker, Christof, *Canon Law and the Letters of Ivo of Chartres*, Cambridge Studies in Medieval Life and Thought, Fourth Series 76 (Cambridge, 2010).

Rolker, Christof, "The Hot and the Cold Language: Incest Discourses in the Twelfth and Thirteenth Centuries," in *Proceedings of the Fourteenth International Congress of Medieval Canon Law, Toronto, 5–11 August 2012*, ed. Joseph Goering, Stephan Dusil, and Andreas Thier (Vatican City, 2016), pp. 651–65.

Roßhirt, Conrad Franz, *Geschichte des Rechts im Mittelalter. Erster Theil: Canonisches Recht* (Mainz, 1846).

Roumy, Franck, "Remarques sur l'œuvre canonique d'Abbon de Fleury," in *Abbon, un abbé de l'an mil*, ed. Anne Dufour and Gilette Labory, Bibliothèque d'histoire culturelle du Moyen Âge 4 (Leuven, 2008), pp. 311–42.

Rubenstein, Jay, *Guibert of Nogent: Portrait of a Medieval Mind* (New York and London, 2002).

Ruppert, Stefan, *Kirchenrecht und Kulturkampf. Historische Legitimation, politische Mitwirkung und wissenschaftliche Begleitung durch die Schule Emil Ludwig Richters*, Ius Ecclesiasticum 70 (Tübingen, 2002).

Ryan, John Joseph, *Saint Peter Damiani and his Canonical Sources: A Preliminary Study in the Antecedents of the Gregorian Reformw*, Pontifical Institute of Medieval Studies. Studies and Texts 2 (Toronto, 1956).

Ryan, John Joseph, "Observations on the pre-Gratian Canonical Collections: Some Recent Work and Present Problems," in *Congrès de droit canonique médiéval: Louvain et Bruxelles 22–26 Juillet 1958*, ed. Stephan Kuttner, Henri Wagnon, and Gérard Fransen, Bibliothèque de la revue d'histoire ecclesiastique 33 (Löwen, 1959), pp. 88–103.

Savigny, Friedrich Carl von, *Geschichte des römischen Rechts im Mittelalter*, 6 vols (Heidelberg, 1815–31).

Schieffer, Theodor, *Die päpstlichen Legaten in Frankreich vom Vertrage von Meersen (870) bis zum Schisma von 1130*, Historische Studien 263 (Berlin, 1935).

Schulte, Johann Friedrich (von), *Das katholische Kirchenrecht*, 2 vols (Giessen, 1856–60).

Schulte, Johann Friedrich (von), *Die Geschichte der Quellen und Literatur des canonischen Rechts*, 3 vols (Stuttgart, 1875).

Schwarz, Willi, "Der Investiturstreit in Frankreich," *Zeitschrift für Kirchengeschichte* 42 (1923), 92–150 and 255–328.

Seckel, Emil, "Pseudoisidor," in *Real-Encyklopädie für protestantische Theologie und Kirche*, 24 vols (Berlin, 1896–1913), 16:1265–1307.

Singer, Heinrich, "Neue Beiträge über die Dekretalensammlungen vor und nach Bernhard von Pavia," *Sitzungsberichte der kaiserlichen Akademie der Wissenschaften, Wien, philosophisch-historische Klasse* 171 (Vienna, 1913).

Singer, Heinrich, "Friedrich Thaner," *Zeitschrift der Savigny-Stiftung für Rechtsgeschichte, kanonistische Abteilung* 6 (1916), V–XI.

Smalley, Beryl, *The Study of the Bible in the Middle Ages*, 3rd ed. (Oxford, 1983).

Smith, Lesley, *The Glossa ordinaria: The Making of a Medieval Bible Commentary* (Leiden, 2009).

Somerville, Robert, *Pope Alexander III and the Council of Tours (1163)* (Berkeley, 1977).

Somerville, Robert, "Canon Law, Inspired Law, and Papal Authority," in *Neti'ot Le David: Jubilee Volume for David Weiss Halivini*, ed. Yakov Elman, Ephraim Bezalel Halivni, Zvi Arie Steinfeld (Jerusalem, 2004), pp. 119–34.

Somerville, Robert, in collaboration with Stephan Kuttner, *Pope Urban II, the* Collectio Britannica, *and the Council of Melfi (1089)* (Oxford, 1996).

Sommar, Mary E., "Gratian's Causa VII and the Multiple Recension Theories," *Bulletin of Medieval Canon Law*, n.s. 24 (2000), 78–96.

Southern, Richard W., *Scholastic Humanism and the Unification of Europe, 1: The Foundations* (Oxford, 1995), 2 (with notes and additions by Lesley Smith and Benedicta Ward): *The Heroic Age* (Oxford, 2001).

Sprandel, Rolf, *Ivo von Chartres und seine Stellung in der Kirchengeschichte*, Pariser historische Studien 1 (Stuttgart, 1962).

Stehr, Nico, "Wissensgesellschaften," in *Handbuch der Kulturwissenschaften*, ed. Friedrich Jaeger and Jörn Rüsen (Stuttgart and Weimar, 2004), pp. 34–49.

Stickler, Alfons Maria, *Historia iuris canonici latini*, 1: *Historia fontium* (Turin, 1950).

Stickler, Alfons Maria, *Der Klerikerzölibat. Seine Entwicklungsgeschichte und seine theologischen Grundlagen* (Abensberg, 1993).

Stolleis, Michael, "Der lernfähige und lernende Staat," in *Wissenskulturen. Über die Erzeugung und Weitergabe von Wissen*, ed. Johannes Fried and Michael Stolleis (Frankfurt and New York, 2009), pp. 58–78.

Taliadoros, Jason, *Law and Theology in Twelfth-Century England: The Works of Master Vacarius (c.1115/1120–c.1200)*, Disputatio 10 (Turnhout, 2006).

Taliadoros, Jason, "Synthesizing the Legal and Theological Thought of Master Vacarius," *Zeitschrift der Savigny-Stiftung für Rechtsgeschichte, kanonistische Abteilung* 95 (2009), 48–77.

Tellenbach, Gerd, "'Gregorianische Reform'. Kritische Besinnungen," in *Reich und Kirche vor dem Investiturstreit. Vorträge beim wissenschaftlichen Kolloquium aus Anlaß des 80. Geburtstags von Gerd Tellenbach*, ed. Karl Schmid (Sigmaringen, 1985), pp. 99–113.

Tellenbach, Gerd, *Die westliche Kirche vom 10. bis zum frühen 12. Jahrhundert*, Die Kirche in ihrer Geschichte 2, F1 (Göttingen, 1988); English trans. by Timothy Reuter, *The Church in Western Europe from the Tenth to the Early Twelfth Century* (Cambridge, 1993).

Thaner, Friedrich, *Abälard und das canonische Recht; Die Persönlichkeit in der Eheschliessung. Zwei Festreden* (Graz, 1900).

Theiner, Augustin, *Über Ivo's vermeintliches Decret. Ein Beitrag zur Geschichte des Kirchenrechts, und ins Besondere zur Critik der Quellen des Gratian. Nebst einem Quellen-Anhang* (Mainz, 1832).

Thier, Andreas, "Dynamische Schriftlichkeit. Zur Normbildung in den vorgratianischen Kanonessammlungen," *Zeitschrift der Savigny-Stiftung für Rechtsgeschichte, kanonistische Abteilung* 124 (2007), 1–33.

Tomea, Paolo, *Tradizione apostolica e coscienza critica a Milano nel medioevo: la leggenda di san Barnaba* (Milano, 1994).

Ullmann, Walter, *The Growth of Papal Government in the Middle Ages*, 3rd ed. (London, 1970).

van de Wiel, Constant, *History of Canon Law* (Louvain, 1991).

Van den Eynde, Damien, "William of Saint-Thierry and the Author of the Summa Sententiarum," *Franciscan Studies* 10 (1950), 241–56.

Vanderputten, Steven, *Monastic Reform as Process: Realities and Representations in Medieval Flanders, 900–1100* (Ithaca, N.Y., 2013).

Viejo-Ximénez, José M., "'Concordia' y 'Decretum' del maestro Graciano: in memoriam Rudolf Weigand," *Ius canonicum* 39 (1999), 333–57.

Violante, Cinzio, "La réforme ecclésiastique du XIe siècle: une synthèse progressive d'idées et de structures opposées," *Le Moyen Âge* 91 (1991), 355–65.

Wasserschleben, Friedrich Wilhelm Hermann, *Beiträge zur Geschichte der vorgratianischen Kirchenrechtsquellen* (Leipzig, 1839).

Watt, John A., "The Theory of Papal Monarchy in the Thirteenth Century: The Contribution of the Canonists," *Traditio* 20 (1964), 179–317.

Wei, John C., "A Reconsideration of St Gall, Stiftsbibliothek 673 (Sg) in Light of the Sources of Distinctions 5–7 of the De penitentia," *Bulletin of medieval canon law*, n.s. 27 (2007), 141–80.

Wei, John C., "Peter Abaelard and the *Collectio sancte Genoveve*," *Zeitschrift der Savigny-Stiftung für Rechtsgeschichte, kanonistische Abteilung* 94 (2008), 21–37.

Wei, John C., "Gratian and the School of Laon," *Traditio* 64 (2009), 279–322.

Wei, John C., "Penitential Theology in Gratian's *Decretum*: Critique and Criticism of the of the Treatise *Baptizato homine*," *Zeitschrift der Savigny-Stiftung für Rechtsgeschichte, kanonistische Abteilung* 95 (2009), 78–100.

Wei, John C., "The Sentence Collection *Deus non habet initium uel terminum* and its Reworking, *Deus itaque summe atque ineffabiliter bonus*," *Mediaeval Studies* 74 (2011), 1–118.

Wei, John C., "A Twelfth-Century Treatise on Charity: The Tract 'Vt autem hoc euidenter' of the Sentence Collection *Deus itaque summe atque ineffabiliter bonus*," *Mediaeval Studies* 72 (2012), 1–50.

Wei, John C., "Gratian's *Decretum* in France and Halberstadt," in *Rechtshandschriften des deutschen Mittelalters. Produktionsorte und Importwege*, ed. Patrizia Carmassi and Gisela Drossbach, Wolfenbüttler Mittelalter-Studien 29 (Wiesbaden, 2015), pp. 363–83.

Wei, John C., "The Importance and Influence of Gratian's *De penitentia*," *Zeitschrift der Savigny-Stiftung für Rechtsgeschichte, kanonistische Abteilung* 101 (2015), 373–388.

Wei, John C., *Gratian the Theologian*, Studies in Medieval and Early Modern Canon Law 13 (Washington, D.C., 2016),

Wei, John C., "The Later Development of Gratian's *Decretum*," in *Proceedings of the Fourteenth International Congress of Medieval Canon Law, Toronto, 5–11 August 2012*, ed. Joseph Goering, Stephan Dusil, and Andreas Thier, MIC Subsidia 15 (Vatican City, 2016), pp. 149–61.

Weigand, Rudolf, "Gandulphusglossen zum Dekret Gratians," *Bulletin of Medieval Canon Law* 7 (1977), 15–48; repr. in idem, *Glossatoren des Dekrets Gratians* (Goldbach, 1997), pp. 181*–214*.

Weigand, Rudolf, "Magister Rolandus und Papst Alexander III," *Archiv für katholisches Kirchenrecht* 149 (1980), 3–44; repr. in idem, *Glossatoren des Dekrets Gratians* (Goldbach, 1997), pp. 73*–114*.

Weigand, Rudolf, "Die Dekretanhänge in den Handschriften Heiligenkreuz 44, Pommersfelden 142 and München 28175," *Bulletin of Medieval Canon Law, new series* 13 (1983), 1–25.

Weigand, Rudolf, "Burchardauszüge in Dekrethandschriften und ihre Verwendung bei Rufin als Paleae im Dekret Gratians," *Archiv für katholisches Kirchenrecht* 158 (1989), 429–51.

Weigand, Rudolf, "Die Dekretabbreviatio 'Quoniam Egestas' und ihre Glossen," in *Fides et ius. Festschrift für Georg May am 65. Geburtstag*, ed. Winfried Aymans, Anna Egler, and Joseph Listl (Regensburg, 1991), pp. 249–65.

Weigand, Rudolf, *Die Glossen zum Dekret Gratians. Studien zu den frühen Glossen und Glossenkompositionen*, Studia Gratiana 25–26, 2 vols (Rome, 1991).

Weigand, Rudolf, "Zusätzliche 'Paleae' in fünf Dekrethandschriften. Domenico Maffei zum 65. Geburtstag gewidmet," *Zeitschrift der Savigny-Stiftung für Rechtsgeschichte, kanonistische Abteilung* 78 (1992), 65–120.

Weigand, Rudolf, "Versuch einer neuen, differenzierten Liste der Paleae und Dubletten des Decretum Gratiani," *Bulletin of medieval canon law*, n.s. 23 (1999), 95–106.

Weigand, Rudolf, "Causa 25 des Dekrets und die Arbeitsweise Gratians," in *Grundlagen des Rechts. Festschrift für Peter Landau*, ed. Richard H. Helmholz, Paul Mikat, Jörg Müller, and Michael Stolleis, Rechts- und Staatswissenschaftliche Veröffentlichungen der Görres-Gesellschaft N.F. 91 (Paderborn, Munich, Vienna, and Zurich, 2000), pp. 78–96.

Weigand, Rudolf, "The Development of the *Glossa ordinaria* to Gratian's *Decretum*," in *The History of Medieval Canon Law in the Classical Period: From Gratian to the Decretals of Pope Gregory IX*, ed. Wilfried Hartmann and Kenneth Pennington, History of Medieval Canon Law (Washington, D.C., 2008), pp. 55–97.

Weigand, Rudolf, "The Transmontane Decretists," in *The History of Medieval Canon Law in the Classical Period: From Gratian to the Decretals of Pope Gregory IX*, ed. Wilfried Hartmann and Kenneth Pennington, History of Medieval Canon Law (Washington, D.C., 2008), pp. 174–210

Weiß, Stefan, *Die Urkunden der päpstlichen Legaten von Leo IX. bis Coelestin III. (1049–1198)*, Beihefte zu J.F. Böhmer, Regesta Imperii 13 (Cologne, 1995).

Werckmeister, Jean, "Les deux versions du 'de matrimonio' de Gratien," *Revue de droit canonique* 48 (1998), 301–15

Wilmart, André, "Une rédaction française des sentences dites d'Amselme de Laon," *Recherches de Théologie ancienne et médiévale* 11 (1939), 119–44.

Winroth, Anders, "The Two Recensions of Gratian's Decretum," *Zeitschrift der Savigny-Stiftung für Rechtsgeschichte, kanonistische Abteilung* 83 (1997), 22–31.

Winroth, Anders, *The Making of Gratian's Decretum*, Cambridge Studies in Medieval Life and Thought, Fourth Series 49 (Cambridge, 2000).

Winroth, Anders, "Recent Work on the Making of Gratian's Decretum," *Bulletin of medieval canon law*, n.s. 26 (2004–06), 1–29.

Winroth, Anders, "Roman Law in Gratian and the *Panormia*," in *Bishops, Texts and the Use of Canon Law around 1100: Essays in the Honour of Martin Brett*, ed. Bruce Clark Brasington and Kathleen Grace Cushing, Church, Faith and Culture in the Middle Ages (Aldershot, 2008), pp. 183–90.

Winroth, Anders, "Marital Consent in Gratian's *Decretum*," in *Readers, Texts and Compilers in the Earlier Middle Ages: Studies in Medieval Canon Law in Honour of Linda Fowler-Magerl*, ed. Martin Brett and Kathleen Grace Cushing, Church, Faith and Culture in the Medieval West (Aldershot, 2009), pp. 111–21.

Winroth, Anders, "Where Gratian Slept: The Life and Death of the Father of Canon Law," *Zeitschrift der Savigny-Stiftung für Rechtsgeschichte, kanonistische Abteilung* 99 (2013), 105–28.

Wojtowytsch, Myron, "Die Kanones *Henrici regis*. Bemerkungen zur römischen Synode vom Februar 1014," in *Papsttum, Kirche und Recht im Mittelalter. Festschrift für Horst Fuhrmann zum 65. Geburtstag*, ed. Hubert Mordek (Tübingen, 1991), pp. 155–68.

Zattoni, Girolamo, "La data della 'Passio S. Apollinaris' di Ravenna," *Atti della Reale Accademia delle Scienze di Torino* 39 (1904), 364–78; repr. in idem, *Scritti storici e ravennati*, ed. Mario Mazzotti (Ravenna, 1975), pp. 113–28.

Zeimentz, Hans, *Ehe nach der Lehre der Frühscholastik. Eine moralgeschichtliche Untersuchung zur Anthropologie und Theologie der Ehe in der Schule Anselms von Laon und Wilhelms von Champeaux, bei Hugo von St. Viktor, Walter von Mortagne und Petrus Lombardus*, Moraltheologische Studien. Historische Abteilung 1 (Dusseldorf, 1973).

General Index

Abelard 29, Chapter 6 (esp. 106–12, 125). *See also* Scholasticism
and Gratian 13 n. 31, 29, Chapter 6 (esp. 108–12, 115–16)
and School of Laon 111–13
Fournier on 29, 109
Adrian IV, pope 158, 166–67
Alexander II, pope 134, 142
Alexander III, pope 134, 142, 146 n. 5, 149, 152, 159–60, 164, 166. *See also* Papal letters
misattributions to 163–64, 168 n. 83
Alger of Liège, *see* Index to canonical collections
Ambrose of Milan, saint 80, 97, 99. *See also* Church Fathers
Ansellus, bishop of Beauvais 65–66, 69
Anselm of Laon 110, 111, 113. *See also* Laon, School of
Anselm of Lucca, bishop 29. *See also* Index to canonical collections
Atto of San Marco, cardinal 29. *See also* Index to canonical collections
Augustine of Hippo, saint. *See also* Church Fathers
De trinitate 86
in Abelard's *Sic et non* 118, 125–26
in canon law 41, 51, 66, 80, 86, 88, 118, 125–26, 159
in sentence collections 121
Retractationes 118, 125–26

Ballerini, Pietro and Girolamo 10
Beauvais, church Chapter 4 (*passim*). *See also* Saint-Quentin
cathedral dignitaries 63–65, 69, 70, 72–73
Benedict, cardinal-priest of Santa Pudenziana 64 n. 23
Berman, Harold 1, 2, Chapter 3 (*passim*)
Bernard of Pavia, *see* Index to canonical collections (*Breviarium extravagantium*)
Bernold of Constance 83–85, 101–04
Bible
biblical law as 'old law' 160
books/parts of
Epheseans 141
Exodus 160
Ezekiel 67, 73
Gospel 86
Leviticus 160
Matthew 16:18–19 86–87, 98
Old Testament 95, 160
Song of Songs 158
Timothy 133
Gloss on 112, 113, 116
Bishops
and canon law 14–15, 19–20, Chapter 2 (esp. 37, 40, 43), Chapter 4 (esp. 60, 76, 78–80), 129–30. *See also* Ecclesiastical jurisdiction, Investiture, Index to canonical collections (Anselm, Burchard, Ivo)
as reformers 37, 62, 78, 132
Fournier on 21, 24 n. 73, 24 n. 75, 26
episcopal elections, in modern France 8. *See also* Investiture
medieval 8, 9, 17, 20, 21, Chapter 4 (*passim*)
medieval, Roman intervention in 67, 71, 74–77, 78
metropolitans, *see* Hugh of Lyon, Manasse of Reims, Willigis of Mainz. *See also* Ecclesiastical jurisdiction
networks 19–21, Chapter 4 (esp. 62–63, 72–73)
Bliemetzrieder, Franz 110
Brett, Martin 36–37, 54, 84
Brocards, *see* Index to canonical collections
Burchard of Worms, and Salian emperors 15, 37. *See also* Index to canonical collections

Canon law. *See also* Bishops
and pastoral care 34, 43, 84, 128. *See also* Penance
and theology 10, 29, 36, 43, 49, 105, 109, 112–18, 128, 143–44. *See also* Abelard,

Gandulphus, Penance, Index to canonical collections (Gratian)
Code of (1917) 54
conflicting authorities in 26, 49–50, 84–85, 101, 105–09, 111, 113, 116, 130, 134–35, 137, 139, 158
databases 145 n. 1, 148 n. 9, 170
historiography on. *See also* s.v. Brett, Duggan, Cheney, Fournier, Fowler-Magerl, Gaudemet, Holtzmann, Kuttner, Landau, Le Bras, Pennington, Thaner
handbooks 4 n. 1
on turning points 1–2, 13, 27–31, 53–54, 36, 48, 56, 145, 147–48, 166
mercy and justice (rigor) in 65–66, 67, 70–71, 79 n. 85, 109, 116
procedures 7, 45 n. 5, 53, 64, 76, 79
sources. *See also* Councils and Papal letters
authenticity 27–28, 101–04
conciliar and papal legislation 15, 18, 56, 71–72, 79, 85, 97, 101–02, 131, 146, 156–57
criticism of transalpine councils 24, 41
forgery 12, 14–15, 24, 130
Canonical collections and decretal collections. *See also* Index to canonical collections
Carolingian 22–26, 48–49, 74. *See also* Capitularies, Index to canonical collections (*Hadriana*, Pseudo-Isidore, Regino)
definition of 'decretal collections' and 'Dekretanhänge' 149–51, 158, 154, 166–67
editions of 148, 176–79
'farraginous' ones 25 n. 85, 154, 169
'Gregorian' Chapter 1 (esp. 18–19, 19–22, 27–31), 59. *See also* Index to canonical collections (Atto, Anselm, Deusdedit, *74T*)
pre-Gratian
Fournier on Chapter 1 (esp. 10–13, 27). *See also* Index to canonical collections
influence after ca. 1140 33–34, 42–43, 114, Chapter 8 (esp. 148, 158, 160–61, 165, 169)
definitions 10, 149
'Reform collections' 14, 16–17, 22, 23, 27–31, 59
Capitula iudiciorum, *see* Penance and penitential books
Capitularies 23 n. 70, 49, 74
Cardinals, *see* Atto of San Marco, Benedict of Santa Pudenziana, Deusdedit, John of Santa Anastasia, Laborans, Peter Damian
Celibacy, *see* Marriage and sexuality
Cheney, Christopher and Mary 148 n. 9, 153
'Church and State' 8–9, 32, 78, 80
Church Fathers 57, 109. *See also* Ambrose, Augustine, Gregory the Great, Jerome
Civil marriage, *see* Marriage
Code, Justinian's, *see* Roman law
Constantinople, as 'second Rome' 95
Corrector sive Medicus, *see* Index to canonical collections (Burchard)
Councils. *See also* Canon law (sources)
'apostolic' 102
authority of 15, 24, 27–28, 41, 71, 79, 101–04, 156–57
criticism of transalpine councils 24, 41
Eastern churches 135
individual councils
Ankara (314) 134, 135, 136
Constantinople, Fourth Council of (869–70) 74
Gangra 135, 136, 141
Lateran Council (1059) 132 n. 16
Lateran Council (1139) 132, 142
Lateran Council (1179) 160, 162 n. 62, 163
Melfi (1089) 75
Melfi (1100) 67 n. 31
Neocaesarea (314/325) 134
Nicea, Second Council of (787) 80
Pisa (1135) 132 n. 18
Poitiers (1100) 64, 66, 70
Quinisextum 136
Ravenna (?) (1014) 26
Reims (1148) 154
Rome (1078) 132 n. 17

Councils (cont.)
Rome (1099) 68 n. 38
Saint-Omer (1099) 74
Seligenstadt (1023) 39
Soissons (1121) 107
Soissons (before August 1100) 64, 67 n. 31, 68, 71–72
Toledo 159
Tours (1163) 154 n. 33, 160, 163, 164 n. 70
Tribur, Peter Damian on 100–01
Vatican, First (1869–71) 8
Cousin, Victor 106–08

Decretum Gelasianum 39, 86, 98, 101, 103
Denifle, Heinrich 108
Descartes, René 107–08
Deusdedit
cardinal, *see* Index to canonical collections
pope 29
pope (?), attribution to 159–60
Deus itaque summe, Sentence collection 112–13, 116, 119
Digest, *see* Roman law
Drogo, cantor of Beauvais 64 n. 21, 72
Due process, *see* Canon law, procedures
Duggan, Charles 146–47, 149–50, 153, 155, 157

Ecclesiastical jurisdiction. *See also* Marriage and sexuality, Canon law (mercy and justice), Papal primacy, and Penance
alternatives to 60, 69–70, 79–80
courts 8, 43
discretion of judge 50, 66, 80
episcopal and metropolitan 62, 66, 69–70, 71–72, 74, 78–79. *See also* Milan and Ravenna
historiography on 6–8
judges delegates 43
papal 43, 66, 69, 73, 85–87, 97, 98
papal legates 21 n. 63, 64–70, 77, 84. *See also* Peter Damian, Hugh of Lyon, Galo of Paris
Episcopal elections, *see* Bishops
Epitome Iuliani, *see* Roman law
Esmein, Adhémar 7, 9
Eugenius III, pope 154, 166

Fliche, Augustin 27, 32 n. 111
Florilegia 112–13, 118–19, 126, 154, 169
Fournier, Paul
academic career 5–7
and Harold Berman Chapter 3 (*passim*)
influence 1–2, Chapter 1 (esp. 4–6 and 32), 34–35, Chapter 3 (esp. 45), 84, 109
on individual collections, *see* Index to canonical collections
on Roman law 6, 8, 35, 44–45, 51, 54, 109
'Premier manuel' article 4 n. 3, 21 n. 61, 28 n. 99, 59 n. 6
'Un tournant' article 4 n. 3, 12, 13 nn. 30–31, 28–30, 44, 83–84
Fowler-Magerl, Linda 59, 81, 154, 170
French Revolution 6–7, 9
Friedberg, Emil 8, 11, 150
Fulgentius of Ruspe 126

Galo of Paris 61–62, 73–74, 76–80
and Ivo of Chartres 61, 73–74, 77
as abbot of Saint-Quentin 61
as bishop-elect of Beauvais 65–78
as papal legate 77
transfer to Paris 78
Gandulphus
decretist 34, 115, 117
theologian 115
Gaudemet, Jean 142–43
Gelasius, pope. *See also Decretum Gelasianum*
confusion with pope Hormisdas 39
Glosses, *see* Bible. *See also* Index to Canonical collections (Gratian and *Panormia*)
Grabmann, Martin 109–10, 119
Gratian, *see* Index to canonical collections
Gregory of Catino, *see* Index to canonical collections (*Farfa Collection*)
Gregory of San Grisogono, *see* Index to canonical collections (*Polycarpus*)
Gregory the Great, pope. *See also* Church Fathers and Papal letters
in canon law 2, 30 n. 110, 41, 141, 157, 159–60, 162–63
Gregory VII, pope 2, 18–19, 19–22, 27–32, 131–32. *See also* Councils and Reform, 'Gregorian'
and Peter Damian 86–88
on clerical celibacy 131–32

Haskins, Charles Homer 1
Henry II, emperor 15, 22, 25–26
Henry III, emperor 20
Henry of France, archbishop of Reims 151
Hinschius, Paul 11, 14 n. 36
Holtzmann, Walther 148–49, 152–54, 155, 162, 164, 166, 168
Honorius II, pope 166
Hugh of Lyon, archbishop 65, 67, 69
Hugh of Saint-Victor 110
Huguccio, *see* Index to canonical collections

Innocent II, pope 158, 160
Investiture 7, 17, 73, 131. *See also* Bishops
'Investiture Contest' 7–8, 16 n. 41, 21 n. 63, 32, 58 n. 1, 78, 109
Isidore of Seville, Pseudo- 135, 138, 141. *See also* Index to canonical collections
Ivo of Chartres, bishop. *See also* Index to canonical collections
  and Beauvais Chapter 4 (esp. 61, 65–78)
  and Galo 61, 73–74, 77
  Fournier on 8, 21, n. 23, 29–31, 35, 84. *See also* Index to canonical collections

Jasper, Detlev 35, 85
Jerome, saint 80, 103, 141
John, cardinal-priest of Santa Anastasia 64 n. 23
John, bishop of Thérouanne 62, 72, 79
Justinian, *see* Roman law

Kulturkampf 8
Kuttner, Stephan 84, 110, 111, 127, 149, 154, 155

Lambert of Guines, bishop of Arras Chapter 4 (esp. 62–63, 68–73, 78–80)
Landau, Peter 33, 130 n. 14, 146, 148
Laon, School of 112–14. *See also* Anselm of Laon, Bible (*Glossa* on)
Le Bras, Gabriel
  and *Histoire* 1, 4 n. 1
  on Alger 13, 20, 29
Leo IX, pope 2, 27, 29, 131
  Fliche on 27
Letters and letter collections 39, 63–80, 86–88, 97–101, 106. *See also* Papal letters
Libelli de lite, *see* Reform, Gregorian, polemics
Liber pontificalis, *see* Index to canonical collections
Linus, pope 87, 99
Louis the Pious, kings of the Franks 74
Louis VI, king of France 61, 72
Lucius III, pope 159

Maassen, Friedrich 11 n. 23
Maitland, Frederic William 11 n. 25, 13 n. 33
Manasses II, archbishop of Reims 62–66, 71–81
Manuscripts, *see* Index to manuscripts; for manuscripts of Burchard, Gratian, and *Panormia, see also* Index to canonical collections
Marriage and sexuality. *See also* Walter of Mortagne
  (medieval) canon law on 7–8, 116, 146 n. 5
    bigamy 133
    clerical marriage and celibacy 17, 55, 65–67, 99–100, Chapter 7 (esp. 131–44)
    incest 130, 132 n. 17
    officialities 6–7
    remarriage and orders 133
  civil marriage 8
  clerical fornication and adultery 59, 65, 67
  King Philip's marriage affair 63 n. 17, 72 n. 58, 77, 79
'Mercy and justice', *see* Canon law
Metropolitans, *see* Bishops
Michelet, Jules 6
Milan, church 86–87, 97, 98–100
Mirbt, Carl 16 n. 41
Monks, and canon law 19–20, 26, 36 n. 12, 38, 40, 59–60, 129
Monod, Bernard 9 n. 15, 61, 63, 78, 79
Moore, Robert Ian 1
Mother, churches as 69–70, 95–101

Nicholas II, pope 86, 97, 131, 142

Officialities, *see* Ecclesiastical jurisdiction and Marriage
Otto III, emperor 15, 37

Palea, *see* Index to canonical collections (Gratian)
Papal legates, *see* Ecclesiastical jurisdiction
Papal letters 12, 15, 18, 56, 71–72, 79, 85, 97, 101–02, 131, Chapter 8 (*passim*). *See also* Canon law (sources)
  definitions 151–52
  in registers 11, 41, 157, 160, 162–63. *See also* Gregory the Great
  individual ones (by Jaffé and Holtzmann numbers)
    JE † 1944 141 n. 42
    JL — [WH 332] 166 n. 77
    JL — [WH 353*] 167 n. 79
    JL — [WH 366] 167 n. 79
    JL — [WH 417] 168 n. 82
    JL — [WH 454] 167 n. 79
    JL — [WH 533*] 167 n. 79
    JL — [WH 656*] 166 n. 78
    JL — [WH 752] 166 n. 78
    JL — [WH 943] 166 n. 78
    JL 4405 and 4406 132 n. 16
    JL 5383 84
    JL 5867 73 n. 60
    JL 5976 and 5979 79 n. 87
    JL 8289 158 n. 49
    JL 8959, 8963, 9506, 9653, 9656, 9659, and 9667 166 n. 78
    JL 10062 167 n. 79
    JL 10444 158 n. 49, 167 n. 79
    JL 10445 and 10459 167 n. 79
    JL 11338 159 n. 53
    JL 11660 167 n. 79
    JL 11872 159 n. 53
    JL 12020 158 n. 47
    JL 12180 151 n. 20
    JL 12293 and 13162 158 n. 47
    JL 13166 159 n. 52
    JL 13792/14190/14202 168 n. 82
    JL 13898 159 n. 52
    JL 14173 151 n. 21
    JL 14216 166 n. 78
Papal primacy 8, 14, 17, 21 n. 63, 24–26, 59, 71–72, 85–87, 97–98, 129
  Bernold on 85–86
  in *74T* 59
  in *Anselmo dedicata* 17 n. 46, 25
  in Burchard 17
  in Pseudo-Isidore 14, 24
  Peter Damian on 87, 97–98
Paris, Galo as bishop 77
Paschal II, pope 2, 27, 62. *See also* Councils
Pastoral care, *see* Canon law, pastoral care. *See also* Penance
Patristic writings, *see* Church Fathers
Paul, apostle 87, 99, 133
Penance and penitential books 10, 23, 24, 39–41, 41 n. 25, 42, 116. *See also* Index to canonical collections (Anselm, book 11, Burchard, *Corrector*, Gratian, *De penitentia*), *Summae confessorum*
Pennington, Ken 34 n. 6
Peter, apostle 87–99
Peter Damian 39, 86–88, 94–104
  and Bernold 101–04
  and Hildebrand 86–88
Peter Lombard 29, 107, 115
Philip I, king of France, Beauvais election 61, 63, 72–74, 76, 78–79
  marriage affair 63 n. 17, 72 n. 58, 77, 79
Pollock, Frederick 11 n. 25, 13 n. 33
Popes and papacy, *see* Ecclesiastical jurisdiction, Papal letters, Papal primacy, Reform (papal), and the entries on individual popes

Ravenna, church 87–98
  apostolic tradition of 87–89
  as 'second Rome' 95
Reforms
  Carolingian, Fournier on 22–24
  definitions of 23–24, 55, 58–59, 61, 80–81
  'Gregorian reform'
    and Roman law 53–54
    Berman on 2, Chapter 2 (esp. 44–45, 49, 50, 52–54),
    Fliche on 27
    Fournier on Chapter 1 (esp. 18–19, 19–22, 24, 27–32, 35), Chapter 2 (esp. 44–45, 49, 50–54), 59–60, 83–84, 104
    'Gregorian collections' Chapter 1 (esp. 18–19, 19–22, 27–31), 59, 100. *See also* Index to canonical collections (Atto, Anselm, Deusdedit, *74T*)
    polemic in 16 n. 41, 19, 21, 29 n. 104, 35, 86, 100
    Tellenbach on 59–60

imperial 24 n. 73, 26–27, 37
institutional and legal 37, 60, 79–81
papal 2–3, 24, 27–31, 49–50, 55, 109, 131
role of bishops 37, Chapter 4, esp. 60–64 and 79–81. *See also* Bishops as reformers
Reform collections, Fournier on 14, 16–17, 22, 18–19, 21–22, 27–31, 35, 44–46, 49–50, 59, 104, 109. *See also* Index to canonical collections (esp. for Atto, Anselm, Deusdedit, *74T*)
Reims, church Chapter 4, 81, 167. *See also* Councils, Henry of France and Manasse of Reims
canon law activity 40, 81, 151, 156
as 'mother' 69–70
Richter, Emil Ludwig 8 n. 13, 150
Roman law 6, 12, 34 n. 6, 44–45, 48, 51, 53–54, 56, 109, 114
and Gregorian reform 53–54
Code 41
Digest 11–12, 34, 51
Epitome Iuliani 41
Fournier's studies on 6, 8, 44–45, 48, 53, 109
in Burchard 15
in Gratian 1, 35, 51, 114
Institutes 41
Rome, and reform 24–25
church. *See also* Councils
apostolic tradition of 87–89, 96, 98–102
appeal to 69, 77
and Milan 86–88, 97–100
and Ravenna 91–94, 95
as 'mother' 69–70, 95–101
Constantinople and Ravenna as 'second Rome' 95
primacy 97–100. *See also* Papal primacy

Sacraments, *see* Marriage and Penance
Saint-Quentin near Beauvais 61–63, 64 n. 21, 78 n. 81. *See also* Galo and Ivo
Savigny, Carl von 11 n. 20
Scholasticism 1, 35–36, Chapter 6 (esp. 106–08, 116–18). *See also* Abelard
'pre-', 'proto', and early 35, 44, 50–51
Schulte, Johann Friedrich (von) 11 n. 23, 150
Secular law, *see* Capitularies and Roman law
Sentence collections Chapter 6 (esp. 110, 112–13, 118–26)
and Gratian 113, 122–26
in *Histoire* 10
Sententiae magistri A. 42
Simony 55, 59, 69, 77, 131
Singer, Heinrich 149–50, 158
Southern, Richard W. 1
Stephen of Garlande, archdeacon of Paris 61–63, 65–72, 75, 79
Summae (canon law) 130, 144, 146, 148, 152, 157. *See also* Index to canonical collections
Summae confessorum 43
Summa sententiarum, sentence collection 119–21
Synods, *see* Councils. *See also* Canon law (sources)

Tellenbach, Gerd 58–59
Thaner, Friedrich 106, 108–09, 111, 114–16
Theology and canon law 10, 29, 36, 43, 49, 105, 109, 112–18, 128, 143–44. *See also* Abelard, Gandulphus, Penance. *See also* Index to canonical collections (Gratian)

Urban II, pope 65, 75, 104. *See also* Councils
Fournier on 20, 44–45, 83–85, 104, 109

Via Francigena 81

Walter of Mortagne, *De coniugio* 120
Weigand, Rudolph 33, 38
William of Saint-Thierry 106
Willigis of Mainz, archbishop 37
Winroth, Anders 42, 145

Index of Canonical Collections and Decretal Collections

Works attributed to named authors or compilers are listed under the name of the latter; anonymous works are normally listed under their Latin titles.

Abbo of Fleury 19, 25, 49
Alger of Liège 109, 116
  and Abelard 13 n. 31, 109
  and Gratian 13 n. 31, 42
  Fournier and Le Bras on 13, 20, 29
Anselm of Lucca 39–41, 42, 47, 126
  Book 11 (penitential) 41–42
  Fournier on 18, 20, 28–29, 46, 126
Appendix concilii Lateranensis 164, 165
Atto of San Marco, Fournier on 28, 29, 30, 41

Baldo, master 119
Bernard of Pavia
  Breviarium extravagantium 34, 151, 153, 155–57, 159–62, 165, 169
  Summa decretalium 157
Bernold of Konstanz, *De fontibus* 13, 84–87, 102
  dating of 85
  Fournier on 20, 83–84
Bonizo of Sutri 30 n. 108
  Fournier on 20
Brocards 34, 157
Burchard of Worms, *Decretum* 15, 18–22, 26, Chapter 2 (*passim*). *See also* Brocards
  and *5L* 26, 39, 40–41
  and decretists 40, 158
  and Gratian 22, 42, 147, 158
  and *Panormia* 57
  and *Polycarpus* 42
  and Regino of Prüm 57
  Atto of San Marco on 41 n. 25
  Fournier on 17–18, 20–21, 28, 34–35
  its *Corrector* 40–41, 43 n. 31
  manuscripts of 33–34, 37–40, 40–41, 147
  versions of 30 n. 110, 39, 40–41

Canones apostolorum 102, 103, 135
Canterbury Collection, *see Collectio Cantuariensis*
Code of Canon Law (1917) 54
Collectio Abrincensis 149
Collectio Ambrosiana 166 n. 74
Collectio Anselmo dedicata 17, 25, 49
  Fournier on 17, 25
Collectio Atrebatensis 30 n. 110, 39, 81
Collectio Bambergensis and related collections 152 n. 26, 156, 165
Collectio Barberiniana 38, 41
Collectio Belverensis 152, 161
Collectio Berolinensis I 162
Collectio Britannica 11 n. 21, 65 n. 27, 84
Collectio Brugensis 151
Collectio Burdegalensis 30 n. 110
Collectio Caesaraugustana 19
Collectio canonum of Vat. lat. 3830 25 n. 85, 38–39, 41
Collectio Cantuariensis 161, 164, 166
Collectio capitula Veronensis 38
Collectio Compendiensis 149
Collectio Dacheriana 23
Collectio Dunelmensis 153, 162, 166–68
Collectio Fontanensis 152, 161, 162
Collectio Francofortana 156, 162, 165
Collectio Hadriana-Dionysiana 23
Collectio Hibernensis 23 n. 66
Collectio Hispana 23
Collectio Lipsiensis 150, 153, 165
Collectio Parisiensis I 164 n. 68
Collectio Parisiensis II 156 n. 39, 159–60
Collectio Remensis, see *Collectio Sinemuriensis*
Collectio Sangermanensis (12th c.) 149
Collectio Sinemuriensis 81
Collectio Tarraconensis 30 n. 110
Collectio Wigorniensis (12th c.) 149, 164 nn. 68–69, 168

Collectio Wigorniensis altera 164 n. 68, 167
Collection in 2 Books/8 Parts 39
Collection in 3 Books 42, 141 n. 42
and Gratian 42
Collection in 4 Books 30 n. 110
Collection in 5 Books, and Burchard 26, 39, 40–41
Collection in 9 Books / Collectio Sangermanensis IX voluminorum 81
Collection in 9 Books (Saint-Victor) 30 n. 110
Collection in 10 Parts 81
Collection in 12 Parts 25 n. 86, 50
Collection in 13 Books 30 n. 110
Collection in 17 Books 30 n. 110
Collection in 74 Titles (74T) 7, 18, 21, 30 n. 110, 30 n. 110, 31, 39, 41, 59–60, 129–30
Fournier on 7, 12 n. 29, 18, 21, 28–29, 46, 59
Collection in 183 Titles 38
Compilatio prima, see Bernard of Pavia

Dekretanhang in Heiligenkreuz 44 166
Deusdedit 47, 129, 130
Fournier on 20, 28–29, 46

False Decretals, *see* Pseudo-Isidore
Farfa Collection 18, 21–22

Gandulphus, decretist 34, 115, 117
Gratian, *Decretum* 1, 8, 11, 12, 29, 30
and Abelard 13 n. 31, 29, Chapter 6 (esp. 109, 111–12, 115–16)
and Anselm of Laon 110, 111, 113
and Anselm of Lucca 42
and Burchard 22, 42, 147
and *Collection in Three Books* 42
and *Glossa ordinaria* 112
and *Panormia* 42, 137–39, 147–38
and *Polycarpus* 42, 138
and Roman law 114
and School of Laon 110, 111–13
and *Sententiae magistri A.* 42
and theological collections 112–13, 118–19, 122–26
and *Tripartita* 29, 42, 138–39
dating of 111–12, 127–26
De penitentia 112–13
Fournier on 12, 35, 44, 109
glosses on 115, 116, 144, 146
Gratian 1 and 2 42, 111–12, 118, 126, Chapter 7 (*passim*)
Gratian as 'mediocre compiler' 12
manuscripts of 34, 38, 118 n. 64, 123, 125–26, 154, 161, 161 n. 60, 166
paleae in 33, 138, 139, 147, 153
Quoniam egestas abbreviation of 154
Treatise on Laws 156

Huguccio, *Summa Decretorum* 157

Ivo of Chartres
Decretum 35, 40, 42, 126
Prologus 84
Ivonian collections (Ivo's *Decretum, Tripartita, Panormia*) 7, 13, 20, 33
and Abelard 13 n. 31, 109
dating of 84
Fournier on 8, 20, 21, 28–31, 35, 39–40, 84–85, 109

Laborans 152–53
Lanfranc, Fournier on 30 n. 110
Liber extra 11 n. 25, 36, 150, 158, 160, 162–63, 168–69
Liber pontificalis 30 n. 110

Omnebene 115

Panormia 20, 31, 33, 51, 84, 119. *See also* Ivonian collections
and Burchard 57
and Gratian 42, 137–39, 147–48
Fournier on 30, 31, 44
glosses on 147–48
influence of 33, 38, 147–48
manuscripts of 147–48
versions of 56–58, 147–48
Paucapalea 156
Polycarpus 42, 138
Pseudo-Isidore 41, 130, 149, 157
Fournier on 11–12, 14–15, 22, 24–25, 26, 35, 41

Quoniam egestas 154

Regino of Prüm 50, 57
  and Burchard of Worms, *Decretum* 57
  Fournier on 23
Reverentia sacrorum canonum 115
Roland, canonist and theologian 115, 117

Sententiae magistri A. 42
Simon of Bisignano 158
Summa Parisiensis 156–57
Summa Parisiensis II 156 n. 39

Tripartita. See also Ivonian collections 74
  and Gratian 29, 42, 137–39

Ubaldus 119

Vacarius 115

Worcester Collection, see Collectio Wigorniensis

Index of Manuscripts

Library names are abbreviated; for full names, see the individual entries in the footnotes.

Admont, Stiftsbibliothek, 43 118 n. 64
Arras, BM, 964 151, 151 n. 23–24

Berlin, Staatsbibliothek, Phill. 1742 166 n. 74
Bernkastel-Kues, Hospitalbibliothek 229, 161, 161 n. 60, 166 n. 74
Biberach, Spitalarchiv, 3515 118 n. 64

Cambridge, Gonville and Caius, 6/6 118 n. 64
Cambridge, Mass., Harvard Law Library 64, 118 n. 64
Cologne, Dombibliothek 127 118 n. 64
128 118 n. 64

Douai, BM, 590 166 n. 74
Durham, Cathedral Library, C.III.1 166, n. 75, 168, n. 83

Erlangen, UB, 342 161, 161, n. 60

Florence, BNC, Conv. Soppr. A.1.402 118 n. 64

Heiligenkreuz, Stiftsbibliothek, 43 118 n. 64
44 118, n. 64, 166

Innsbruck, UB, 80 168, 168 n. 83
90 118 n. 64

Leipzig, UB, 975 156 n. 39, 165 n. 71
London, BL, Arundel 490 161, 161 n. 60
Royal 10.A.ii 149 n. 11, 163 n. 66
Royal 10.B.iv 161
Royal 10.C.iv 166 n. 74
Royal 11.B.ii 164 n. 68, 167 n. 80

Mainz, Stadtbibliothek, II.204 118 n. 64
Milan, Archivio capitolare, M.57 166 n. 74
Milan, Biblioteca Ambrosiana, A 46 25 n. 85
Montecassino, Archivio dell'Abbazzia, 216 41
Munich, BSB, Clm 4505, 13004, and 28161 118 n. 64

Paris, BnF, lat. 1566 156 n. 38, 160 n. 55
lat. 1596 164 n. 68
lat. 3890 118 n. 64
lat. 15001 154, 154 n. 34
lat. 18221 39
nouv. ac. fr. 1921 61 n. 12

Reims, BM, 15 81
673 81
674 147 n. 6
Rome, Biblioteca Casanatense 2010 41
Biblioteca Vallicelliana, F2 41
F8 41
Salzburg, Stiftsbibliothek Sankt Peter, a.XI.9 118 n. 64, 153 n. 29
a.XII.9 118 n. 64
Sankt Florian, Stiftsbibliothek, III.5 166 n. 74
Sankt Gallen, Stiftsbibliothek, 673 118 n. 64, 128 n. 5, 166 n. 74
Trier, Stadtbibliothek, 906 (1141) 118 n. 64
Troyes, Médiathèque, 103 167, 167 n. 80
246 25 n. 86
Vatican City, BAV, Vat. lat. 1345 119
Vat. lat. 3830 25 n. 85, 38–39, 41
Verona, Biblioteca Capitolare, CLXXXIV (164) 166 n. 77

Printed in the United States
By Bookmasters